IN DENIAL

IN DENIAL

By Larry Hancock

In Denial: Secret Wars with Air Strikes and Tanks?

Copyright 2020

All Rights Reserved.

Larry Hancock

ISBN: 978-1-7341393-3-4

This text was created and printed in the United States of America. No portion of this book is to be used or reproduced in any manner without express written permission except in the case of brief quotations embodied in critical articles or reviews. All intellectual property is the possession of the author and licensed to Campania Partners, LLC with associated rights and commercial properties therein.

CAMPANIA PARTNERS, LLC.

www.campaniapartners.com

First Edition: 2020

Praise for Larry Hancock's previous national security books:

Surprise Attack

"In clear and detailed writing, the author focuses on the widespread American command and control networks that examine strategic/national and tactical/local intelligence... An important topic for everyone to comprehend, as the threat of a new attack is constant, both from home-grown extremists as well as foreign groups." — Library Journal Starred Review

"Hancock, a veteran national security journalist is not shy about suggesting improvements, but admits that since American leaders may never get their act together, more surprises are likely in store." — Publishers Weekly

"A valuable examination of U.S. national security crises past and present... A timely, pertinent study emphasizing the fact that when it comes to military or terrorist attacks, 'there are always be warnings.'" — Kirkus Reviews

Shadow Warfare

"A grim yet trenchant portrait of American imperial reach – Kirkus Reviews

"The authors' attention to tactical methods, such as the use of front companies, may interest readers of intelligence history, while those concerned with the constitutionality of this subject will be sated with discussion of its legal aspects. Because its extensive research is wrapped in politically neutral prose, Shadow Warfare engages a range of readers with a controversial topic." – Booklist Review

Creating Chaos

"Hancock shows how age-old tactics have moved into new forms of cyber technology as governments on both sides have sown disinformation in order to create chaos. Creating Chaos makes startling charges but it is matter of fact, never veers towards sensationalism" — Kirkus Reviews

Table of Contents

Forward 1
Covert Action / An Introduction 5
Chapter 1: The Cuba Project 32
Chapter 2: Propaganda and Political Action 67
Chapter 3: Insurgency 103
Chapter 4: Decisions and Deniability 135
Chapter 5: Plan Zapata in Action 181
Chapter 6: Mission Failure 222
Chapter 7: Hidden Measures 260
Chapter 8: Aspirations vs. Capabilities 295
Chapter 9: Inertia 348
Chapter 10: In Search of Deniability 397
About the Author 462
Other Books Published By Campania Partners 463
Index 464

Secret Wars With Air Strikes And Tanks?

Forward

This is a book about covert action, specifically in its military form. It delves deeply into its practices, its failures, and its successes. It's also a book about the fundamental assumption – and temptation – that such covert action can be conducted deniably, with no exposure and no consequences. Although you might find that notion strange, it was presented to most American presidents during the Cold War of the 20th Century, and approved by them. And now it has resurfaced in the 21st Century, in new practices by the Russian Federation, China and Iran. Could it once again become the preferred tool for national leaders in a new century?

Covert action remains a constant temptation simply because it offers leaders an option to engage, to do something, when it appears that national security – or political pressure – dictates action. Yet few modern leaders, especially in the nuclear age, want to run the risk of full scale military combat and the possibility of uncontrolled escalation. This means that old or new, the one constant for all covert military action is that (to paraphrase President Dwight Eisenhower) the hand of the actor must not show. Or at least it must not show in a technical sense. We will explore exactly what that involves, but in the broadest sense it means that while the public, domestic politicians, the operations target and even the international community may full well know who is behind the operation it can't be proved – which means it can be officially denied, adamantly and sincerely.

    Covert action is a challenging subject. In order to fully understand it *In Denial* travels around the globe from Tibet and Indonesia through Zaire and Angola during the Cold War and on to the Ukraine, the Persian Gulf and the South China Sea in contemporary times. On the way, a great deal of time and a number of chapters are devoted to exploring American covert military action against the regime of Fidel Castro in Cuba. The reason for that focus is simple – that operation was a disaster both for the president's involved, the Central Intelligence Agency, the nation and most definitely for the Cuban volunteers who participated in its various efforts, including the disaster at the Bay of Pigs. And because it was such a disaster, it was examined and documented in extensive detail, by a Presidential inquiry panel, by the CIA's own Inspector General and later by the CIA's official historian. No other covert action provides the amount of documented detail as the Cuba Project, at least none in which thousands of pages of documents have been released for public study. Of course, it literally took decades for that documentation to become public, to be researched – and even reviewed with some of the most senior participants. That proved to be a shock for all involved. The documents now available provide a totally different picture of that project, and of the landings at the Bay of Pigs than that which initially entered the history books, and which became the standard soundbite in any conversation about the Kennedy Administration.

Secret Wars With Air Strikes And Tanks?

In Denial covers a great deal of territory, and the better part of eight decades, right up to the present. It also provides a great deal of context as background to the overall discussion of covert military action, including an overview of the process by which American covert action is authorized, funded, and subject (or not subjected) to oversight. It also provides an overview and examination of the legislation and legal statures under which that all happens. In order to prepare readers who are not familiar with the subject, that is offered in a rather lengthy introduction – if you are familiar with such things and want to jump right into the deep water of actual operations you might want to skip the Introduction and proceed directly to Chapter 1, The Cuba Project.

By the time you have finished the chapters on Cuba you will be more than ready to proceed with the decades of American operations around the globe and suitably alerted to the risks and realities of covert military action – starting with mission creep and continuing through the tragedies of inertia. You may be surprised to find successful covert military action in the Congo, initiated under President Kennedy, and shocked by how quickly the lessons of the Cuba Project were forgotten, from Laos to Angola. It's all deep, it's all controversial, and some of it is shocking. More importantly, covert action in new forms and with new twists is coming back – it is playing an increasingly important role in today's world and we all need to be able to recognize it.

Acknowledgements: I would like to extend my appreciation for the work that historians and researchers have done to make this work possible. I've tried to cite them extensively in the references, but I would like to especially mention both the in-depth document research done by Dr. John Newman and his seminal writings on the Kennedy Administration in regard to both Vietnam and Laos. The research of journalist Don Bohning and historian Peter Kornbluh provided critical context related to the American engagement with the Castro regime, and the various inquiries into the failure of the Cuba Project. Other invaluable resources include Frank Villafana's work on the Cuban Volunteer Group in the Congo, Kenneth Conboy and James Morrison's research and writing on covert action in both Tibet and Indonesia, and a number of historical studies of covert action in both Laos and North Vietnam by authors such as Richard Schultz and Robert Gillespie.

In regard to *In Denial*, very special thanks go out to my friends David Boylan and Bill Simpich, who have spent hundreds of hours analyzing new Cuba Project documents and "breaking" cryptonyms and pseudonyms - which allows us to understand the CIA activities in that operation at a level of *detail* never previously possible. Finally, Mike Swanson and Carmine Savastano played an invaluable role in editing and fact checking my work, and bringing this book into existence. It would not have happened without them.

Thanks to you all,
Larry Hancock

Secret Wars With Air Strikes And Tanks?

Covert Action / An Introduction

Throughout the Cold War virtually every American president authorized programs of covert action - both political and military - conducted against foreign governments around the globe. Covert action, involving psychological warfare and deniable military action, was carried out to oust leaders and governments seen to be under the influence of America's major geopolitical adversaries – Soviet Russia and Communist China. In the 21st Century covert action continues, with new actors, new tactics, and new tools. One constant in all such actions is that they are designed to be executed so as to conceal any trace of national sponsorship, and always to provide official government deniability. Nonetheless, virtually all covert projects have been exposed and become visible to the general public, both domestically and internationally.

In the years following World War II, during the Truman Administration, American covert action came to involve a complex mix of overt propaganda, covert psychological warfare, and various types of paramilitary action. Many of its tactics and practices were adapted from military measures carried out during the recent war, but conducted in a much more complex peacetime, political environment. In a recent work historian Sarah-Jane Corke detailed the extent to which Truman's covert action operations - focused primarily on the explosive growth of Russian political influence in Europe - were handicapped by the lack of a consistent, unified policy toward the post-World War II Soviet Union.

Truman's State Department descended into a series of internal debates on the appropriate "strategic vision" for confronting the expansion of Soviet influence. At the same time State Department personnel engaged in sometimes bitter exchanges with the American post-war intelligence services as to the immediacy of a Russian military threat. In addition to that ongoing discord, conflicts in roles and reporting among those assigned to covert action projects added considerable confusion for the individuals actually operating overseas.[1] In contrast to the ongoing debates within the State Department and intelligence community, the American military was unified in its view of both the Soviet threat and its own role.

The military perception of real and imminent danger had begun to solidify even as World War II was ending. Wartime concerns were reinforced by incidents such as the failure of the Russians to respond to American requests to return three B-29 bombers which diverted to a Russian base during an air action over Manchuria. While the aircrews were eventually repatriated, the aircraft themselves were taken apart piece by piece and copied, within a short time providing Russia with a highly advanced weapon, the T-4 long range strategic bomber.[2] Such actions, combined with Joseph Stalin's public declaration that "whoever occupies a territory imposes its own social system" moved American military commanders to begin contingency planning against the Soviet Union, in anticipation of a likely military confrontation with Russia.[3]

Secret Wars With Air Strikes And Tanks?

As early as May, 1945, a photomapping effort designated as "Casey Jones" was instituted over western and south-central Europe. The goal of the missions was to develop comprehensive terrain maps which would be needed if the Red Army was ordered to continue its advance to the west following Germany's defeat. The concerns of such a move were so great that by August, 1945 the American Army Air Forces planning staff prepared a document titled "A Strategic Chart of Certain Russian and Manchurian Areas" – in essence an early targeting study which anticipated the need for strategic bombing of the Soviet Union. The following month the Joint Chiefs of Staff expressed the possible need for a first strike strategic bombing policy, including the use of atomic weapons. By October a plan had been prepared for a strike delivering twenty to thirty such weapons. The plan included details of B-29 staging areas and flight paths against Russian targets.[4]

In concert with the very real fears of a continued Red Army advance across Western Europe, quite possibly to the English Channel, in July 1946 the Joint Chiefs of Staff also began to explore the creation of underground armies that could be called upon in any open conflict with the Soviet Union. By August, 1946 a highly secret effort to collect intelligence on armed resistance movements within the emerging Soviet bloc was underway.[5] The military view of an imminent Russian threat and increasingly assertive remarks from Soviet leader Joseph Stalin continued to drive demands for covert intelligence collection, leading to conflicts in priorities between American military groups and State Department personnel. In her Truman era study, Corke describes the quandary of an American Foreign Services officer dispatched to Hungary in 1946, assigned to work on uncovering Nazi assets and locating Nazi personnel still in hiding. At that point in time – and until 1949 – there simply was no official Truman Administration policy towards the nations of Eastern Europe. Yet in spite of any established policy, the State Department officer was approached by an American covert military intelligence mission operating inside Hungary to assist in the secret organization of an underground resistance network to remove the new communist government of Hungary.[6]

Even within the State Department there were ongoing calls for covert paramilitary options and action. In October 1949 one of the more aggressive proposals circulating within State was to commence direct covert action against not only the emerging Soviet Bloc nations, but Russia itself. The proposed action called for not only propaganda, but deniable operations designed to promote guerilla action against the Soviet communist regime inside Russia. The proposal also called for recruiting small groups of anti-communist refugees, training them in guerilla warfare, and dropping them inside Russia in the event of war.[7] During the following years various factions within the State Department, as well as personal policy advisors to President Truman, would cycle between strategies involving: a) simply containing Soviet expansion beyond its new bloc of Eastern European states; b) undermining Russian political and military influence over the new satellite nations; and c) beginning an active covert action campaign targeting the Russian state.

In contrast to those competing strategy proposals from within the State Department and from competing political factions within the administration (each with access to Truman and their own ideas on foreign policy), the American military maintained its earlier view of continuing to lobby for the creation of covert intelligence collection and resistance networks in the east, and pursuing its own initiative of establishing what were described as "stay behind networks" in the nations most exposed to further Red Army advance. The highly secret networks included well concealed weapons and supply caches. Such stores would have been used to aid in the recovery of downed American aircrews, to sustain American Special Forces inserted into denied territory, and in support of indigenous resistance groups. With or without a unified administration policy, the American military remained focused on what it was going to face in the event of actual combat with the Soviet Union.

President Truman was also personally convinced of a very real Russian/communist threat. So much so that he authorized covert political action across Europe. That effort included a successful Italian election propaganda and political action campaign (including secret funding of some $1,000,000 dollars to select Italian political parties). The operation was conducted with great caution and concern for deniability. A combination of American and locally produced media materials was brought into play, however great care was taken to ensure that only local actors – political parties, media companies, spokespersons – actually conducted the messaging to the Italian public. Operationally both propaganda and psychological activities was treated strictly as the province of the Italian government and the political parties supporting it.[8] The Italian action was felt to have been quite effective, defeating communist party hopes of gaining control over Italy in 1948.

Truman also supported a series of propaganda and psychological warfare campaigns targeting newly communist Eastern European regimes. That effort included covert efforts intended to organize Eastern European refuges and expatriates in political opposition to the emerging, Soviet orchestrated communist governments. Covers for those early projects were carefully developed - with the names of prominent American businessmen, lawyers, and philanthropists being associated with highly visible public entities such as the National Committee for a Free Europe (NCFE). The NCFE was openly supported by a host of well-known American public figures such as Dwight Eisenhower (five-star General), Arthur Schlesinger, Jr (historian), Cecil B. DeMille (movie magnate) and Allen Dulles (future Director of the CIA). One of its major missions was fund raising, conducted by the Crusade for Freedom. Donated monies ostensibly went to support a number of very public activities, and the Crusade for Freedom was very visible on the public stage - producing donations of two to three million dollars annually through the early 1950s. In comparison, the covert government funding for the NCFE effort was some thirty million dollars.[9]

Under this very public initiative, propaganda operations were carried out so secretly that board members of the Crusade for Freedom and Radio Free Europe had no idea that considerable financial backing, including funds for organizing and supporting a number of expatriate groups, were coming from the CIA. It would not be until 1971, when the CIA's relationship was exposed, that Agency funding ceased.[10] Eventually, released documents revealed that the offices (in a well-appointed space on the third floor of the Empire State Building) of the National Committee for a Free Europe routinely received a weekly support payment in the form of a CIA funded check - carried to them from the offices of the Wall Street Investment firm of Henry Sears and Company.[11]

Eastern European paramilitary operations were also conducted with extreme deniability, using expatriate and refugee volunteers for infiltration.[12] The goal was to insert single agents and teams into the new Soviet satellite nations, both for intelligence collection and with the hope of sustaining the limited number of guerilla and resistance groups still opposing the new communist regimes. Ultimately the paramilitary initiatives proved almost entirely unsuccessful; dozens of teams and hundreds of volunteers simply disappeared into the East. Some were heard from briefly as coerced or fake radio messages lured in new individuals and teams – who were immediately captured.

It was years before it was confirmed that most missions were compromised by Soviet agents with access to operational plans but ultimately those CIA denied area insertion actions proved to be a horrific fiasco, yet deniability was maintained. Americans were involved only in the preparation and dispatch of the teams. One retired American Army officer who had been involved with the "black" insertion efforts into Eastern Europe summarized the experience – "I went down to the airfield each time an agent team was to be inserted into a target country….to do a final equipment check and wish them luck…at the time none of them I was responsible for made contact after being inserted."[13] Corke's detailed study of covert action during the Truman Administration ultimately concludes that it failed largely due to the lack of a consistent, coherent foreign policy which could be translated into a strategy suitable for driving effective action against either Russia or the emerging Soviet Bloc. As a consequence, the degree of Soviet control over its new satellite nations was actually stronger in 1953 when Truman left office than it had been in 1948, when the first covert actions had been authorized.[14]

The one standard practice which did emerge under the Truman Administration was that covert action - especially its paramilitary elements - was to be organized by American personnel, but carried out by surrogates. The dual guidelines of distance and deniability came to dictate operations for decades. Throughout the Cold War, CIA covert projects would be organized and logistically supported through the efforts of its Plans Directorate (later designated the Operations Directorate), and by officers within the P/P (propaganda and paramilitary activities) section. Standing orders were that the CIA personnel themselves were never to participate directly in military actions. In order to ensure deniability, any such activities would be conducted by volunteers - expatriates, exiles, resistance fighters - supported but not led into actual combat by Americans. One officer, broadly experienced in such covert projects described it all quite succinctly: "In a tactical sense, that's what the Cold War was about; the two major powers fencing, and taking their lumps, through proxies, with the local people picking up the tab, at least in terms of bloodshed."[15]

In 1954, former General Dwight Eisenhower and his new administration's National Security Council staff undertook the same past debates and posturing regarding Soviet strategy and policy. Beyond policy and strategy concerns, there were also calls for a broader involvement in the process of authorizing and monitoring covert action projects. President Truman had left operational matters largely to the heads of a series of evolving intelligence organizations – and ultimately under sole charge of the CIA Director. In some instances that had proved challenging for the military/logistics support of the projects, as well as embarrassing for the State Department. In at least one instance, a major regime change project, in 1952, was compromised and canceled with virtually no discussion. The cancellation left major shipments of weapons and ammunition (destined for use against the government of Guatemala) in transit. The logistics for that project were no small matter. In total over 28,000 pounds were being shipped by air, another 124, 000 pounds were in an early boat shipment, and a total of 917,000 pounds had been assembled for follow-on shipment out of the Port of New Orleans. As we will see, the CIA was often quite enthusiastic about equipping its surrogate forces.

The Guatemala project involved only some 200 fighters, but they were being initially supplied with 750,000 rounds of pistol and rifle ammunition and 2,200 hand grenades – as well as high explosive and armor piercing artillery rounds (but no artillery pieces).[16] As it happened, the son of a Nicaraguan leader that was covertly supporting the operation happened to encounter the American Assistant Secretary of State for Inter-American Affairs and casually inquired as to whether the "machinery" being shipped to his father was on the way. When the conversation was relayed to Secretary of State Dean Acheson, he immediately protested to President Truman that the CIA's operation had likely been compromised and was becoming a potential diplomatic risk.[17] In response Truman almost immediately canceled the operation. Incidents such as that had produced concerns within both the military and diplomatic community, concerns which carried over into the Eisenhower Administration. Both the State

Department and the Joint Chiefs expressed the position that they had very legitimate reasons for being informed (and consulted) in regard to the CIA's covert operations.

Under President Eisenhower the initial step towards addressing such issues was the issuance of National Security Directive 5412, creating the Operations Coordinating Board (OCB).[18] That directive included the provision that the CIA Director was responsible for ensuring that operations were planned and conducted in a manner consistent with US foreign and military policies – acknowledging this to be a special challenge considering that officially stated foreign policies and even international agreements would increasingly be at odds with Eisenhower Administration covert action programs. The OCB's initial role was to ensure that notice of all covert action would be provided to the Departments of State and Defense, with the Board having the responsibility to review and approve operations conducted by the CIA. In reality the group remained primarily a communications vehicle, although it did create a forum for the State Department and the Joint Chiefs of Staff to review activities which might lead to policy problems and compromise the public deniability of covert projects. Over the decades this policy oversight group would continue its basic functions, consistently receiving new names: The Planning Coordinating Group and then The Special Group under President Eisenhower; The Special Group Augmented under President Kennedy; The 303 Committee under President Johnson; The 40 Committee under President Nixon, and more from then on. Despite the name changes its basic role would remain relatively consistent.

While the CIA sometimes proposed covert actions, in other instances even the directive to develop a proposal came from the Commander in Chief, approvals to initiate an action and funding require presidential directives. The president's own authority to order covert action was - and remains - based on the constitutional role of Commander in Chief and the justification of national self-defense. Precedents extending back to the earliest years of the nation held that it was not deemed necessary to wait until the nation had been attacked, preemptive self-defense was a necessary option, an option which included both overt and covert action. [19] In terms of operational constraints, the legal authorization for covert action rests largely in the provisions of the National Security Act of 1947. That 1947 legislation, the follow-on 1949 Central Intelligence Agency Act, and the related Title 50 legal code governing intelligence and covert actions, describe and sanction clandestine activities of the Central Intelligence Agency.[20] Those authorities also allow clandestine action to be conducted outside the laws and legal code governing conventional warfare.

The legal interpretation of this body of national security legislation has been that it allows the president the digression to conduct clandestine action without the need for Congressional approval. That interpretation has been questioned at times. In 1962, the CIA's own counsel offered an opinion that there was no statutory authorization for covert action – but also noted that there was no explicit prohibition.[21] Given its attractions virtually all administrations have found reason to regard deniable operations as an available option, sustaining the repeated use of both covert political and military activities. The National Security Act and Title 50 code are also key to authorizing clandestine action in which American citizens, including members of the military, may be ordered to perform acts not normally authorized in peacetime - as proscribed by the Title 10 Code and the rules contained in the Uniform Code of Military Justice. During the Cold War, this convention provided legal cover for a number of otherwise illegal acts of CIA paramilitary personnel – including murder and political assassination. In the 21st Century it has come to serve as the authorization for the combined, clandestine operations of regular American military and CIA personnel in joint anti-terrorism missions.[22]

Legal experts have offered the opinion that counterterrorism missions are more easily and quickly authorized if the primary authority is "clandestine," given to the CIA and conducted as a national security operation even if it primarily involving regular military forces. Designation of such operations as national security missions also allows increased levels of operational security and classification, including legal control of information related to the mission. It was for such reasons – rather than specifically in pursuit of deniability - that President Obama ordered the 2011 mission to seize Osama bin Laden to be conducted as a clandestine operations project.[23] The melding of covert/clandestine missions involving both CIA personnel and regular US military has become the norm in contemporary American clandestine military action.

That practice has raised a number of issues in regard to gray areas between Title 50 and Title 10 legal protections for the personal involved, as well as the requirements for notification of Congress. While there have been objections and legal issues raised in regard to the use of regular military forces in clandestine operations (especially when Congress has passed no declaration of war) as of this writing, the constitutionally of the practice - much less of the original 1940s national security legislation - has neither been legally challenged, much less ruled on by the United States Supreme Court. It remains as the fundamental justification for 21st Century American covert/clandestine action. The option of deniable operations obviously provides the Commander in Chief a great deal of flexibility to take preemptive action against both regimes and groups which may be designated as national security threats. Beyond that it has proved particularly attractive as a means to act without the involvement of or even the notification of Congress. During the Truman Administration, presidential directive NSC 20/5 affirmed the presidential mandate for covert action and gave the CIA absolute authority in its conduct. At that point no group or officer outside the President or the Director of Central Intelligence had authority or oversight over covert action.[24]

Although official presidential policy directives were issued to authorize covert operations, the nature of that communication was strictly up to the president and on numerous occasions the directives were broad, with little detail. When President Eisenhower issued a directive to oust an elected but leftist leaning regime in Guatemala, he included no definitive goal, no specification of funding and no operational restrictions. Decades later, President Ford issued a directive for covert action which was intended to bring about regime change in Angola, however that directive merely stated that the action was necessary to the national defense and specified only that it involved Africa, not even identifying the targeted country.[25] Clearly presidents desire a great deal of flexibility in regard to covert action; history also suggests that they also desire as little involvement as possible from Congress in such decisions.

In fact, during the initial two decades following the passing of the 1947 national security legislation, the legal interpretation was that the president was not even under a specific requirement to inform Congress of such projects – ensuring both maximum operational security and deniability. On occasion there were private briefings for select Congressional leaders, in other instances the president's acted totally unilaterally. President Eisenhower, who turned to covert action perhaps more frequently than any other American president with the possible exception of Ronald Reagan, was known to be especially averse to having Congress involved with the oversight of any of his foreign policy decisions and programs, including covert action. He also made it a practice to avoid participation by the Foreign Intelligence Advisory Board. While Eisenhower, Kennedy, and Johnson all continued the use of the designated special groups for policy level oversight of covert operations, those groups were composed strictly of individuals within their own administrations.

In later decades, as under President Eisenhower, senior members of Congress received private briefings - increasingly so as the United States broadened covert military action in Southeast Asia. During 1969, when American military involvement in Laos began to receive major media coverage, Senator Stuart Symington expressed his outrage and announced that he was prepared to accuse high government officials of withholding information from Congress. His position became compromised when it was revealed that Symington himself had been personally briefed multiple times, including on a tour of the main base of the CIA's major surrogate military commander – inside Laos.[26] As a follow up the CIA announced it had secretly briefed as many as 67 Congresspersons on its operations in Laos and that some briefings had begun as early as 1963. However, such briefings, and even tours, were strictly discretionary. There was no legislation or legally binding mandate for Congressional reporting or oversight of the projects.

It would only be when CIA military action in Laos and Cambodia became so extensive and so publicly exposed by the media that Congress asserted itself to the point of passing legislation requiring at least a minimal level of notification. Beginning in 1974 and extending through 1980, a series of bills were passed (over presidential veto) to establish that practice. In 1974 the Hughes-Ryan Amendment to the Foreign Assistance Act directed that the president must report all covert operations of the CIA to designated Congressional committees within a set time limit. Each action had to be certified as critical to national security. The amendment also prohibited monies being used for covert operations without such a "finding" being submitted to the committees.[27] Only on very rare occasions has Congress actually moved to restrict covert action through control of budget monies going to such operations, the most significant being in the restrictions placed on funding of the second Reagan administration's regime change effort against the Sandinista government of Nicaragua in the mid-1980's. While Congress passed subsequent legislation restructuring the overall intelligence community in both 1990 and in the 21st Century, in terms of reporting and oversight of covert action there has been little change in the status quo.[28]

There is reason to suspect that 21st Century Commanders in Chief are no more enthusiastic about revealing all their covert actions to Congress than their predecessors. As an example, in 2009 the House Intelligence Committee announced that it had terminated an unspecified but very serious CIA program which had not been reported to Congress for over eight years.[29] Subsequent media investigation suggested that action had involved a directive from President George W. Bush issued in 2001 – to find and kill Al-Qaeda operatives. Given the attacks on America in 2001, the question remains as to why such an easily justified and unobjectionable program would not have been advised in a finding to the appropriate intelligence committees? The House Intelligence Committee concluded that the action had indeed not been reported, had no oversight and had intentionally not been issued as a finding. In addition, a series of CIA Directors had consciously decided to continue the action while not reporting their activities to Congress. CIA Director Leon Panetta subsequently advised the committee that Vice-President Dick Cheney had ordered that Congress not be briefed on the program.[30]

The perceived threats and political considerations which led to the explosive expansion of American covert action programs in the years immediately following World War II have been explored in great detail by numerous historians, and in books by John Prados, Peter Kornbluh and Sarah-Jane Corke, among others. Another view, illustrated in the work of political scientist James David Barber, considers the effects of presidential personality. Barber's book "The Presidential Character: Predicting Performance in the White House" offers insight into how variations in executive personality appear to affect decision making on highly sensitive issues – including decisions to directly order deniable actions or to commit to covert project proposals from the intelligence community, particularly the CIA. Barber's studies suggest that President Eisenhower, motivated by a strong sense of duty, preferred set procedures and routines to politics, making him more comfortable with making decisions outside the extended give and take of political discourse.[31] Certainly that view is consistent with Eisenhower's frequent approval of covert action projects and in comparison Barber describes President Kennedy as having a far more public, activist personality type.

Kennedy was by nature more comfortable with broader dialogs – including consideration of multiple options – during the decision-making process. While something of a risk taker, Kennedy's nature was to evaluate all options and learn from his mistakes. That trait is confirmed by Kennedy's orders for a broad review of the CIA proposals for a major covert military action against Cuba in 1961, in the earliest months of his presidency. Kennedy only approved the operation after forcing extended discussions, and some level of military review. He also demanded a number of additional operational restrictions in what proved to be a vain pursuit of increased deniability. Barber's assessment of Kennedy's character in regard to decision making also helps explain JFK's pursuit of alternative approaches to covert action following the CIA's disastrous failure at the Bay of Pigs.

Beyond the authorities and the decision making that goes into committing to covert action, there remains a final and extremely serious decision which may occur during any project. That is the decision that a particular project's goal has become unattainable in terms of policy, objectives or degree of deniability. In her study of Truman Administration activities, Corke notes that in addition to the lack of definitive administration policies, the failure to reconcile "aspirations and capabilities" not only presented a fundamental challenge to covert action in the earliest post-war years, but would become an enduring challenge - faced not only by Truman but by virtually all of his successors.[32]

In Denial will explore the particular dangers of reconciling aspirations and capabilities in projects involving a major covert military element, dangers which can result in significant "mission creep," in project failure, and ultimately in exposure. The Cuba Project of 1960/61 provides a particularly important illustration of all three risks. The project continued for over a year, continually expanding, from deniably enabling an insurgency against Fidel Castro into something far more overt, launching a highly visible amphibious landing at the Bay of Pigs. That landing was more than six weeks beyond the ultimate deadline for success identified by its military chief. The Cuba Project also reveals certain inherent problems particular to covert military action – risks involving restricted chains of command, compartmentalized methods of communication, and a reliance on verbal instructions for high risk and particularly sensitive activities (including political assassination). *In Denial* also examines the constraints of deniability in regard to covert military action, constraints which can significantly vary according to the personalities of the presidents who authorize such operations.

Technically the fundamental criteria for deniability in covert and deniable programs has remained consistent from Truman's first operations to the present day: 1) all government funding for such projects has to be totally disconnected so that monies actually disbursed in the operations cannot be traced back to the CIA or the American government, 2) any equipment used in the operations was to be "sanitized" and made untraceable to US military stocks, and 3) no serving American personnel were to participate in combat operations where they could be killed or captured. Yet in terms of actually judging acceptable deniability, Truman was willing to respond to State Department concerns and cancel the first Guatemala regime change operation (PBFORTUNE) over a high level but relative minor leak of American sponsorship.

In contrast Eisenhower not only reauthorized a new regime change effort (PBSUCCESS) against Guatemala, but was willing to accept a CIA effort which included "mercenary" air support - including bombing and strafing missions - and intense psychological warfare which included open threats of political assassinations. He even authorized the deployment of an American naval force off Guatemala and directed the establishment of a blockade intended to support the CIA regime change mission. The Navy mission, Operation Hard Rock Baker, was quite public, and quite intimidating. United States Navy ships stopped and boarded all inbound shipping to Guatemala, even ships of allied nations. In addition, a force of five amphibious assault ships, backed by a full marine battalion, stood immediately off the coast of Guatemala – posing a clear and obvious threat of overt American military intervention. In one incident a "mercenary" fighter bomber actually attacked and sank a British commercial vessel, the Springfjord. In retrospect it appears that Eisenhower's criteria for deniability were significantly different from those of his predecessor. As we will see, major differences in President Eisenhower and President Kennedy's views as to what constituted acceptable deniability were to have a dramatic impact on the Cuba Project.

There is no doubt the conduct of American covert action has varied under different presidents – not necessarily in the practices and "tradecraft" used, but rather as to the degree of overtness and readiness to accept compromise in regard to the degree of deniability in the operations themselves. A broad examination of covert action projects over the decades reveals that deniability, and the operational restrictions imposed in its pursuit, have been a major variable associated with the success or failure of covert action. *In Denial* is devoted to the exploration of this critical element of covert action - and to exploring two additional questions which surface in regard to such projects.

First, largely because of its ostensible deniability, covert action has its obvious attractions to national leaders, yet the historical record suggests that to a great extent such benefits are most often illusionary. The majority of all covert actions are exposed, operational deniability is not maintained, mission creep escalates paramilitary action from the use of a limited number of surrogates to full scale conventional combat, the sponsoring nation becomes the topic of international condemnation, and political leaders suffer the consequences. All of which raises the question of why the proposals for such actions have been repeatedly requested, accepted, and endorsed by national leaders? Second, given the obvious challenges of actual deniability, why have so many experienced members of the intelligence community committed themselves both professionally and personally to deniable operations over the years -

developing proposals, championing them to national leaders, organizing and managing operations which fail, and bearing the consequences of that failure?

The first question may be partially answered simply in terms of temptation. Covert operations allow preemptive action short of openly declaring war or deploying conventional military force – both of which required American presidents to engage with Congress and obtain some measure of approval. The very concept of "deniability" is attractive in terms of both allowing multiple levels of national policy (simultaneously pursuing both overt international policies and covert action which are totally at odds with each other). Perhaps foremost, covert action is imminently attractive from a political standpoint, protecting presidents from failures and distancing them from Congressional interference. Yet such temptation needs to be balanced by actual experience, and by the lessons of history. It is those lessons *In Denial* explores - lessons illustrated by the extensive and painful official investigation of one of the most sensational failures of the American covert action – the Cuba Project. In the end that operation (officially directed to be totally deniable) involved a full infantry brigade, a tank unit, paratroop drops, and air strikes and this brutal failure was highly embarrassing for the United States. The result was a series of official inquiries and the creation of an operational history which provides a unique resource for the study of key issues pertaining to the conduct and feasibility of covert, deniable military action.

Notes

[1] Sarah-Jane Corke, *U.S. Covert Operations and Cold War Strategy; Truman, secret warfare and the CIA 1945-1953*, Routledge, London and New York, 2014, 4

[2] William Burrows, *By Any Means Necessary; America's Secret Air War in the Cold War*, Farrar, Straus and Giroux, New York, 2001, 45

[3] Quoted in Joseph Persico, *Roosevelt's Centurions; FDR and the Commanders he led to Victory in WWII*, Random House, New York, 2013, 462

[4] Richard Rhodes, *Dark Sun; The Making of the Hydrogen Bomb*, Simon and Schuster, New York, 1995, 23-24

[5] Sarah-Jane Corke, *U.S. Covert Operations and Cold War Strategy; Truman, secret warfare and the CIA 1945-1953*, 25

[6] Ibid, 27

[7] Ibid, 79

[8] Mario Del Pero, "The United States and Psychological Warfare in Italy; 1948-1955," *The Journal of American History*, March 2001, 1307-1308
http://www.academicroom.com/article/united-states-and-psychological-warfare-italy-1948-1955

[9] Sarah-Jane Corke, *U.S. Covert Operations and Cold War Strategy; Truman, secret warfare and the CIA 1945-1953*, 86

[10] "The National Committee for a Free Europe," *A Look Back, Central Intelligence Agency*, 2007, Washington, D.C. https://www.cia.gov/news-information/featured-story-archive/2007-featured-story-archive/a-look-back.html

[11] Michael Nelson, *War of the Black Heavens; The Battles of Western Broadcasting in the Cold War*, Syracuse University Press, 1997, 49

[12] Extensive recruiting programs were developed by the CIA to identify intelligence assets, infiltration assets, and even individuals who could be activated for military operations in the event of open warfare with the Soviets. A number of defectors with pilot, navigator and maintenance experience were also recruited into a pool which was used for deniable air operations. In some instances, programs such as AEDEPOT were authorized to provide foreign trainers for surrogate forces. AEDEPOT (formerly AEREADY) (1957-65) was developed to provide a trained "Hot War" cadre of Eastern European volunteers who could be used during a period of heightened tensions/increased alert or during actual hostilities against the Soviet Union. AEDEPOT personnel were made available to other functions within the CIA at the Director's approval - for instance personnel from that unit were used in training Cuban volunteers at bases in both Panama and Guatemala for the JMMATE project against Castro's regime in Cuba. An extensive collection of documents is now available for research into these programs:
https://numbers-stations.com/cia/AEDEPOT_/AEDEPOT%20%20%20VOL.%201_0015.pdf
https://that1archive.neocities.org/subfolder1/early-cia.html

[13] Richard H. Schultz Jr. *The Secret War against Hanoi; The Untold Story of Spies, Saboteurs and Covert Warriors in North Vietnam*. Harper Perennial, New York, 2001, 11

[14] Ibid, 2

[15] Richard Secord with Jay Wurts, *Honored and Betrayed*, New York, John Wiley and Sons, 1996, 48

[16] Unnumbered report issued September 1, 1952, titled *Intermediate Report on Plans for Guatemala*, 2003 Release under CIA Historical Review Program, 5

[17] Nicholas Cullather, *Operation PBSUCCESS; the United States and Guatemala 1952-1954*, History Staff, Center for the Study of Intelligence, Central Intelligence Agency, Washington D.C.

[18] "Note on U.S. Covert Actions," *Foreign Relations of the United States, 1962-1968, Volume XII, Western Europe, XXXI-XXXV*, April 16, 2001
https://fas.org/sgp/advisory/state/covert.html

[19] In its earliest years the American Congress had debated the concept of national self-defense, with Alexander Hamilton arguing that while Congress held the responsibility to authorize the initiation of war, the president did not need special authorization to engage an adversary who was already attacking the nation. Congress accepted that position during their debate over the predations of the Barbary Pirates; in more contemporary times the same conceptual justification was for covert action against the existential threat of international communism during the Cold War of the 20th Century. Dave Brenner, "Jefferson and the Barbary Pirates," The Abbeville Review, Abbeville Institute, January 26, 2016
https://www.abbevilleinstitute.org/review/jefferson-and-the-barbary-pirates/

[20] Titles 10 and 50 are part of the overall legal code referred to as the Code of Laws of the United States. Title 10 outlines the role of the Armed Forces and provides the legal framework for the organization, missions, roles of the Department of Defense and the individual services; it includes the Uniform Code of Military Service which governs the conduct of all military personnel. Title 50 relates more generally to war and the defense of the nation. It addresses espionage, alien enemies, classified information and authorities of the of the intelligence community including the Central Intelligence Agency and the National Security Agency. A full listing of the code is available from Cornell University:
https://www.law.cornell.edu/uscode/text

[21] The actual language in the relevant Act includes a general statement regarding authorization of "other duties and functions," with the contextual implication those related to intelligence activities rather than military operations. Up to this point in time no administration has chosen to go with a strict interpretation which would prohibit it from conducting covert action.

[22] Andru E. Wall, *Demystifying the Title 10-50 Debate: Distinguishing Military Operations, Intelligence Activities and Covert Action, National Security Journal*, Harvard Law School, Volume 3, 86-132
https://harvardnsj.org/wp-content/uploads/sites/13/2012/01/Vol-3-Wall.pdf

[23] John Rollins, Coordinator Specialist in Terrorism and National Security, *Osama Bin Laden's Death: Implications and Considerations, CRS Report to Congress*, Congressional Research Service, May 5, 2011

https://nsarchive2.gwu.edu/NSAEBB/NSAEBB410/docs/UBLDocument14.pdf

[24] "Note on U.S. Covert Action Programs," *Foreign Relations of the United States, 1969-1976, Volume E-10*
https://history.state.gov/historicaldocuments/frus1969-76ve10

[25] John Stockwell, *In Search of Enemies: A CIA Story*, New York, W.W. Norton Company Inc, 1978, 45-46

[26] John Prados, *President's Secret Wars; CIA and Pentagon Covert Operations from World War II through the Persian Gulf War*, Chicago, Ivan R. Dee, 1996, 164-166

[27] Note on U.S. Covert Actions, *Foreign Relations of the United States, 1977–1980, Volume XVIII, Middle East Region; Arabian Peninsula*, Office of the Historian, State Department of the United States
https://history.state.gov/historicaldocuments/frus1977-80v18/notes

[28] James S. Van Wagenen, DIA Chair at the Joint Military Intelligence College, "A Review of Congressional Oversight; Critics and Defenders," *Central Intelligence Agency Library*, Jun 27, 2008
https://www.cia.gov/library/center-for-the-study-of-intelligence/csi-publications/csi-studies/studies/97unclass/wagenen.html

[29] Siobhan Gorman, "CIA had Secret Al Qaeda Plan," *The Wall Street Journal*, July 13, 2009

[30] "Cheney Ordered intel withheld from Congress – Senator," *Reuters*, July 12, 2009

[31] James D Barber, *The Presidential Character: Predicting Performance in the White House (Longman Classics in Political Science),* Pearson, London, July 11, 2008, 19-20

[32] Sarah-Jane Corke, *U.S. Covert Operations and Cold War Strategy; Truman, secret warfare and the CIA 1945-1953*, 161-162

In Denial

Chapter 1: The Cuba Project

The defeat suffered by the American organized and equipped Cuban Expeditionary Brigade at Cuba's Bay of Pigs in April, 1961 remains one of the most dramatic exposures of a covert action by a major geopolitical power during the Cold War. The landing of Brigade 2506, and its failure to hold a beachhead (designated as a "lodgment") inside Cuba, resulted in over 100 of the 1,500 plus man unit killed in action, and over 1,100 of the volunteers taken prisoner and sent to Cuban prisons. Large amounts of American equipment (including tanks, heavy weapons and a variety of military landing craft) were abandoned on the beaches and recovered by Cuban forces. Efforts to support the amphibious landing also resulted in the death of volunteer American Air National Guard pilots, killed in aerial combat over the beachhead. The failure of the operation was a tragedy for the Cuban volunteers, a huge psychological victory for the Castro regime, and resulted in tremendous damage to the reputation of the Central Intelligence Agency. One of the things that made the failure so shocking was that the Central Intelligence Agency had come to assume not only a highly trusted position with American presidents, but as an organization, something of a legendary status. The American public viewed the CIA as mysterious, but extremely capable. That was an image that the CIA itself had begun to actively promote as early as

1954, based on its claimed success at regime change in Iran.

The CIA's Iran operation (TPAJAX)[33] had been authorized to ensure that Iran would be led by a figure viewed as positive towards American and British interests in the region, offering the Russians no opportunity to use Iran as a path to post war power in the Middle East. The operation had been the first in which both the CIA's Directorate of Operations and the US State Department had introduced the "domino theory," maintaining that growing Soviet influence over Iran could cost the Western Bloc its access to gulf oil resources. During the prior Truman era the CIA had maintained an extremely low public profile, however by 1954 its success in regime change (with extensive details very possibly leaked by the agency itself)[34] was touted in a widely read *Saturday Evening Post* article. The piece carried the title "The Mysterious Doings of the CIA."[35] The article began by referring to the recent political events in Iran as a "CIA triumph" with the "successful overthrow...of old, dictatorial Premier Mohammad Mosaddegh...and a return to power of this country's friend Shah Mohammad Riza Pahlavi." The *Post* article went on to justify the American political action as a response to a "blackmail" effort by Mosaddegh, which had been rejected by President Eisenhower with appropriate consequences for him.

The article glamorized CIA involvement, touting mysterious trips abroad and meetings with the twin sister of the Shah of Iran, meetings secretly conducted in Switzerland by CIA Director Allen Dulles and the Ambassador to Iran, Loy Henderson. For added effect the article maintained that the Dulles meetings in Switzerland had occurred while Mosaddegh himself was "consorting" with the Russian diplomatic delegation in Tehran. The Post article went into extensive detail in regard to the events and individuals associated with the CIA's activities, ending with effusive praise for the CIA in its success - "the strategic little nation of Iran was saved from the closing clutch of Moscow" due to action of the CIA in developing and nurturing "indigenous Iranian legions" within Iran. Alan Dulles had himself been personally active in promoting the CIA's successes directly with President Eisenhower.

The process became even easier with the virtually bloodless regime change in Iran that was followed by another supposed outstanding CIA success – orchestration of a successful coup against the democratically elected Guatemalan President, Jacobo Árbenz. The CIA's relatively quick success in Guatemala was particularly impressive due to the fact that the surrogate military force trained and deployed as the paramilitary element of the operation consisted only of some 170 men – a mix of Guatemalan exiles and volunteers made available from the governments of Nicaraguan President Anastasio Somoza, and the leader of the Dominican Republic, Rafael Trujillo, both longtime supporters of the United States. The effort was especially notable as the first covert action in which the CIA had successfully deployed a deniable air combat unit. The air group was organized by Whiting Willauer, formerly the senior manager of Civil Air Transport (CAT), the CIA affiliated company utilized by the CIA for deniable air operations against Communist China.[36]

The "rebel" air unit operated out of Honduras and was comprised of a dozen aircraft, including three bombers, fighters, and fighter bombers; it proved especially effective in projecting the image of a much stronger and well-equipped rebellion against Arbenz than actually existed. Fortunately for the CIA none of the rebel planes was downed during strafing and bombing attacks; it would have required a very creative explanation to explain why Chinese pilots were flying the aircraft. CIA success in Guatemala was also aided by the fact that after initial clashes (in which three of the four rebel ground forces were crushed, with well over 100 men killed or captured) Arbenz ordered his military not to oppose their further advance, apparently fearing direct intervention by the American Marine amphibious force just offshore. In the end Arbenz fled his capital and Director Dulles flew the primary CIA officers involved in the project to Washington D.C., for personal introductions and victory commendations from President Eisenhower.

Some six years later in 1960, when Eisenhower approved the Cuba Project, he accepted a CIA proposal quite similar to PBSUCCESS in Guatemala. Several of the original PBSUCCESS personnel would be assigned to the Cuba Project but others were not available as they were already engaged in support of other covert action paramilitary projects. By this time CIA covert military activities had grown quite significantly, with its officers deployed to organize and support anti-communist forces in Tibet, Laos and South Vietnam. It had also begun to significantly escalate covert intelligence collection and sabotage operations against North Vietnam.

In the years before President Eisenhower authorized a specific operation to remove the Castro regime, Cuba had been an area of routine CIA foreign intelligence collections and political influence (anti-communist) efforts. Those activities had been in progress since the early 1950s. Following the Castro revolution, the new Cuban government was increasingly of concern to both the CIA and the State Department. Eisenhower had tasked oversight of Cuban matters to the Special Group as early as 1958 and this nation had been an ongoing subject of discussion. The CIA itself began actively conducting "foreign influence" programs in Cuba in the mid 1950's, providing financial support for anti-communist groups and circulating anti-communist propaganda.[37] By December 1958, President Eisenhower had become seriously focused on revolutionary activity in Cuba, instructing the Special Group to meet weekly on its evolving political crisis.[38] In turn the CIA became adamant that Cuba under a populist leader such as Fidel Castro could open the door to Russian influence, and the Special Group began discussion of contingencies ranging from overt military action with American Marines to having the United States formally designate a new interim junta to govern Cuba. In support of such options the US Army began using commercial covers to secretly place officers inside Cuba to collect military intelligence.[39]

As domestic Cuban resistance to the pro-American Batista government grew there was an abortive U. S. government effort attempted to persuade President Fulgencio Batista to transfer power to an interim military junta – and at the same time the CIA placed agents inside both resistance groups and the Cuban military.[40] Clandestine CIA activities escalated towards the end of 1958 as CIA Western Hemisphere Chief J.C. King initiated plans to identify dissidents who were both anti-Castro and anti-Batista. Two CIA paramilitary officers were sent into Cuba to identify groups and prepare drop zones to supply them. In January, 1959 two aircraft were designated and arms loads were rigged for covert supply to the resistance groups.[41]

Despite those early concerns and clandestine activities, it was over a year before a covert operation was formally approved by President Eisenhower - on March 17, 1960. The CIA proposed the project based on its internal study ("A Plan of Covert Action against Cuba"). The study had been initiated by J.C. King, the head of the CIA's Western Hemisphere division. King had headed the Western Hemisphere during the CIA's successful regime change operation in Guatemala and tasked this new Cuba study to Jake Esterline, who himself had served as Deputy Chief of the earlier Guatemala project.[42] Esterline prepared the CIA's Cuba proposal over a period of some 90 days, beginning in January, 1960. It was initially reviewed by the Special Group on March 14, and submitted to President Eisenhower in a joint meeting of the Special Group and the National Security Council.

As of March, 1960, when the Cuba Project was authorized, Special Group members included the Under Secretary of State, the Assistant Secretary of Defense, the Director of Central Intelligence, and the president's advisor on national security matters - as well as designated representatives from the Joint Chiefs of Staff. While presidents were verbally briefed on Special Group activities (by their national security advisors), the presidents themselves were not expected or encouraged to participate in the group's regular meetings. That practice was quite intentional, providing a level of political deniability for the president personally as well as for the nation's official foreign policy positions. During the Cuba Project, CIA Director Dulles himself advised the Special Group to preserve that separation, urging them to address the project's plans without the necessity of involving President Eisenhower.

With Eisenhower's approval, the Cuba Project plan called for: a) propaganda activities; b) the development of a Cuban exile organization as a highly visible public front for the anti-Castro effort; c) clandestine intelligence collection inside Cuba, and d) the covert recruiting and training of a relatively small paramilitary cadre of Cuban expatriates and anti-Castro resistance fighters. Members of the resistance cadre were to come out of the large Cuban community in Miami, others would be clandestinely exfiltrated out of Cuba itself. The goal was to stimulate an insurgency which would remove the Castro government and that goal was to be met by identifying and sustaining on-island resistance groups. Those groups were to be encouraged, led by highly trained paramilitary volunteers infiltrated into Cuba, clandestinely equipped to conduct activities designed to encourage defections and widespread public opposition to the Castro regime.

This initial project time line called for the new anti-Castro political front to be established within approximately one month, and a powerful propaganda effort to be organized within two months. In regard to paramilitary action, a covert intelligence collections effort was to be in place within two months, providing intelligence both for the propaganda efforts, and for targeting individual defections from the Castro military as well as other key state positions. The Cuban volunteer cadre was to be recruited, trained and deployed inside Cuba within six to eight months (September/October, 1960) to support what was anticipated to be a growing resistance movement. In addition, as with the Guatemala operation, there were to be deniable combat aircraft on call for selective air strikes – in support of resistance attacks and to provide highly visible air strikes in support of the psychological warfare program. Such airstrikes were felt to have been a major contributing factor to success in the Guatemala project, and had become a key element in a number of follow-on CIA operations - most recently with the Agency covertly organizing the Revolutionary Air Force (AUREV) used in support of its regime change effort in Indonesia (Operation Haik) during 1958.[43][44]

All elements of the new Cuba Project were to be fully operational and producing results by November, 1960.[45] CIA Plans/Operations officers with direct experience in the Guatemala project would manage the project within a specially tasked group of the CIA's Western Hemisphere Division (WH/4), organizing its logistics and recruiting as well as managing its intelligence collection, political action and psychological warfare elements. Veteran CIA paramilitary officers would be detailed to oversee training for the Cuban volunteer cadre in guerilla operations and intelligence collection practices. The overall project was to be conducted with total deniability, pursuing United States foreign policy objectives, but concealing its activities to the extent that the president and State Department could plausibly deny any official responsibility – including both basic deniability (in regard to funding or the use of American military equipment) and the denial of any sanctioned participation of American citizens in military activities.

That was the CIA plan as officially authorized to support the directive signed by President Eisenhower in March, 1960. Anyone "read into" or briefed on the project at a policy level during much of 1960 would only have become aware of a highly secret, deniable project intended to use a relatively small number of Cuban volunteers in generating a domestic counter-revolution and ousting the Castro regime. Only a close examination of the actual Paramilitary Plan (Operations Plan 60) developed during the July/August time frame would have revealed that the original concept had already evolved into something increasingly overt. At that point the plan had come to include the creation of a deniable revolutionary air force composed of 12 to 16 B-26 fighter bombers. The B-26's were to be flown by volunteer Cuban pilots and deployed to conduct tactical air support for resistance groups inside Cuba beginning by November 1. Those combat air strikes were projected to continue for a period of at least six months.[46] As with the Guatemala project, the psychological impact of an active anti-regime air campaign was seen as a vital part of the overall project, with air strikes conducted over an extended period.

It is critical for any thorough examination of the Cuba Project to clearly delineate the fact that during its 13-month time span, the paramilitary aspects of the project dramatically changed. Significant "mission creep" began occurring in November 1960 - what had begun as a plan for enabling an insurgency morphed into a plan for amphibious landing of a heavily armed infantry brigade on Cuban beaches. Given the extent to which "mission creep" occurred during the life of the project, we will explore the project in its separate phases:

Phase 1   Insurgency / March – October, 1960

Phase 2   Transition / November – January, 1960

Phase 3   Amphibious Force proposal (Trinidad Plan) - January/February, 1960

Secret Wars With Air Strikes And Tanks?

Phase 4   Amphibious Force (Zapata Plan) – March/April, 1960

The Cuba Project (assigned the CIA codewords/cryptonyms JMARC/JMATE) evolved from what was a limited military effort – directly modeled on PBSUCCESS in Guatemala – into something entirely different. As initially planned, it was to have utilized a group of no more than a few hundred volunteers, larger but comparable to the force organized for Guatemala.[47] Several of the PBSUCCESS project officers were assigned to lead the Cuba Project, including Tracy Barnes, the chief aide to CIA Deputy Director of Plans and Cuba Project head Richard Bissell. In addition to relatively standard political action and psychological warfare activities, the project ultimately came to involve the largest combined air, sea, and ground military operation ever organized by the CIA up to that time. Although military personnel were detailed to the final phase of the operation, the project leadership had no experience with the level of combat, command, and control which became key to the final amphibious landings in Cuba.

Guatemala operation alumnae assigned to the Cuba Project included David Phillips, much admired for his propaganda and psychological warfare campaigns in PBSUCCESS. Phillips was assigned to head those activities against Cuba (he had previously been working as a contract undercover officer inside Cuba for some two years). Howard Hunt, a political action veteran of Guatemala, was tasked with working with the Cuban expatriate leadership committee, and maintaining relations with the numerous exiled political figures vying for a role in a new Cuban government.

In Denial

    Guatemala operation paramilitary officers David Morales and Rip Robertson were assigned to key support roles in the project. Morales was charged with organizing and training a Cuban intelligence group and Robertson was delegated first to establishing a key strike base to be used in launching offshore military operations against Cuba; later he became directly involved with the amphibious operation and sailed with the Cuban Expeditionary Force, providing leadership during the actual landings at the Bay of Pigs. Following its approval, the Cuba Project, remained under the policy oversight of the Special Group, as all covert operations did. In terms of its operational policies, several new constraints were placed on the project, limiting its access to clandestine logistics and military support. In those respects, it would become quite different from earlier CIA operations - and quite unlike a recent regime change operation in Indonesia. The origin of those polices remains unclear, but there is no record of any strong protest from the project's head, Richard Bissell (at least at the time they were being enforced). In contrast, the new policies - which took many of the clandestine military assets used in earlier operations out of play for the Cuba Project – did draw immediate and significant criticism from the field personnel inside its operations.

    Certainly, the Special Group was concerned about deniability, and one of its expressed concerns was the risk of using active American military personnel in missions over the island of Cuba. Yet it would only be in October that the group was briefed that U-2 photographic reconnaissance missions over Cuba were already in progress. At that point the group directed it be consulted in advance of any further planned overflights. In December, 1960 when preparations had finally been completed for actual supply and propaganda leaflet drops into Cuba, the Special Group directed that it be advised in advance of each mission.[48]

It remains uncertain as to what degree President Eisenhower was involved with the operational details of the project, and to what extent he was personally monitoring its progress or timetables during its first months. The best insight available appears to come from the Taylor Commission, which reviewed the project after its failure. That official study notes that Eisenhower's involvement with the program had dropped off sharply by the July/August 1960 time frame when the military elements of the insurgency plan were being finalized. His interest on the project only returned in November, following the presidential elections of 1960.[49] It is understandable that Eisenhower may well have left the project to essentially start up under CIA management without his personal involvement – both to protect deniability and because he had considerable confidence in its abilities. Eisenhower had been impressed by the CIA's performance during his presidency and there were other secret interventions demanding his attention at this time - happening across South East Asia and especially in Laos.

Eisenhower had authorized the covert deployment of 107 Green Berets to Laos in 1959. Operating in civilian clothes and under cover as contract employees of the Program Evaluations Office, a civilian aid mission, the Green Berets acted as advisors to the twelve battalions of the Royal Lao Army. In addition, they recruited Laotian tribesmen for reconnaissance and intelligence collections missions against the routes through eastern Laos which were already being used by North Vietnam for infiltration into South Vietnam. That project was expanding during

1960, with American military authorized to enter combat against communist insurgents if their advisory role demanded it.[50] In 1960, Eisenhower further expanded the covert effort in Laos, allowing the CIA to deploy field personnel. An arrangement was made for CIA operations officer Bill Lair to bring in some one hundred Thai Border police to assist in recruiting Hmong tribal fighters to create and arm a guerilla force to collect intelligence and begin military harassment missions against Laotian communist rebels - as well as the North Vietnamese forces being deployed to expand the supply route through eastern Laos into South Vietnam. Over 2,000 rifles were initially supplied to the Hmong, and air supply drops to the Hmong militia (using the CIA proprietary Air America) were first made in January, 1960. [51] Equally importantly, the CIA had begun covertly building up its own aerial strike force in Laos, composed of the same type of B-26 fighter bombers which would ultimately become the aircraft of choice for the Cuba Project. Officials sent four "sanitized" B-26's from Taiwan into Laos in preparation for strikes against communist forces in the Plaine de Jarres (Plain of Jars) region of Laos.

Eisenhower's focus on Laos during 1960 is particularly well documented – he referred to it as the "Cork in the Bottle." He felt that preserving Laos from communist control was key to communist domination of the entire Far East.[52] With covert operations already quite active in Laos, Southeast Asia would become a topic for the conversation Eisenhower would have with the newly elected president, John Kennedy, in January 1961 as he welcomed him to the White House. Eisenhower's warnings to Kennedy on Laos were sufficiently stern that Kennedy later approved a major B-26 air strike in Laos. CIA planners would ultimately set the date for those missions to occur at the same time as the landings in Cuba.53 Given the events at the Bay of Pigs the Laotian air strikes were not carried out as planned. However, President Kennedy continued to support the covert operations in Laos and the CIA air strike force in Laos doubled in size during the spring of 1961.54

Kennedy later expressed surprise that the first major decisions his administration had to deal with related to the Cuba Project, as Eisenhower had not raised Cuba as a major topic. Cuba was mentioned during the transition conversation, although apparently in no particular detail and only with an admonition from Eisenhower to Kennedy that he must remain strong in facing the problem of Castro, taking whatever action might be necessary.55 At first such an omission appears either curious or mysterious. As we will see, it is much less so given the fact that the initial Cuba Project had essentially failed in its mission as of November, 1960. During the transition between administrations, the CIA leadership was desperately searching for new options, and a new approach for the project. It only began to explore a new concept with the Special Group in December, expanding on it in early January. However, at the end of Eisenhower's term, all the CIA really had in progress was a group of some 500 military trainees in Guatemala, and an aerial element only just becoming operational for the dropping propaganda leaflets into Cuba.

It is important to note that President Eisenhower had again personally taken up the subject of Cuba and specifically the Cuba Project beginning in late November, 1960. He continued to put pressure on the CIA during December, urging them to be creative and bold, yet no new plan was submitted, and no new presidential directive was issued. In reality, during the final months of Eisenhower's presidency the CIA's Cuba team leaders were searching for a concept that might salvage the entire project. One of the team's two top leaders, Jake Esterline, recommended to project team chief Richard Bissell that they simply hold in place until the new Kennedy Administration established itself, and resume planning in an orderly fashion under the policies of the new administration. Esterline would later state that he "got nowhere" with the idea of a temporary hold (and was quite uneasy about that).[56]

A new concept was briefed to President Kennedy after he took office in January, 1961 and it was something far different than what had been authorized in Eisenhower's initial project. The concept itself appears to have been largely a creation of Richard Bissell, working with Jake Esterline, and with the advice of Colonel Jack Hawkins, the new Marine military officer detailed to the project only in October, 1960. The proposal now involved the amphibious landing of a full brigade (four battalions) of troops trained for infantry action, transport aircraft dropping a paratroop unit during the landing, and the use of military landing craft to bring in tanks and heavy weapons to support the overall effort. It was also planned to include air strikes on a broad range of military targets, as well as ongoing combat air cover over the beachheads. One of the first responses from President Kennedy was to ask whether or not the proposal had been reviewed in any detail, including evaluation by the military. When told it had not, he directed that the proposal be put into writing for review; the result became known as the Trinidad Plan.

Clearly the Trinidad plan was nothing like the paramilitary activities (Operations Plan 60) initially developed for the Cuba Project during the summer of 1960.

Secret Wars With Air Strikes And Tanks?

The amphibious landing referred to in the plan focused on establishing what was termed as a "lodgment" in the Cuban port city of Trinidad. That "lodgment" would be defended by the volunteer Cuban Expeditionary Force, supported by ongoing air strikes, and maintained for sufficient time - an estimated two weeks - to trigger a major uprising throughout Cuba, as well as the defection of large segments of the Cuban Army and militia.[57] A later addition to the plan acknowledged that such an uprising might not occur, in that event it would be possible to move the political leadership of a new exile leadership group (still to be formed at that time, but subsequently organized and designated as the Cuban Revolutionary Council) onto the island. The CRC would then declare itself a "provisional government" to be recognized by the United States and then given some unspecified form of conventional American military support. Along with the anticipated uprising and defections, that would bring down Castro and his regime.

Objectively, even in concept, the Trinidad Plan is difficult to conceive as either a covert or deniable action. The vessels required for such an amphibious assault took it far outside the scale of operations that any private group such as the Cubans in the FRD/CRC could support. Beyond that the details of the plan included main line American military equipment such as US Army M41 "Bulldog" tanks, and the involvement of naval assets such as the LST tank landing craft. In addition, the planned US Navy support of the landings at Trinidad, and the proposed rules of engagement designated for those landings, would almost certainly have taken the US Navy into direct combat with Cuban forces. Yet in the initial directive for the Cuba Project, President Eisenhower had demanded total deniability, stating that "our hand should not show up in anything that is done." The plan he had officially approved did not even hint at landing a conventional military force; it only called for placing trained Cuban volunteers on the island to stimulate guerilla warfare against the Castro regime.[58] It is true that Eisenhower appears to have been prepared to accept some level of overt American action, but he had never approved anything in the form of the proposal that the CIA eventually presented to President Kennedy.

In early November, in a Special Group meeting held only days before the presidential election, Gordon Gray, Eisenhower's national security advisor and his conduit to the group, offered the opinion that it would be impossible to oust Castro from power without the use of overt American military force. In what could only have been a reflection of Eisenhower's own views, Gray went so far as suggesting that the CIA use its Cuban exile volunteers in a staged attack on the American Guantanamo Navy base in order to create a false provocation sufficient to justify American military intervention in Cuba.[59] Speculation that Eisenhower himself had become frustrated by the CIA's lack of progress is further suggested by his urging (expressed in a November 29 White House meeting) that the CIA attendees be more imaginative and more aggressive. It is further reinforced by Cuba Project chief Richard Bissell's remarks that Eisenhower had suggested to Bissell that the president would authorize a military move against Castro before January 20, 1961 (the inauguration of President Kennedy) if "we could think of manufacturing something that would be generally acceptable."[60]

Secret Wars With Air Strikes And Tanks?

There is no sign that CIA Director Dulles or Cuba team Chief Richard Bissell responded to Eisenhower on that point. However, it is increasingly clear that the Eisenhower Special Group, as well as the Cuba Project Team, had begun thinking in terms of overt American involvement, as early as the end of November. In his work on an official history of the project, CIA Historian Jack Pfeiffer uncovered what he termed a "strange" note which had been produced following a November staff meeting of the Cuba Project task force (WH/4). The note stated that the original concept of the project was felt to be unachievable in light of the rapid escalation of Castro's internal security controls – "There will not be the internal unrest earlier believed possible, nor will the defenses permit the type of strike first planned. Our second attempt (1,500 – 3,000-man force to secure a beach with an airstrip) is also seen to be unachievable except as a joint Agency [CIA] / DOD [Department of Defense/military] action."[61]

It must also be noted that the CIA's enthusiasm for covert action in Cuba consistently outpaced the estimates of other segments of the intelligence community - as well as that of the military. [62] Before the CIA had even offered a formal Cuba proposal to the Special Group, much less to President Eisenhower, a Special National Intelligence Estimate of December, 1959 had registered the assessment that no serious domestic threats against the Castro regime were seen emerging during 1960 and that any American intervention in Cuba would simply unify the Cuban people behind him. It warned that "most Cubans, including the military, would react violently" to American intervention.[63] Even after the concept of what later became the Trinidad Plan was floated to the Special Group in December, Colonel Hawkins officially advised that there would be no early advance from the lodgment secured by an amphibious landing. Only in the event of a general uprising on the island - or "overt military intervention" by the United States – could the plan succeed.[64] Hawkins's view of the necessary actions for success was crystal clear. His concern was whether or not the new president would accept the necessity of moving on Cuba by March 1 - and of supporting the operation with military action by American forces.

Yet with the records and interviews now available, it appears that Hawkins's advisory memorandum was never circulated outside the Cuba Project. Neither was his position on the absolute necessity of extensive air support presented at any of Kennedy's briefings – or even during the landings themselves. In later years, Hawkins was also quite explicit on that particular point:[65]*"I don't believe that anyone was explaining to the President [Kennedy] that you can't take a thin-skinned troop transport on to a hostile beach and drop anchor with hostile fighters and bombers overhead. It can't be done. Nobody in the administration seemed to know that and nobody made it clear to President Kennedy that I know of."* We will examine that particular issue as well as the overall issue of command and control within the Cuba Project in a following chapter – and present verification that Hawkins's professional military concerns were not being shared with the president, even by the most senior CIA heads of the Cuba Project.

In the days following JFK's taking office, he required that the CIA put its lodgment proposal into written form, including the actual insertion of the Cuban Expeditionary Force. President Kennedy then insisted that the plans be circulated and evaluated by the Joint Chiefs and their designated staff. That review did address certain issues with the Trinidad plan, including the risk of Cuban military aircraft attacking the force's ships and Kennedy himself continued to express his own concerns over the issue of deniability in such an overt move against a Cuban city. Hawkins had correctly anticipated that the issue of overt American military involvement could prove to be a sticking point with the new president, and Kennedy's reaction to the Trinidad plan confirmed that concern. Kennedy's deniability issues, including the choice of the landing site and issues related to proposed air strikes led to significant revisions and the development of a new plan, designated as Zapata. Changes included moving the operation to a more remote and isolated beach area (with no docks for unloading the transports), a night time rather than day light landing, and a series of iterations in what was to be allowable in terms of the timing, number and types of air strikes. The discussions, and revisions related to generating a new operations plan resulted in a slip of the landings well beyond Hawkins's March 1 deadline – the date based on his assessment that ongoing Russian military shipments to Cuba would put the military operation at real risk.

Ultimately the landing was moved some six weeks beyond Hawkins's March 1 deadline. It also became clear that President Kennedy was not about to accept the degree of overt action that had been anticipated in the CIA proposal for the lodgment option. In consequence, after the revisions to the Trinidad plan, both Esterline and Hawkins offered their resignations to project head Bissell - rather than committing to what they anticipated could become a disaster at the Bay of Pigs.[66] Hawkins and Esterline's warnings were neither heeded by Bissell nor sent further up the chain of command but instead Bissell convinced both men to stay with the operation, promising that he would persuade Kennedy to approve a larger air attack and additional air strikes. That promise was not kept - far worse was the fact Bissell actually assured the president that the attacking force could be cut in half and did not inform Hawkins and Esterline of that decision until the late afternoon of the day before planned strikes of the following morning.[67] As Esterline and Hawkins had feared, the landing of the Cuban Brigade at the Bay of Pigs proved to be both a tragedy for those involved, and a political disaster for both the United States and the Kennedy Administration. The dramatic failure of the CIA's thirteen-month Cuba Project immediately brought into question the planning, practices, tools and the decision making associated with American covert operations in progress around the globe.

Those ongoing operations involved a number of covert military initiatives being run by the CIA and given the dramatic failure of the Cuba Project Kennedy was faced with the need for an immediate reevaluation of those programs and of the CIA's involvement. As of May, 1961, the outstanding question for the new Kennedy Administration was whether or not tasking the CIA with military operations - as compared to a much greater involvement of the Department of Defense in covert operations - had been the right decision. President Kennedy and the CIA Director both issued orders for inquiries into the Cuba Project failure – with the goal not of actually suspending covert action projects, but rather of isolating weaknesses and drawing the lessons necessary for success in future deniable operations particularly those which involved covert military activities. The inquiry ordered by President Kennedy was chaired by General

Maxwell Taylor; its report would subsequently be referred to as the Taylor Commission Study.

General Taylor chaired the commission with others members Attorney General Robert Kennedy, Admiral Arleigh Burke of the Joint Chiefs of Staff, and CIA Director Allen Dulles. In itself the report of the Taylor Commission is extremely valuable because General Taylor was tasked with not only examining the manner in which the Cuba Project had been conducted, but the overall approach to covert operations as part of the nation's total spectrum of military options. President Kennedy clearly intended that the study would drive future decisions about the use of the CIA and the respective roles of both the Agency and the Department of Defense - roles not just in regard to future action related to Cuba, but in respect to the rapidly escalating challenges the United States faced globally. Concerns over the CIA's conduct of large-scale military operations were sustained in the final Taylor Report, which proved to be highly critical of the CIA's management of the Cuba Project. In fact, because of likely morale damage the report was not circulated within the CIA and never fully released publicly – it remains held confidentially at the JFK Presidential Library to this day. Extremely limited portions of the report were released in 1977 and in 1979 but apart from that, the CIA's own historian managed to obtain a full copy for use in an internal CIA study and it is heavily referenced in the Official History of the Bay of Pigs (a five-volume work). It was only in 2000 that the National Archives and Records Administration obtained and made a declassified copy of the Official History of the Bay of Pigs available for historical review.

In addition to the broadly-based Taylor Commission study of 1964, the CIA's Inspector General, Lyman

Kirkpatrick, was ordered to conduct an internal review of the Cuba Project. After some six months of work that report, "The Inspector General's Survey of the Cuban Operation," was selectively circulated inside the CIA for comment and the Kirkpatrick report proved to be critical of many aspects of the project including its organizational structure and management. It was immediately viewed by those who had been personally involved in the project as being both inaccurate and intentionally brutal. In response, the CIA's Director allowed Cuba Project leader Richard Bissell (Deputy Director of Plans/Operations) to prepare a detailed rebuttal to the IG report. Much of the material in that rebuttal was accumulated and drafted by Tracy Barnes, Bissell's chief aide on the Cuba Project. Both the IG's report and the Bissell rebuttal paper were seen by a very limited number of senior CIA personnel, however they are particularly important given that they document contemporary inside views of the overall project. The rebuttal also identifies perceived major lessons from the experience by calling out specific changes that should be made in assigning and organizing any future deniable/covert projects. Largely because of the heated nature of exchanges (relating primarily to the landings at the Bay of Pigs) within the CIA, certain issues and suggestions raised by the project's own officers appear not to have gotten the higher-level discussion that they deserved. Yet these arguments did not address the primary issue of establishing a set process to be used for documenting the criteria for deniability and reporting on potential exposures during an operation.

Another highly sensitive matter was the question of whether or not the Cuba Project had faced undue restrictions on its paramilitary activities – in the form of operational constraints far more stringent than in earlier covert actions. When taken as a body, all the Cuba Project inquiries, reports and commentaries are extremely valuable in regard to the study of both historical and current day military operations, whether deniable, clandestine or simply "low profile." Unfortunately, the CIA's internal reports themselves have to be studied with the caution given that they include a significant amount of pointed, and at times acerbic disagreement, extending to personal recriminations and an obvious amount of bitterness. What senior policy makers saw as lessons to be learned were viewed by many CIA personnel as finger pointing. Those individuals almost universally felt that they had received unfair blame assigned for what were failed policies and decisions imposed on the Agency - in particular by the new Kennedy Administration. With careers at risk, organizational roles potentially to be redefined, and substantive policy decisions in play, there were heated objections and pointed accusations expressed at virtually all levels of the CIA's Directorate of Plans/Operations.

The extent of that disagreement, and what can only be called "attitude," appears throughout the CIA's own history of the Cuba Project, researched and written between 1979 and 1984. CIA staff historian Jack Pfeiffer prepared that history in five separate volumes that offered extensive technical and operational detail in hundreds of pages of work and Volume I, over 400 pages, is largely devoted to aerial operations and the Bay of Pigs landings. Fortunately, Pfeiffer's work also contains the original Bissell rebuttal to the original IG report, as well as Pfeiffer's own deconstruction and virtually total rejection of the Taylor Group Study.[68] While the Pfeiffer's Official History is extremely useful as a source of operational detail, his own personal views are made quite clear throughout his work – most especially in Volume V. In fact, the CIA determined that Volume V was not publishable as a finished report because of its obvious polemics and accusatory tone and in 2016 it was made available for public review as a draft paper only.

The good news is that from a historical perspective the various studies and reports provide a point – counterpoint exchange, based in multiple perspectives.[69] Such critical analysis is vital to a comprehensive understanding of any complex and controversial piece of history, especially so when dealing with a challenging subject like covert/deniable operations – projects in which both documents and communications are intentionally compartmentalized and coded with cryptonyms in order to facilitate operational security. In order to conduct the official inquiries, much of that security had to be sacrificed in order to provide the level of detailed and factual information presented in the point-counterpoint exchanges found in the exchanges and rebuttals in the Taylor Study, the CIA IG Report (including the internal Bissell rebuttal) and finally in the Official History of the Cuba Project. The amount of historical detail and the existence of what amounts to a detailed peer review of each study by those contesting it available in the competing studies of the Cuba Project is virtually unique.

In addition, we now have resources which allow us to take a critical exploration of the project even further. Those resources are found in literally thousands of pages of day to day operational reports, internal project memoranda, individual mission directives, and even debriefings. It's a wealth of information which has only become available during the first two decades of the 21st Century, largely due to declassification and massive release of CIA files. Equally importantly, new research has made it possible to determine the true identities of both CIA personnel and Cuban volunteers, identities which were originally protected by the cryptonyms and aliases that are routinely used in covert operations files. We can now read and understand documents which were previously unintelligible, or at best obscure, by now knowing the identities of the individuals involved. From a historical perspective, the value of such personnel identification includes the fact that many of the project related documents were released and became available in time to allow them to be shown and discussed with several of the original participants. That exercise was nothing less than a revelation as it proved to be the first time that key individuals in the project's chain of command learned of communications, directives, and policy decisions which were totally unknown to them during some of the most critical periods of the project - including the actual Cuban air strikes and landings. In several instances the information proved shocking to those individuals, allowing important new insights into the overall failure of the operation.[70]

    A detailed examination of the operational documents, combined with newly available oral histories, has also surfaced the fact that at the highest levels of the project a series of decisions were made to initiate multiple efforts to decapitate Cuban leadership prior to the insertion of the Cuban Expeditionary Force. Those decisions and actions were withheld from all the initial government inquiries and reports and certain ones were also withheld from later Congressional investigations of the CIA. Beyond that new

In Denial

finding, we have also learned that a highly aggressive set of rules of engagement (ROE) for American Naval forces were developed for the initial plan (the Trinidad plan) for inserting the Cuban volunteer force into Cuba.[71] Based on currently available information it appears that President Kennedy was not briefed on either the Castro assassination efforts (which continued after he took office) or given details of the full military effort actually deployed in support of the operation, in particular the Navy element. Both the plans for attacks on the Cuban leadership, and the aggressive rules of engagement had been discussed only verbally by those directly involved; they remained essentially "hidden" outside the special group oversight and were not part of the initial verbal briefings on the Cuba Project given to President Kennedy. Neither the full picture of the Castro assassination efforts nor the various independent activities of senior US Navy officers were actively discussed or commented on in the Taylor Study or the CIA IG report.

With this new, much more detailed body of information, it is now possible to develop a much more comprehensive picture of both Cuba Project and what were actually its two separate failures. That picture includes the early restrictions placed on the project's operations as well as the highly compartmentalized and "hidden" aspects of the project. There were lessons learned at the Bay of Pigs, lessons that led first to serious questions within the new Kennedy Administration, and then to policy changes and revisions in covert project tasking and management. They also led to new experiments such as the concept of "autonomous" covert action - paramilitary operations logistically and operationally divorced from virtually all the standard practices of CIA involvement and paramilitary control. Yet among the options explored by President Kennedy, neither he nor his successors pursued the alternative of totally abandoning either regime change or covert, deniable action. Existing projects remained in play in some instances significantly escalated – even in regard to regime change targeting of Cuba and Fidel Castro.

The temptation of deniable action remained – and remains still. Even the professionals assigned to such projects run the risk of deluding themselves, moving into a virtual state of denial. In remarks made after the failure of the Cuba Project its project chief – Richard Bissell – blamed the failure on operational restrictions and poor policy decisions. But to the end he also maintained (in his formal response to the CIA IG report) that the project itself had been conducted so as to be "technically deniable."[72] There is much still to be learned – and relearned – from the failure of the Cuba Project.

Was its project chief correct - did the root cause of its failure lie in restrictions placed on the project from its very inception? Or was the CIA IG correct in his assessment that a fundamental failure of project management had occurred? Perhaps the Taylor Commission was right and the CIA had simply gotten in over its head, driven by hubris to embark on a complex, essentially military, operation which was beyond its own expertise and resources? We will explore each of those contentions, beginning with the complaint that even under President Eisenhower, the project had been restricted far beyond previous CIA regime change efforts. Exploring that claim will take us into propaganda, political action and deniable military engagements around the globe during the 1950's, from Latin America to Southeast Asia and even to the Himalayan mountains of Tibet.

Notes

[33] As an aid to readers who would like to delve more deeply into actual reference document research, CIA project and individual code names/cryptonyms will be noted in parenthesis in the text (crypto). For document security purposes CIA personnel and assets were also assigned pseudonyms and those will be identified in a similar fashion (pseudo). A comprehensive list of CIA cryptonyms developed though document research is also available at the Mary Ferrell Foundation.
https://www.maryferrell.org/php/cryptdb.php

[34] The depth of detail in the article seems to suggest either a concerning leak of operational security information (especially with the actual naming of Norman Schwarzkopf and Fazlollah Zahedi, as key CIA assets in TPAJAX) – or a CIA leak intentionally planted with the domestic media for the purposes of propaganda. It certainly made the CIA appear virtually omnipotent, able to carry out regime change with at most a handful of meetings and a few weeks of political action. The article did not mention that the US State Department was also deeply involved in the coup activities.

[35] Richard and Gladys Harkness, "The Mysterious Doings of the CIA," *The Saturday Evening Post*, November 6, 1954, 66-68
https://www.cia.gov/library/readingroom/docs/CIA-RDP60-00321R000100090002-0.pdf

[36] John Prados, *President's Secret Wars*, New York, William Morrow and Company Inc., 1986, 100-103

[37] Jack Pfeiffer, *Official History of the Bay of Pigs Operation, Volume 3, U.S. Governments' Anti-Castro Program Central Intelligence Agency*, Central Intelligence Agency, Washington D.C., October 13, 2016, Document Number: 5076ddc4993247d4d82b58da, 43

Secret Wars With Air Strikes And Tanks?

[38] The Special Group - a high level policy committee created to conduct oversight over covert foreign actions – was tasked with ensuring that the Cuba Project would not be publicly revealed, or if it did become visible, could at least be plausibly denied. The Special Group had been created and authorized by NSC Directive 5412/2 to conduct policy supervision of all covert foreign activities.

[39] Jack Pfeiffer, *Official History of the Bay of Pigs Operation, Volume 3, U.S. Governments' Anti-Castro Program Central Intelligence Agency*, Central Intelligence Agency, Washington D.C., October 13, 2016, Document Number: 5076ddc4993247d4d82b58da, 16-18

[40] Ibid, 6-9

[41] Ibid, 13

[42] Ibid, Appendix B, Project Organizational Chart, 105

[43] The CIA had assembled a "rebel" air force of some dozen military and civilian aircraft (including fighters and fighter bombers) to support its operations against Guatemala. The aircraft had flown out of an abandoned air base in Nicaragua, with full approval by that nation's president, Luis Somoza. Somoza had provided the commercial cover for covertly purchasing aircraft, which were then flown by CIA contract pilots transferred from its Far Eastern proprietary company, Civilian Air Transport (CAT). The same location, Puerto Cabezas, would later be used as the forward strike base for the Cuba Project. Ibid, 50-51

[44] Tom Cooper and Marc Koelich, *Clandestine US Operations: Indonesia 1958, Operation "Haik*, February 10, 2008 https://www.indopacificimages.com/wp-content/uploads/2010/12/Operation-Haik.pdf

⁴⁵ Jack Pfeiffer, *Official History of the Bay of Pigs Operation, Volume 1, Part 2, Appendix 1, U.S. Governments' Anti-Castro Program Central Intelligence Agency*, Central Intelligence Agency, Washington D.C., October 13, 2016, Document Number: 5076ddc4993247d4d82b58da, , 408 – 412 https://www.cia.gov/library/readingroom/collection/bay-pigs-release

⁴⁶ Ibid, 96

⁴⁷ Nicholas Cullather, *Operation PBSUCCESS; The United States and Guatemala 1952-1955, Appendix A, PBSCUCCESS Timeline*, History Staff, Center for the Study of Intelligence, Central Intelligence Agency, Washington D.C., 1994, 97-103 https://www.cia.gov/library/readingroom/docs/DOC_0000134974.pdf

⁴⁸ Jack Pfeiffer, *Official History of the Bay of Pigs Operation, Volume 1, Part 1 U.S. Governments' Anti-Castro Program Central Intelligence Agency*, Central Intelligence Agency, Washington D.C., October 13, 2016, Document Number: 5076ddc4993247d4d82b58da, 31,68-69,78

⁴⁹ Jack Pfeiffer, *Official History of the Bay of Pigs Operation, Volume 4, Part 1 U.S. Governments' Anti-Castro Program Central Intelligence Agency, citations to the Taylor Committee Report*, Central Intelligence Agency, Washington D.C., October 13, 2016, Document Number: 5076ddc4993247d4d82b58da, 2-3

⁵⁰ John Prados, *Fighting the War in Southeast Asia, 1961-1973*, National Security Archive Electronic Briefing Book No. 248, Posted - April 9, 2008
https://nsarchive2.gwu.edu/NSAEBB/NSAEBB248/

Secret Wars With Air Strikes And Tanks?

[51] Thomas L Ahern Jr. *Undercover Armies; CIA and Surrogate Warfare in Laos, 1961-1963*, CIA History Staff, Central Intelligence Agency, Washington D.C., 2006, Approved for release 2009, 27
https://www.cia.gov/library/readingroom/docs/6_UNDERCOVER_ARMIES.pdf

[52] Ibid, XIII

[53] Kevin Conboy, *Shadow War; The CIA's Secret War in Laos*, Paladin Press, Boulder, Colorado. 1995, 51

[54] Warren A. Trest, *Air Commando One; Heinie Anderholt and America's Secret Air Wars*, Smithsonian Press, Washington and London, 2000, 110

[55] Irwin F. Gellman, "It's Time to Stop Saying That JFK Inherited the Bay of Pigs Operation From Ike," *History News Network*, Columbian College of Arts and Sciences, The George Washington University, December 12, 2015
https://historynewsnetwork.org/article/161188?fbclid=IwAR3UDyVX8q3tC-LDZRTV2Kur19x2RN4yCBqVHeorb0Bh81uBOROfyD0VdbM

[56] Peter Kornbluh, Interview with Jacob Esterline and Col. Jack Hawkins, October, 1996 as presented in *Bay of Pigs Declassified*, edited by Peter Kornbluh, The New Press, New York, 1996, 261

[57] Ibid, 260

[58] Jack Pfeiffer, *Official History of the Bay of Pigs Operation, Volume 3, U.S. Governments' Anti-Castro Program Central Intelligence Agency*, Central Intelligence Agency, Washington D.C., October 13, 2016, Document Number: 5076ddc4993247d4d82b58da, 72-74

[59] Minutes of the Special Group Meeting, 11/3/1960

[60] Richard M. Bissell Jr., *Reflections of a Cold Warrior*, Yale University Press, New Haven, Connecticut, 1996, 161

[61] Jack Pfeiffer, *Official History of the Bay of Pigs Operation, Volume 3, U.S. Governments' Anti-Castro Program Central Intelligence Agency*, Central Intelligence Agency, Washington D.C., October 13, 2016, Document Number: 5076ddc4993247d4d82b58da, 149-150

[62] Ibid, 30

[63] Eric Rosenbach and Aki J. Peritz, *National Intelligence Estimates*, Belfer Center for Science and International Affairs, Harvard Kennedy School, July 2009
https://www.belfercenter.org/publication/national-intelligence-estimates

[64] Memorandum from the Chief of WH/4/PM (Hawkins) to Chief of WH/4 Directorate of Plans (Esterline), *Foreign Relations of the United States, U.S. State Department, 1961-1963, Volume X, Cuba*, Document 9

[65] Peter Kornbluh, Interview with Jacob Esterline and Col. Jack Hawkins, October, 1996 as presented in *Bay of Pigs Declassified*, edited by Peter Kornbluh, The New Press, New York, 1996, 262

[66] Don Bohning, interviews and correspondence with Jake Esterline and Jack Hawkins, *The Castro Obsession; U.S. Covert Operations Against Cuba*, 34

[67] Op cit, 34

[68] Jack Pfeiffer, *Official History of the Bay of Pigs Operation*, Central Intelligence Agency, Washington D.C. https://www.cia.gov/library/readingroom/collection/bay-pigs-release

[69] The CIA Inspector General's Survey of the Cuban Operation and Richard Bissell's rebuttal (An Analysis of the Cuban Operation by the Deputy Director Plans) are available in an extremely useful document collection prepared by Peter Kornbluh. Peter Kornbluh, editor, *Bay of Pig's Declassified; The Secret CIA Report on the Invasion of Cuba,* The New Press and the National Security Archive, New York, 1998.

[70] Don Bohning, interviews and correspondence with Jake Esterline and Jack Hawkins, *The Castro Obsession; U.S. Covert Operations Against Cuba,* Potomac Books, 2005, Chapter 2, 35-41

[71] Gordon Calhoun, "Task Force Alpha at the Bay of Pigs," *The Day Book, Volume 9, Issue 1,* 8-14
www.history.navy.mil/museums/hrnm/files/daybook/pdfs/vol9issueone.pdf

[72] Jack Pfeiffer, *Official History of the Bay of Pigs Operation Draft Volume V, CIA's Internal Investigation of the Bay of Pigs,* Central Intelligence Agency, Washington D.C., 2016, 100
https://www.cia.gov/library/readingroom/document/0001254908

In Denial

Chapter 2: Propaganda and Political Action

    The Cuba Project changed so dramatically during its yearlong span that it could properly be considered as two different and separate operations. The first phase was an effort to grow and support an expanding anti-Castro resistance inside Cuba, supported by a deniable air offensive comparable to the earlier Guatemala project or the more recent CIA covert air operations in Indonesia. The second phase of the project was something vastly different, a large-scale amphibious landing involving a full brigade of infantry troops, supported by a tank unit, a heavy weapons unit, and paratroop drops - an operation totally unlike anything previously attempted by the CIA. Evaluating the project as a whole presents a major challenge given the two dramatically different phases, with some elements such as propaganda and political action common to both, in contrast to the changing military element which constantly evolved throughout the entire span of the project. The failure of the amphibious landings at the Bay of Pigs had been so disastrous that even in the official inquiries (especially the Taylor committee study) it tended to become the primary focus in discussion of the overall operation, both at the time and over the following decades. Even the project's officers generally focused their assessments and comments on the failed landings, painfully fresh in their minds in the months immediately following the loss of virtually the entire Cuban Expeditionary Force.

In an effort to obtain a deeper view of the entire project it seems more productive to examine the propaganda and political action elements separately from the military activities. While certainly linked to the military efforts, the CIA's efforts in propaganda and political action were relatively consistent during the full-time span of the project. Unlike the amphibious military effort, they remained closely tied to the original, official directive for the project, as approved by the Special Group and authorized by President Eisenhower. Separating these elements will also help in judging the extent to which any new policy directives or operational restrictions were applied to the propaganda and political action activities which might have constrained their use in the Cuba Project - as compared to previous, successful regime change actions. If such changes were imposed on the project it will be especially important to determine their origins, whether at the level of presidential direction, from the Special Group, or within the Cuba project group itself, either from the project's chief Richard Bissell or the head of the Western Hemisphere task group (WH/4), Jake Esterline. The issues raised in regard to restrictions and policy directives related to the military phases of the project will be explored in the following chapters.

In its earliest form the Cuba Project assumed a group of expatriate leaders capable of forming a highly public Cuban media voice opposing the Castro regime that would comprise a political action committee with the goal of creating a revolutionary front. This group would enact a propaganda campaign designed to undermine confidence in the Castro regime, be committed to restoring democracy in a free Cuba, and be directly involved with openly recruiting volunteers for military action against the Communist nation's government. The CIA's initial role was to train the Cuban volunteers, deploy them inside Cuba, and supply them with the quantities of weapons, explosives, and supplies needed to spur island wide guerilla action.

Propaganda:

To fully appreciate the practices employed in the project, and to help identify whether or not new restrictions or constraints were placed on project activities, we need to review it in reference to previous operations carried out during the Eisenhower Administration during the 1950s. In terms of propaganda, undermining confidence in the Castro regime in 1960 proved to be an exceptional challenge compared to earlier CIA operations – largely due to two issues. Castro himself had recently been part of a general revolution which deposed a widely unpopular government, that of Fulgencio Batista. The Castro regime's socialist political polices and increasingly brutal security practices had diminished support among the established business and professional classes, however Castro had countered public criticism by establishing total media control and essentially quashing any organized political resistance. He also remained personally popular, and had been able to leverage Cuban nationalism to maintain control of the Cuban military, and to create a large island wide militia force. Due to Castro's centralized political control, opposition political parties were forced to operate largely underground and without media access. Both broadcast and print media were under constant regime scrutiny and in effect the entire island of Cuba had become a denied territory in terms of media access. Setting up relatively low power opposition radio broadcast in stations just across the border, as some had in Guatemala, was not an option.

By comparison, covert propaganda and political action opposing communist political gains in Italy circa 1954 had been relatively easy, with no media access problems and domestic Italian political parties as well as the governing regime itself providing venues for its anti-communist messaging. Pro-American communications were endorsed and carried out by the Italian government, an example being active in the broad distribution of a newsreel titled "Thanks America," developed by the Italian firm of Pallavicini newsreels.[73] The program intentionally avoided controversial issues and was essentially a "friendship program" featuring well known American performers including Bing Crosby, Walter Pidgeon, and Dinah Shore. All the personalities made at least limited remarks in Italian with a broad variety of communications media readily available for public consumption. Some were offered freely by the government and the rest could be purchased for widespread dissemination. The CIA was able to conduct its propaganda and psychological warfare through the Italian government and the political parties being supported.[74] CIA officers in Italy carried out their missions with no security challenges, no government surveillance and with no personal risk. There were no constraints to political action. CIA political officers were easily able to provide at least a million dollars in direct funding for favored, centrist political parties. The payments enabled a burst of meetings, leafleting and advertising activities immediately prior to the national elections and arguably forestalled a communist party victory.

Open media access had also been available to the first CIA regime change program, targeting the elected leadership of Iran. The CIA station in Iran focused on "increased subsidization for selected Iranian newspapers, extending guidance and money to Iranian elements opposed to ultra-nationalism and terrorism...taking steps to discredit and if possible disrupt forces hostile to US security interests. In pursuit of that effort it also pursued the idea of "the possibility of establishing...a radio station for clandestine broadcasts which would reach at least certain parts of Iran."[75] In the end political action in Iran progressed so quickly that an extended propaganda campaign proved unnecessary, and an American orchestrated domestic military coup carried out the regime change without the need for a broad based, popular revolution.

The closest comparison to the challenge the Cuba Project faced was the CIA's propaganda campaign in Eastern Europe. By 1953 some 26 transmitters were broadcasting to the Soviet Bloc and Russia itself – with over 1,500 foreign employees devoted to the individual national language broadcasts.[76] Even at the time it was difficult to determine the degree to which that extensive campaign had any significant effect on public opinion in the targeted countries. There were a few notable successes, and one of the major lessons learned was that the impact of the propaganda was significantly improved if the broadcasts contained detailed, real time news. Real names, real people, real events – news worked, even if the news was massaged to fit the propaganda goal. In one Eastern European example the CIA managed to recruit a former Polish intelligence officer who had prior access to dossiers on leading communists currently in senior positions in the

Polish government. Those files included specific details of personal and financial corruption. Broadcasting "news" with that intelligence, targeting specific regime figures, was so effective that a purge resulted – with the final result of a more "moderate" regime coming into power.[77] That lesson had also been reinforced in the Guatemala regime change operation.

In PBSUCCESS propaganda was both personalized and news oriented and the personalization took the form of intimidation, specifically targeted to individual regime political leaders and communist sympathizers. In one instance "mourning" cards were mailed to communist leaders, referencing purges and containing death threats. Wooden coffins, hangman's nooses, and phony bombs were used as part of the campaign; targeted individuals were treated to finding slogans placed on their houses such as "Here Lives a Spy" and "You have only 5 days."[78] CIA officers also supported the use of political assassination in the project, but cautioned that such murders should be restricted to those "irrevocably implicated in communist doctrine and policy...to individuals proven to be communist leaders," or "those few individuals in key government and military positions of tactical importance whose removal for psychological, organizational, or other reasons is mandatory for the success of military action." The CIA project chief also advised that for maximum effect such assassinations should be timed to occur only during the actual invasion and coup.[79]

The news side of the Guatemala propaganda involved setting up an "opposition" radio station outside the country to broadcast what was presented as local news as if the station was located in Guatemala City itself. Its news broadcasts incorporated real time information, particularly stories of air attacks and sabotage. "Counter" propaganda was also used quite successfully; in one instance radio broadcasts claimed to be delivering official government announcements that the capital city's water supply had not been poisoned – assuring citizens the water was safe to drink. The fake emergency notice broadcasts immediately spun off a widely circulated series of rumors that the water had indeed been poisoned by the rebels. The CIA felt that the Guatemala propaganda effort had significantly raised public and regime leadership fears – particularly since the actual military element of the project had gone rather poorly. In what was broadcast as a major invasion, CIA-backed, armed Guatemalan exiles (operating from border camps in Honduras) had crossed into Guatemala from geographically remote points. What was broadcast in propaganda news bulletins as a major invasion consisted of only four groups, crossing at five separate points and involving less than 500 men.

The rebel groups advanced cautiously until opposition was met and then were roundly defeated. In the first battle 122 rebels faced some 33 Guatemalan soldiers and only 28 of the rebels managed to escape being killed or captured following combat. In a second battle a local police chief rallied workers to successfully oppose the rebels and within three days two of the advancing rebel groups had been taken out of action. In spite of this reality, a combination of alternative news broadcasts and ongoing air strikes managed to present a picture of ongoing, successful military action against the central government. The propaganda campaign developed for the Guatemala project was viewed as a huge success. The CIA employee in charge – David Phillips – gained the reputation of being a psychological warfare and propaganda prodigy and he was among the group taken to Washington D.C. for a secret victory session with President Eisenhower. Phillips also received a personal CIA commendation for his efforts and he would be the individual assigned to develop and lead the propaganda element of the Cuba Project, applying the practices from Guatemala against the Castro regime.[80]

Phillip's challenge in Cuba faced many of the same "denied area" access problems encountered in earlier CIA propaganda operations against Eastern Europe which included that – as in Guatemala – the regime in power had a good deal of public popularity. In the earliest Cuba Project meeting (March 9, 1960) of the new Cuba Project task force it was estimated that some 60-70 percent of the Cuban population was supportive of the Castro regime and the revolution that had brought it into power.[81] In addition the anti-Castro opposition movement was highly fragmented, with competing political factions and even competing resistance groups. Unlike the CIA's earlier regime change efforts in Iran and Guatemala, there was no single leader standing out as the champion for the opposition to the government in power.

In terms of restrictions, the issue of Phillip's funding definitely faced no limitations. The resources assigned for psychological warfare against Cuba matched the challenge of the mission, with a budget of well over one million dollars and the authorization to set up 8 different broadcast stations. But two constraints did emerge, one a policy decision and the other something quite different. The project's first major broadcast station, Radio Swan, went on the air quite early, in May, 1960, with coverage of the entire island of Cuba. However an operational decision was made to position it as a neutral, commercial news outlet rather than an anti-Castro opposition station (certainly not as an alternative national news outlet as in Guatemala).[82] It was determined that the station would switch to aggressively anti-regime broadcasts only at the point that a militarily active insurgency was enabled inside Cuba – a point at which there would be important messages to include in the broadcasts.

That transition strategy might have proved effective if the initial projections for the planned insurgency had come to fruition. The initial project timetable called for an aggressive and well supplied island wide resistance in action by October/November, 1961. That resistance effort would have been continually supported by targeted air strikes, as in Guatemala and there would have been a good deal of real, opposition-oriented news for propaganda broadcasts. Instead, by September/October, the only news was that Cuba itself was protesting to the United Nations that Radio Swan was pirating its assigned radio frequencies and had placed its propaganda broadcasts at the disposal of "war criminals." Well before the end of 1960, months before the proposal for an amphibious invasion had developed, the CIA itself was forced to admit that the effectiveness of its Cuban radio campaign had been limited and was already diminishing.[83] While there was still a large listening audience on the island, Radio Swan's reputation had suffered because its broadcasts did not have a broad popular appeal. There had been no real military news to broadcast, and the station's credibility had also suffered when certain of its more sensational news had been quickly and easily found to be untrue.

While unrestricted and well-funded, the effectiveness of the radio propaganda effort against the Castro regime suffered greatly from the delay in the project's military efforts. Of course, the Guatemala strategy might have eventually proved out in Cuba. In conjunction with the landing of the Cuban Expeditionary Force in April, 1961 Radio Swan did move into an aggressive agitation role, touting a popular revolt in progress with calls for defection, sabotage and resistance. But by that point Castro's own news outlets were broadcasting details of a United States supported invasion and calling for national unity. The rapid defeat of the landings at the Bay of Pigs literally closed the window on the type of psychological warfare campaign Phillips had waged in Guatemala – that window in Cuba only opened briefly, over less than 72 hours.

Other than radio broadcasts, the only other major tool of propaganda used in the project was the distribution of leaflets. The first challenge was getting them onto the island in some quantity, much less bringing about a broad public distribution and it was only late in 1960 that project air elements became available for the Special Group to authorize air drops of propaganda leaflets into Cuba. On December 11, 1960 two B-26 fighter bombers and one C-54 made leaflet drops into western Cuba and dropped some 3,700 pounds of material. During the period of December to March, twenty-three separate air missions delivered some 12 million leaflets onto the island.[84] These air drops were high risk and high visibility missions that clearly represented a significant effort. Yet the operational reports and after-action assessments provide no details on any special arrangements for dissemination of the printed materials. It remains unclear as to what extent the material was actually circulated, much less if it had any notable effect on segments of the Cuban population.

Political Action:

An aggressive political action program supported by the creation of a united anti-Castro political front was viewed as critical to the success of the Cuba Project and President Eisenhower had made it clear that he wanted Castro ousted by a Cuban led resistance movement. That was to be the key to deniability, distancing the United States from regime change in Cuba. As with propaganda, political action was well funded; the initial proposal to the Special Group and President Eisenhower called for over four million dollars in CIA political action funding along with efforts to stimulate private donations, with a goal of some two million dollars. Although the government funded was provided for, the private donations for the political front never emerged.[85]

As with the propaganda mission, successful political action faced the fact that a good portion of Cuba's population had supported the revolution against Batista - against a government and an establishment which was felt to be fundamentally corrupt. Any anti-Castro opposition effort would also have to reach into the on-island resistance movement (much of which was anti-Castro but remained equally anti-Batista). It also had to face the issue of involving political Cuban exiles and expatriates inside the United States, many of whom had at one time been involved with pre-revolutionary Cuban governments. Some of those individuals had held government positions under the Batista regime with many of the most financially and politically influential members of the expatriate community heavily in the financial infrastructure of pre-revolutionary Cuba.

In Denial

As of 1960 this included a number of wealthy Cubans living in New York City and Miami who long had strong ties to the United States, children attending college there, and generally their politics were conservative. They had been very much involved in Cuban politics before and during the Batista government and all of them wanted Castro out – many also wanted a role in the government which would succeed him. The same could be said for their American business associates, a number of the most rich and important had been well positioned inside the Batista government. Of course, they wanted to maintain their influence with any government which might succeed to power following the ouster of Castro, yet associating them by name with any new anti-revolutionary opposition initiative had its political downside, especially with the segment of the Cuban population that had carried out a revolution against Batista and his government's corruption.

In contrast, as early as 1959 and increasingly during 1960, a number of younger Cubans (some still of university age) who had supported the revolution and whose views were fundamentally populist and more liberal, had begun to turn against Castro due to concerns over communist influence as well in reaction to the regime's increasingly draconian security measures. Their view was that Castro was becoming a traitor to the revolution and they wanted a new Cuba, with agricultural reform, with improved access to education and public services, but without the corruption of the Batista era and with Castro and his clique gone. Those Cubans, many of them quite independent (revolutionaries and true Cuban patriots in their own eyes) tended to be suspicious of the United States due to its former diplomatic relationships with the Batista government. They were also the type of activists who increasingly became involved in actual military resistance against Castro, creating their own groups of trusted followers. In many instances it would be those younger Cubans who would either defect or be assisted out of Cuba by the CIA during 1960 and some of them would also be among the first to volunteer for the Cuba Project's military activities. However, bringing all these factions together in some sort of unified political or military opposition proved to be exceptionally challenging.

The CIA had attempted something similar before in its efforts to form "liberation" committees from the exiles and refugees coming out of the new regimes the Soviets had forced into place in Eastern Europe at the end of World War II. The goal for those liberation committees was to serve as the public face and media voice for protests against the new totalitarianism in their native countries. The new Cuban "front" was intended to serve the same purpose. It would also provide a cover for recruiting military volunteers for CIA directed covert military activities.[86] That earlier liberation committee effort had encountered a variety of ultimately overwhelming problems, largely based in the diversity of views among the refugees and their constant, contentious jockeying for leadership positions in the groups. CIA case officers had found it simply impossible to reconcile pre-existing political and personal differences in order to create new leadership councils for the Yugoslav, Polish, and Romanian exiles. Beyond that the committees that had been formed for the Czechoslovaks and Hungarians were fractionalized and eventually dissolved in disarray.

A CIA internal review of the overall political action effort against the Soviet bloc nations concluded that it was virtually impossible to organize effective national councils due to the continual "bickering" and "jealousies" among the member politicians. [87] It also noted that the political leaders in the various groups were more than willing to publicly boast of American support to make their individual cases to the media and beyond. [88] This is exactly the same behavior that can be said to characterize the Cuban politicians involved in the CIA's political action efforts. Given the CIA's own prior challenges in organizing united political opposition fronts, it appears that expectations for an anti-Castro revolutionary leadership organization – ultimately intended to be either a government in exile or possibly a provisional government on the island itself – were unrealistic. The same has to be said for the expectation that the Cuban front might actually be able to play a major role not only in recruiting, but in directing military activities. If the military element of the project had remained as limited as originally specified – simply identifying and supporting an on-island insurgency – perhaps the political front group would have been effective in coordinating and directing military actions. However, based on later remarks from senior Cuba Project officers, it appears that there simply had not been sufficient awareness of the depth of the ideological differences among the various anti-Castro factions as well as the extent of the old grudges and personal vendettas which existed amongst the exiled Cuban political leaders.

The original CIA political action plan had been ambitious, calling for a united council (junta) to be formed within one month. The council was expected to quickly develop the ability not only to serve as a media front for the anti-Castro program, but to assume an active role in the creation of a covert intelligence network which would reach inside Cuba to obtain hard intelligence on conditions and Castro's military capabilities. It would also facilitate infiltrations, exfiltration's, distribution of propaganda, and the promotion of defections. The initial progress did seem encouraging and the project proposal was made on March 16 with the overall project receiving President Eisenhower's approval on March 17, and following a May 11-12 meeting in New York City, an anti-Castro political council – the Cuban Democratic Revolutionary Front (in Spanish the Frente or FRD/Frente Revolucionario Democrático) was organized. Certainly, that was in line with Eisenhower's directions as he wanted Castro to fall from power based on a Cuban resistance effort, with anti-Castro leaders and anti-Castro fighters doing the work.

In that context, project Chief Richard Bissell (supported by the State Department) appears to have instituted his own policy of "non-interference" in FRD/Frente political matters that included rejecting any involvement in its leadership decisions, which Bissell termed as "strictly unilateral exile Cuban affairs." Yet as the months passed, CIA officers became increasingly frustrated by the degree of bickering and jousting for influence among the Cuban political leaders because each seemed only interested in supporting their particular party, lobbying specifically for assistance for their own resistance groups inside Cuba and all too often painting an exaggerated picture of their own group's size and capabilities.[89] The effort to grow a coordinated military resistance movement via the FRD also proved to be challenging. It was not that individual Cuban leaders were not willing to take the initiative, it was more a matter of them wanting to work with virtually anyone and everyone.

This can be observed in a memorandum from one of the senior CIA political action officers, dated September 6, 1960.[90] The memo relates a meeting involving Manuel Artime and three other individuals with General Graves Erskine, head of a special Joint Chiefs staff unit assigned to support covert operations. Two months earlier, in June, Artime himself had already played a key role in recruiting some of the first Cuban volunteers for the CIA's guerilla cadre training. He had personally accompanied them, and the chief CIA paramilitary trainer, to the CIA Useppa Island screening facility. Prior to the August meeting with General Erskine, Artime and the others had attended a VFW convention in Detroit and were in Washington, independently meeting with high level government officials including Vice-President Nixon and several US Senators, including Senator Kennedy.[91]

In the meeting with General Erskine, Artime and his companions focused on the immediate need of American support for their movement and the FRD. Issues raised included the challenges of direct communications between the FRD and their agents in Cuba – they were seeking a powerful radio transmitter of their own. As part of the related discussion they noted their lack of ability to conduct their own broadcast propaganda messages into Cuba and made a plea for more training and for the immediate delivery of demolitions materials directly to the FRD. Yet the problem was that these Artime meetings were occurring at the same time that the CIA's own military operations plan was being finalized with recruiting and volunteer vetting already underway, including initial CIA radio training for the first volunteers. The operational timeline was being set, resources allocated, and the initial

Secret Wars With Air Strikes And Tanks?

Radio Swan propaganda broadcasts were already in progress.

At the same time that the CIA Cuba team was establishing its own specific anti-Castro propaganda and military operations plans (utilizing the FRD as a resource), Artime and the other FRD representatives were personally visiting and lobbying for direct FRD support from the Joint Chiefs staff, the American Vice-President and senior Senators. They were even making specific requests, including not just for additional training, but for their own radio equipment and supplies, including explosives. Beyond that, the FRD itself had designated its own military leadership group, assuming that it would play a major role in planning and coordinating operations. Yet while the Cubans involved with the FRD clearly desired a major role in operations, they faced ongoing internal conflicts involving political and military issues, such as contending views as to the form of any new government of Cuba. Some of the younger, more populist anti-Castro activists were suspected of having either socialist or communist leanings. There were also disagreements as to the pace of military operations and those exiles with active resistance fighters on the island were especially focused on obtaining supplies and directing CIA support to their own groups.

Manuel Artime, one of the members of the FRD Executive Council, had been selected largely due to his leadership of a very active on-island resistance group, the Movement to Recover the Revolution (MRR). However, during the course of 1960 he largely withdrew from FRD political activities, volunteered to personally join the CIA military element, and repeatedly urged the CIA project team to infiltrate him into Cuba in an effort to spur the armed resistance movement on the island.[92] It was only in

1961, in the weeks immediately before the landings in Cuba that Artime was brought back into the FRD political effort, as one of the leaders in the newly formed Cuban Revolutionary Council (CRC). The revolutionary council itself was organized by the CIA, only weeks prior to the April attempt to establish a lodgment inside Cuba. Given the early and ongoing political and military jousting going on within the FRD, even at its executive level, it is not terribly surprising to find that the CIA leadership had rather quickly taken full charge of virtually all activities related to the effort against Castro – including both propaganda and military action. Richard Bissell's decision for the CIA to assume comprehensive operational planning and control did eliminate what could have become an increasing confusion over roles (even within the US government), but it quite definitely restricted the activities of the Cuban political leadership.

By September, 1960 CIA officers were planning and managing the training activities of the Cuban military element as well as running propaganda and field intelligence collection. Cuban volunteers were infiltrated into Cuba to collect intelligence and report it back to CIA headquarters, but there is little indication that they were involved in the detailed planning of missions into Cuba; they were simply briefed on them. As to the FRD, it became little more than a true front, a public vehicle for propaganda statements and anti-Castro declarations, but with no operational authority or role. Bissell stated in the CIA Inspector General's report that his only choice had been to accept the fact that the idea the FRD could actually run field activities had proven to be "illusionary." In order to maintain operational initiative, it had been absolutely necessary to initiate CIA control over both propaganda and military operations. As a result, during the fall of 1960, and most importantly during the second (lodgment) phase of the project, the CIA rather than the FRD became the single channel for contacts with volunteers and sources within the general Cuban exile community and the only true point of contact and support for resistance groups inside Cuba.

In contrast, at the same time that the CIA was taking full operational and military control, it continued to distance itself from political involvement. That became clear in September when the FRD requested that the United States designate a particular individual to serve as General Coordinator, effectively to head the exile leadership committee and become the public face of anti-Castro action. That request came at a time of increased internal competition and strife within the exile leadership (Bissell himself described the level of contention as having developed into "internal warfare"). At that point Bissell declined (in a decision supported by the State Department) to make a unilateral decision and rejected the request, continuing to assert a policy of non-interference in exile political affairs and leaving the FRD leaders to resolve their own problems. Following the failure of the project, the policy decision of assuming military control over resistance operations - while not asserting a similar degree of direct political involvement - drew a good deal of discussion and criticism. Bissell was forced to reassert and defend his political action policy decisions in his rebuttal to the criticisms appearing in the CIA Inspector General's study.[93]

In those remarks Bissell commented at length on how much political case officer time and energy were consumed sustaining the "non-interference" policy and he also described its negative effects on day to day propaganda activities.[94] Perhaps more importantly, both Bissell and the

State Department called out the exile political leaders "incessant preoccupation with political advantage" as a source of delay in recruiting officers and volunteers for the military effort within the project timeframes.[95] Bissell also noted that many of the younger, more military active, but progressively oriented anti-Castro Cubans were very much at odds with several of the older, more conservative Cuban establishment political figures. Ultimately, as new resistance groups and new Cuban military activists emerged (and as internal conflicts continued among the Cuban exile leaders) by November, 1960 Bissell had determined that it would be the CIA rather than the FRD which would make all the decisions about which resistance groups it would work with and how resources would be allocated.[96] While this was understandable from an operational standpoint, that decision was a further source of discord among the FRD leadership.

The limited role of the FRD, the lack of a single, designated opposition military leader (as had been standard practice in earlier, successful CIA regime change efforts), and the competition between exile political factions became increasingly visible and of more concern during the fall of 1960. Internal strife within the exile leadership mounted as the volunteer force in training grew in size, and began to transition from a relatively small cadre of resistance leaders into a more conventional military unit. A study of Cuban volunteer debriefing documents containing actual remarks from the Cubans themselves reveals that there was discord over roles from the very beginning of the training effort. A good deal of the dissatisfaction lay in volunteer expectations in regard to the military chain of command. The FRD had established its own military staff and clearly expected to have a role in training and military operations.[97] That view was reflected in the volunteers recruited by the various affiliated FRD groups, who each expected to encounter chains of command running back through their own groups or at least to the FRD. In contrast, volunteers recruited by the CIA appear to have understood that they would be fully under CIA military command.

The Cuba Project team chief's later remarks on issues related to chain of command issues appear to understate the ongoing problems with the volunteer training effort. Internal political conflicts in the Guatemala military training camp had come to a point of open confrontation as early as September, 1960 and what CIA project reports referred to as a "dissident problem" was documented in a memorandum on a training camp meeting of September 25. In that meeting certain trainees were accused of being involved with slander, gossip, rumors and agitation, which had risen to such a level that the CIA officers involved felt that an actual conspiracy appeared to be in play, undermining the military effort of the project.[98] The individuals identified as dissidents were described as continually expressing their opposition to the former Cuban Army personnel who had been delegated by the CIA to run the camp on a daily basis. The "dissidents" referred to those Cuban leaders as worse than Castro, and statements were made that if the Castro was ousted there would need to be another revolution against the "Army men."

The CIA officers suspected that the "dissidents" had intentionally infiltrated the training in an effort to undermine it or at least delay its progress. They were described as specifically targeting personnel who were either former Cuban Army members or volunteers from the

MRR group (Artime's group). They had reportedly threatened to break off once inside Cuba and eliminate those individuals, then join with their own groups for unilateral actions. A number of the very early Cuban volunteers that had been personally recruited by Manual Artime presumed they would find him in a command position, but that never occurred. Although Artime was quite involved with the American military commanders – even being considered by them for a special mission into Cuba – he played no role in the training or leadership of either the early infiltrations missions or the final infantry training.

The CIA meetings on what was obviously a serious morale problem resulted in the decision to separate and detain what were described as nine "hard core agitators," as well as to maintain a watch on three others. Initially nine of the dissidents were put under a special watch, until a detention area could be prepared. The CIA reports also noted that there were others in training who were viewed as undesirables as they were either criminals out of New York or Miami or individuals planted by various political factions. The trainers were pushing to have a contingent ready to go into Cuba in October, but noted that it was a real challenge given the quality of the volunteers and that any initial force would have to be selected from the "relatively few good men on board."[99] Beyond incidents with individual "dissidents," over the entire period of training volunteers recruited by different FRD leaders openly expressed conflicting political views. They also advocated for advanced positions for their preferred political leader, or his designated representatives in the military effort, and protested when that did not occur. By November, 1960 CIA memoranda dealing with the camps reflect a lack of both political connection between the trainees and the FRD, as well as trainee concerns that new CIA military appointments within the Cuban force were being made to appease and pacify political factions rather than on the individual's own merit and skills.[100]

Bissell himself was ultimately forced to acknowledge that there was sufficient discontent and contention both among FRD leaders and with the volunteers that the CIA itself "actively intervened to prevent visits by the political leaders during December and January....this was deeply resented by the political leaders...and lack of contact with the political leadership left the Cuban military unsure of what and for whom they were going to have to fight." [101] The reason for the ban was that up to the last moment various political leaders were trying to secure future positions inside Cuba by maneuvering to have their political supporters appointed into military leadership positions. Bissell even expressed the view that exposure to the exile political figures might well have fragmented and disrupted the entire Cuban Expeditionary Force – at a time when it had become the only real CIA asset for regime change in Cuba. In early 1961 Bissell and the Cuba Project leadership were forced to face the fact that discord within the FRD had prevented it from functioning in a military leadership role. It had served as a propaganda cover, but had totally failed from an operational standpoint and it was impossible to view its undertakings as effectively directing any united military effort. With that in mind, and with the new goal for the force being an amphibious landing and the creation of a lodgment inside Cuba, a new political action effort was made to create an exile leadership group which might serve as a credible provisional government.

In Denial

During the final months before the landings, CIA political officers reached out to virtually all anti-Castro opposition leaders in an attempt to move them into a group which could present itself as a governing body prior to new elections in Cuba (elections clearly not involving members of the Castro regime). Following constant negotiations with all the prominent leaders during February and March, the formation of a new leadership council (the Cuban Revolutionary Council) with Miro Cardona as its head was finalized on March 22, 1961 – less than a month prior to the actual landings in Cuba. Yet even Bissell acknowledged that, as with the early FRD executive committee, certain members of the new Cuban Revolutionary Council would have not been welcomed in the Guatemala infantry training camp - and the new CRC leadership council was not allowed direct contact with the infantry brigade. Bissell went so far to say that by the time of the landings at the Bay of Pigs, the political/military relationship with the Cuban Expeditionary Force was the best it ever had been, yet he admitted that the Cuban force had only "superficially" accepted its relationship to the Cuban Revolutionary Council. The most positive characterization he could give was that the creation of the council had been a step forward in the political action effort.[102] There is reason to believe that even with that qualified statement, Bissell was painting an over optimistic view of what were deep and ongoing conflicts within the groups participating in the military operation. A CIA internal memorandum of March 30, 1961 reports on intelligence of a purported conspiracy among certain establishment oriented anti-Castro factions and former Cuban Army officers within the Brigade. The report described a clandestine effort to align support within the expeditionary force towards Manuel Artime, so that after the invasion and ouster of Castro they would replace the CRC and Miro Cardona with an Artime regime largely controlled by former Batista era political figures.[103]

Another rumor circulating within the exile community was that a plan existed to eliminate the more socialist and populist volunteers within the military force, including those affiliated with Manuel Ray. Ray had been persuaded to join the Cuban Revolutionary Council only weeks before the landings (he was strongly opposed by main line factions and leaders such as Artime). The task was reportedly to be carried out by a specially CIA trained group of intelligence personnel, volunteers who had been trained to go into Cuba with the mission of locating and neutralizing Castro's leadership cadre and prominent communists as the first step in establishing a new post-Castro civil administration program.[104] A reading of the various official debriefings and interviews with the Cuban volunteers provides further confirmation of political conflicts and leadership difficulties in the military training camps. Those insights are more detailed and arguably more realistic than the remarks in the CIA operations memoranda (or in Bissell's remarks). It appears that ongoing protests about the lack of direct FRD leadership involvement in military affairs actually continued through January and into February, 1961. Actual desertions began to occur in February.[105]

While the formation of the Cuban Revolutionary Council and the installation of Miro Cardona as the chief of the council (hence the leader of the FRD) had provided some level of relief, personal opposition even to the elevation of Cardona was expressed by a number of the trainees. In retrospect and with a view of matters from inside the Cuban volunteer ranks, it appears that the political conflicts and leadership issues had indeed not been truly resolved prior to the dispatch of the Cuban Expeditionary Force to the Bay of Pigs, they had simply faded into the background as final movements and preparations for the force's landings in Cuba became the focus of attention.[106] The view that political reconciliations were still tenuous seems confirmed by the reality that the CIA actually felt it necessary to isolate the CRC leadership during the actual landings in Cuba, with CIA personnel even preparing and issuing political statements in the CRC's name. The chief of the CRC, Miro Cardona (a former Cuban government Prime Minister), presumably the head of the new Cuban provisional government, remained in the United States with the rest of the CRC leadership.

The only member of the CRC to actually accompany the Brigade and land with the military force was Manual Artime, who was an early FRD executive council member and perhaps the most militarily active political leader. Yet Artime had no command role with the Brigade, nor in the landings themselves, which were effectively managed by the CIA military advisors on the landing craft command ships. Artime's designated position within the CRC carried no military endorsement; he had been designated as the Economic Administrator in the new, provisional Cuban government. Miro Cardona had announced him as simply the CRC "delegate" of the military force. The Brigade had its own CIA designated Cuban military leaders. Those leaders were in communications with the CIA field officers who sailed with the expeditionary force, however only the CIA officers themselves were in direct communications with the project's senior CIA leadership or the Brigade's air unit at the Nicaragua strike base.

Ramifications:

This examination of both the propaganda and political action aspects of the Cuba Project reveals that while there were no funding restrictions, there were a number of policy decisions which did constrain both activities. Propaganda operations were further limited by the pace of the project as well as the failure to produce an expanding insurgency inside Cuba. The "real time" propaganda and psychological warfare tactics (based on air strikes and the advance of rebel forces towards the capital) which had proved effective in Guatemala simply never came into play in Cuban operations. In regard to political action, policy decisions were made which did have a considerable operational impact.

In prior covert actions, the CIA had directly involved itself with selecting political leaders, negotiating with those individuals directly, and effectively designating them as the new political leaders of the nations being targeted. In Iran, were a military coup was organized, the CIA had identified an opposition figure with extensive support within the Iranian military - Major General Fazlollah Zahedi - as the American champion. It was clearly understood that CIA efforts were intended to place him in political control of Iran as its Premier. And in regard to the military elements of the coup, it was Zahedi who was in charge, with a series of identified army units supporting him. Although it had been challenging, there had been no political or military disconnects in the successful Iranian effort. During a debriefing on that action, the CIA officer in charge, Kermit Roosevelt Jr., had summed up the lessons learned in the very first CIA regime change project: *"If we, the CIA, are going to try something like this again, we must be absolutely sure that the people and the Army [in the targeted country] want what we want. If not, you had better give the job to the marines."[107]* Although it was offered with the voice of experience, Roosevelt's advice certainly did not become institutionalized in American covert action policy.

The CIA's next regime change project, in Guatemala, also involved selecting a single individual to lead both the military and political elements. Carlos Castillo Armas had received military training in the United States at Fort Leavenworth, Kansas and served on the Guatemalan Army General Staff. Later, in its 1958 Indonesian operation, the CIA contacted specific Indonesian Army officers (on different islands) and provided them each with support. Acting on their own, the officers formed an independent provisional government – the Revolutionary Government of the Republic of Indonesia - with its own cabinet. The scope of that insurgency, extending over a number of large but scattered islands in the Indonesian Archipelago, placed a real limitation on the opposition's military efforts. The central government was able to independently move against each military group, reducing them one by one. In some respects that tactic foreshadowed the Castro government's defeat of individual resistance groups inside Cuba, engaging and eliminating them one by one and on occasions with thousands of troops and militia deployed against vastly smaller guerilla forces.

As compared to the earlier Iranian, Guatemalan, and Indonesian operations, the Cuban Project's political action efforts were both exceedingly complex and ambitious. Rather than specifically identifying select military figures (designated for both resistance and political leadership) the "non-intervention policy" implemented under Richard Bissell attempted to distance the CIA from the political aspect of replacing the Castro regime. Yet for over a year CIA political action officers remained constantly engaged in simply maintaining a level of coexistence among the political front which they had organized so quickly in the first month of the project. That ongoing discord among the political factions led Bissell to operationally divorce the FRD first from the propaganda effort and within months from the planning and control of military operations. This led to a much more extensive involvement of CIA personnel than had been anticipated.

Earlier regime change projects had been carried out by very small numbers of CIA political and military personnel, with active US military involvement in transportation and logistics. Initially the Cuba Project had been structured in the same mold – with the original organization specified as involving only some 40 CIA personnel and with the number of trained Cuban resistance fighters estimated at no more than 500 volunteers. Yet, over the span of the project, the CIA participation had expanded to 588 individuals, not counting personnel assigned from the CIA's own air operations group.[108] In terms of Cuban volunteers the infantry brigade dispatched to the landings at the Bay of Pigs involved some 1,500 men. In addition, some 60 volunteers were dispatched as a diversionary force under Nino Diaz. That force arrived in Cuban waters in the vicinity of Baracoa, near the US base at Guantanamo, but failed to even send anyone onshore. Additionally, some 100 highly trained personnel intended to serve as military intelligence and civil administration groups under a Cuban provisional government had been prepared and dispatched, but were unable to be deployed into Cuba after the defeat on the beaches (those groups were designated as AMOTS, AMCHEERS, and AMFASTS).[109] Finally, an estimated 100 paramilitary personnel had been selected to conduct covert intelligence collection and military infiltration missions in advance of the landings. A number of those individuals had been inserted onto the island. Some of them were captured, but others managed to extract themselves out of Cuba in the months following the failure at the Bay of Pigs.

In the end the very first estimate of some 60 specially trained Cuban cadre had grown first to 500, and ultimately to something on the order of 1,800 volunteers. During its 13 months the Cuba Project had expanded at an unprecedented rate, evolving through two distinct phases into a military effort beyond anything the CIA had ever attempted up to that point in time. While policy decisions within the project had led to some restriction of the propaganda effort, in terms of effect the result was to place CIA personnel in virtually total control of propaganda, political action, and military operations. The impact of that approach on the overall project can be debated as the report of the CIA Inspector General and rebuttal of the Cuba Project team leader clearly illustrate disagreement on the issue. What cannot be debated is that there were very significant constraints and restrictions placed on both the political action and the actual military operations of the project. These were restrictions that had never been applied to prior covert CIA action projects and certainly not to prior regime change operations and we shall explore the specifics of the military restrictions in the next chapter.

Secret Wars With Air Strikes And Tanks?

Notes

[73] The Secretary of State to the Embassy in Italy, Gala showing "Thanks America," Washington, March 24, 1948, *Foreign Relations of the United States, 1948, Volume III*, Office of the State Historian, United States Department of State
https://history.state.gov/historicaldocuments/frus1948v03/d532

[74] Mario Del Pero, "The United States and Psychological Warfare in Italy; 1948-1955," *The Journal of American History*, March 2001, 1307-1308
http://www.academicroom.com/article/united-states-and-psychological-warfare-italy-1948-1955

[75] Memorandum Prepared in the Office of National Estimates, Central Intelligence Agency, Washington, March 9, 1951, Memorandum of Information Number for the National Estimates Board, Subject: The Situation in Iran. *Foreign Relations of the United States, 1952-1954, Iran, 1951–1954,* Office of the Historian, Department of State, United States of America
https://history.state.gov/historicaldocuments/frus1951-54Iran/d3

[76] Walter Hixon, *Parting the Curtain: Propaganda, Culture and the Cold War,* 63

[77] Hugh Wilford, *The Mighty Wurlitzer: How the CIA Played America,* 35

[78] Foreign Relations of the United States, *Dispatch to [ ],* "Training," 6 June 1954, Box 75 (Secret, PBSUCCESS, Rybat). [ ] and Memorandum to LINCOLN Station, 16 May 1954, "Tactical Instructions (part II)" (S) and To LINCOLN "Instructions" Nerve War Against Individuals," 9 June 1954, Box 50 (S) Cited in Gerald K Haines, CIA and Guatemala

Assassinations Proposals 1952-1954, CIA History Staff Analysis, 1995
https://www.cia.gov/library/readingroom/docs/DOC_0000135796.pdf

[79]Foreign Relations of the United States, *Chief, Economic Warfare, [ ] memo to All Staff Officers, "Selection of individuals for Disposal by Junta Group." 31 March 1954, Box 145 (S). Cited in Gerald K Haines, CIA and Guatemala Assassinations Proposals 1952-1954, CIA History Staff Analysis, 1995*

Document location, Foreign Relations, Guatemala, 1952-1954, Released by the Office of the Historian Documents 104-132; U.S. Department of State Archive; *Item #119*
https://2001-2009.state.gov/r/pa/ho/frus/ike/guat/20178.htm

[80]David Phillips, *The Night Watch*, New York, Atheneum, 1977, 36

[81] Colonel J.C. King, "First Meeting of the Branch 4 Task Force," *WH/4*, March 9, 1960
https://www.maryferrell.org/showDoc.html?docId=197408&relPageId=2&search=stanulis

[82] David Atlee Phillips, *The Night Watch*, Ballantine Books, New York, 1989, 122

[83] "Brief History of Radio Swan, *Taylor Committee Study, Annex 2*

[84] Jack Pfeiffer, Official *History of the Bay of Pigs Operation, Volume 1 Air Operations Part 1, U.S. Governments' Anti-Castro Program, Central Intelligence Agency*, Central Intelligence Agency, Washington D.C., October 13, 2016, Document Number: 5076ddc4993247d4d82b58da, 146

Secret Wars With Air Strikes And Tanks?

[85] Proposal to the Special Group, "A Program of Covert Action Against the Cuban Government," March 16, 1960 as presented in *The Inspector General's Survey of the Cuban Operation, October 1961, Annex A*

[86] "Office of Policy Coordination 1948-1953"; CIA History Document, Released March 1997, 12
https://cryptome.org/2012/05/cia-opc.pdf

[87] Walter Hixon, *Parting the Curtain: Propaganda, Culture and the Cold War* (Palgrave McMillian, 1998), 66, Also The Report on the President's Committee on International Information Activities, also known as the "Jackson Committee"
https://www.cia.gov/library/readingroom/docs/DOC_000047693 9.pdf

[88] Hugh Wilford, *The Mighty Wurlitzer: How the CIA Played America*, 7

[89] John Prados, Editor, *Bay of Pig's Declassified; The Secret CIA Report on the Invasion of Cuba*, New Press and National Security Archive, New York, 1998, 33

[90] CIA Office Memorandum, Meeting with Artime and General Erskine, September 6, 1960
https://www.maryferrell.org/showDoc.html?docId=21067&search=droller#relPageId=3&tab=page

[91] Democratic Revolutionary Front (FRD), Federal Bureau of Investigation, New York, New York, September 20, 1960
https://www.maryferrell.org/showDoc.html?docId=83062#relPageId=3&tab=page

[92] Memorandum for Director CIA, Subject: Artime Buesa, Manuel Francisco, , via Deputy Director of Plans (Richard Bissell), from Chief Western Hemisphere (J.C. King), February 1, 1961

https://www.maryferrell.org/showDoc.html?docId=62352&search=%22lacks_facilities+for+accomplishing+this%22#relPageId=54&tab=page

[93] Richard Bissell, The FRD Political Element, "An Analysis of the Cuban Operation by the Deputy Director (Plans) Central Intelligence Agency, January 18, 1962, 33, 216 Sourced from Peter Kornbluh, *Bay of Pigs Declassified*, 133-234

[94] Ibid, 218-219

[95] Ibid, 220 - 222

[96] Richard Bissell noted that by early fall, 1960 there were over sixty "active and vocal" anti-Castro political groups operating in the Miami, Florida area. Some involved only three or four people and no group activities inside Cuba at all. Beyond that, the initial on-island groups identified in the original CIA proposal as offering the best hopes for on-island military action had largely been suppressed, with new groups replacing them. Ibid, 216-218

[97] Memorandum of an interview conducted at Coral Gables, Subject: Training Bases, Florida, February, 1961, Artime File, CIA Historical Records release, 5-11
https://www.maryferrell.org/showDoc.html?docId=62352&search=%22lacks_facilities+for+accomplishing+this%22#relPageId=54&tab=page

[98] Message to Director/CIA from WH/9, Dissident Problem, September 30, 1960, 81-82
https://www.maryferrell.org/showDoc.html?docId=55260&relPageId=81&search=2523

[99] Ibid, 82-83
https://www.maryferrell.org/showDoc.html?docId=55260&search=2523#relPageId=83&tab=page

Secret Wars With Air Strikes And Tanks?

[100] Memorandum to Director, JMTRAV trip report (infantry training camp, Guatemala), November 29, 1960
https://www.maryferrell.org/showDoc.html?docId=17589&search=enzel#relPageId=2&tab=page

[101] John Prados, Editor, *Bay of Pig's Declassified; The Secret CIA Report on the Invasion of Cuba*, 220-221

[102] Ibid, 221

[103] Cable, Miami Station [JMWAVE) to Cuba Project headquarters (BELL), Conspiracy Sponsored by Batista Followers, March 30, 1961
https://www.maryferrell.org/showDoc.html?docId=17589&#relPageId=2&tab=page

[104] White House Memorandum, Schlesinger to Goodwin, Sam Halpern information on Operation 40 and Sanjenis, June 9, 1961

[105] "Interview with former prisoner of war" (former Bay of Pigs prisoner), Central Intelligence Agency, December, 1962, 1-4
https://www.maryferrell.org/showDoc.html?docId=61514#relPageId=3&tab=page

[106] Ibid, 5-6

[107] Kermit Roosevelt Jr., senior officer Middle Eastern Division, White House debriefing remarks on Iranian Coup/Operation Ajax, 1954

[108] John Prados, Editor, *Bay of Pig's Declassified; The Secret CIA Report on the Invasion of Cuba*, 27

[109] Separate groups of Cuban volunteers were extensively trained by the CIA as intelligence and civil administration officers. Designated by the cryptonyms AMOT and AMCHEER some of

these volunteers were inserted prior to the infantry landings, others were prepared to go in with the landing force and proceed with the identification and neutralization of Castro regime and his supporting communist party cadre. They were expected to form the initial core of the provisional government's intelligence service and support its civil administration operations. Following the failure of the landings, the group was reformed as a domestic Cuban focused domestic intelligence service – with its members continuing to be designated as AMOTS. Memorandum for the Record, Interview with the Chief of WH/4's Intelligence Section, June 5, 1961 and Memorandum for Chief WH/4, CI Program for JMATE Project, April 20, 1961
https://www.maryferrell.org/showDoc.html?docId=16200&relPageId=42
https://www.maryferrell.org/showDoc.html?docId=16200#relPageId=60&tab=page

Chapter 3: Insurgency

In late June, 1960 the National Security Council was briefed on the plan for the Cuba Project and the briefing paper for the meeting described the recruiting and training of some 500 Cuban volunteers, a force comparable in size although a bit larger than the number of CIA surrogate fighters involved in the Guatemala project. The Cubans would be split into 25 teams or "action cadres," each of which would be highly trained in guerilla tactics and supported by a radio operator. The goal would be to infiltrate them into Cuba to serve as trainers and leaders for on-island resistance groups which would be supported by a guerrilla air campaign. Those activities were expected to lead to defections and an island wide insurgency, resulting in the overthrow of the Castro regime. The original operations plan developed for the project called for aerial supply missions to the insurgents as well as an extended period of tactical air strikes supporting their military actions. The initial air operations schedule specified the schedule for acquisition and preparation of air operations facilities (July 20-Aug 15), aircraft acquisition/crew training/operations planning (August 15-October 1), and tactical air operations to be conducted over a minimum of three months (October - December).[110]

In Denial

If that original operations planning time table had come to fruition, by the end of October, 1961 a number of aggressive new guerilla assaults would have been underway inside Cuba. Resistance groups would have been well supplied with weapons and ammunition, led by CIA trained volunteers and in routine contact by radio for the coordination of supply efforts as well as ongoing air strikes. Those ground and air campaigns would have provided the news required for an aggressive propaganda campaign designed to weaken confidence in the Castro regime and encourage defections. The FRD political front would have been able to take credit for the growing armed opposition in Cuba, advancing its reputation and giving it the status to assert itself as a legitimate opposition government.

The project's aggressive operations timetable was driven by two concerns - the growing effectiveness of Castro's internal security controls and the pace at which his regime was increasing its military capabilities. In a National Security Council briefing on June 22, CIA officers had cautioned that those were the main risks to the project. At that point resistance groups were known to be conducting some sabotage activities on the island, including setting fire to sugar cane fields, but no military opposition of any real strength had yet emerged, even among the groups with which the CIA had ongoing contacts. It was going to be critical to quickly train and infiltrate guerilla force cadres, supply a number of groups inside militarily denied territory, and conduct ongoing tactical air strikes to enable sustained resistance activities sufficient to demonstrate a credible military opposition to Castro's government. This was all challenging, but well within the CIA's existing skill set and by 1960 the CIA was well experienced in all the required activities, including paramilitary training, covert supply missions into denied territories, and deniable combat air operations.

During the Korean War, the CIA had initially used American military pilots and aircraft to fly clandestine missions over mainland China; missions including agent parachute drops. After one such flight over China was shot down in 1952, US military personnel were banned from China overflights. At that point the CIA turned to using personnel from its own proprietary cover company – Civil Air Transport (CAT), headquartered in Nationalist China on Taiwan. CAT had been established as a CIA commercial cover in 1950.[111] By 1951 the CIA was using CAT aircraft and crews to clandestinely support Nationalist Chinese forces operating along the remote border areas of Burma and China. Enabled with CIA air drops of some 3,000 rifles and 160,000 pounds of ammunition, Republic of China troops actually moved across the Chinese border and occupied portions of Chinese territory for some months.[112]

In the Guatemala regime change operation of 1954, the CIA fielded its own paramilitary officers for ground forces training and coordination of "guerilla air force" air strikes. That air effort began with the use of surplus B-26 fighter bombers for leaflet drops over the capital of Guatemala City. Once the surrogate infantry groups actually moved into Guatemala actual combat air operations began. A dozen military aircraft were used to conduct air strikes against Guatemalan military bases and targets in the capital city - in conjunction with the groups advancing into the country. A dozen different combat aircraft including both bombers and fighters were used against Guatemala, flown by Nationalist Chinese pilots. The "guerilla" air campaign in Guatemala had been something of a scratch effort, lasting only a few weeks, using WWII surplus bombs, and even improvised explosives dropped from the aircraft. However, within a few more years the CIA would significantly advance the sophistication of its deniable air operations.

In 1949, the CIA recruited Czech pilots living in Britain (they had flown for the British during the Battle of Britain) to fly clandestine missions over the Ukraine. In 1950 six Poles who had also flown for the British were recruited for Albanian missions, and in 1955 Polish pilots were used for the first CIA clandestine air missions into Tibet. The Tibetan missions were conducted in hopes of encouraging military resistance to the ongoing Chinese incursions into that country.[113] Early missions were flown using aircraft (all black B-17's) out of Taiwan, flown though Clark Air Base in the Philippines, and then staged into Tibet out of a field in East Pakistan. The aircraft carried out covert air supply drops to resistance fighters in Tibet.[114] The early Polish air crews were eventually replaced first by Nationalist Chinese military pilots and later by American aviators flying for CAT out of Taiwan. By 1958 the clandestine CIA air missions were successfully dropping paramilitary volunteers into Tibet - as well as hundreds of deniable .303 Lee Infield rifles and cases of ammunition. At the end of the year some 18,000 pounds of weapons, ammunition, and communications equipment had been ferried into Tibet, one of the most challenging terrains on the planet.[115]

The CIA had also established an effective partnership with the US Air Force in regard to logistics support for its clandestine missions. During the 1950's the Air Force had organized its own units to support clandestine operations, beginning with the neutrally named Air Resupply and Communications Service (ARCS), intended to have a global reach. It also established regional units such as the 322nd Troop Carrier Squadron operating out of Kadena Air Base in Okinawa – the unit which provided primary transport and logistics support for the CIA's clandestine Tibet missions. In addition to ferrying supplies for the missions into Tibet, the Air Force provided clandestine transportation for the Tibetan guerilla volunteers, all of whom needed basic military training as well as advanced training in guerilla tactics and in portable radio operations. The Tibetan volunteers were initially taken to a secret US Navy facility on Saipan (designated as the Navy Technical Training Unit). Beginning in 1950 that base had been used for training Chinese Nationalists, South Koreans, and other Asian volunteers as agents, paramilitary operatives, and resistance fighters and it would continue to be used in later years to train Laotians and South Vietnamese.

In training the Tibetans for mountain operations, the CIA decided a more realistic facility was required and moved to set up a new training base for them in Colorado.[116] Training in the Colorado camp was conducted during 1958 and through 1960, with air operations into Tibet continuing through the entire period. With the number of missions increasing, a support base for the supply line into East Pakistan was established in Takhli, Thailand. The overall logistics operation was under the control of the Operational Evaluation and Training Group, commanded by an Air Force officer (Heine Aderholt), detailed to the CIA for covert air operations. Aderholt would go on to become the mainstay of CIA Air Operations in Laos, beginning with its initial Mill Pond clandestine air operations during the early 1960s.

With even this brief overview of the CIA's clandestine air operations, including extremely high-risk missions into denied territories, it becomes clear that the Cuba Project would have been able to call on extremely competent and experienced Air Force resources for its logistics, air transport, and personnel insertion missions. Air Force officers were available upon request and personnel such as Aderholt were routinely detailed for such clandestine projects. The project could also have turned to its own clandestine assets, companies such as CAT/Air America. As a last resort it could even have simply contracted independent pilots and air crews as in previous operations. As recently as 1958 the CIA had called upon its own clandestine resources, hired contract pilots, and turned to the United States Navy in support of the Indonesian regime change project. With those assets its field officers had organized not only major supply efforts to a number of resistance groups on islands across the Indonesian Archipelago, but fielded yet another "guerilla" air force. That deniable air effort was larger and far more aggressive than the earlier Guatemala action. CIA "revolutionary" aircraft carried out an extensive air campaign against both central government ground forces and commercial shipping in the island chain.

An overview of the Indonesian operations provides a very useful benchmark of what the CIA was able to accomplish in a very brief period of time and with only a handful of its own personnel. It also provides a critical reference into the degree that the Cuba Project was indeed constrained in virtually all its military activities. President Eisenhower had officially committed the United States to a program of support for opposition and resistance groups across Indonesia in September, 1957. The goal was to either totally oust the Indonesian central government (felt to be too communist leaning) or to at least pressure it into

Secret Wars With Air Strikes And Tanks?

moving away from its stance of neutrality in foreign relations as a way to thwart potential Soviet influence.[117] In support of that effort the CIA deployed a limited number of its military personnel from Singapore, from Taipei on Formosa, and from CIA headquarters in Washington D.C. Covert action to sufficiently strengthen the various opposition groups required a considerable military effort as the Indonesian government was well equipped, with its own air force of light bombers and fighter aircraft, paratroop transports, heavy weapons and a capability for moving its forces by sea.

In an effort to quickly build up the insurgent forces, the CIA turned to the US Navy. The Navy began shipments of weapons and ammunition in November, 1957. The first deliveries (Operation HAIK) were made by submarine (the US Navy submarine Bluegill) and on barges towed by the landing ship U.S.S. Thomaston, sailing out of Subic Bay in the Philippines.[118] The Thomaston's cargo included supplies for over 8,000 fighters. As in the Guatemala operation, American aircraft and ships would transport weapons and supplies into Indonesia far in excess of anything required by the actual numbers of resistance fighters involved in military combat. By early 1958 regular clandestine supply flights had begun, with aircraft chartered by the CIA flying out of the Philippines. In March, 1958 large amounts of combat material was being carried in not only by aircraft but in a new Navy barge towing effort (Operation HANCE).

In addition, the CIA arranged for Nationalist China to support the insurgency, and Taipei responded by committing transport and attack aircraft as well as sending in cargoes of supplies by freighter.[119] Later in 1958, in the face of central government military successes, the Navy organized Task Force 57, consisting of two destroyers with a cruiser and aircraft carrier scheduled to follow. The Navy proposed "bloodying the nose" of a planned Indonesian government military initiative which might have involved air attacks on oil company facilities employing American civilians. The Navy offer was rejected, largely due to the shared position of Secretary of State John Foster Dulles and Alan Dulles that American civilian casualties would offer major leverage for official protests against further military action against the insurgencies.[120]

Covert operations in Indonesia and across South East Asia illustrate that both the US Air Force and US Navy were experienced, and in fact eager to support CIA missions, both with clandestine operations and if necessary, more overtly. One of the most striking policy restrictions placed on the Cuba Project was not only that it was not allowed to use any Air Force or Navy assets in support of its supply and paramilitary operations, but that personnel detailed from the services (in particular the Air Force) would not be allowed to participate even in non-combat supply activities. Beyond that, the Cuba Project was also not allowed to use one of the most significant clandestine military assets that the CIA had called repeatedly during the decade of the 1950's – experienced military pilots flying on contract or under commercial cover. That is particularly striking given the Indonesian experiences of 1958, only a short time before the Cuba Project started its operations in 1960. President Eisenhower himself had proposed and authorized providing covert air support to the Indonesian effort and had even authorized hiring American contract pilots.[121] In terms of Cuba, it is unclear that similar practices were actually broached with the National Security Council or the president.

In Indonesia, CIA officers had assembled and fielded what amounted to a full guerilla air force, composed of contract aircrews and fighter and bomber (B-26) aircraft obtained via the Air Force's Clark Field in the Philippines.[122] The aircraft were purchased under war surplus cover, stripped of Air Force markings and sent on strafing and bombing attacks across the Indonesian archipelago – positioned as the Revolutionary Air Force (AUREV), a fictional organization headed by insurgents formerly associated with the Indonesian Air Force. CIA support of the effort was so enthusiastic (and visible) that the Navy delivered barge loads of bombs and aviation fuel directly to the aerial strike base in the Philippines.[123] The Indonesian air effort had been authorized in March and aircraft began ground attack missions within little more than a month. By May the CIA air group was retargeted on to commercial shipping, carrying out attacks on Panamanian, Greek, and British flagged oil tankers and transport ships as well as oil production and shipping facilities. The air attacks were actually quite effective, causing commercial carriers including Dutch vessels to order a cessation of shipping in Indonesian waters.[124] Beyond that, strikes were also conducted against central government naval units sailing against opposition forces.

In authorizing the CIA air strikes against the Indonesian government ships, President Eisenhower had even raised the possibility of dispatching Navy submarines to deal with the problem.[125] During the extended series of Indonesian air attacks, carried out over some three months, one American CIA contract pilot was shot down, captured, and exposed. But by that time American involvement had already been made visible in a number of instances — in one incident pallets of captured weapons clearly showed shipping labels listing their transshipment from Taiwan via Clark Air Force Base in the Philippines. No particular concerns over the exposure were expressed by the president, and CIA Director Allen Dulles arranged for the award of the CIA's prestigious Intelligence Star to the project's team leader, even though the regime change project ultimately failed in its mission. [126]

Given the approval and encouragement of President Eisenhower, his National Security Council, and the CIA's own director for the 1958 covert operations in Indonesia, it is something of a surprise to find how severely the Cuba Project of 1960 was restricted in regard to its efforts to develop, supply, and support armed resistance inside Cuba. Clearly it progressed slowly compared to the Indonesian operations, and employed virtually none of the military resources that had been used in Guatemala, Tibet, or Indonesia. In fact, it appears that these project policy and operational decisions may well have slowed the pace of the first phase of the project to the point of mission failure in regard to its original timetable for the creation of a broad insurgency by November, 1960. That failure involved all three military elements of the original operational plan including a) contacting active resistance groups and inserting trained guerilla cadre to lead them, b) supplying them with quantities of weapons, ammunition and explosives, and c) supporting them with tactical air strikes (initially targeting airfields and barracks, but with combat air support on call).[127]

In retrospect, the actual pace of the project's first phase (Insurgency) never came close to supporting the project's earliest planning timeline. The initial date specified for the volunteer cadre training in Panama had been May 1 and it had been emphasized that third country training locations would be absolutely necessary for the larger groups of ground and air volunteers. Starting up training outside the US, at brand new locations, became even more of a challenge when the number of volunteers to be inserted into Cuba was dramatically increased from an original 60 men to some 500 in June. At that time the initial recruiting and security vetting of the very first volunteers, the core of the Cuban training cadre, was still in progress. It was only on June 2 that the first eight Cuban volunteers had been taken from Miami to Fort Meyers for a boat trip to Useppa Island (crypto JMPICK) where they were interviewed and evaluated. The new volunteers were accompanied by Manuel Artime, a former anti-Batista resistance fighter active in the Castro revolution. [128] During 1959 Artime had become a professor at the Havana Military Academy, only to break with Castro's new regime to become actively involved in forming the Movement to Recover the Revolution (/MRR) prior to being assisted out of Cuba by the CIA.

CIA documents reveal that these first key CIA recruits were both suspicious and tense and the men had traveled with personal weapons and there was an issue of trust and a definite hesitancy to surrender them upon arrival. It was only the assurances of the Cubans traveling with them – Artime and Manuel Blanco – rather than from the CIA officer accompanying them, Carl Jenkins - that turned around what was briefly an armed standoff. Some three weeks later, Jenkins was able to take the first volunteers to Fort Glick, in Panama, for their initial preparation as training cadre. Carl Jenkin's (pseudonym James D Zaboth[129]) background illustrates the extent to which the

In Denial

CIA already had experienced military staff available for such tasks. Jenkins was a WWII veteran who had become a paramilitary instructor for the CIA in 1952. His specialties were maritime infiltration and guerilla/resistance tactics, as well as evasion and escape. Jenkins had earlier conducted paramilitary training for Thai and Nationalist Chinese personnel before moving on to perform similar duties in Malaysia and the Philippines and Indonesia.

As we have seen, the CIA had previously conducted extensive paramilitary training (including radio operations and various types of sabotage) at American military facilities, ranging from the US Navy installation on Saipan to the Tibet training camp in Colorado. The first Cuban volunteers received radio operations training on Useppa Island but the exact details of the training decision remain unclear because the policy was established that third country training was mandatory. The major training for the guerilla force would be conducted in Guatemala at a location where facilities would need to be constructed almost entirely from the bare ground. The decision not to use established training centers on American facilities, either in the United States or overseas, led to significant delay in the start of actual training, as did the lack of sufficient military training personnel.[130] While CIA paramilitary officers such as Jenkins might well have been able to handle training for what had initially been planned as only some 60 experienced individuals (many of them former Cuban military) the lack of trainers became critical with the change of plan to some 500 trainees. It was only in September, 1960 that the Cuba Project managed to conclude an agreement to bring in more trainers – not from the American military, but rather 26 individuals from the CIA's own AEDEPOT program.

Secret Wars With Air Strikes And Tanks?

That program involved a special unit established in Europe, with personnel including Soviet defectors and expatriates. It had been formed to carry out clandestine missions in support of American Special forces in the event of Soviet military combat in Europe.[131] Yet even with the agreement for very special AEDEPOT support, the foreign trainers did not arrive and begin actually working with the Cuban volunteers in Guatemala until December. It would not be until the focus on insurgency had been abandoned for the amphibious landing plan that American Special Forces trainers would arrive to work with the Cuban trainees in February, 1961. Details and criticisms of the early months of training received some attention in the CIA Inspector General's report, primarily in regard to the total lack of facilities and it was noted that when the CIA project officer arrived in Guatemala he literally had to locate sites, contract supplies and equipment, and do everything with only three assistants - two contract employees and a communications aide.

Bissell's rebuttal to the IG criticism focused largely on the Guatemala bases as they were operated to support the final phase of the project (Amphibious Landings). His remarks in reference to Guatemala contain frequent reference to the project's military commander, Marine Colonel Jack Hawkins. In reality Hawkins was only detailed to the project in October, at the point in which the project plan began to morph from insurgency and paramilitary action into the insertion of a conventional infantry force.[132] Hawkins himself stated that he was told only that "the CIA wants to land a few Cuban exile troops in Cuba and they have asked for a Marine Colonel to give them some help on this."[133] Ultimately Hawkins would be directed to develop a constantly expanding number of recruits into a 1,500 man force. That force was expected to function as a fully trained infantry brigade (complete with a tank group, which he opposed). With the extensive and detailed information in the CIA Historian's work, as well as details from actual debriefing records from the Cuban volunteers, it becomes clear that the Inspector General's criticisms were justified. The paramilitary training for the project had indeed gotten off to a slow and challenging start.

CIA military officer Carl Jenkins had taken the first training cadre volunteers from Useppa Island, off Florida, to the Panama training camp at Fort Glick in July. At the same time regular Cuban volunteers were being screened and moved to what would become the main training base in Guatemala (JMTRAV). As of August 23, the Guatemala camp housed some 60 volunteers in very primitive facilities, as a training base for hundreds of men it would literally have to be built from scratch and some 47 additional trainees arrived form Useppa Island at the end of August as well as the initial 25 training cadre from the Panama camp.[134] But the camp itself had to be completed before any military training could begin and the Cuban volunteers were assigned to build camp facilities, including barracks, buildings, latrines, and roads. They were even tasked with building a dam in order to provide sufficient water for the camp.

By September paramilitary training had actually begun and teams of 8-15 men were established. Select team members were given special training in demolitions, weapons, map reading, navigation, camouflage, air drop reception, and parachute training. That training continued into October. However, beginning in October new arrivals were not taken into paramilitary training, but rather first into basic military training and then conventional infantry preparation. Despite the challenges, some 100 trainees were certified as ready for infiltration into Cuba by the end of October. By November, 1960 (some ten months after the initial proposal of the project) 10 paramilitary teams consisting of 178 men, including radio operators, were available for insertion into Cuba, but still awaiting orders.[135] Those orders never came.

Instead, on November 4, the base was advised that 60 men would be detailed for future resistance work and segregated from the larger group. Those men were taken out of Guatemala for special assignments (which will be discussed in a following chapter) and Carl Jenkins, the first Chief of Base at the Guatemala camp also left for special assignment in December.[136] During December the AEDEPOT instructors finally arrived in Guatemala and began working with the Cuban volunteers, because of the language difficulties, much of that was simply devoted to basic physical training. In December, the Guatemala base was advised that a new proposal for operations was under consideration and that the trainees were to be organized into a single large assault force to be inserted into Cuba and supported with an air assault group. In reality, that concept had been discussed by the Special Group only on December 5, in a meeting in which the Deputy Secretary of Defense challenged whether such a force could be effective, even with a dramatic increase in the size.

In response, in a meeting three days later, the CIA had its new military chief, Colonel Hawkins, brief the Special Group on the idea of an amphibious landing of some 700 men in Cuba with the unit equipped with exceptionally heavy firepower. The force would hold a limited territory and provide the impetus for defections and a general uprising.[137] It was at that meeting that a group of Army trainers was finally authorized for the new infantry unit and by the end of December special Cuban brigade formations began to be organized. Individuals were selected to receive specialty instruction in heavy weapons, paratroop drops, and armored combat with American army tanks.

This timeline provides us with a more complete picture of the evolution of the project's military element. In terms of aiding or inciting an insurgency within Cuba the very earliest concept of infiltrating some 60 cadre to assist active resistance groups was certainly feasible. In fact, that many individuals were prepared and eventually inserted during the course of the project. President Eisenhower's August 1960, approval of an expanded effort, involving some 500 trainees (forming some 25 action teams) and requirement for training in Guatemalan certainly became a major challenge for what had originally been a limited training task.[138] Still, a substantial group of volunteers were in training, and at least some units could have been taken into Cuba to begin driving an insurgency by the end of October. Cuba Project headquarters was advised of that fact, yet it appears that no concrete infiltration plan had even been prepared up to that point in time. That may well have been due to the fact that the air and maritime supply elements of the operation plan had lagged far behind the expectations of the original timeline.

In contrast to all its earlier CIA covert military projects, the Cuba Project was restricted from using any of the air operations and sea supply assets that the CIA had come to rely on in its earlier paramilitary operations. As with the commitment to offshore training, it remains unclear exactly who made that particular decision, but it became established project policy that only Cuban pilots would be used in all air supply and combat support activities. No CIA cover or contract pilots would be allowed on such missions and the Air Force would not be requested to participate in any form, even in serving in an air crew advisory role on the highly demanding, long range nighttime supply drops over Cuba.

Initial training for the Cuban pilots and air crew appeared to get off to a positive start, primarily because so many of the volunteers were former Cuban military or commercial pilots. The military pilots were generally familiar with two engine aircraft such as the B-26's, and the commercial pilots with the types of transports to be used in the project. It was with some confidence that the initial air operations timeline called for training facilities to be in place by August, 15, aircrew and pilot training to be completed and aircraft prepared by October 1, and both supply and tactical air support to be in progress between October 1 and December 1, 1960.[139] The CIA began training with two instructors brought in from CAT, tasked with both training and certification of over 50 Cubans. The first group of 44 air unit trainees arrived in Guatemala in late August, with another 14 arrived on Sept 9, 1960. The training field itself (JMADD), was near the town of Retalhuleu, Guatemala – some ten miles away from the ground forces training location and similar to the infantry camp, the facility at Retalhuleu required a good deal of construction to become usable. The first trainees lived in a coffee warehouse until barracks and other facilities could be prepared.[140]

Initially it was assumed that preparation of the commercial pilots for transport operations would be largely a matter of retraining and familiarization, given the commonalities in aircraft. However, by the end of September, two different transport planes had been heavily damaged in routine landings and approaches to the base. Another aircraft was lost to the project on an early mission and errors led to the cargo being dropped onto a Cuban power plant, with the aircraft making an emergency landing in Mexico, at which point it was impounded.[141] Those incidents weakened the air training staff's confidence in the Cuban transport pilots, leading to an ongoing series of requests to allow American pilots to be used in air supply missions and in air combat training. Those requests were routinely rejected by project headquarters.

It was only in November that the first successful air drop was made into Cuba and overall the air supply effort proved to be almost totally unsuccessful, due to a number of problems including the difficulties of accurately making cargo drops under challenging conditions. Of the 68 missions flown between September, 1960 and April, 1961 only 7 actually delivered cargoes to the designated resistance groups.[142] Worse yet, a number of the drops actually carried out were recovered by Cuban forces, exposing the existence and general location of the most active groups with whom the CIA had made contact. Developing frustrations within the Cuban air group itself were reflected in November requests by the Cuban chiefs of both the C-54 and C-46 groups to leave the program and return to Miami. A dozen pilots left the group and several pilots who had gone back to Miami on rest and relaxation leaves had gone absent without leave. At that point CIA air group memoranda describe "insurmountable security problems and a lack of discipline" and by December the head of the training group actually recommended closing the Guatemala air training facility.¹⁴³

In terms of enabling military action inside Cuba, the air supply effort not only fell well outside the original operations plan time table, but proved ineffective at sustaining or growing the limited number of groups the CIA had established contact with on the island. Certainly, it would have fallen woefully short of sustaining the growing insurgency which had been envisioned in the original project plan. The same could also be said for the tactical air support envisioned in the original insurgency plan as the training for the B-26 combat pilots was not completed until December, 1960.¹⁴⁴ On December 5, the first operational B-26 mission into Cuba was a supply effort to an MRR resistance group. Although the pilot did an exact job of navigation and identified the drop zone lights, he failed to open his bomb bay door for the supply drop. That apparently spooked the resistance fighters who turned off their lights and ultimately the pilot returned to base with the supplies. Later, on December 12 the first propaganda leaflet missions were conducted using two B-26's and one C-54, among them the three aircraft dropped some 3,700 pounds of leaflets into Cuba.

In contrast, the pace of Castro military buildup anticipated in the earliest planning meetings was proceeding in line with the planner's original concerns. On September 10, 1960 the first major shipments of Soviet arms had arrived in Cuba, including anti-aircraft guns, machine guns and even ten tanks. By October 20, CIA Director Dulles advised the National Security Council that three such shipments had arrived and another was on the way. It was also increasingly obvious that the resistance groups active on the island were under increasing pressure

In Denial

and that Castro's internal security apprentice was becoming both more aggressive and more effective. CIA Director Dulles reported to the National Security Council that some 1,000 resistance fighters were present in the Escambray Mountains of Cuba, but that they were poorly armed, had little in the way of supplies, and were fragmented operating without any unified leadership.[145]

Yet it was in October that the military trainers in Guatemala had expected to begin sending volunteers into Cuba. The training base had notified headquarters that personnel were ready for operations and requested insertion plans. Infiltration teams had been organized and the Cuban team leaders were already preparing their groups for insertion.[146] At headquarters level, there was discussion of inserting several small groups or possibly even larger groups of up to 200 men. The thought was that larger groups could defend themselves and even advance against Castro's forces and that might be sufficient to stimulate a broader insurgency. When Guatemala base advised project headquarters that it had 100 men ready to go, headquarters replied that it was proposing boat infiltrations of several teams in November.

How such maritime infiltration could even have been an option for proposal remains unclear. In previous operations the CIA had relied almost entirely on the Navy for maritime transport and supply, but the CIA's own Inspector General could find no indication that the Cuba Project had even approached the Navy for assistance in any of its activities during 1960. The CIA itself had no maritime unit or experience. During the period of March-December 1960, it operated only one boat in clandestine missions – the 54-foot pleasure cruiser Metusa Tine, on loan from a friend of a CIA officer.[147]

Secret Wars With Air Strikes And Tanks?

Somewhat incredibly, given the critical issue of supplying the growing resistance movement specified in the initial plan, no maritime supply missions occurred prior to September 30, 1960. In that first trip only 300 pounds of materials were taken to the island. Through the end of 1960 the single CIA operated boat made five more trips to Cuba, offloading a total of 10,000 pounds of cargo and inserting only a single infiltration agent. Some six small boat missions did go into Cuba during November and December but they were totally uncoordinated and consisted merely of individual Cuban exiles offering their own boats to CIA officers. No specific records were kept of the loads carried on those trips nor how effectively they might have been distributed. Due to the small size of the private boats, all such trips were to the northern coast of Cuba, the only region within small boat range, rather than to the southern coast and the Escambray, where the majority of what resistance remained was located.

Cuba Project maritime operations received exceptionally blunt criticism from the CIA Inspector General, and with the statistics so obvious Bissell could make no effective rebuttal. In what can only be considered obfuscation, Bissell failed to even comment on maritime supply as being critical to the planned insurgency. He simply focused on the maritime missions which were conducted during the initial months of 1961, and acknowledged that the startup of the maritime effort had been slow. He positioned that as of no particular significance because intelligence agents could be sent into Cuba legally up to January, 1961.[148] Bissell made no reference to the initial insurgency operations plan or the project's failure to develop air and sea resources as scheduled to support it. He only acknowledged that the effort to place trained radio communicators, trained paramilitary cadres, and other agents inside Cuba, in direct contact with resistance groups, had hampered the air supply effort and that "the buildup of the guerilla groups had never caught up with Castro's improving security measures."[149]

By November it was clear that the original plan to stimulate and enable a growing, militant insurgency inside Cuba had failed. As early as the end of October an internal CIA operations memo advised that the "recent wrap up of several groups" (who had been in contact with CIA personnel sent into the island under various covers) indicated that Cuban security had a good ability for "locating and apprehending armed counter-revolutionary groups." It advised the risk of infiltrations was great and would be especially so for a high-profile individual such as Manuel Artime.[150] While there were trained and available Cuban paramilitary cadre, there was no credible air or maritime operations force to infiltrate or supply them even in high risk missions. As the CIA Inspector General described it, November was a time of choice for the Cuba Project, especially so as its operational security worsened and the deniability of American involvement with the Cuban resistance movement lessened.[151] Further action would almost certainly have to become more overt, and less deniable. That issue became the central point of the Special Group policy discussions in its meeting on November 3, 1960.

In that meeting the Deputy Secretaries of Defense and State both challenged Bissell (Director Dulles did not attend the meeting) as to the odds of success for any further covert action. President Eisenhower's representative to the committee took the position that the problem of Castro would be virtually impossible to "clean up" without the use of overt US military force. He went so far as to suggest staging a provocation attack on Guantanamo which would justify American military intervention.[152] The internal discussions that followed within the Cuba Project and at the highest levels of the CIA remain clouded, with extremely minimal documentation. President Eisenhower had reengaged with the Cuba problem following the November elections and definitely pressured the CIA for options. In a special meeting on Cuba he urged them to be more imaginative, to be more aggressive, and to be prepared to take more chances. President Eisenhower also informed the group that he had a meeting with President-elect John Kennedy scheduled on December 6 and was going to urge him to continue with the action against Castro.[153]

The first sign of what could be described as a new, aggressive, and bold CIA plan — or alternatively a high stakes bet it all on one roll of the dice gamble — surfaced in the Special Group meeting of December 8, 1960.[154] In that meeting (with CIA Director Dulles in attendance), the new military chief of the project (Colonel Hawkins) verbally briefed the special group on the concept of landing up to 750 of the Cuban volunteers in Cuba, equipped with extraordinarily heavy fire power. Air strikes from a base in Nicaragua would proceed the insertion and both supply flights and combat air strikes would continue to support the force. As noted previously, the goal of the landings would be to hold a limited territory and communicate that the overthrow of Castro had begun in order to draw enough dissidents to the force to stimulate a general uprising. The Special Group proved receptive to the concept outlined by Hawkins, and authorized American Special Forces trainers for the force.

In Denial

To what extent the new approach was actually briefed or discussed beyond the Special Group, either to the National Security Council or President Eisenhower, remains a matter of debate. In fact, there is some doubt that any detailed plan was put into writing at that stage. As late as January 4, Colonel Hawkins generated a memorandum to Jake Esterline (head of WH/4 operations) simply laying out the general concept and adding that if a general uprising did not occur, the landing area could be temporarily held as a "lodgment," allowing FRD council members the opportunity to use it as a base to declare a provisional government. This provided the United States the opportunity to respond to a call from them for military intervention. [155]

Hawkins's memorandum was also definitive in setting a deadline for any such operation, noting that Castro had already received a significant amount of Soviet military equipment including both medium and heavy tanks, artillery, and anti-aircraft weapons - and more shipments were on the way. At any point after March 1, 1961 Castro would have not only a dramatically increased military capability, but the possibility of newly trained jet pilots. The anticipated appearance of Soviet MIG fighters on the island could doom any landings. Hawkins was explicit and as the head of the military element of the project his concerns should have been given considerable weight. Hawkins had also done his best to stress the absolute necessity that the new president be thoroughly briefed and commit to both the level of support and the deadline involved. However there remains no proof that Hawkins's concept memorandum and warnings were ever distributed beyond the Cuba Project itself nor later to President Kennedy.

Secret Wars With Air Strikes And Tanks?

Even if the new amphibious landings approach only existed in concept, in the last days of the Eisenhower Administration the Special Group was definitely behind it. Its members were going beyond simple encouragement, calling for the preparation of contingency plans covering the possible overt use of American military forces in support of the landings. At its final meeting, on January 19, the Eisenhower Administration Special Group noted that a force of only 750 men would likely not be enough, that additional personnel would be needed, and that a decision was required from the incoming administration on overt support for the action. CIA Director Dulles, who was in attendance, commented that a number of policy problems would need to be addressed, and that the new president and his National Security Council would need to affirm the basic concepts under discussion.[156] As the Eisenhower era ended, the Cuba Project leaders had come up with a new concept – an amphibious landing - which was arguably more overt than covert. As a strategy it was far outside the presidential directive governing the Cuba Project.

In terms of risk it had to be characterized largely as a gamble. If all the elements came into place it just might work. Regarding deniability there had been a noted shift since the earliest months of the project and the early focus on insurgency. Within the Cuba Project leadership there had been discussion that any move against Castro would now have to be more overt. The Special Group had discussed the same issue – even approving contingency planning for the use of American military force. President Eisenhower had encouraged boldness and even suggested justifying overt military intervention with some type of provocation.

In Denial

The incoming president had campaigned on the United States providing support for the anti-Castro opposition inside Cuba, and had warned against a growing Soviet military presence on the island. In October, Kennedy had issued a press statement affirming the need to strengthen democratic anti-Castro forces in exile and inside Cuba, and the urgent need for the United States to provide assistance. He had taken that stance again in his final campaign debate with Richard Nixon.[157] There was no doubt that JFK supported the Cuban resistance and he had even mentioned possible unilateral action during the presidential campaign but the real question was whether he would accept something as strikingly overt as an American supported amphibious landing of a large, heavily armed anti-Castro force in Cuba itself. As Hawkins had anticipated, in the end, the discussion, the concerns, and Kennedy's decisions would focus largely around a single issue - deniability.

Secret Wars With Air Strikes And Tanks?

Notes

[110] Jack B. Pfeiffer, *Official History of the Bay of Pigs, Volume 1 Air Operations, Part 1 March 1960-April 1961*, Central Intelligence Agency, Washington D.C., September, 1979, 6-8

[111] Originally a Chinese commercial transportation company, CAT was moved to Taiwan along with the retreating Nationalist Chinese government. By 1950 it was in serious financial difficulties and the CIA acquired stock in CAT via the Airdale Corporation, a private Delaware company. CAT continued flying regular commercial passenger and air transport flights but CAT personnel and aircraft were increasingly used by the CIA for clandestine missions, first against mainland China, then into Thailand and eventually across Asia and Southeast Asia. Renamed as Air America in 1959 it flew an immense number of clandestine transport missions into the 1970's. *CIA's Clandestine Services: Histories of Civil Air Transport*, Central Intelligence Library
https://www.cia.gov/library/readingroom/collection/cias-clandestine-services-histories-civil-air-transport

[112] Richard Gibson and Wen H. Chen, *The Secret Army: Chiang Kai-shek and the Drug Warlords of the Golden Triangle*, Wiley, Hoboken, New Jersey, 2011, 105-106

[113] Kenneth Conboy and James Morrison, *The CIA's Secret War in Tibet*, University Press of Kansas, 2002, 58-59

[114] Ibid, 55-61

[115] Ibid, 77

[116] Ibid, 107

[117] Charles Triebel, Memorandum from the Special Assistant: Washington, February 10, 1959. In *U.S. Department of State, Indonesia, Vol. 17 (1958-1960), Foreign Relations of the United States*, Washington D.C., 31

[118] Kenneth Conboy and James Morrison, *Feet to the Fire, CIA Covert Operations in Indonesia, 1957-1958*, Naval Institute Press, Annapolis, Maryland, 1999, 31-32; 180

[119] Ibid 43-44, 130-131 and 153-154

[120] Allan Dulles and John Foster Dulles, telephone conversation on March 4, 1958, In *U.S. Department of State, Indonesia, Vol. 17 (1958-1960), Foreign Relations of the United States*, Washington D.C., 52

[121] Kenneth Conboy and James Morrison, *Feet to the Fire, CIA Covert Operations in Indonesia, 1957-1958*, 84, 99

[122] Ibid, 132

[123] Ibid, 142

[124] Ibid, 115-118

[125] Ibid, 110

[126] Ibid, 155 - 156

[127] *Official History of the Bay of Pigs Operation, Volume I: Air Operations, March 1960 - April 1961*, JMADD: Air Training Base, Retalhuleu, Guatemala, 81

[128] "AMBIDDY and Nine Heavily Armed Young Officers Arrived," CIA Cable from JMPIC to Director (Headquarters), 06/-4/60

Secret Wars With Air Strikes And Tanks?

https://www.maryferrell.org/showDoc.html?docId=20962&relPageId=1=104-10240-10087

[129] Operational communication on AMBIDDY-1 [Manuel Artime] infiltration team, Cuba Project, January 21, 1961 https://www.maryferrell.org/showDoc.html?docId=21090&#relPageId=2&tab=page

[130] *Official History of the Bay of Pigs Operation, Volume II: Participation in the Conduct of Foreign Policy, Current Section: G. The Special Forces Trainers -- Pragmatism and Patience*, Jack Pfeiffer, *Official History of the Bay of Pigs Operation, Volume 1 Air Operations Part 1, U.S. Governments' Anti-Castro Program*, Central Intelligence Agency, Central Intelligence Agency, Washington D.C., October 13, 2016, 57-63 https://www.maryferrell.org/showDoc.html?docId=146517&relPageId=68

[131] P Crookham, AEDEPOT Training Plans for Summer 1963, CIA Memorandum, July 23, 1962 https://www.cia.gov/library/readingroom/docs/AEDEPOT%20%20%20VOL.%203_0100.pdf

[132] John Prados, Editor, *Bay of Pig's Declassified; The Secret CIA Report on the Invasion of Cuba*, New Press and National Security Archive, New York, 1998, 210

[133] Ibid, "An Interview with Jacob Esterline and Colonel Jack Hawkins," 258-260

[134] "Former Bay of Pigs Prisoner Interviewed, CIA Report, December 23, 1964, 3-7 https://www.maryferrell.org/showDoc.html?docId=32493&#relPageId=3&tab=page

[135] CIA Inspector General's Report as cited in John Prados, Editor, *Bay of Pig's Declassified; The Secret CIA Report on the Invasion of Cuba*, 92

[136] *Official History of the Bay of Pigs Operation, Volume II: Participation in the Conduct of Foreign Policy*, Current Section: C. Cover, Security and Latin Pride, 15

[137] *Foreign Relations of the United States, 1958-1960, Volume VI*, Cuba, Document 621

[138] Memorandum of a Meeting with the President in the White House, *Foreign Relations of the United States, 1958-1960, Volume VI, Cuba, August 25, 1960*, Document 577

[139] Op. cit.

[140] *Official History of the Bay of Pigs Operation, Volume I: Air Operations, March 1960 - April 1961*, JMADD: Air Training Base, Retalhuleu, Guatemala, 7-8
https://www.maryferrell.org/showDoc.html?docId=146516&#relPageId=139&tab=page

[141] Ibid, 113-115

https://www.maryferrell.org/showDoc.html?docId=146516&#relPageId=142&tab=page

[142] Ibid, 117
https://www.maryferrell.org/showDoc.html?docId=146516&#relPageId=146&tab=page

[143] Ibid, 128

[144] *Official History of the Bay of Pigs Operation, Volume I: Part I Air Operations, March 1960- 1961*, 41

[145] Memorandum of the Discussion of the 464th Meeting of the National Security Council, *Foreign Relations of the United States, 1958-1960, Volume VI, Cuba*, October 20, 1960, Document 596

[146] CIA Inspector General's Report as cited in John Prados, Editor, *Bay of Pig's Declassified; The Secret CIA Report on the Invasion of Cuba*, 91-92

[147] Ibid, 82

[148] An Analysis of the Cuban Operation by the Deputy Director of Plans [Richard Bissell] Central Intelligence Agency, January 18, 1962, as cited in John Prados, Editor, *Bay of Pig's Declassified; The Secret CIA Report on the Invasion of Cuba*, 144

[149] Ibid, 145

[150] "Artime Pre-Mortem," Memorandum for Chief WH/4/PA, October 20, 1960
https://www.maryferrell.org/showDoc.html?docId=21033&#relPageId=2&tab=page

[151] CIA Inspector General's Report as cited in John Prados, Editor, *Bay of Pig's Declassified; The Secret CIA Report on the Invasion of Cuba*, 55

[152] Minutes of Special Group, November 3, 1960 as cited in John M. Newman, *Countdown to Darkness*, 2017, 346

[153] *Foreign Relations of the United States, 1958 – 1960, Volume VI*, Cuba, Document 613

[154] *Foreign Relations of the United States, 1958 – 1960, Volume VI*, Cuba, Document 621

[155] Memorandum from the Chief of WH/4/PM, Central Intelligence Agency (Hawkins) to the Chief of WH/4 of the Directorate for Plans (Esterline), Washington, January 4, 1961. Source: *U.S., Department of State, Foreign Relations of the United States, 1961-1963, Volume X, Cuba, 1961-1962* https://www.mtholyoke.edu/acad/intrel/baypig.htm

[156] *Foreign Relations of the United States, 1961-1963, Volume X, Cuba*, Documents 617, 21 and 23; Memoranda prepared by the Central Intelligence Agency

[157] Kennedy Campaign press release, cited in *New York Times*, October 19, 1969 also Kennedy/Nixon Final Television Debate, October 21, 1960

Chapter 4: Decisions and Deniability

It seems fair to say that the extent of the military effort called for in the CIA's Cuban Expeditionary Force landings/lodgment plan was both a shock and a surprise to the new Kennedy Administration, especially since the CIA was moving towards executing the operation within a matter of weeks to the start of the administration. While some authors have written that Kennedy had himself been briefed in detail on the operations and the landings, even prior to the November election, there is no historical record to substantiate that premise. In fact, the concept of the amphibious operation only began to develop within the Cuba Project team in late November, first being presented at an overview level to the Eisenhower Special Group in December, 1960. President Kennedy did not participate in his first actual overview of the Cuba Project until a meeting with the CIA on January 28, 1961

And in December, 1960 the CIA had no force in readiness to support its new proposal. The Cuban volunteers in Guatemala, some 500 of them, were in the first stages of being switched from preparation as guerilla fighters to conventional infantry training. Yet by January, hundreds more were being recruited and trained for a beach landing and before the first briefings of the new Kennedy administration, the military element of the Cuba

Project was already making a transition to combat. This would involve heavy weapons, tanks, and paratroop drops as well as air strikes to eliminate the Cuban air force and provide combat air support for the proposed landing. What happened to the Cuba Project during December-January can only be described as major "mission creep" – a shift in objective from covertly supporting an indigenous guerrilla campaign to landing a conventional military force in an operation which could itself trigger a broad insurgency against the Castro regime. By definition, "mission creep" results in an unplanned commitment. However, in this instance something more dangerous happened, a major change in a covert project without a specific commitment from President Eisenhower, or any new directive (and budget) to authorize the change. Perhaps most dangerously, the mission creep occurred during a transition in political administrations, a transition which involved the replacement of virtually all the National Security and Special Group figures involved in decision making and oversight of the initial project approved by President Eisenhower.

As noted earlier, following the November election, WH/4 Operations Chief of the Cuba Project (Jacob "Jake" Esterline) had attempted to convince Richard Bissell that project activities should go on hold until discussions could occur with the incoming Kennedy Administration – that attempt was totally rebuffed by Bissell. It appears that instead, based strictly on verbal encouragement from the Eisenhower Special Group, plus a much more general push for some sort of action from President Eisenhower himself, Alan Dulles and Richard Bissell began to shift to the landings/lodgment operation well before introducing it to President Kennedy or the incoming administration. That shift provides us with considerable insight into just how mission creep occurs, even with the special Group engaged and with presidential oversight. It seems to have begun in a Special Group meeting of December 3, 1960, a meeting which involved considerable dialog about the increasing challenge posed by Castro's rapidly growing military and security forces. Concerns caused some participants to propose a substantial expansion of the proposed volunteer infantry force, perhaps doubling it to 3,000 fighters.

In response, but with no special request from the group, on December 8, Bissell brought the project's new military chief to a Special Group meeting to present the new landing/lodgment proposal, which included a series of preliminary air strikes. The group responded positively, approving American military trainers and calling for contingency studies for actual American military support. Based on that reception, during December and early January, Bissell moved ahead with a number of major operational activities including recruiting, diplomatic negotiations, construction projects, and the acquisition of aircraft, weapons, and naval vessels. Effectively the Special Group endorsement was being used as the authorization to initiate activities and acquisitions well beyond the scope of the original project which President Eisenhower had authorized and beyond its official project directive, original budget, and initial operations plan.

Details of the new military proposal were not briefed directly to President Eisenhower, possibly based on the advice Dulles had given to the Special Group in the earliest days of the project. In a meeting on January 2, 1962 (following Castro's demand that the US reduce its embassy staff in Havana) President Eisenhower reviewed the Cuban situation, and pushed the CIA for more creative and prompter action. He even raised the idea of a provocation incident to justify an American military action. While specifics of the new landing/lodgment proposal were apparently not presented in the January 2 meeting (at least for the record), Dulles touted the exile "army" in training, while at the same time maintaining that it could not be ready for action prior to March.[158] Dulles also introduced the need for new training locations for the additional troops, and Secretary of Defense Thomas Gates "wanted to decentralize trainees throughout American bases."[159] President Eisenhower reportedly raised no objection – another indication that certain of the restrictions imposed on the original project were no longer in play, at least as of the last month of the Eisenhower Administration.

On another point, President Eisenhower directed that the Cuban volunteers be immediately equipped with recoilless rifles and commented that it would be important to "mobilize a stronger invasion force so that a failure in the first effort would not wipe out the whole project."[160] There were also remarks indicating that American military support was going to be required for the force being trained. It is also worth noting that Dulles's statement, on January 2, that the force could not be prepared and ready until sometime in March, is not at all consistent with the internal CIA message from Hawkins to Esterline which was sent only two days later, on January 4. In that message Hawkins (as military chief of the volunteer force) warned that the insertion of the force had to occur prior to March 1, otherwise the rapid advances in Cuban military capability would likely overwhelm it. While not critical in itself, this inconsistency raises the issue that the project's best-informed military leaders were often not included in strategic discussions and this problem would become increasingly serious in the following months.

During the following weeks the Eisenhower Special Group continued to meet on Cuba. On January 5 all parties in the meeting agreed that the overt involvement of American forces should be considered.[161] And in a follow-on meeting of January 12, there was a proposal that contingency plans for overt use of military force be prepared; that theme was reinforced again in a meeting of January 19. A review of the Special Group meetings of January, 1961 clearly shows that the Eisenhower Administration, if not personally the president, was clearly open to the direct use of American military in support of the CIA's landing/lodgment plans. Given the encouragement coming from the Special Group, CIA officers from headquarters were dispatched to Nicaragua to begin negotiations related to establishing a site for a strike base in that country. The base would be necessary to sustain combat air missions against Cuba, and Nicaragua would also be important in actually launching the ships and equipment of the amphibious force. There is simply no doubt that the CIA and the Cuba Project Team were aggressively proceeding with the landing/lodgment operation even before the first meeting with senior staff from the new Kennedy Administration, which occurred only on January 22, 1961.[162]

The new Secretary of State, Dean Rusk, chaired that first meeting and began by asking for a military review of the situation. Joint Chiefs Chairman, Lyman Lemnitzer, described Cuba as an "armed camp" – the Cuban Army had 32,000 men, the militia over 200,000, and the National Police some 9,000. Over 30,000 tons of arms and equipment had been received over the previous few months and in turn the CIA Director described the Cuba Project's propaganda, political action, and military efforts to date. He estimated the active resistance inside Cuba as involving only some 1,000 men, in scattered groups and Dulles characterized the current Cuba Program military status in terms of some 500-600 volunteers who were being trained by a small Army Special Forces contingent in Guatemala - the plan had been to insert them into Cuba in paramilitary teams of six to eight men, to work with Cuban resistance groups. Beyond that he offered the opinion that a much larger force could be put ashore in Cuba to possibly hold a beachhead long enough for the US to recognize a provisional opposition government and openly aid it with military support. The remarks from Dulles failed to detail the extent to which the CIA had already moved forward on preparation for just such an amphibious landing operation without any specific presidential directive or formal modification of the official Cuba Project mission's description. He also failed to describe the CIA's ongoing foreign relations contacts and negotiations, which were vital to the plan being operationalized.

    Negotiations with foreign leaders were normally outside the CIA's province, so far from its normal role that the CIA's Historian devoted a full section (Volume 2 / Foreign Policy) to it in his study of the Cuba Project. Given the need for an air base close enough to support extended combat strikes into Cuba, project officers had begun working towards a Nicaraguan base as early as October, 1960. Their groundwork went so far as to identify two American companies operating there as possible covers for the clandestine effort – Nicaraguan Long Leaf Pine and Standard Fruit Company.[163] CIA foreign policy efforts and diplomatic activities with Nicaragua were also notable because they were largely conducted by a CIA contract employee, William "Rip" Robertson. Robertson had served as a paramilitary officer in the earlier PBSUCCESS Guatemala regime change effort, coordinating military activities staged out of Nicaragua directly with Luis Anastasio Somoza, the president of that nation. Afterwards he had operated a private business in Nicaragua for a number of years. In August, 1960 he had written the CIA that his businesses (gold mining and water wells) in Nicaragua was closing and that he was in search of employment. Based on his experience and personal connections, he was given the responsibility of serving as the primary American liaison to Somoza – effectively serving as the senior Cuba Project officer in Nicaragua; he was ordered to that position on December 2, 1960[164]

As with the Guatemala ground force training bases, the Nicaraguan air strike base, Porto Cabezas, some 650 miles due west of Havana, also required substantial development. It was designated as JMTIDE and construction work on the facility actually began only in February, 1961. The base would not become fully operational until early April, 1961 only weeks before the amphibious force was sent towards Cuba.[165] From December and through March all air operations over Cuba (primarily leafletting missions) continued to be flown from the air training base in Guatemala (JMADD). Apart from dropping propaganda and messages, some to specific groups, those flights confirmed that the shipments of Soviet 37mm anti-aircraft guns had indeed begun to be emplaced in Cuba. As propaganda leaflet drops increased during early 1961, ground anti-aircraft fire became noticeably more common even outside military targets. One C-54 was badly damaged by ground fire during this

In Denial

period and clearly the air support resources for what was being proposed as effectively the second phase of the Cuba Project did not exist in December when the idea was enthusiastically received by the outgoing Eisenhower Special Group. Nor did it actually exist at the very end of January when President Kennedy was first briefed on the Cuban volunteer force and the new landing/lodgment plan.

However, as those discussions were literally just getting underway during January and early February (and before any review of the CIA plans by the Joint Chiefs of Staff), CIA teams were aggressively proceeding with a number of additional activities, including a major increase in maritime operations and training of Cuban volunteers at several new facilities, including bases inside the United States. While these activities are mentioned in the official inquiries, details and timing are often lacking. Fortunately, we now know much more about them directly from the individuals involved and from CIA field/operations documents. In terms of training, Cuban volunteers would be taking the Army's M-41 tank into its first actual combat – against the heavier Soviet tanks supplied to Cuba.[166] The Cuba brigade tank unit was equipped with five of the M-41 tanks and received their armor/tank training from the United States Army School at Fort Knox, Tennessee.

Another special volunteer unit – frogman and underwater demolitions - was taken first (in late November) into initial underwater training at a US Marine Reservation on Vieques Island in Puerto Rico. That group was then moved to a new facility for advanced training, conducted at a former US Navy facility near Belle Chase, some ten miles from New Orleans, Louisiana. It remains unclear as to whether the Special Group specifically authorized each new American facility for Cuba Project use. What is clear is that in December and January, many of the restrictions placed on the first phase of the Cuba Project were no longer a consideration. The new Belle Chase base outside New Orleans stands out as particularly important given that it was used to train a variety of maritime infiltrations personnel, including a special group to be deployed for diversionary action during the amphibious landings. The facility itself had to largely be rebuilt from scratch, under the direction of Grayston Lynch, a CIA paramilitary officer, who along with Rip Robertson, would serve as the two officers participating in the amphibious landings at the Bay of Pigs.

Lynch arrived at the Belle Chase camp in January, 1961 to find it overgrown with bushes and trees and the base swimming pool (to be used for the underwater training) clogged with algae. After several days of clearing and clean up actual weapons training began, both at Belle Chase and at an island some six miles out in the Gulf.[167] By early February Belle Chase was fully operational and some 300 Cuban volunteers were in various types of training. At that point in time Lynch was ordered to Key West to take over a vessel which had actually been purchased by the CIA from the United States Navy. That vessel was the Blagar, a surplus Landing Craft Infantry (LCI) and the second LCI (the Barbara J) was already at the CIA Key West base, under the control of Rip Robertson. These vessels would ultimately serve to insert the frogmen and underwater demolition teams designated to reconnoiter and prepare for the landings. The .50 caliber machine guns which Lynch and Robertson had mounted on the LCI's while at Key West would prove to be the only significant air defense for the Brigade ships and landing craft during operations at the beachhead in Cuba

In Denial

At the time that the Cuban volunteers were going into these new types of training at American facilities, the CIA had yet to present its new military plans to the Joint Chiefs and that became clear during President Kennedy's first meeting with his Joint Chiefs on January 25, 1961. The CIA did not attend that meeting and when he asked the Pentagon participants about the Cuba situation, Kennedy was told that their opinion was that a clandestine approach simply was not going to work as it would be necessary to put "troops" on the island. That would encourage guerilla action and the military would then directly support the revolutionary forces. The position of the Chiefs, in favor of overt American involvement, was clear. It was also clear that the CIA had not reviewed its new plans with the Joint Chiefs and this was verified in the first CIA meeting with the new president, on January 28, 1961. At that time Director Dulles noted that the Pentagon's view was that "no currently authorized action" (the original Eisenhower approved insurgency plan) was going to be successful in ousting Castro, which of course had actually become the CIA's own view.[168] Senior CIA officers had been actively preparing an alternative action of conventional military operation for over two months with no specific presidential authorization.

In a late January meeting, President Kennedy did endorse the basic concept of preparing anti-Castro volunteers to be inserted into Cuba. He issued no new directive but he did order the CIA to document its plan and review it with the Pentagon, yet up to that point in time the Cuba Project Team had not involved the military in its planning, in particular it had not sought out Navy expertise in developing what was an increasingly complex full scale conventional amphibious operation. However, some word of the CIA's preparations had apparently filtered through the Eisenhower Special Group meetings. According to Admiral Arleigh Burke, Chief of Naval Operations, the Joint Chiefs of Staff first heard of the amphibious landing proposal in January, 1961.[169] As Burke described it, the CIA initially had made it adamantly clear that the operation was not a military one and that the military was not to be involved but military leaders became formally involved only in February/March, when the president directed the CIA to present their plan (which was designated as the Trinidad plan, as it involved a landing at the Cuban city of Trinidad) to the Joint Chiefs for review.

Burke noted that there were few details in the Trinidad proposal and it was largely a concept with very limited information on combat operations and logistics so concrete evaluation was challenging. This was a concern from a military perspective due to the lack of detail and open issues, he himself had given it no better than a 50% chance of success. He also noted that the follow-on plan (Zapata) was evaluated as having even less of a chance of success for a number of reasons, including the landings being closer to the Cuban air force's fields, and it's having been reworked to be more clandestine and less of a standard military operation.[170] In contrast, the Joint Chiefs February 3, initial assessment of the Trinidad plan (prepared after no more than 3-4 days study) was somewhat more encouraging; the plan was given a "favorable" evaluation, concluding that there was a "fair chance" of landing the volunteer force.[171] However the Chief's assessment noted that the plan assumed a virtually unopposed landing, the supply logistics for the plan were "austere," and resupply efforts would likely fail if any determined opposition appeared. In the event that no popular uprising occurred or without some immediate influx of local volunteers (1,500 were being assumed by the CIA in the plan) any determined Cuban resistance would overwhelm the beachhead.

A supplemental air study of the plan warned that total suppression of the Cuban air force was absolutely mandatory – if a single Cuban combat aircraft was operational over the beachhead it would expose the supply ships and potentially doom the entire effort. The Joint Chief's study provides us with a useful illustration and a caution in regard to how military issues which are supremely important operationally can essentially become buried behind the summaries that serve as the main points of policy level discussion. In this instance, the critical issues with the CIA plan were covered in detail in the Joint Chief's report, but not strongly reflected in the summary which rated the plan as "favorable." If the issues had been developed into a checklist to monitor the evolution of the plan, and later the real time command of the operation, there is a strong chance that the operation would have been canceled or the landing of the force aborted following evaluation of the initial air strikes on Castro's air force. There is no doubt that command and control of the military elements of covert action is especially challenging and we will explore that point in detail in the following chapter.

In terms of detail (and reality) at the time of the early February plan assessment by the Joint Chiefs, both the maritime and air activities of the Cuba Project were still far from being ready to support an immediate operation, certainly not one which would have met Hawkins's original March 1 deadline. A new cadre of American military trainers only began appearing in Guatemala in late

January/early February and the specialty tank, parachute, and underwater team training was still in progress.

Construction at the new air strike base in Guatemala and the Belle Chase camp was also just underway in February. And there was no CIA maritime element operational other than a group of CIA personnel in Miami and the Florida Keys, engaged in running clandestine small boat infiltration/exfiltration and minor supply missions into Cuba - missions which had been extremely limited up to that point in time. However, well before the Navy had been notified of the amphibious operation and months before the Joint Chiefs performed their evaluation of the Trinidad Plan, CIA officers had attempted to obtain military vessels by verbally requisitioning Navy vessels for its use. Two CIA officers approached the Little Creek office of the Atlantic Amphibious Command and expressed the need for a large amphibious assault ship. When questioned as to their need they refused to provide details, simply saying that the president had personally endorsed the request. The commander declined, instead calling the Joint Chiefs and expressing outrage over such a demand.[172]

In the end Cuba Project Chief Bissell personally intervened and the Navy did sell three LCI's (Landing Craft Infantry) to the CIA, for $125,000 each. However, the CIA found the craft to be virtually inoperable and CIA personnel spent the winter months making them seaworthy enough to sail from Hampton Roads to Puerto Rico. Later the Naval officer detailed to the project discovered that the CIA employees initially assigned to move the LCI's had little to no experience with them and offered the opinion that it was fortunate that the LCI's actually made it across the Caribbean to Puerto Rico.[173] As much as the Cuba Project team might have liked to proceed entirely on its own, the scale of the amphibious operation being developed had evolved to something which could not be carried out without Navy assistance and without specialized military craft of the size and capability of transporting tanks and infantry landing craft. Of course, in terms of deniability, the transport and landing of tanks, trucks, and heavy weapons was something far beyond what the FRD could have conceivably managed on its own. In itself the appearance of multiple infantry and tank landing craft unloading large military trucks, tanks, and huge quantities of weapons and ammunition at the Bay of Pigs demonstrated American government sponsorship. This obviously was a primary reason why President Kennedy was so consistently adamant that the entire operation had to be conducted in at night, with all craft withdrawn during daylight hours.

The Navy vessel assigned for the heavy transport duty was the LSD (landing dock craft or dock landing ship) San Marcos stationed at Little Creek, near Hampton Roads Virginia. The World War II era San Marcos had been built in 1944 and was covertly deployed by the Navy to Vieques, Puerto Rico where it was ultimately loaded with M-41 tanks, trucks, machine guns, and ammunition for the landings.[174] The San Marcos also carried specialty utility landing craft (LCU's) capable of transporting cargo to and from other vessels or directly on to beaches. The LSD, a large and specially equipped vessel, was operated by regular Navy personnel and its crew as well as the crews of a number of destroyers and an aircraft carrier, were certainly going to be well aware of the extent to which the Cuban force was being directly supported by the American military. For that matter, the officers and crews of the LCI's (Blagar and Barbara J), which would go directly into Cuban waters to support the landings, included engineers, radio operators, and mates, all of whom were Americans on loan to the CIA from the Military Sea Transportation Service (MSTS). They were experienced civilian mariners, but definitely not combat veterans and while the CIA officers sailing with each LCI (Lynch and Robertson) were combat experienced, they themselves were not in charge of the vessels, that command remained with the civilian captains of each LCI.[175]

Acting on its own initiative the CIA had also arranged for additional transport ships, including the freighter (designated as a troop carrier) Rio Escondido and three Cuban registered ships, with Cuba crews. Those three ships were essentially loaned to the project by one of the owners of the Garcia Line (Eduardo Garcia) which operated out of Havana and the arrangements for crewing those ships also spoke against any reasonable expectation for the long-term deniability of US involvement in the landings. The Houston, Caribe, and Atlántico were effectively taken over by the CIA while in American ports, with all pro-Castro seaman removed and detailed by US Immigration.[176] The ships were then sailed to Porto Cabezas in Nicaragua and Garcia himself visited each of them in turn, explaining that they would be involved in an action against Castro. Anyone declining to participate (as did one captain and five crewmembers) was detained in Nicaragua. The three Cuban freighters were designated to carry the force's troops, weapons, and ammunition, however neither the ship's captains and crews were experienced or prepared for what turned into extremely dangerous combat mission. That lack of experience - and commitment – became tragically apparent during the actual landings when two of the transports (Atlántico and Caribe) fled the area and failed to return to deliver desperately needed ammunition during the landings. The Caribe had to be stopped in flight some two hundred miles south of Cuba and turned back by a Navy destroyer and the Atlántico was only discovered and returned following an aerial search by aircraft from the Navy aircraft carrier supporting the operation.[177]

The extent of the maritime support required for the amphibious operation, the size and quantity of the vessels involved, the number of American's (both military and civilian) actually participating, and the involvement of Cuban crews who had not volunteered for combat clearly exposed the amphibious operation in terms of long-term deniability. Yet for some reason none of those elements appear to have been of serious concern during the February/March discussions of the operations. Even the landing of American Army tanks on to the beaches appears not to have emerged as an issue. Throughout the debate over the operation, and even during the final landings, the only real concern was over exposure of US involvement as it related to air strikes on Cuban targets and combat air cover for the landings. As of February 18, the new president had not been at all convinced that a massive amphibious operation was the correct approach to the problem of Fidel Castro, despite all the preparations which were underway for just that operation. As of that date, Kennedy was still looking at options and dealing with contending agendas, including anti-Castro political coalitions to mass "infiltration" of the Cuban volunteers.[178] President Kennedy had still made no definite decision to commit to the amphibious landing/lodgment operation and the CIA was quite well aware of that fact.

However, the Joint Chiefs had given a qualified endorsement, all the elements of the plan were going into place and the Navy had come on board, assigning an amphibious operations specialist to the project. During February, 1961 US Navy Captain Jack Scapa was detailed to the Cuba Task force from the Atlantic Fleet's Amphibious Training Command, as a special assistant for military matters. Scapa became personally involved in the maritime aspects of the amphibious landing, first in regard to the initial CIA plan (Trinidad), and later as the liaison for the actual US Navy support of the final landing operation (Zapata/Bay of Pigs). His first hand comments on the naval involvement and the evolution of the operational plans, including the Navy's rules of engagement, are of considerable interest and come from his extended interview with *The Daybook*, a publication of the Hampton Roads Naval Museum, operated by the Commander Navy Region Mid-Atlantic.[179] Scapa's observations are also quite useful in fully appreciating how the first CIA proposal (Trinidad) compared to the final plan (Zapata) and how the initial Navy Rules of Engagement would have very likely led to almost immediate combat between the US Navy and Cuban forces. Scapa's remarks also described a Navy element of the amphibious plans totally missing from the official inquiries – the preparations made to enable American jet fighter bomber strikes across the island of Cuba. We will explore that, the apparent lack of any contingency plans for removing and re-landing the force, and certain CIA activities, none of which were discussed in the official inquiries in a following chapter.

Trinidad

The simple reality is that what President Kennedy was seeking – the clandestine insertion of the Cuban volunteers into Cuba to stimulate internal resistance to Castro – was far more in line with the official mission of the Cuba Project than what was being proposed to him. Neither the initial Trinidad plan nor the final Zapata plan for landings at the Bay of Pigs were fully clandestine or even "deniable" in any practical sense, certainly not in the political sense of the United States being the active sponsor for the Cuban expeditionary force. To that point, by February, 1961 the fact that the United States had been training an anti-Castro military force had already been widely reported in both the international and domestic press. Beginning in January the presence of the Cuban volunteer force inside Guatemala had been so heavily covered in the media that it had become a domestic Guatemalan political issue, leading to constant government pressure on the United States to remove the Cuban volunteers. CIA officers had even been forced to hide in the woods near the camps when local and international press appeared with Director Dulles addressing the exposure in Guatemala in the first Cuba Project meeting with President Kennedy, on January 26, 1961. In March a *Washington Post* article wrote of an army of thousands of volunteers being trained by Americans in Guatemala.[180]

The massive build up at the strike base in Nicaragua also clearly revealed American involvement but the exact nature and extent of that support remained a matter of speculation up to the point of the actual operation. At that point the arrival of a series of freighters, the embarking of a brigade sized military force, a surge in air transport flights, and the constant coming and going of combat aircraft fully exposed the operation. The CIA military officer charged with setting up the JMTIDE strike base in Nicaragua (who sailed from there with the force on one of the two command ships) made that perfectly clear, stating that once the shooting started the American effort would all be perfectly obvious and totally undeniable.[181] Robertson's remarks were ultimately confirmed by the CIA Director himself, who stated that the CIA should have informed President Kennedy as early as November that plausible deniability was an impossibility.[182]

The composition and size of the amphibious force, including a variety of military landing craft and command ships, was something that the Cuban political front group could never have assembled or financed on its own. Beyond that American involvement was certainly visible in the deployment of a carrier task group, scheduled for an April exercise off Rhode Island but "secretly" redirected to the Caribbean for tropical exercise instead. Justification for the size of the naval force deployed in support of the Cuban Expeditionary Force was never detailed nor is it clear that President Kennedy received any detailed briefing on its composition. One version of the task force assignment suggests that the CIA was concerned about the security of the expedition's transports as they sailed across the Caribbean from Nicaragua, although security from what type of threat was not specified. As Scapa described it, the Navy force's concept of its primary role was not only that of screening the expedition's ships during passage, but also providing protection for them as they approached Cuba. The freighters, transports, and the two LCI's were to sail independently and then rendezvous with the LCD San Marcos at sea, proceeding to a point offshore from Trinidad. The San Marcos would unload its landing craft and transfer the tanks, trucks, and heavy equipment needed for the landings. The Cuban force would then land and seize the town of Trinidad and its adjacent port facilities and the transports would be able to unload at the docks during daylight hours, rapidly discharging their cargos and departing.

While the insertion of the force progressed the US Navy would provide air cover for the operation (how much air cover is unclear but certainly protection for the ships). In a related point, something not discussed in the follow-on official inquiries, the Trinidad Plan had also called for a series of B-26 strikes against Cuban fields containing combat aircraft – the strikes were to be flown by American pilots.[183] The option of using American pilots generated considerable debate and was rejected over issues of deniability. In the event of any unanticipated opposition or a rapid Cuban counter-attack, the force was expected to withdraw into the adjacent Escambray Mountains, joining with resistance groups in that relatively remote area. There were no plans to attempt an evacuation once the force had landed. On February 8, Kennedy met personally with the Navy CINCLANT (commander in chief / Atlantic) Admiral Robert Dennison. Dennison asked the president if he wanted a Navy "bail out" plan for the landing at Trinidad and Kennedy had responded that would not be needed as the force would move into guerilla action if it was unable to hold the Trinidad lodgment.

Following a field review of the infantry force in Guatemala, the Joint Chiefs provided its evaluation of the Trinidad Plan to Secretary of Defense Robert McNamara on March 10, 1961. Its conclusion was that from a strictly military point of view the expeditionary force could be expected to establish a lodgment at Trinidad but holding that position over the longer term would require support in the form of an anti-Castro uprising throughout Cuba. It also cautioned that surprise was absolutely necessary to the plan, and estimated the odds against such surprise were on the order of 85%.[184] The evaluation also noted that the CIA plan assumed a total destruction of the Cuban air force as a given for the success of the operation. The Joint Chiefs offered no estimate of the number of planes to be used nor number of air strikes needed to accomplish such a mission. The report simply warned that the destruction of the Cuban air force was absolutely vital to any successful effort. Given that apparent military endorsement, but lacking any specific recognition of the Joint Chief's cautions, Cuba Project chief Bissell submitted a final proposal for the Trinidad operation on March 11.

In spite of the concern over total destruction of the Cuban air, the final CIA proposal did not call for any air strikes other than those to be made on the day of the landings. In addition to lacking any elaboration of exactly how the plan would guarantee total control of the air, the proposal presented no detailed information on the current state of the on-island resistance movement or intelligence on the likelihood of an island wide uprising. Richard Bissell only noted that if no lodgment could be established or held the expeditionary force could withdraw into the mountains and pursue guerilla action. However, no mention was made of the fact that the majority of the force had not received any training in guerilla operations nor were they equipped to go into the mountains – they had been trained as a conventional integrated infantry force with heavy weapons and armor units and they were being deployed for such combat.

It was on March 11 that the divergence between the president's priorities and that of the Cuba Project team, especially its military officers, became obvious. President Kennedy's reaction, which would be consistent throughout the operation, was that what he wanted was an extremely low-profile insertion of the force into Cuba, to support a Cuban insurgency. What the CIA and Navy planners were presenting to him was a conventional and very overt military operation and his questions and directions during the following weeks would all be in line with minimizing the visibility of the landings and the air strikes required to enable them. In turn the officers actually charged with the landings would continue to be focused on turning the landing into a supportable lodgment that could be maintained for weeks at a minimum. The strategic policy discussion which should have occurred would have involved the overall concept the CIA was promoting, the lodgment as a trigger for an island wide uprising. That would have led to pragmatic estimate of the reality of an island wide insurgency and the ability of Castro's forces to deal with it. As the Joint Chiefs had pointed out, Trinidad might well be held, but not for an extended time unless such an uprising occurred to divert a major effort against the expeditionary force.

Those questions were not asked, issues of resistance and insurgency did not become the focus of the ongoing decision making and none of the military officers involved with the plan were consulted. Instead, President Kennedy rejected the Trinidad proposal on the basis of it being too overt, too visible – a broad daylight show of force with American military support too obvious to deny. The CIA was told to come up with a more covert version of the plan, not from a point of military concealment or operational security but for political deniability. Cuba Project mission creep had led the CIA to the point of having no real solution other than an overt, undeniable military action, but at the highest level of Dulles and Bissell, there was a lack of willingness to state the obvious. The contrast in what they were proposing and what President Kennedy actually wanted should have been quite clear by that point in time. In fact, Kennedy put his priorities into a National Security Action Memorandum – NSAM 31. The NSAM was essentially a single page position paper which described a combined military, political, and propaganda campaign and contained no mention of American military support for actions against Cuba.

In a single paragraph it stated that President Kennedy is "expected to authorize support for an appropriate number of patriotic Cubans to return to their homeland" and that new proposals were required from the CIA in regard to meet that objective.[185]Actually NSAM 31 was also quite consistent with Kennedy's own election campaign, focused on supporting anti-Castro Cubans and resistance to the Castro regime. It was all about American support, but not direct involvement and in substance the Kennedy directive was little different than the Eisenhower insurgency directive which had authorized the Cuba Project some twelve months before. Further indication of what appears to have become a major disconnect between what the president wanted (and felt he was approving) and the extent of the military operation which was actually underway appears in his remarks to his own National Security Council on April 22, 1961, following the disastrous landings at the Bay of Pigs and the capture of the majority of the Cuban Expeditionary Force:[186] "This was not a United States intervention. It is wise that we all keep this in mind. The responsibility was a Cuban responsibility. The United States did give some support to the freedom fighters and did have some knowledge of the operation." Given that those remarks were made to the senior members of his own administration, it remains unclear as to what extent the president had indeed been fully and effectively briefed by the senior officers of the Cuba Project as to the military and logistics aspects of either the initial Trinidad plan or the Zapata plan which followed.

Zapata:

Based on Kennedy's directives about lowering the visibility of the landings, Richard Bissell, apparently with Director Dulles's support, did indeed go back to his military officers and craft a less visible plan for inserting the expeditionary force. In only three days the daylight landing at Trinidad, a town with a port and docks available, and with unencumbered access to the Escambray Mountains, was changed to a night landing which required all men, materials, and supplies to be landed directly on the beaches. To some extent the plan offered more geographic protection for a lodgment given that the beaches were surrounded by swamps, with only a few undeveloped roads offering access to them. However, the location selected moved the force well away from the mountains and effectively eliminated the guerilla option that President Kennedy still seemed to anticipate. It also made it significantly more difficult for any indigenous fighters to link up with the volunteer force unless they quickly broke out and moved beyond the swamps, something not anticipated in the lodgment plan.

No plans were presented for a Navy extraction of the force and re-landing of the force should the lodgment be met with any significant military opposition. The Zapata plan called for the occupation of an airfield adjacent to the beach and the immediate operation of the force's aircraft following the landing. The proposal presented to the president made no mention of reduction in air strikes (although they had actually been reduced by over 25% as compared to Trinidad). It did mention that a few attacks would be carried out against Cuban airfields prior to the landings. A very brief Joint Chiefs' assessment of the new plan limited itself to declaring that in its essentials it still did appear feasible that a force could be landed and sustained for some limited time, but that the isolated location could well restrict any indigenous support. In turn President Kennedy's National Security Advisor McGeorge Bundy praised the CIA for its steps towards making the revised plan quiet and less "spectacular." He also described it as "plausibly Cuban" in its essentials, with no elaboration on that point. To some extent Bundy appears to have fallen back on the standard concept of deniability, which had been in play since the CIA began its covert actions – if American's are not involved in the combat then it's not officially an American intervention.

To a great extent the meetings of the two following days, and the concerns and restrictions raised by the president over what became the Zapata plan, perfectly highlight the fundamental limitations of both covert action and political deniability. They also illustrate – in dramatic fashion – the differences in priorities and mindsets between the personnel who manage covert paramilitary action and those who lead military operations. Two White House meetings were held to review Bissell's Zapata proposal, on March 15 and 16th and neither explored the most critical military aspects of the plan in any detail, including the air campaign to eliminate the Cuban air force and the Navy maritime operation to insert the expeditionary force. Neither meeting included participation by the project's military operations chiefs. The first meeting on March 15

In Denial

was quite brief – President Kennedy simply remained adamant that the force should be inserted covertly, with the appearance of guerilla activity. He specifically directed that all craft had to clear the beachhead by dawn. If necessary, they could return the following night, but they had to be out of view and outside Cuban waters during the day. Kennedy's position was forceful and again consistent, but it raises the question of whether or not he fully understood the full nature of the force, including tanks, trucks, heavy weapons, and a very large amount of ammunition. His comments would continue to reflect a view of the operation more in line with the landing of a large guerilla force, not a fully equipped and armed conventional army brigade.

The following day, March 16, a review of the changes was conducted with the only Pentagon representative being Admiral Burke (Chief of Naval Operations) and with none of the Cuba Project's military personnel present. It has to be noted, as the CIA's own historian reported, that only Hawkins and Esterline were fully aware of all the operational details of these plans and that President Kennedy was not truly being briefed at an operational level.[187] For that matter, the air elements of the operation were managed not by Hawkins, but rather by officers from the CIA's Air Operations Directorate, neither of whom participated in the operational review meetings. Hawkins had protested the divided command structure when he was detailed to the project in October, with little result. Cuba Project Chief Bissell was adamant in regard to keeping air operations separated and Hawkins bid for direct command of air operations was rejected.[188]

The functional problem for the Cuba Project was that the views and attitudes of President Kennedy were largely

160

isolated from the individuals actually charged with the military actions, including the extremely vital air campaign. Over the following weeks, and during the landing itself, critical elements of the air strike plan would repeatedly be debated and both strategic and tactical decisions reached by individuals without either full knowledge of the overall military operation or, even worse, with virtually no experience at all with combat air campaigns.[189] As previously noted, the Joint Chiefs of Staff had assessed the air campaign critical to the landings (just as a general uprising was critical to maintaining the lodgment) but the JCS had not offered any opinion on the number, type, or timing of air strikes that would be required. That situation was exacerbated by the fact that both Esterline and Hawkins had become increasingly concerned that the changes being made to make the operation less "noisy" were seriously compromising its chances of success. Largely because of his adamant position on the necessity for sufficient air strikes, Esterline himself had been banned from attending strategic planning sessions with White House representatives and he later concluded his sidelining by Bissell occurred because of his assertiveness, and, because as an experienced CIA officer he tended to express himself more strongly than Hawkins.[190] Esterline also had combat military experience including paramilitary and guerilla operations leading units of battalion strength and had come to the CIA from a position as chief instructor at the Army's Guerilla Warfare School at Fort Benning. The general use of Esterline in what amounted to an administrative support role, focused on inventory and logistics issues, was described as "unbelievable" in the CIA's official history of the project.[191]

In Denial

Although the March 16 meeting was just one of many that took place over the weeks prior to the actual landings, it was especially significant in two ways. First, as noted, the project's military leaders were not in attendance, only Dulles and Bissell represented the CIA. That meant that the two key operations officers did not hear President Kennedy's pointed confrontation with Admiral Burke – a confrontation in which Burke expressed only a 50/50 assessment that the landing/lodgment would succeed, and in response to Kennedy's question about contingency plans in the event the landing stalled on the beach replied there were none. Burke stated the force would not be re-embarked and there were no plans to take them elsewhere.[192] In response Kennedy directed the Chairman of the Joint Chiefs of Staff to prepare a plan to recover the force and land it at another location should the landing be blocked, yet it remains unclear whether such a plan was actually prepared. Given that there was little to no discussion of follow-on plans for the lodgment, the establishment of a provisional government, or contingency plans for American intervention in support of such a provisional government, it appears that by mid-March virtually all the attention was being given to the landings rather than to the overall strategy for ousting Castro. Even when the topic of an uprising – still described as vital to the success of the operation – was raised, there were no challenges to the assumption that the landing would trigger it. There was no in-depth discussion of the current state of on-island guerrilla activity or specifically of the level of resistance in the vicinity of the new landing area at the Bay of Pigs. Dulles and Bissell brought forth no new information in the meetings regarding any of those issues.

Secret Wars With Air Strikes And Tanks?

That same pattern of discussion continued in a number of meetings during the following two weeks and President Kennedy continually repeated his desire for an operation that would insert the Cuban volunteers in groups of 200-500, developing them into a larger force inside Cuba. Everything was to be done to present the appearance that the volunteers were joining an active resistance, being supported from inside Cuba.[193] The president's views were expressed to all concerned, including Dulles, Bissell, and in one meeting Colonel Hawkins. In that instance Hawkins did make an attempt to push back against Kennedy's concept of smaller group landings, stating that units of 200-250 men would simply be overwhelmed but the president responded simply by stating his priority that the operation must look like part of an internal uprising. In follow-on meetings President Kennedy was even more specific.

On April 6 he directed that any air strikes had to appear to come from inside Cuba, flown by Cuban air force defectors. Such strikes could be made before the landings, if a satisfactory cover story of defection could be established. That cover was acceptable as being consistent with his order that combat flights during the operation were to be flown from the lodgment area seized during the landings.[194] President Kennedy consistently focused on operational details which would support that stance - air strikes had to be limited to absolutely essential targets, the landings had to occur later at night, ships had to be out of the landing area by dawn, a diversionary landing was acceptable since it would speak to a broader insurgency. If the landings at the Bay of Pigs appeared to be failing than there had be a contingency plan to abort them, to re-embark the force, and to covertly land them somewhere else in Cuba.

In turn, during all those meetings the senior CIA officers failed to discuss the critical issue of air strikes in any level of detail - or to protest the restrictions being placed on them by the president. They also failed to give any new update on the status of the resistance movement on the island, which at that time was suffering major losses in its leadership due Castro's increasingly effective security practices. No new intelligence or estimates of the likelihood of an uprising were given as the Zapata plan continued to be discussed. The CIA's own infiltration of agents into Cuba had become more active in February, but its personnel were continually at risk and radio communications were difficult to maintain in the face of increasing Cuban security.[195] Even more importantly on March 22 word was received that the on island efforts to create a unified resistance had suffered a major blow.[196]

The resistance organization Unidad Revolucionaria (UR) represented the most serious attempt to connect and organize opposition to Castro's regime and it had just been decapitated. Unidad involved some 27 independent groups operating inside Cuba, including all those with any significant number of actual fighters. It had been formed in March, 1960 and involved the most effective and active opposition forces on the island. Unidad had been given pledges of support by the CIA as well as by certain American corporations, and had begun to receive some military aid during the earliest months of 1961. Its priorities were penetrating the Cuban Navy, police units, and the military forces and to identify potential defectors and undercover assets willing to support an insurgency.

Secret Wars With Air Strikes And Tanks?

UNIDAD groups were the primary recipients of the CIA boat supply missions which had begun in February and March and the group was evaluated by the CIA as having grown substantially, with the capability of carrying out broad based sabotage and even seizures of government military and policy installations. However, intelligence sent back to the CIA indicated that Unidad was not yet ready to support any wide scale military action and therefore was not advised in advance of the landings nor brought into any organized effort to support them.[197] The reality was that UNIDAD groups would have been key to any general island uprising in the event the landing and lodgment was successful but the potential for support largely disappeared in mid-March when Cuban security raided a UNIDAD leadership meeting and subsequently arrested 38 of the group's most active figures. The survivors maintained that the raid and arrests very possibly resulted from their contacts with CIA infiltration personnel.[198] Whether or not that was true, the impact on the possibility for any organized resistance was dramatic, especially, because the group's trusted military leader, Humberto Sori Marin, was arrested and executed. The news of the UNIDAD arrests and the compromise of its potential to support any uprising appears not to have been shared in the White House meetings or communicated to President Kennedy. That in itself is shocking as it represented a major factor in evaluating Castro's internal security capabilities as well as the likelihood of the spontaneous uprising that was being touted as critical to the landing and lodgment in strategy sessions with the president.

It needs to be repeated that the issue of the uprising was extremely critical. It had been noted as one of the two key elements to the plan's success during the Joint Chief's military review and continued to be a part of the discussion during almost all the high-level meetings during March and April. Admiral Burke stated that there had been a major planning emphasis on the uprising, including how to put supplies for some 30,000 insurgents into Cuba in support of a general insurgency triggered by the landings.[199] In contrast the CIA's own estimates ranged from a stated figure of 1,200 guerillas on March 11 to as many as 7,000 "potential insurgents" on April 12, but with the caution that as of that late date individual resistance groups were quite small and very inadequately armed.[200] Project chief Bissell repeatedly promoted the idea of a general uprising. Yet the actual intelligence supporting such an idea appears to have been slim at best. WH/4 head Esterline is on record as saying only that they "believed" that the landings might precipitate an uprising, but that there was no definitive intelligence to confirm that belief and that belief was primarily related to general anti-Castro sympathies among the rural population of the Escambray mountain region, not any assessment of the situation on the entire island or the area surrounding the capital of Havana. In regard to concrete intelligence for the likelihood of a broader insurgency, the Inspector General's inquiry specifically sought records which would have supported the concept of a potential uprising. Its report concluded that no intelligence information was found to support the belief that "...*Cubans in significant numbers could or would join the invaders or that there was any sort of effective and cohesive resistance movement under anybody's control let along the Agency's.*"[201]

The degree of disconnect which developed between the highest-level decision makers and the actual field personnel involved with the operation is striking. While

Secret Wars With Air Strikes And Tanks?

Esterline simply believed that the landings might stimulate an uprising, it appears never to even have been a consideration by the military personnel directly involved. "Rip" Robertson, one of the two CIA paramilitary officers who went in with the expeditionary force during the landings at the Bay of Pigs, testified and remained adamant that at the actual field levels of the operation there was no expectation of any insurgency at all. Their expectation was that only after holding the beach lodgment for weeks, and with ongoing air attacks continuing across the island, would the Cuban people come to accept and support the fact that the Castro regime was doomed and join in the effort to oust Castro.[202] Such severe disconnects were not something that occurred strictly during the last weeks in the White House meetings of March and April. In the earliest days of the new landings/lodgment plan (as early as late November) Esterline and Hawkins projected the need for a two-week period of air strikes prior to the landings. However, they did appreciate that such a protracted period of sorties, which had been in the phase one insurgency plans for months at that point in time, might well be unlikely to be approved due to political concerns and objections from the State Department, especially in a new administration.

During December their first actual military proposals appear to have called for three days of air strikes but that month Bissell's aide, Tracy Barnes, wrote to Jake Esterline (WH/4 Operations), and recommended dropping even that level of air activity due to anticipation of State Department objections. As an alternative, Barnes proposed sabotage operations targeting Cuban Air Force planes, combined with a very limited number of airstrikes only on the day of the landings carried out by no more than three aircraft flying out of the staging area in Nicaragua. Barnes also noted that air strikes beyond a very limited number of aircraft would also present an issue of deniability since it would obviously be something far beyond what the Cuban front (FRD) could reasonably accomplish on its own. Esterline responded to Barnes' proposed restrictions with a memorandum on December 28, 1960 that advised that while he and Hawkins felt that a three day campaign of air strikes was preferable, they could support a compromise which involved a series of heavy air attacks on the Cuban Air Force (FAR) and other key targets the day prior to the actual landings (D-Day minus 1 / D-1).[203] That same day Barnes, very likely reflecting Bissel's views, continued to push back on air strikes, suggesting that an option might be establishing an "enclave," with no air strikes at all. Well before the new president and his cabinet appeared on the scene, a serious split had emerged within the Cuba Project – a split which would continue to pit military needs against deniability.

Those December exchanges between the senior management of the project (Bissell and Barnes) and the operational/military leadership of the project (Esterline and Hawkins) confirm that the overall lodgment operation was still in a concept/proposal state as of the end of December. They also document what was to become a major command disagreement in the project in regard to the degree of air support required. This disagreement would seriously compromise the operational chain of military command in the project and the exchanges and debates on what would and would not be acceptable in terms of air strikes and air support over the beaches continued on through the months and days prior to the landings. It was still occurring even as the Cuban volunteers were embarking on the transports taking them towards the beaches at the Bay of Pigs. However, there were other military issues in which there was virtually no attention or discussion beyond the Cuba Project team itself and one of the most critical of those related to the capabilities of the volunteer air unit.

On January 4, Hawkins sent an exceptionally negative memorandum to Esterline in regard to the project's air element and in it he noted that of the available 10 B-26's there were only 5 highly qualified pilots for them. Matters were even worse in regard to transport aircraft, the planes which would certainly bear the burden of supplying the lodgment for some time once it was established. There were 13 C-54 and C-46 cargo planes, but only one crew qualified for the C-54's and three crews for the C-46's. Hawkins recommended hiring contract crews and pilots but his request was denied and appears not to have been considered outside the project.[204] The disparity between the number of aircraft and the number of qualified crews later became a significant concern and similar to the limited number of B-26 crews, it would have posed a huge problem in maintaining any successful lodgment over the period of several weeks. In the days immediately before the amphibious operation began, a communication to project headquarters described a "critical shortage" of transport aircraft commanders and crews and the need was felt to be so great that all Cuban volunteers available in the Miami area were requested to be dispatched to the strike base. Later, in post Bay of Pigs comments, that memorandum and the severe crew shortages were downplayed, but only in the context that more transport flights would likely have been scrubbed due to the ultimate Cuban Air Force control over the beaches.[205] No comments were offered as to what would have been the impact on air supply to a successful lodgment, or how that would have been achieved with the personnel available.

The senior officers – Dulles, Bissell, and Barnes – regularly meeting with the president and his chief advisors apparently isolated themselves from a number of the realities being communicated to them from their military planners who would actually be directing the landings inside Cuba. Even worse, to some extent that isolation can now be seen to have been intentional. It is only relatively recently that we have come to learn that both the project's military leaders, Esterline and Hawkins, believed that senior CIA officer compromises with President Kennedy over deniability, especially in regard to air strikes, had gone too far and that the entire amphibious operation was in serious jeopardy. That had become so clear to the operational leaders that on April 9, 1961, both men privately visited Bissell, advising him that as it now stood the operation would be a "disaster" and submitted their resignations.

As context to such a drastic action it has to be pointed out that Bissell had blocked Esterline's attendance at the ongoing strategic White House meetings, and that neither Bissell nor Hawkins had been given the opportunity to do detailed operational briefings for the top decision makers.[206] Later the two men would neither be present nor participate in vital the communications with senior administration figures and the president during the actual landings in Cuba. Those contacts were limited to Dulles and Bissell along with Bissell's aide Tracy Barnes and the chief of WH/4 (Esterline's chief) General Charles Cabell - individuals which both the Inspector General's report and the CIA historian describe as having had limited exposure to operational details. Esterline himself stated that Barnes did not understand the operational plans well enough to do briefings, and that Cabell was never "deeply informed."[207] The result of the private, April 9 Esterline/Hawkins meeting with Bissell was that the two men were told that the amphibious operation would go on even without them, and that their departure would further jeopardize the men who they had trained and were personally committed to supporting. At that point Bissell promised them that he would go back to President Kennedy and convince him to assign more aircraft and commit to more air strikes. As a very minimum he promised the two that there would be no further reductions in the planned air strikes.

It would be decades before both men learned that no push for additional aircraft or more air strikes had been made. Instead Bissell had further agreed to Kennedy's concerns – repeatedly reducing both the number of aircraft used and the type and number of air strikes both before and during the landings. Within two to three days of the April 9 meeting Bissell had actually cut the air attack force by half. Bissell did not communicate the reduction to Esterline or Hawkins, and when they were notified – only on the late afternoon of the day preceding the airstrikes – he told them it was a last minute, arbitrary decision by President Kennedy.[208] Bissell's own accounting of the change, made in his memoirs, relates that Kennedy simply asked him to keep the strikes minimal and that it was Bissell's own decision as to how many planes would actually be used.[209] There is no record of the specific concerns of either Esterline or Hawkins being expressed to the president or in any of the ongoing White House meetings. In later years, when shown the actual records of those meetings, both men concluded that operational issues were "deliberately being misrepresented" to the president and that Bissell had lied to both Kennedy and to the men reporting to him. Esterline was actually forced to conclude that for reasons he could not understand, Bissell had been "lying down and lying up."[210] The consequences of Bissell's actions in regard to air support led to not only decades of misunderstandings, but to a tragedy of command and control errors during the briefings of the Cuban force leaders, and during the actual landings at the Bay of Pigs.

In the final high-level meetings, air strikes were either mentioned only briefly or increasingly minimized to comply with the president's concerns over deniability and even as the ships of the force were under direct attack at the Bay of Pigs. When Bissell was given a last-minute opportunity to persuade the president of the urgency for combat air cover, he passed on the opportunity and later Bissell himself admitted to viewing control of the air as important, but not critical.[211] Clearly his views did not match that of his military officers – at any level. The apparent lack of openness of the most senior CIA officers in regard to both the on-island resistance situation, and the likelihood of an uprising has to be viewed as questionable if not incompetent. Bissell's failure to accurately represent the importance of totally eliminating Cuban air capability is even more damning.

At best the senior officers appear to have become trapped in a very fundamental risk of all covert action – operational fixation. No more and no less than the tendency of anyone committed to a mission over an extended period of time to consume themselves with succeeding, despite the realities involved. Historian Sarah Jane Corke characterized it as an intrinsic problem in covert action – the gap between aspirations and capabilities. McGeorge Bundy described it even more pointedly and succinctly during one of the follow-on Bay of Pigs inquiries: "I think the men who worked on this got into a world of their own."[212]

Notes

[158] Irwin F. Gillman, *The President and the Apprentice, Eisenhower and Nixon 1052-1961*, Yale University Press, New Haven and London, 2015, 553

[159] Ibid, 554

[160] Op. Cit.

[161] Memorandum prepared by the Central Intelligence Agency, January, 12, 1961, *Foreign Relations of the United States, 1961-1963, Volume X, Cuba*, Document 17 also John M. Newman, Countdown to Darkness, 2017, 357-358

[162] Memorandum prepared by the Central Intelligence Agency, *Foreign Relations of the United States 1961-1963, Volume X, Cuba*, Document 24 also John Newman, *Countdown to Darkness*, 2017, 358-359

[163] Jack B. Pfeiffer, *Official History of the Bay of Pigs, Volume 2, Foreign Policy*, Central Intelligence Agency, Washington D.C., September, 1979, 107

[164] Ibid, 109-111

[165] Jack B. Pfeiffer, *Official History of the Bay of Pigs, Volume 1 Air Operations, Part 1 March 1960-April 1961*, Central Intelligence Agency, Washington D.C., September, 1979, 152-154

[166] The M-41 had actually gone into production during the Korean War but arrived too late to see combat in that conflict. It served as the Army's main light tank during the 1950's, but was

taken out of front-line service during the 1960's as the U.S. Army faced more heavily armed and armored Soviet tanks.

[167] Grayston Lynch, *Decision for Disaster; Betrayal at the Bay of Pigs*, Brassey's, New York and London, 1998, 52

[168] Memorandum prepared by the Central Intelligence Agency, *Foreign Relations of the United States 1961-1963, Volume X, Cuba*, Document 27 also John Newman, *Countdown to Darkness*, 2017, 361

[169] James E. O'Connor, Arleigh A. Burke, Oral History Interview, Administrative Information, Washington D.C., January 20, 1967, 21-22
https://www.jfklibrary.org/sites/default/files/archives/JFKOH/Burke%2C%20Arleigh%20A/JFKOH-ARB-01/JFKOH-ARB-01-TR.pdf

[170] Op. Cit.

[171] "Military Evaluation of the [CIA] Cuban Plan, Joint Chiefs report to Secretary of Defense Robert McNamara, February 3, 1961 also Memorandum prepared by the Central Intelligence Agency, *Foreign Relations of the United States 1961-1963, Volume X*, Cuba, Document 35 also John Newman, *Countdown to Darkness*, 2017, 364-365

[172] John T. Mason, Jr., Oral History interview with Admiral Robert Lee Dennison, November 1962-July 1963, United States Naval Institute, 1975

[173] Gordon Calhoun, "Task Force Alpha in the Bay of Pigs," *The Daybook*, Hampton Roads Naval Museum, Vol. 9, Issue 1, 2003

[174] Op. Cit.

[175] Grayston Lynch, *Decision for Disaster; Betrayal at the Bay of Pigs*, Brassey's, New York and London, 1998, 55-56

[176] John T. Mason, Jr., Oral History interview with Admiral Robert Lee Dennison, November 1962-July 1963, United States Naval Institute, 1975

[177] Grayston Lynch, *Decision for Disaster; Betrayal at the Bay of Pigs*, Brassey's, New York and London, 1998, 119-120

[178] Memorandum prepared by the Central Intelligence Agency, *Foreign Relations of the United States 1961-1963, Volume X, Cuba*, Document 47 also John Newman, *Countdown to Darkness*, 2017, 369

[179] Gordon Calhoun, "Task Force Alpha in the Bay of Pigs," *The Daybook*, Hampton Roads Naval Museum, Vol. 9, Issue 1, 2003 https://www.history.navy.mil/museums/hrnm/files/daybook/pdfs/vol9issueone.pdf

[180] Jack B. Pfeiffer, *Official History of the Bay of Pigs, Volume 2, Foreign Policy*, Central Intelligence Agency, Washington D.C., September, 1979, 74-78

[181] Ibid, 121

[182] Jack B. Pfeiffer, *Official History of the Bay of Pigs, Volume 4*, Central Intelligence Agency, Washington D.C., September, 1979, 160

[183] Jack B. Pfeiffer, *Official History of the Bay of Pigs, Volume 1*, Central Intelligence Agency, Washington D.C., September, 1979, 178

[184] Memorandum from the Joint Chiefs of Staff to Secretary of Defense McNamara, *Foreign Relations of the United States 1961-1963, Volume X, Cuba*, Document 56 also John Newman, *Countdown to Darkness*, 2017, 387

[185] Memorandum of Discussion on Cuba, National Security Action Memorandum Number 31, March 11, 1961, John F Kennedy Presidential Library and Museum https://www.jfklibrary.org/asset-viewer/archives/JFKNSF/329/JFKNSF-329-006

[186] Memorandum for the Record, N.S.C. Meeting at the White House 10 A.M. 22 April 1961 https://www.maryferrell.org/showDoc.html?docId=165&#relPageId=3&tab=page

[187] Jack B. Pfeiffer, *Official History of the Bay of Pigs, Volume 1 Air Operations, Part 1 March 1960-April 1961*, Central Intelligence Agency, Washington D.C., September, 1979, 283-286

[188] Ibid, 10-13

[189] In response the CIA Inspector General's criticisms of project staffing, Richard Bissell attached a synopsis of project personnel backgrounds with his rebuttal paper. Interestingly, he neither listed nor provided any information on the project's air staff. In regard to maritime staff he listed only U.S. Navy Captain Jacob Scapa, who was detailed to the project only in February, 1961, having little more than a month's service with the project.

[190] Don Bohning, *The Castro Obsession / U.S. Covert Operations Against Cuba 1959-1965*, Potomac Books, Inc., Washington D.C., 2005, 28-29

[191] Jack B. Pfeiffer, *Official History of the Bay of Pigs, Volume 2, Foreign Policy*, Central Intelligence Agency, Washington D.C., September, 1979, 124

192 Editorial Note, *Foreign Relations of the United States 1961-1963, Volume X, Cuba*, Document 66 also John Newman, Countdown to Darkness, 2017, 393

193 Editorial Note, *Foreign Relations of the United States 1961-1963, Volume X, Cuba*, Document 80 also John Newman, *Countdown to Darkness*, 2017, 395

194 Editorial Note, Foreign Relations of the United States 1961-1963, Volume X, Cuba, Document 84 also John Newman, *Countdown to Darkness*, 2017, 396

195 AMDIP-3 Courier arrived WAVE [Miami station] from Havana, AMAZE [infiltration operations], WAVE to Bell (Cuba Project headquarters), February 15, 1961
https://www.maryferrell.org/showDoc.html?docId=23686&#relPageId=1&tab=page

196 Memorandum from acting Chief of Station Havana, December, 28, 1960, Central Intelligence Agency, Record Information Number 104-10166-10226
https://www.maryferrell.org/showDoc.html?docId=47414&#relPageId=2&tab=page

197 Chief of Station JMWAVE Dispatch to Chief Special Affairs Staff, Central Intelligence Agency, Information on Counter-revolutionary organization Unidad Revolucionaria, August 30, 1963, 7-9
https://www.maryferrell.org/showDoc.html?docId=155773&relPageId=1

198 Cable from JMWAVE [Miami Station] to BELL [project HQ], Arrest of MRR and UNIDAD revolutionary members, March 22, 1961, Central Intelligence Agency, Record Information Number 104-10226-10262

https://www.maryferrell.org/showDoc.html?docId=47391&relPageId=2

[199] Jack B. Pfeiffer, *Official History of the Bay of Pigs, Volume 4*, Central Intelligence Agency, Washington D.C., September, 1979, 119

[200] Peter Kornbluh, *Bay of Pigs Declassified; The Secret CIA Report on the Invasion of Cuba*, The New Press, New York, 1998, 49-50

[201] Ibid, 121

[202] Grayston Lynch, *Decision for Disaster; Betrayal at the Bay of Pigs*, Brassey's, New York and London, 1998, 163 and 168

[203] Ibid, 91-92

[204] Ibid, 144

[205] Ibid, 168-169

[206] Jack B. Pfeiffer, *Official History of the Bay of Pigs, Volume 1 Air Operations, Part 1 March 1960-April 1961*, Central Intelligence Agency, Washington D.C., September, 1979, 286

[207] Ibid, 247 and 283

[208] Don Bohning, *The Castro Obsession / U.S. Covert Operations Against Cuba 1959-1965*, Potomac Books, Inc., Washington D.C., 2005, 34

[209] Ibid, 35

[210] Peter Kornbluh, *Bay of Pigs Declassified; The Secret CIA Report on the Invasion of Cuba*, The New Press, New York, 1998, 263-264

[211] Jack B. Pfeiffer, *Official History of the Bay of Pigs, Volume 1 Air Operations, Part 1* March 1960-April 1961, Central Intelligence Agency, Washington D.C., September, 1979, 275

[212] Ibid, 5

Chapter 5: Plan Zapata in Action

With Plan Zapata approved the mission's success was going to depend on the organization to which it was assigned as well as upon the personnel actually carrying out the mission. Covert action is challenging in all its aspects – propaganda, psychological warfare, or political action - but covert military action has some unique issues. One area of particular challenge is its mix of participants because chains of command which are clearly defined within conventional military organizations can easily become confusing in clandestine efforts which involve a changing combination of civilians, detailed regular military, and volunteer surrogate forces. Ranks and reporting are often unclear when CIA officers, paramilitary contractors, and military detailees routinely appear in civilian clothes or quasi-military apparel. Rank and command authority can be quite confusing in such situations, as with the Cuba Project, when surrogate fighters are in uniform, within their own unit military command structures and with their own ranks. Command authorities become even less clear when CIA officers of various government service "ranks" are directing detailed (on temporary duty) military personnel (in uniform or not). The question of who takes orders from whom then becomes unclear and even more so when surrogate forces within their own ranks and chains of command are brought into the picture. Conflicting (or competing) authorities between offices within the CIA can complicate things as well given that multiple Directorates, Stations, and field offices (each with their own independent communications channels and operational security guidelines) all can become involved in common tasks.

A second area of particular challenge comes from the extreme compartmentalization (carried out due to concerns over both operational security and political deniability) of covert operations. Excessive compartmentalizing can fragment mission directives, conflict the chain of command, and even restrict normal military communications, especially at the point in which clandestine actions evolve into conventional military operations. Under normal circumstances, and given enough time, the confusion and disconnections caused by compartmentalization can be reconciled. But when operations move into actual combat, when there is limited time for decision making and no room for communications errors, limits on mission knowledge assume a far greater risk. At that point confusion over mission and roles within the chain of command (policy makers/civilian managers/military advisers/surrogate forces) can become fatal, especially in combined operations where tactical coordination of air, sea, and land forces is vital. As we follow the Zapata Plan into its execution, one of the most basic questions to be explored is whether or not the actual force structure and operations guidelines, which were implemented, actually conformed to the Commander in Chief's guidance for the mission.

Plan Zapata Mission

In his review of the Trinidad Plan, the president had made it clear that the primary mission objective was the clandestine insertion of the Cuban volunteers into Cuba to stimulate internal resistance to Castro. The Trinidad Plan was rejected specifically because it was not significantly clandestine and would have quite visibly revealed the extent of American involvement with the Cuban Expeditionary Force. The basic mission definition for the plan was made quite clear in President Kennedy's National Security Action Memorandum – NSAM 31. This NSAM authorized an ongoing, combined military, political and propaganda campaign. It contained no mention of overt American military action against Castro. In regard to the Cuban volunteer force in training, President Kennedy was focused on authorizing "an appropriate number of patriotic Cubans to return to their homeland."[213] It seems clear that the president believed that he had definitely directed Plan Zapata to be a support operation to deliver a Cuban anti-Castro force into Cuba, under command of its own military leaders and with political leadership from the Cuban Revolutionary Council.[214]

American military visibility in the effort was a significant concern because of the extent to which press coverage had already revealed the fact that the United States was training Cuban volunteers to fight against Castro. Beyond that as of early March virtually the entire Cuban community in the United States (as reported to the FBI by its own sources) was talking about CIA support and imminent CIA backed military action in Cuba.[215] Even the preservation of "technical deniability" required that no Americans be involved in the landings and that no American military presence appeared in Cuban waters, and certainly not inside Cuba itself, during the insertion of the volunteer force. The president had also ordered that the Cuban leaders of the volunteer force be told that the American military was not going to participate in or support its combat operations. They were to be made aware and accept that they would be fighting on their own. In addition, the military effort involved in the landings (at least the visible element) would have to be limited to the degree that it could be claimed to have been organized and carried out by the anti-Castro front, under the direction of the Cuban Revolutionary Council. That meant staging the air attacks in a manner which would allow claims that they were carried out by Cuban Air Force defectors to be credible and that meant minimizing both the suppression air strikes and the combat air cover over the beachhead at a level which could have been organized by the anti-Castro organization itself.

In the event that the initial landing in the Zapata area faced unanticipated military opposition, the president had ordered a contingency plan be prepared to reload the initial elements of the force and shift its insertion to a backup area. If the force seized the beachhead but became unable to hold its position, especially if the landings did not trigger a general anti-Castro uprising, it was to move into the Escambray mountains, link up with resistance groups already there and intensify an on-island insurgency. President Kennedy consistently remained adamant that the force had to be inserted covertly, with the appearance of simply being an extension of already existing on island anti-Castro resistance movement. Beyond that, to limit visibility he ordered that all landing craft and transports had to clear the beachhead by dawn. They could return the following night if necessary, but they had to be out of view and outside Cuban waters during the day. President Kennedy's position was forceful and consistent – the real question is whether it was at all consistent with the military effort already being prepared and the operations plan being briefed down the chain of command?

Plan Zapata Force Structure

The maritime element of the Cuban Expeditionary Force involved the freighters Houston, Caribe, and Atlántico which carried supplies and also served as troop transports. Initially they were loaded with some 1,600 tons of supplies, ammunition and vehicles in New Orleans and then sailed to the strike base in Nicaragua. In Nicaragua they joined two large former US Navy infantry landing craft (LCI's), which were to assist in landing troops, but were also equipped as communications and command ships. The LCI's were manned and captained by commercial civilian personnel and were also armed with .50 caliber machine guns; each carried an underwater team to mark beach landing areas and for all practical purposes were under the direct control of a CIA contract paramilitary officer, serving as an advisor and "troubleshooter." The Cuban Expeditionary Force (Brigade 2506) infantry element of almost 1,500 volunteers was shuttled from their training area in Guatemala to the strike base by brigade transport planes over some three days and nights. The Cuban force leaders and the CIA advisors were personally briefed on the Zapata plan by the Cuba Project military chief, Colonel Hawkins. The air element of the force, including both transport and combat pilots/ crew was not under Hawkins's command or control and its personnel were briefed separately. As noted previously the project's air operations were controlled by officers from the CIA's Air Operations Directorate - none of whom had participated in the White House project discussions.

As described by the CIA advisor attached to the LCI command ship (Blagar) the amphibious landing plan was relatively complex, with the force to be deployed on three separate beaches around the Bay of Pigs.[216] The ground force was composed of six infantry battalions, a heavy weapons battalion (4.2 inch mortars, .75mm recoilless rifles and .50 caliber machine guns), an armored truck battalion, a tank company with 5 M-41 light tanks, and a paratroop unit. Each infantry unit was undermanned in the conventional sense, in anticipation of filling each to regular strength as volunteers were added inside Cuba. The overall military commander of the force was Jose "Pepe" San Roman, an experienced officer and graduate of the Cuban Military Academy. The men in each unit varied as to their length of actual training, those in the sixth infantry brigade were given additional weapons training at sea, in route to the landings.

The bay itself was surrounded by the Zapata swamps, with only two roads joining it to the interior, blocking actions were planned for both roads with the main threat coming down the road at the north end of the Bay (Red Beach). That road offered direct access to the beachhead to forces from a regular Cuban Army base which housed a battalion sized group of over 1,000 men. That base was only eighteen miles away so blocking the roads and isolating the beachheads was a major priority for the overall "lodgment" aspect of the operation. Blue Beach, at the outlet of the bay and with the adjacent airfield, was designated as the main expedition lodgment, with its commander (San Roman) establishing his command there.

Secret Wars With Air Strikes And Tanks?

Two battalions (4th and 6th) were to land just after midnight and establish the main beachhead at the mouth of the bay, with the 4th advancing to block a secondary road coming into the beach area at the village of San Blas. Two battalions (2nd and 5th) were to land at Red Beach at 3 AM and perform blocking of the main road into the beach, assisted by troops from a parachute drop at daylight. The 3rd battalion was to land to the east of the bay (Green Beach) after the Blue Beach landing was completed, securing against any advance down the beach from the east towards the main beachhead and airfield.

After the infantry, vehicles, tanks, and heavy weapons had been landed, the transport ships would then unload ammunition and supplies – first to unload would be the Rio Escondido which carried aviation fuel, rockets and bombs for the brigade aircraft that were to immediately begin operating from the airfield at the bay. All the ships coming into the operation, including those sailing from Vieques in Puerto Rico (including the large Landing Dock ship, the LSD San Marcos, originally out of Hampton Roads, Virginia) were to rendezvous some eighteen miles at sea at a point twenty-seven miles from the entrance to the Bay. Sailing in line and led by the command ship, the LCI Blagar, the group would meet the large San Marcos at sea. The San Marcos carried the utility landing craft (LCI's) and vehicle landing craft (LCVP's) already loaded with weapons, vehicles and tanks. The LCUs were offloaded by CIA instructor crews and then handed off to the trained brigade crews with the San Marcos departing to sea.

A point not mentioned by Grayston Lynch in his personal history of the landings, but later described by the Navy liaison to the project, Jake Scapa, is that the two Navy destroyers (USS Eaton and Murray) were assigned to

In Denial

actually accompany the brigade LCI's into Cuban waters and lead the transports into the bay.[217] The two destroyers then withdrew to refuel from a tanker (USS Elokomin) which had accompanied the Navy task group. The task group officially assigned to the project under Navy operation Bumpy Roads was led by the aircraft carrier U.S.S. Essex. Based on Scapa's comments, the destroyer escort into the beachhead had been part of the Trinidad plan as well, however in that proposal the Navy's suggested rules for engagement had also called for providing Navy combat air cover over the landing itself.[218] The rules of engagement (ROE) which had been finally established for the Zapata landing were far different, and had become incrementally more strict based on repeated White House concerns over deniability.

The ships of the Navy task group were to maintain strict radio silence and if any ship was spotted which might approach one of the Brigade freighters a destroyer was to position itself in between the ship and the freighter. Navy ships could only fire if fired upon and if shots were exchanged the overall operation was to be cancelled. Navy task group Task Force Alpha (deployed in a support operation designated "Bumpy Road), consisted of a destroyer group led by the aircraft carrier Essex. Task Force Alpha and the Essex normally functioned in an anti-submarine warfare (ASW) role. The aircraft complement routinely carried by the Essex included a number propeller driver anti-submarine aircraft, carrying light weight torpedoes and rockets, as well as single rotor helicopters equipped for submarine detection and tracking. A small complement of fighters was also carried, to provide protection for the carrier and its ASW aircraft. While its normal aircraft certainly could have been used in the simple screening and security over-watch role designated to the task group (shadowing the various ships of the landing force across the Caribbean), the Essex actually sailed from Hampton Roads, Virginia with no aircraft on board. That immediately raised questions among its crew, as did the fact that the aircraft weapons ordinance loaded prior to sailing was clearly that used for ground attack missions, not at all comparable to its normal ordinance load out for the carrier.[219]

The ground attack ordinance load became more understandable when 12 A-4 Skyhawk fighter bombers flew onto the Essex at sea; the Skyhawk was capable of carrying a load of bombs, missiles, and other munitions with the equivalent striking power of a World War II era B-17 bomber.[220] The Essex sailed toward Cuba for deployment off the southern coast of the Zapata region with an immense ground attack capability, offering not just the capability of providing security for the expeditionary force while at sea, but the potential for conducting devastating ground strikes in support of the beachhead, or across the island of Cuba but neither of those options had been called for in the president's guidance for the mission. This review of the ground and naval elements of the force gives us much of what we need to move forward in following the action of the Plan Zapata as it became operational. But one critical element is still missing, the air element. Control of the air during the landings had been identified as a key to success of the operation in the Joint Chief's staff assessment, and it is critical to fully follow its actual execution as compared to the plan.

The air element of the Cuba Project was initially planned to focus on supporting the small team "action cadres" which were to be inserted into Cuba. As early as March 17,

In Denial

1960 the WH/4 working group had made a request to the CIA's Development Project's Division (the CIA air arm was headed by US. Air Force Colonel Stanley Beerli, reporting directly to the Deputy Director of Plans, Richard Bissell) for establishing an air transportation element to serve the Cuba Project.[221] A DPD officer (Lt. Colonel Gaines) was assigned to overall Cuba Project responsibility and the initial mission for the air element focused on recruiting and training to support infiltration, propaganda, and supply drops and transportation of volunteers to the training sites in Panama and Guatemala. By the end of summer 1960 the air element's role had been expanded to include ground air strikes in support of the resistance activities. In order to address that new aspect of the air mission, B-26 fighter bombers were added to the transport aircraft planned for the air unit. The B-26 was a long range, medium bomber with the capacity to carry up to some 5,000 pounds of bombs and it also mounted forward firing machine guns, primarily used in ground attack missions. It has to be noted that the B-26 was primarily designed as a light bomber, and that the training for the project's pilots focused on tactical/ground attack missions, not fighter operations and air to air combat.

What was essentially a divided chain of command between the project (JMATE) and DPD staff, did raise a series of administrative issues during the early months of the project, but did not produce significant operational problems. Through October and during phase I (Insurgency) air element activities were devoted primarily to training, and the earliest operational missions over Cuba were individual supply flights of which there were relatively few in number up to November, 1961. However in November, as the project began its change into a conventional military operation, aimed at landing and supporting combat operations of a large amphibious force inside Cuba, the new Cuba Project's military officer (Hawkins) immediately saw the issue of having divided operational command as a problem, especially so during intense, real time military action. He registered his concerns and requested authority over the air element to WH/4 (Esterline and J.C. King). His request was referred to Richard Bissell – and denied.[222] That decision also meant that the ground element (even during the amphibious operation) would be restricted to using the DPD's radio communications and cable network for its communications; dependence on message relay inserted a delay factor, always an issue in real time communications during combat operations.

From the earliest phase of the Zapata operation through days of combat on the beaches, Hawkins had to rely on passing messages back and forth at headquarters, and then anticipating they would be quickly and accurately communicated. In retrospect it can be seen that the isolation of the communications did significantly affect field operations – two of the most dramatic examples being the delay in advising the ground force about changes in the timing and amount of air strikes going into Cuba as well as the D-2 post strike bomb damage assessment that showed that half of Castro's air force was still operational prior to the actual landings. Both Hawkins and Esterline later identified the separation of the air element and the related lack of real time command and control as a very real contributing factor to the failure at the Bay of Pigs.[223] Neither man was hesitant in stating his opinions for the CIA history, with Esterline saying "I never felt we had adequate control of our air arm" and expressing that he was never certain that the orders being issued within DPD were fully supportive of his own direction.[224] An associated problem noted in the history was that few of the DPD air or higher level Air Force personnel associated with the project had any real experience with tactical air operations.

In terms of compartmentalization, another group which appears to have been almost totally isolated from the military mission at the Bay of Pigs was the project's small boat group, which operated out of its clandestine Key West facility. That group was used to support covert boat infiltrations into Cuba, both on supply missions and to insert specially trained paramilitary Cuban volunteers for intelligence collection and to establish contact and communications with resistance groups. Their full role with the project will be examined more closely, but it appears that they provided no support for the Bay of Pig's landings in terms of contacts with the resistance groups in the Zapata region nor any of the normal pre-operational reconnaissance (often referred to as "pathfinder" work) of the general area of the landings. Given that one of president's directives was that the force should be prepared to fall back into guerilla operations with resistance groups in the Escambray, the lack of paramilitary contact with those groups raises questions as to how seriously his order, which had been agreed to and endorsed by the senior CIA officers in the White House strategy sessions, was actually taken.

In following the Zapata operation from the conception of an amphibious landing through the landing itself, we will find that command and control became a major issue for the entire operation. Given the strong personal feelings about what happened at the Bay of Pigs, as well as the political and personal career concerns involved, it is more than a little challenging to objectively differentiate the actual issues with command and control from the personalities involved. It is also challenging not to become so immersed in the issues of the air strikes and air support that the overall mission and issues related to the landings themselves become obscured. In an attempt to avoid that problem, the following examination of the amphibious operation will involve decisions and issues related to all three elements of the operation – land, sea, and air – and present them in a chronological manner. It will also attempt to compare and contrast the mission directives (as established by President Kennedy as the Commander in Chief) with elements of the operation which appear to have become seriously out of sync with those directives. Special attention will be given to planning issues and apparent command and control disconnects which occurred among at all four major levels of the operation – strategic (President/National Security Council Adviser/CIA Director), Cuba Project Leadership (Bissell/Cabell), Cuba Project Military Operations (Esterline/Hawkins), the Cuba Project personnel at the Bay of Pigs (Paramilitary advisors Lynch and Robertson) and the Cuban force commanded by San Roman. In that respect, delving into the actual Zapata operation actually has to begin with one of the most fundamental conflicts and disconnects related to virtually all levels of project command - the type, amount, and importance of combat air support required for the mission.

December: Cuba Project Air staff become aware of the fact that the Cuban air force (FAR) T-33 jet aircraft were equipped with machine guns and were fully operational as fighters. Cuban air force fighters of all types posed a serious threat to the B-26 ground attack aircraft of the expedition's air element as well as to its transports, which were planned to be used for sustaining the beachhead with air drops and supply missions. But the greatest threat would come from the Cuban jets. Yet none of the White House discussions, JCS staff reviews, or air strike plans specifically addressed the T-33 threat or focused on destruction of those aircraft.[225]

January 4: Hawkins advised Esterline that in addition to a limited number of both Brigade combat and transport aircraft, there were only 5 highly qualified Cuban volunteer B-26 pilots (6 others were of "questionable proficiency"), and only 4 qualified crews for the thirteen C-45 and C-54 aircraft. Hawkins made an appeal for hiring U.S pilots on contract – the appeal was refused. The availability of qualified transport pilots and aircrews would become a major factor in sustaining operations inside Cuba since the planned lodgment would have to be largely supplied by air in order to maintain deniability. As of December, 1960, the air element was anticipating some six months of ongoing Cuba Project operations during 1961.[226] Plans and projections for sustainment of the lodgment would not become part of any of the following White House discussions and strategy sessions during the following months prior to the actual landings.

April 5/6: Ongoing concerns about the exposure of the force to Cuban air attacks were called out in the Joint Chiefs of Staff study and the Department of Defense review as well as in messages from the project's military chiefs (Esterline and Hawkins). The result was a compromise plan for deniable pre-landing (D-2) air strikes against Cuban air force bases. Such an attack would alert Castro to imminent military action, but in the interest of deniability it could be positioned as an attack by rebellious Cuban Air Force pilots. President Kennedy remained concerned that any large-scale strike could not be associated with defecting Cuban pilots and he requested that Bissell limit the strike as much as possible. Later Bissell himself arbitrarily reduced the number of aircraft flown in the attack by 50%, giving that order directly to the air element commander.

    It also appears that the senior administration officials, including the president, may not have been aware that the original air staff estimates of the full-scale Brigade preemptive strike (as described by DPD Chief of air operations) projected taking out only 50% of Castro's combat aircraft in the first D-2 attacks. Within the project that figure was viewed as acceptable, preserving some level of deniability, but they also planned for a follow-on series of strikes the early morning of the landing to take out all the remaining aircraft that could "hurt the ground troops and the ships."[227] The senior military staff assigned to the project accepted the concept of dividing the air strikes into two separate series of attacks, however it is seems clear that actual projections showing the critical nature of both strikes were not presented in the higher level White House discussions. A very limited amount of detail (ostensibly due to the covert nature of the project) was presented in the policy level meetings and no details at all were put into writing. Despite considerable research it remains unclear whether the president personally approved the two phased strike plans but National Security Advisor McGeorge Bundy clearly did support it. President Kennedy appears to have been made generally aware of plans for air strikes both before and on the day of the landing if not on the actual mission projections for each. In terms of command and control, a point to be noted is that while discussion of such strikes had actually begun in March none of the project's air staff including those at the strike base in Nicaragua were involved in the discussions or dialog. The directive was not actually passed to the air commander of the strike base until the actual decision was reached on or about April 6, only days before the D-2 strike was to be carried out.[228]

April 8: Strike base (JMTIDE) protested a major change in the air element mission – "original mission distorted beyond recognition." Instead of acting simply as a forward air base for air strikes and air supply, its tasking changed to that of a maritime support base with its personnel consumed by cargo operations and handling huge parts shipments. It became a logistics nightmare, including unanticipated personnel additions double what the base had been built to support.[229] As of early April serious shortages of pilots and flight crews were still a major issue, reports from the strike base point out "a serious shortage of Cuban pilots for the planned air operations." While more B-26's were in the pipeline, the correspondence pointed out that while the aircraft might be resolved there simply were not crews to fly them and the prospect of additional personnel was dim - there was no backlog of trainees and prospecting for new candidates had proved largely fruitless, "we just can't find them." Given that support for the planned lodgment was to be primarily by air drops and actual landings at the beachhead, this raises questions as to what extent planning had actually been done for the post-landing mission.[230]

April 9: Project military leaders Esterline and Hawkins met with Bissell and advised him that in their professional military opinion the overall Zapata Plan as approved had become fundamentally unsound. Ground operations beyond the beachhead would not be feasible due to the strength of Castro's ground forces and while the swamps and available roads would protect the lodgment, they also allowed Castro's forces to block any break out towards the resistance groups in the mountains almost one hundred miles away. While the force itself might hold the beachhead for a limited time (given the total destruction of Castro's air power) the landings would accomplish nothing significant militarily without general defections from within the Cuban military and a broader uprising.[231] In addition they stressed that the available air element B-26's, to be flown by a very limited number of highly qualified Cuban pilots, were insufficient to ensure the destruction of Castro's air force (FAR) in a single 16 plane preemptive air strike on D-2 before the landings. Failure to totally decimate FAR would place the entire landing operation at risk and they reminded Bissell (as the JCS air staff had previously noted) that any Cuban combat aircraft operating over the beachhead endangered not only the ships, but would make air resupply of the beachhead virtually impossible. The two men then offered their resignations and subsequently Bissell promised them that he would go back to President Kennedy and convince him to assign more aircraft and commit to more air strikes – at a minimum promising no further reduction in the 16 plane D-2 strike package. There is no record that Bissell shared that military advice within the project, with CIA Director Dulles, with the White House, or any of the president's senior advisors. The April 9 appeal to Bissell was not disclosed during any of the official inquiries; only years later was it was revealed to the CIA historian by both men.

April 10: Lt. Colonel George Gates, of DPD, traveled to the Nicaragua strike base to begin briefings of staff and Cuban pilots on the planned "six" aircraft strike.[232] Given that planning had already been underway for the strikes it appears possible that Bissell may already have cut the strike package more than in half at the time of his meeting with Esterline and Hawkins. The briefings continued through April 12, as the final details of the strikes were completed and later remarks by the senior Cuban pilot observed that absolutely all of the planning for the raids was done by US personnel and that the Cubans were totally excluded and ignored in the process, even though they had far better knowledge of the terrain and the bases (some 20 of the Cuban volunteers were former Cuban Air Force and Navy pilots). The two-day delay between the preemptive strike and the landings was not at all well received by either the strike base's staff or the Cuban volunteers but according to later interviews with the participants all objections were roughly dismissed by Colonel Gates.[233] It should also be noted that while the D-2 strike did target each of the bases which were believed to host Cuban T-33 jets the mission planning and strike orders gave no specific attention to attacking them or otherwise ensuring their destruction. Sabotage operations, which were discussed earlier, appear not to have become part of the planning to eliminate the Cuban air threat.[234]

April 13: Colonel Hawkins, travelled to the strike base in Nicaragua to review the ground element of the Brigade and sent a cable to headquarters confirming that the infantry force was fully prepared. He also confirmed that the force's Cuban officers had been advised there would be no assistance from American military forces and the only further aid to be provided to them after the landing would be covert delivery of supplies. While in Nicaragua Hawkins appears to have had no idea that the large D-2 strike had been dramatically reduced, and that the head of the project's air operation had been briefing the staff and six pilots on the mission since April 10. He would later write that if he had been aware of the extent to which the chain of command was being violated in such decisions he would "have had time to consult with General Shoup, the Commandant of the Marine Corps who had personally assigned him to the mission, explain the untenable military situation and recommend to him that he propose to the Joint Chief of Staff that they intervene.....," informing President Kennedy that the military operation as it was being executed was no longer viable.[235]

April 14: Final orders for the D-2 air strike were transmitted to the strike base in Nicaragua. Esterline and Hawkins were not advised on the reduction until the evening prior to the strike, in informing the two men Bissell "implied" that the 50% reduction had come directly from the president.[236] Years later Hawkins would, in writing, describe Bissell's failure to notify him and Esterline as "departing from the norms of command and staff procedure."[237]

April 15: Initial photographic analysis estimated the air field damage created by the D-2 strike to be relatively limited, all the targeted fields still had operational runways and photos showed that only one B-26 aircraft and three transport aircraft were destroyed or damaged. The photo analysis had to be relayed to project headquarters because the photographic interpretation center was actually at Miami Station. Post-strike debriefing interviews with the pilots were far more positive, although the only specific estimates were one B-26 destroyed and either possible or probable destruction of three T-33's. The positive JMTIDE strike base damage estimate was based on the assumption that significant damage had been caused by bomb fragments and machine gun fire, which was not visible in the photographs.

Yet at that point in time there was no doubt that a number of FAR aircraft might still be operational to face the planned landings on April 17. The Cuban Air Force had been evaluated as having some 36-combat aircraft, including 5 T-33 jets and 13 high speed propeller driven Sea Fury fighters (with a top speed of 460 mph the Sea Fury had a major speed advantage over the 287 mph B-26). If even half of them were operational at the time of the D-2 surprise attack a safe assumption would have been that at least half a dozen high speed fighters, including T-33's and Sea Fury's would remain to attack the beach landings – post landing assessments suggest that would have been a realistic estimate, placing 2 B-26's, 2 Sea Furies and 2 T-33 jets in action over the beachhead. There is no record that the actual post raid damage assessments or any new air threat analysis was shared with either CIA Director Dulles or President Kennedy. CIA Director Dulles had determined to travel to a speaking engagement in Puerto Rico during the operation and there is no evidence that he maintained any sort of communication with project headquarters while he was there or involved himself in any command discussions or decisions upon his return.

April 15: Cuba immediately accused the United States of military aggression and challenged the air strikes on its bases at the United Nations. The cover story of defecting Cuban pilots being behind the attacks was almost immediately exposed by the American and international press.

April 16: In response to the Cuban accusations and the media exposure of the "defecting Cuban pilot" cover story,

Secret Wars With Air Strikes And Tanks?

at 9:30 PM on April 16 President Kennedy ordered a cancellation of a major B-26 dawn strike against Cuban airfields scheduled for the following morning, unless there were overriding "operational reasons" for them.[238] Strikes against Cuban air bases and other targets were still allowed, but only after the landing when they could be represented as coming from the beachhead itself. At that point in time the maritime force was approaching Cuba, although actual movement towards the beachhead had not begun - the first probing of the beach only occurred after midnight. It was at this point in time where one of the most significant command and control disconnects occurred. President Kennedy's directive and the response from the Cuba Project leaders would become a focus of debate and controversy for decades.

What is known for certain is that at 10:15 PM Bissell and WH/4 chief J.C. King met with Secretary of State Dean Rusk and protested the cancellation decision – the president himself was away from Washington D.C. and Rusk pressed the two men regarding the absolute need for the D-Day air strikes given that it would confirm the Cuban UN charges. He then offered to make a call to Kennedy and let them present their case but they declined to do so and simply returned to project headquarters. Exactly why Bissell, having been warned by his own military staff, refrained from making a case to the president remains a matter of controversy. Bissell himself provided less than satisfactory explanations, including stating that he was unaware of any significant threat from the Cuban T-33 jets since it was not known that they were armed (a fact known at all levels of the military command below Bissell).

That particular command level exchange highlights a classic point of potential failure in any covert operation, which moves to the level of conventional military action. In this instance there is no doubt that all the individuals in the project with significant military experience – Hawkins, Esterline, the air operations staff, and the CIA paramilitary officers on the LCI's with the force – all knew the importance of either eliminating the remaining Cuban combat aircraft or seriously disrupting their operations while the landings were in progress. Hawkins, Esterline and the LCI officers were fully aware of the complexity of the landing plan, the challenges in moving tanks, armored trucks, and a massive amount of equipment onto the beachhead in the only opportunity to establish supplies for the lodgment which might have to last for weeks of combat. Yet it appears that Bissell and Barnes had no such real appreciation for the air threat, having proposed even conducting the operation without any air strikes months earlier in December.

Whether or not they appreciated the full risk of the air threat to the amphibious operation itself is questionable. For that matter both Esterline and Hawkins later stated that neither Barnes nor Bissell had sufficient detailed knowledge to do adequate briefings, yet Esterline himself had been largely excluded from the White House strategy sessions during the final weeks and the serious concerns of Hawkins about the overall operation had never been raised with the president or his senior staff. Bissell later admitted that he and Cabell had presented the need for the dawn air strikes as important, but they had not represented them to Rusk as critical to the overall operation. They had stressed that the only risk would be on attacks targeting unloaded ships late leaving the beachhead. This would occur if there were delays in the landings and if Cuban air forces attacked the beachhead itself, but they assumed such attacks would not be decisive.[239] In giving those remarks Bissell appears to have virtually ignored the professional assessments from virtually all the military personnel within the project, including both Esterline and Hawkins who had felt so strongly about issues such as the amount of air strikes that they had offered their resignations. He also appears to have had a poor understanding of the challenges of the actual amphibious landing itself.

His later remarks further appear especially disingenuous in that he implied that the Joint Chiefs had not attached a critical importance to the D-Day air strikes, referring to unspecified general conversations from unnamed individuals. He contrasted such impressions that he might have received as perhaps outweighing the emphasis on the strikes coming from "the Marine Colonel (Hawkins) who really was in charge of the direct planning of the operation."[240] In contrast to Bissell's remarks, the senior officers directly involved in the White House dialogs, Admiral Burke and General Lemnitzer, themselves stated that the D-Day air strikes were critical because the D-2 attacks were "not built or designed to knock out any great amount of the Cuban Air Force" – rebutting Bissell but also demonstrating their own lack of the importance to the D-2 attack as originally planned and projected by the Brigade's own air element.[241] A secondary point to these issues relates to the plan's execution as compared to the overall mission guidelines established by the Commander in Chief. President Kennedy had been specific that the landing be conducted and completed well after dark, with all brigade ships out of Cuban waters and under American air cover in international waters by morning light. He had also authorized that spoiling attacks and tactical air to ground operations against Cuban targets could be launched from the air strip at the Bay of Pigs (including strikes immediately following the landing) and two aircraft were designated to operate from the beach with fuel and weaponry delivered in the initial landing.[242]

While purely speculative, any telephone dialog which could have occurred between Bissell and the president would have had to cover some very dicey issues in respect to Kennedy's orders – including the fact that the complexity of the amphibious landing, the Navy landing craft involved, and the quantity of tanks, trucks, and a massive amount of cargo had actually precluded any real chance of completing the landing and withdrawing all ships (including the command LCI's) by dawn. The true extent of the remaining Cuban air threat would have also had to be disclosed, no doubt raising further questions of the plans for resupply of the beachhead over the longer term, which involved extensive flights out of the Nicaraguan base, something which would almost certainly demonstrate American involvement. The issue of the contingency plans for guerrilla action or even re-landing the force, directed as backup options by the president, might also have been raised by President Kennedy. If that sort of dialog had occurred there is certainly a possibility that the president might have aborted the landing, as he had continually reserved the right to order. At the point in time when Bissell and Cabell determined not to talk to President Kennedy the landing force was still some two to two and a half hours from its scheduled deployment off the transports.[243]

In short, the reality is that despite Bissell's remarks, it had been obvious to the project's military leaders that the Cuban air threat was real and a major danger to the operation. Its air commander (Gaines) said it had been obvious that "we were in trouble after the first strike." He had requested follow-on strikes on D-1 when it became obvious that the T-33's remained a threat. His request was denied.[244] Gaines also stated that there had been an agreement among all the project military commanders that no troops would land if any Cuban air threat remained. That was a position which the military commanders appear to have mistakenly felt was shared by senior project leadership and there is good reason to believe that neither the president nor his National Security Advisor, much less Secretary of State Dean Rusk, had received a thorough operational briefing. While that is generally the case with covert actions – to preserve deniability – the risk is great when the action moves into a conventional military operation. To appreciate that risk it is quite important to have an understanding of how complex and ambitious the Zapata operation actually was, based not only on the plan, but from commentary by the individuals actually involved in the landings.

April 17: The Zapata Plan amphibious operation was clearly ambitious, designed to put two battalions ashore on one beach (Red Beach), two more along with the heavy weapons company, tank company, and headquarters personnel on another (Blue Beach) and a third battalion at another location (Green Beach). The beach landings were to be coordinated with a paratroop drop intended to seal off the two roads coming through the swamps and with the establishment of the brigade air group at a runway behind the beaches. The complexity of the landing and the size and nature of the craft being used, including the very large tank landing craft (LCUs), which required special handling (including the use of winches to get them off the beach), appear not to have been understood or communicated to the senior decision makers.

That is illustrated by the constant discussions in the White House strategy sessions in which President Kennedy repeatedly demanded that the landings would occur at night, with all ships well out at sea and not visible in Cuban waters during the day – a true covert action. Yet according to the CIA advisor on the landing command ship (Grayston Lynch), the operation's unloading schedule was detailed and precise. Following it even with no unanticipated obstacles would have had the LCI's at the beachhead and the landing craft transiting from the freighters to and from the beaches until well after daylight.[245] Offloading the tanks and armored trucks from their large LCU carriers was particularly tricky, especially difficult in darkness on a beach which had not been reconnoitered in advance. Apparently, the planners had not anticipated the difficulties of putting them on the beach in total darkness.

One of the remaining mysteries of the landings is the fact that there was seemingly no clandestine ground level reconnaissance that would have confirmed obstacles such as the coral reefs encountered at the Bay of Pigs. Photographic surveys were provided to the landing force and Cuban force leaders as well as Lynch and they were all concerned that the beaches were surrounded by a ring of black coral extending across the entire area landing zone and out to a hundred yards beyond the beach. Initially there were plans to deploy an underwater team by submarine to scout the landing area, however that was canceled, and the team went in only with the landing force, on Lynch's LCI.[246] At that point it was limited to scouting for defenders and marking the beach with lights for the landings. The lack of advanced scouting missions led to a failure to confirm that most of the landing area was screened by a series of very nasty coral reefs. Reefs which damaged landing craft and slowed the movements of the larger vehicle transports, especially the tank carriers and several of the LCVP's hit the coral at full speed, two had their bottoms badly torn but managed to put their cargos ashore. One sunk as it beached, while the other made it back to the troop ship Atlántico, only to sink alongside it.

Normally in amphibious operations, certainly of the scale involved with the Brigade, "pathfinder" teams would have been inserted to identify such obstacles. While the CIA had spent a great deal of time training a large number of Cuban volunteers in advanced infiltration skills, including underwater training, no record has surfaced suggesting that any of those teams were deployed into the Zapata area, even to coordinate potential linkages to resistance groups in the Escambray. By early 1961 Cuba Project maritime operations had certainly improved and it was operating boats with the capability of reaching the southern coast, beyond that the Navy could certainly have inserted such teams – nothing of that sort appears to have been planned or carried out. The lack of pre-landing reconnaissance in the general area of the Bay of Pigs also contributed to a false estimate of how quickly the brigade would face heavy opposition. In follow-on inquiry testimony Colonel Hawkins confirmed the lack of local intelligence – "we had not known that he [Castro] had coordinated forces [at Zapata] who could close in and fight as they did..."[247] Although some resistance to the landings was anticipated, local militia had begun brief engagements early on, at both Blue and Red Beaches. Before noon of the first day the brigade's second battalion at Red Beach were heavily engaged with the regular Cuban military from its

In Denial

Zapata base, advancing on one of the two roads into the swamp. The Cuban troops, part of a thousand-man battalion, had come some eighteen miles from their military headquarters of the Zapata Zone.

In terms of command of the landing force, to be deployed on three beaches, "Pepe" San Roman was the overall commander. However, to exercise that command he had to establish his command post on Blue Beach and establish a local radio command network before he could exercise any effective control. All long-distance communications beyond the beachhead initially went through the two LCI command ships which accompanied the small fleet of landing craft into the bay. The LCI's did have communication with the landing groups and with project headquarters while nominally under the command of a civilian, Captain Rydberg, who was officially designated as naval commander for the landing group. Rydberg himself was a commercial maritime professional with no combat experience and no military rank and standard practice in military amphibious landings is to have a "beach master" or beach master unit in control of the infantry landing craft, transport landing craft, and vehicles operating on the beach. No brigade personnel had been trained or charged with beach control, nor were any Americans designated in the plan for that function.

Instead, the two CIA contract employees who had sailed the LCI's to the strike base were assigned to sail with those vessels and act as "troubleshooters" and advisors. The two (Lynch and Robertson) were concerned that they held no rank nor official position with the expedition (nor had they trained with it or its commanders, meeting them only on the voyage from Nicaragua). They were told that they were to stay with the LCI's at the beach for three or four days as the lodgment was established (certainly a violation of the several aspects of the plan as it had been discussed at the White House level).[248] Later they would find out that their presence in the landing was actually not known at project headquarters. Lynch's LCI was designated as the command ship, as it carried the brigade commander (San Roman) and his headquarters group. Lynch would later write of his conversations with San Roman and the advice he provided for dealing with the threat of the heavy Soviet Stalin tanks which would be sent towards the beachhead - advice which San Roman put to good use in successfully holding back the early Cuban advances. Manuel Artime also traveled on the Command ship Blagar, but had no military rank or command role with the brigade, he simply went ashore with it, ultimately being wounded and captured.

While not called out in any plan, the two CIA advisors ended up performing the beach master role, serving as communications liaison between the brigade elements and directing the movement of landing craft. That became particularly important when the brigade command structure itself began to experience problems. The 2nd battalion had been successfully landed at Red Beach, but the leader of the second wave of the force refused to debark his troops from the transport Houston – even after direct orders from the brigade's deputy commander who had landed at with the Second Battalion at Red Beach. After observing a brief firefight on the beach, the Cuban Brigade officer remaining on the Houston had disobeyed a direct order from his battalion commander, then turned off his radio, leaving the force on Red Beach without its second unit, and the supplies (including ammunition) which remained to be unloaded from the Houston. Those personnel and brigade command issues at Red Beach (rather than enemy action) significantly delayed the unloading of the Houston, slowing the debarking of troops and seriously delaying the offload of ammunition. The Houston should have been on its way back to Blue Beach well before day light. Instead, much of its ammunition remained on board as the sun rose and the first Cuban aircraft approached the beachhead.

Before the Cuban counter attack arrived, Lynch and Robertson intervened, and with agreement from brigade commander San Roman, ordered the LCI Barbara J and the Houston back from Red Beach to Blue Beach where the LCI's could provide at least minimal anti-aircraft fire with their .50 caliber machine guns. Lynch had only been notified a few hours earlier (after the landings were underway) that Castro still had operational combat aircraft. That was apparently a surprise to Lynch, yet even the most optimistic post D-2 strike analysis had confirmed that an undetermined number of Cuban combat aircraft were still operational. Even if the planned D-Day strike had been launched, there could have been no certainty some surviving Cuban planes would not have attacked the landing area, which had no air defenses other than the machine guns Lynch and Robertson had personally seen to it were mounted on their LCI's. In terms of command and control, following the D-Day brigade airstrike cancellation, neither project headquarters nor the strike base appears to have immediately passed on a warning, issued any modified landing orders or operational adjustments – only Lynch describes personally warning the Cuban force commander and discussing possible tactics with him.

The first Cuban planes had taken off at 5:30 AM that morning and both Cuban B-26's and Sea Fury fighters arrived over the beachheads at sunrise.[249] Troops as well as tanks, trucks, and heavy weapons were still being landed, with progress slowed by the rugged coral beaches. The majority of the ammunition and supplies shipped to support the Brigade was still intact and on board the freighters, it had to be unloaded and transported to the beaches. The first strike to arrive was a Cuban B-26, which attacked and "chewed up" an LCVP, which was landing mortar crews on Blue Beach. It was followed by two other planes - the first a B-26, which was immediately engaged by the Blagar (Lynch) with .50 caliber fire. However, that aircraft was actually a Brigade plane escorting a paratroop transport and while the Brigade B-26 escaped damage, two paratroopers were wounded from the friendly fire. The blue rings painted on the Brigade B-26 proved of little help in differentiating friend from foe during actual combat.

Red Beach was also attacked by a Cuban aircraft at daylight, as the LCI Barbara J (Robertson) and the freighter Houston began moving away from Red Beach. Both the Houston and the Barbara J were repeatedly attacked, with the Houston eventually grounding itself with its remaining infantry came under heavy fire as they left the ship. Despite the air attacks, the Red Beach force had managed to deploy and established itself in positions to defend the main road leading through the swamps onto the beach. Later in the morning they would be reinforced by troops dropped by parachute and by two tanks deployed from Blue Beach

A major control issue, which emerged during the first hours of daylight, was that there was no provision for radio communications between the brigade aircraft and the infantry force on the beachhead or the LCI command ships.[250] That meant that the brigade aircraft could only be ordered (by the strike base) to avoid the ships and landing craft in order not to take friendly fire and it also meant that there was no chance for forward air control over the B-26's from the brigade itself. It also appears that the Brigade itself had received no training in coordinating such ground support strikes. The Brigade aircraft could not be warned nor could targets be identified for them and they were left to find their own targets during the relatively limited loiter time they had over beachhead or its approaches.[251] To illustrate that point, on the day of the landing, twelve B-26 sorties from Nicaragua were flown, however none found any targets and all returned to base with their ordinance.

Still, by late in the morning of D-Day, all vehicles and tanks were ashore, the airfield had been taken and a fuel truck and armaments were ready for the B-26's to begin operations from the beachhead. However due to the presence of Cuban aircraft, none of the B-26's attempted to land and refuel or rearm. One did crash land during the first morning after taking severe air combat damage. As best can be determined no special anti-aircraft weapons were sent with the brigade for defending the airfield, although the heavy weapons groups were equipped with .50 caliber machine guns. At Blue Beach the freighter Rio Escondido still remained offshore and was ordered towards the beach to offload the 6th Battalion as well as its load of 20 tons of ammunition and aviation fuel (the fuel was stored in steel drums on the foredeck). With the troops offloaded, it was almost immediately attacked from the air with hits into the fuel drums. Small boats managed to save the crew, but as the fire spread the ship turned into a huge bomb and violently exploded.

According to Lynch, headquarters had been ordering the ships offshore all morning long, however, with the delays in the offloading, all ships were still directly off the beachhead and far from the Navy combat air cover in international waters. At that point in time, as a Cuban Sea Fury began its attack on Blue Beach, Lynch describes having received a radio message stating that "Castro's Air Force 100% destroyed. Do not fire on our planes. Remember they have blue bands on wings and fuselage."[252] Apparently the Brigade air command at the strike base had received complaints about its aircraft being fired upon – and, worse yet, was strikingly uniformed as to the true status of the Cuban combat aircraft.

 The first Cuban ground attacks, from a militia unit, came shortly after noon, down the main road towards Red Beach. A heavily armed Brigade force ambushed and badly hurt them and it took until mid-afternoon for further attacks to come down the road. That follow on attack was made by troops of a regular Cuban Army unit and they too were badly mauled, by that time two Brigade tanks had deployed from Blue Beach in support of the blocking action along with two brigade B-26's that also joined in with attacks against the column. Yet by afternoon the majority of supplies and ammunition from the remaining freighters was still unloaded and half the total ammunition load had been lost with the Rio Escondido. The remainder would still have supported the beachhead for a considerable time but at that point another headquarters message adamantly directed Lynch to withdraw the ships to the twelve-mile limit, to unload the transports into the LCU's there, and to return to the beach after dark. According to Lynch, the promised Navy air cover never showed up at the twelve mile limit and the ships continued to take sporadic air attacks at sea.[253] As noted earlier, the expeditionary force (although its Cuban commander could only have made requests) had communications with the strike base air

In Denial

element and the US Navy only as relayed though LCI's – yet another command and control issue, one of which would become fatal in the following days.

With the freighters, LCU's and LCI's at sea, the Atlántico and Caribe refused Lynch's orders to slow their speed to the pace of the smaller craft. With Cuban aircraft periodically overhead and no sign of US Navy air cover, the two freighters simply ignored orders (they were commercial ships with civilian crews) and replied that they would continue towards a point some 50 miles off shore. In reality both ships continued at speed. Navy search planes and destroyers finally forced them to stop and return, one a hundred miles offshore, the other two hundred. The Caribe only stopped when a Navy destroyer fired a round across its bow.[254] Lynch was also adamant that even when directly requested, the Navy (via the destroyer Santiago) replied that it had no orders to provide air cover at the 12 mile limit, so Cuban planes continued to harass the LCI's and other ships while at sea. Lynch repeatedly advised project headquarters in Washington of the failure of air cover from the Navy, but received no response.[255]

While much is made of the loss of the Rio Escondido as fatal to the landings, the plan to unload the remaining ships at sea and transport cargoes of ammunition back into the beach with the LCU's and LCI's the first night was perfectly feasible if the civilian freighter crews had not fled the scene during combat – combat which in fact they had never volunteered to face. In fact, during pursuit of the freighters the LCI's and LCU's were so far offshore that they had lost contact with the forces on the beach and could only wait for the return of the freighters. That return took so long that a landing the night of D-Day became impossible and the LCI's could do nothing more than return to a point where radio contact with the beachhead could be re-established, providing at least a single communications link with the Brigade, which was itself fighting aggressively and effectively against Cuban forces attacking the beachheads.

D-Day during daylight had been difficult, but not a total disaster. The Brigade was in place, its units including tanks and heavy weapons were in combat and both roads into the beach were blocked with brigade infantry, heavy weapons, and tanks. The first Cuban forces advancing on the beach had been met successfully and badly mauled. Several issues of military command and control had surfaced, internetworked radio communications being a major area of apparently neglected planning. Friendly fire had been a problem, the lack of any point defense for the airfield was another issue, and there had been no plans to protect the landing craft or ships at all. Lynch and Robertson appear to have equipped the LCI's with machine guns at their own initiative, and headquarters didn't even know it had CIA officers involved in the actual landings.

Given the complexity of landing at multiple beaches as well as the type and amount of equipment and supplies, it remains hard to imagine how anyone could have promised the president that all the brigade craft would indeed be well out to sea by dawn on D-Day (in fact there appear to have been no plans to withdraw the LCI command ships at all), especially when no provisions had been made for reconnaissance of the beach head or for experienced beach master control of the landings. It's hard to imagine how long the process would have taken if Lynch and Robertson had not been in the command LCI's, with the Cuban brigade commander onshore with his troops. There would have been no overall landing coordination at all, none of

In Denial

the brigade officers had been trained or assigned to that function. However, Brigade 2506 was ashore, with all its weapons, its tanks, and even with elements of its paratroop force involved in blocking Cuban army and militia advances. The Brigade troops were fighting aggressively and effectively. They did not have all the ammunition that would be needed to hold the lodgment, but Blue Beach was yet under attack. The landing had succeeded and the force was holding its own, although more and much stronger Cuban attacks would come after midnight.

All of which raises a number of strategic questions. With a beachhead established at the Bay of Pigs, a brigade sized infantry force in place and holding its own that was supplied with ammunition for days if not weeks of fighting still off shore and too be landed – what was going on with the highest-level command of the supply operation? Were defections or uprisings occurring to divert Cuban forces? Where was the Cuban Revolutionary Council and the propaganda initiative - what about the announcement of a provisional government? Finally, what preparations were in place for the worst-case contingency plans - a transition to guerilla warfare in the mountains?

As of the afternoon of D-Day, Brigade 2506 had been successfully inserted into Cuba. The Brigade had established a lodgment and was holding it. Pepe San Roman was in command, he and his officers had been told, by Colonel Hawkins, that there would be no American military support beyond the landing. During the night of D-Day Brigade 2506 faced an imminent threat on the ground – Cuban tanks, artillery barrages, and infantry advances in battalion strength as desperate air supply efforts managed to supply ammunition in quantity to Blue Beach forces. Plan Zapata had established its lodgment, but

Secret Wars With Air Strikes And Tanks?

that was only one element of the overall mission of bringing down the Castro regime with an amphibious landing. Yet in the end it would be the mission, not the Brigade that would fail.

Notes

[213] Memorandum of Discussion on Cuba, National Security Action Memorandum Number 31, March 11, 1961, John F Kennedy Presidential Library and Museum
https://www.jfklibrary.org/asset-viewer/archives/JFKNSF/329/JFKNSF-329-006

[214] Memorandum for the Record, N.S.C. Meeting at the White House 10 A.M. 22 April 1961
https://www.maryferrell.org/showDoc.html?docId=165&#relPageId=3&tab=page

[215] FBI report from New York City to Headquarters, Information from Informant T-1, March 13, 1961
https://www.maryferrell.org/showDoc.html?docId=112947&#relPageId=2&tab=page

[216] Grayston L. Lynch, *Decision for Disaster,* Brassey's, New York and London, 1998, 63-73

[217] Gordon Calhoun, "Task Force Alpha in the Bay of Pigs," *The Daybook*, Hampton Roads Naval Museum, Vol. 9, Issue 1, 2003, 14
https://www.history.navy.mil/museums/hrnm/files/daybook/pdfs/vol9issueone.pdf

[218] Ibid, 7

[219] Gordon Calhoun, "Task Force Alpha in the Bay of Pigs," *The Daybook*, Hampton Roads Naval Museum, Vol. 9, Issue 1, 2003, 8

[220] Ibid, 9

[221] Jack B. Pfeiffer, *Official History of the Bay of Pigs, Volume 1; Part 1, March 1960-April 1961*, Central Intelligence Agency, Washington D.C., September, 1979

[222] Ibid, 9-13

[223] Ibid, 18

[224] Ibid, 18-21

[225] Ibid, 198

[226] Ibid, 28

[227] Ibid, 184

[228] Ibid, 182-186

[229] Ibid, 172

[230] Ibid, 166-168

[231] Don Bohning, *The Castro Obsession; U.S. Covert Operations Against Cuba 1959-1965*, Potomac Books Inc., Washington D.C., 2005, 32-33

[232] Ibid, 193

[233] Jack B. Pfeiffer, *Official History of the Bay of Pigs, Volume 1; Part 1, March 1960-April 1961*, Central Intelligence Agency, Washington D.C., September, 1979 193-197

[234] Ibid, 198-199

[235] Don Bohning, *The Castro Obsession; U.S. Covert Operations Against Cuba 1959-1965*, Potomac Books Inc., Washington D.C., 2005, 40-41

[236] Ibid, 35

[237] Ibid, 40

[238] Ibid, 285-286

[239] Ibid, 270

[240] Ibid, 274

[241] Ibid, 227-228

[242] Ibid, 179

[243] Ibid, 56

[244] Ibid, 215

[245] Grayston L. Lynch, *Decision for Disaster*, Brassey's, New York and London, 1998, 66-67

[246] Gordon Calhoun, "Task Force Alpha in the Bay of Pigs," *The Daybook*, Hampton Roads Naval Museum, Vol. 9, Issue 1, 2003

[247] Jack B. Pfeiffer, *Official History of the Bay of Pigs, Volume 4, March 1960-April 1961*, Central Intelligence Agency, Washington D.C., September, 1979, 34

[248] Grayston L. Lynch, *Decision for Disaster*, Brassey's, New York and London, 1998, 66-67

[249] One question never raised during the official inquires was in regard to the actual timing of the D-Day Brigade airstrikes; we actually have nothing which demonstrates that the first Cuban Air Force attacks – FAR launched its first aircraft at 5:30 AM – would not have arrived at the beachhead before the scheduled Brigade strike even if it had not been cancelled. It would be

interesting to know the exact Time over Target which had been planned for the Brigade strike.

[250] Jack B. Pfeiffer, *Official History of the Bay of Pigs, Volume 1, Part 2, March 1960-April 1961*, Central Intelligence Agency, Washington D.C., September, 1979, 321

[251] Jack B. Pfeiffer, *Official History of the Bay of Pigs, Volume 4, March 1960-April 1961*, Central Intelligence Agency, Washington D.C., September, 1979, 38

[252] Grayston L. Lynch, *Decision for Disaster*, Brassey's, New York and London, 1998, 11

[253] Ibid, 117

[254] Ibid, 120

[255] Ibid, 116-117

In Denial

Chapter 6: Mission Failure

April 17, 1961   D Day at the Bay of Pigs

Brigade 2506 successfully landed on the beaches at the Bay of Pigs, with its tanks, trucks, heavy weapons, and a limited amount of ammunition and supplies. There had been a number of delays due to black coral reefs obstructing access by landing craft, disobedience to orders by one Cuban infantry unit commander, and, after dawn, sporadic attacks by Cuban aircraft – which beached one freighter (the Houston) and sunk a second (the Rio Escondido). The brigade lost both its bulk aviation gasoline and long-range communications equipment in the sinking of the Rio Escondido. The majority of its ammunition and supplies remained intact, carried on the Atlántico and Caribe, and in a much smaller amounts, on the two LCI's with CIA officers Lynch and Robertson on board.

In retrospect, with the lodgment fully in place by noon (and deniability established) the question arises as to why ground air strikes against Cuban airfields were not immediately carried out – as they were that night? Brigade aircraft operated over the beachhead all day, most returned with their full weapons load out. The primary Cuban field being used to rearm and send strikes against the beaches was a matter of only 15-20 minutes flying time from the beachhead.[256] There is no record of any effort to request daylight harassment attacks on the key Cuban airbase, based on the proposition that suitable cover/deniability had effectively been established with the successful landing. Daylight attacks on that base might well have delayed or even reduced the number of attacks on the Brigade ships, attacks which continued as they pulled out to sea during the afternoon. As described by Lynch, on the LCI Blagar accompanying the freighters, the continued appearance of Cuban aircraft – with no sign of the promised Navy air cover outside the 12-mile limit - apparently caused the two freighters containing critical amounts of ammunition to continue in flight over a hundred miles out into the Caribbean. That was the first sign of what would grow into a series of command and communications failures related to Navy support of the operation.

Despite the Cuban air attacks, the Red Beach force had deployed and battered the first Cuban militia advance towards the beach which occurred around noon, causing the militia to retreat. Strikes by two brigade B-26's helped in that effort, to what extent remains in dispute. As the hours passed on the beaches at the Bay of Pigs, command delays and confusion became significant factors in undermining effective support for the brigade. Authorizations for several types of actions including further brigade air strikes and Navy air support were approved, but far too slowly and in far too uncoordinated a manner. Over that period of time it appears that what can be called "strategic" command (at the level of the project leadership, the CIA Director and the White House) was limited. As an example, while CIA Director Alan Dulles did return from Puerto Rico on April 17, he appeared to take little interest in the state of the operation and made no effort to assume any sort of command - or more importantly to facilitate dialogs with the president or his senior advisors. He was met upon his return by an officer from the Cuba Project who attempted to brief him on matters in Cuba; Dulles asked few questions and appeared relatively uninterested.[257]

In a corollary, there appears to have been no organized effort by Cuba Project staff or its officers to meet personally with or hold conference calls with the president or his senior staff based on what was happening on the beaches. Delays were also generated by the fact that any news of what was happening on the beaches had to be transmitted from brigade commander San Roman at Blue Beach to Lynch on the LCI Blagar, and then on to either project headquarters or the strike base in Nicaragua. The same held for any information from headquarters, the strike base, or the Navy which were directed to the brigade. Lynch later stated that in between manning a .50 caliber machine gun to defend against air attacks, he spent a great deal of time simply relaying messages; the CIA officer assigned as project liaison on the Navy command ship U.S.S. Essex appears to have been largely uninvolved in regard to communications.

Once launched, the initial operations plan remained largely fixed in the face of actual combat realities – a fatal circumstance in any conventional military operation. The brigade itself followed the plan for ground combat quite closely, deploying and establishing blocking actions on the roads approaching the beachhead, seizing and taking control over the airstrip and pushing back the initial militia and Cuban Army advances. However, the logistics of the operation never recovered from the fact that the landing debarkation process, especially for the tanks, trucks, heavy weapons, and bulk ammunition, continued throughout the morning and faced the pressure of ongoing Cuban airstrikes. Still, by nightfall on D-Day, the brigade had completed its lodgment, bloodily blunted the first Cuban advance against the beachhead and was awaiting re-supply both by air and the night-time landing of its remaining ammunition by LCU's (which were to be loaded from the freighters at sea). The majority of the brigades' ammunition and supplies remained intact on the Atlántico and Caribe.

The beachhead air strip was ready for use, and a series of nighttime air strikes had been authorized against Cuban airfields. Given that the brigade air transport crews had trained extensively for air drops into denied territory in Cuba and had carried out a number of night time missions, hopes were high that cargoes of ammunition and supplies could be readily air dropped to the forces at the lodgment. Seven transports were sent from JMTIDE, each with 12,000 pounds of ammunition and three loads were dropped at Blue Beach and one on Red Beach for a total of 48,000 pounds. Another transport aircraft dropped some 10,000 pounds at the beachhead airfield providing in total almost 60,000 pounds of extra ammunition delivered to the beachhead in resupply efforts during the night and very early morning of April 18, D+1.[258]

Follow on supply missions were also authorized and prepared for the nights of D+1 and D+2, April 18-19. Beyond that authorization was granted for US Air Force transports to fly supply missions to the beachhead and for the use of napalm in ground attacks including on Cuban air bases (both authorizations which clearly compromised American deniability).[259] Clearly strategic authorizations were being granted by D-Day evening, apparently with

In Denial

serious concessions to political deniability. What is lacking from the record is any history of the exchanges related to those authorizations, any detail as to dialog with the White House, or insight into the overall strategic command process. Activities which had been "off the table" prior to D-Day were now being allowed, unfortunately we have no insight into how or exactly who was involved in those decisions.

Along with the initially successful night time air supply effort, new rounds of airstrikes against Cuban airfields began D-Day night. Six brigade aircraft attempted airstrikes against two major targets, five failed to drop their ordinance, claiming poor visibility and haze but one did fly close enough to bomb and did not inflict any damage. A contributing factor to the failure (beyond haze and base blackouts) may have been the fact, noted earlier, that there were a limited number of Cuban B-26 pilots available and at least some of the crews on the nighttime mission had already been in action over the beaches. With two round trip overseas flights to Cuba, and the ongoing tension of the constant fuel conservation measures necessary on all flights, some brigade pilots were already exhausted by the end of their D-Day and D-Day night missions. After dark, beginning with an artillery barrage (from Soviet 122mm howitzers), the second series of far heavier Cuban attacks began, with another advance down the primary road into the lodgment, towards Red Beach. The artillery pounding continued over some three hours, stopping just before midnight and was quickly followed with a series of Cuban Army tank and infantry assaults; once again each was stopped and bloodied by the brigade forces using bazookas, and with M-41 tank support. Tank and infantry assaults continued until 3 AM in the morning, all were repulsed.

Secret Wars With Air Strikes And Tanks?

With destroyed or damaged tanks blocking the road though the swamp the Cuban forces fell back on heavy infantry attacks, which were also stopped with every evidence of heavy casualties for the Cuban Army/militia.

While the Cuban attacks had been defeated, it appears that the blocking force had not been sufficiently resupplied with ammunition, either from the air drops at Red Beach or the drops at Blue Beach. At least one truck with mortars and heavy weapons ammunition had overturned in the dark going from Blue Beach to the blocking force.[260] Given the size of the Cuban Army units building up for renewed attacks, the brigade blocking unit on the Red Beach road was ordered to retreat to Blue Beach, which up to that point had faced no ground attacks. By the second day (D+1) brigade control was restricted to Blue Beach and difficulties experienced during the landings caused troops initially designated to the third landing area, Green Beach, to instead land at Red Beach.

April 18 D+1

Contrary to the popular image of total Cuban air superiority at the Bay of Pigs, on the second day of the lodgment some 20 Cuban air force attack sorties involving 2 B-26's, 2 Sea Furies and 2 T-33 jets were flown from against the lodgment from San Antonio air field by Castro's forces and no Brigade aircraft were lost to the Cuban fighters. However two Brigade aircraft were lost to ground fire during the combat.[261] With the source of the Cuban air attacks identified, a new series of air strikes were ordered against the San Antonio airfield and permission was received to use American contract pilots to provide air cover over the beaches.[262] Those authorizations were further evidence that the rules were being changed and new authorities were being granted, but yet again we have no clue at all as to the actual exchanges which generated them, where they originated or at what level they were actually being approved.

The Brigade strike base was also directed to launch a major series of attacks against Cuban ground forces approaching the beaches and advised that the air strikes would be given fighter cover by Navy aircraft operating off the carrier Essex. American pilots did fly six B-26's in ground attacks on D+1 (the Brigade pilots were reserved for the night time strikes against Cuban airfields) and heavily damaged a column of an estimated 15-20 light tanks and 20 trunks with infantry troops, using guns, rockets, and napalm.[263] Remarks relating to the Navy combat air cover for the American pilots are found in Grayston Lynch's description of four Navy jets flying over the beach towards the interior, returning over the same route. He had been advised by radio only that Navy jets would be in the area. Lynch's description of his ongoing communications with the Navy reflects considerable misunderstanding and confusion over what type of combat was and was not authorized. This demonstrates a clear command problem and one which affected morale both on the LCI's and with the brigade on the beaches.[264] Given that Lynch and his LCI were the only radio link into the brigade, it is hard to imagine how isolated the Brigade commanders must have felt. There were no direct communications with the aircraft operating over the beaches, with the vital air drops, or with the strike base in Nicaragua. The Brigade ground commanders had no real understanding or control over what support they were getting, might get, or certainly would not get - a command and morale nightmare for any military force.

As of the end of the second day of the lodgment, Blue Beach was being held by Brigade 2506, with the brigade largely intact, having received some resupply of ammunition via air drops and ongoing air supply planned. The LCU's carrying a considerable amount of ammunition from the freighters were expected to bring them in after dark. Even with the slowness of the freighter offloads, the LCU's hoped to arrive at 4:30 AM, offload in an hour and be back at sea by dawn.[265] Combat authorities had changed so significantly that American pilots had flown successful ground attack missions against a Cuban column, with Navy combat air support. Whether the Navy pilots had been authorized to actually engage Cuban aircraft remains a matter of debate as there is considerable confusion on that point in available records, as well as from among those actually involved. Lynch describes having engaged in ground strike planning and targeting (to the level of providing specific map coordinates for the attacks) during his communications with the Navy force.[266]

At the end of D+1 the brigade had established itself inside Cuba, under attack but largely intact and this itself raises a key issue of strategic command and planning. In the Guatemala regime change effort, the CIA's military surrogates had been overwhelmingly defeated in their advance into that country, with half the small force lost and retreating after its first two engagements. Yet the project's propaganda had declared an early victory, claimed to be broadcasting from inside the country – and along with a small number of relatively inconsequential air strikes against highly visible targets – totally intimidated the governing regime. In Cuba, at the Bay of Pigs on the end of the second day (with a member of the Cuban Revolutionary Council on the Beach and others in Florida who could have been made available to the media) nothing similar happened.

There were no highly visible air actions over population centers as in Guatemala, or actions against other Cuban government facilities across the island. There was no spurt of resistance activity, of defections, of sabotage – nothing to feed rumors and gossip of a regime under pressure. All of which raises the question of what the plan for actual success had been? What was the minimum time to announce a provisional government in Cuba and request military protection for it? Would this require days or weeks? Or was there no real plan beyond landing the brigade? Was it all just talk?

April 19 D+2

The air resupply of the beachhead at the end of the first day had been relatively effective, with seven transport planes officially recorded as dropping some 60,000 pounds of ammunition. With the same number of aircraft available, with the beach airstrip having installed lights and not under direct Cuban attack at night, a second series of night-time supply drops should have been even more successful. All available transport aircraft were to be used and the strike base had obtained the authority to use American contract pilots as back up with the Cuban crews.[267] At least one brigade transport was also prepared to land at the beach airstrip itself on the morning of April 19. Beyond that authorization had also been obtained for the United States Air Force to use C-130 aircraft to conduct night supply drops of some 60,000 to 90,000 pounds, flying from Kelly Air Force Base in San Antonio, Texas directly to the Bay of Pigs.

Instead, the second night resupply of the beachhead proved largely fruitless. Although seven aircraft had launched for resupply the previous night, only two aircraft appear to have made drops at Blue Beach on the critical second night, with some of the supplies going into the swamp and others into the water. The scheduled landing of one cargo plane on the beach strip did occur and its cargo was delivered (the mission flown by a Cuban pilot and American co-pilot). No explanation of what appears to have been a major air resupply failure on that second night is readily available, although it must be remembered that the strike base had warned of a severe lack of capable transport aircrews even before the Zapata operation had launched. It is also worthwhile noting, just as in regard to the lack of clandestine reconnaissance of the beaches, the special paramilitary teams that had received months of training, including managing covert night time air drops, sabotage, and diversions, were not deployed to support the Bay of Pigs effort. In addition to the failure of air resupply, the large-scale air strike on Cuban fields scheduled for the same night produced virtually no results, with haze and weather conditions offered as an explanation.

There is no doubt that the brigade's air unit was fully engaged, and under virtually no restrictions but it also appears that by the end of the second day, fatigued and with ongoing exposure to Cuban air attack, the brigade's Cuban pilots had largely reached the end of their effectiveness. The earlier logistics concerns about having sufficient pilots and aircrews to sustain combat operations proved to have been extremely well founded – as were virtually all the warnings from professional military staff detailed to the project. As to the critical US Air Force air supply missions, none were actually flown and the explanation given was that such supply had not been preplanned and there were insufficient parachute riggers (additional riggers had to be flown in from Montana) for the full number of planes and amount of cargo designated in the Day+2 mission. The record contains no explanation as to why, with the critical importance of ammunition to the effort, at least a partial Air Force resupply mission was not launched.[268]

Given the known limits of brigade air transport, this appears to reflect a serious lack of planning for any long-term support of an actual lodgment inside Cuba as well as a total failure of real time command. As with the air strikes on Cuban bases, there simply seem to have been none of the "contingency" plans common to conventional military operations. The final hope for any major resupply lay with bringing loaded landing craft, escorted by Lynch and Roberts on the brigade LCI's. That hope was lost in two fatal command and control failures, both involving project headquarters and the US Navy. As Lynch records, the craft were on the way to the beach and could have offloaded under cover of darkness, although they would have been exposed to air attack on their way back out to sea. Based on his own experiences, the Navy had proved largely ineffective at protecting brigade craft even at the 12-mile distance specified in the rules of engagement.

With the craft on the way to the beach, at 2:30 AM, Lynch received orders to turn back and hold at his position well off shore, some 50 miles off the beach.[269] Hours later he was advised that there would be a major air strike mounted in support of the lodgment that morning, again supported by Navy combat air cover as on the previous day.

Secret Wars With Air Strikes And Tanks?

He was apparently not told that the strike had been authorized to cover air supply drops into the lodgment as well as resupply by his loaded LCU's. In retrospect, if all the supply missions for the night of D+1 and morning of D+2 had actually been executed, the second day on the beachhead would have been something far different than what history now records. Instead, D+2 proved to be disastrous.

There is also little evidence of any improvement in high level strategic control by the second day on the beach. Instead we find an account of a meeting in the very early hours of that day, at around 1:30 AM. It is virtually the only account of a high-level meeting on the Cuba lodgment involving President Kennedy. The meeting included National Security Advisor Bundy, Vice-President Johnson, Secretary of State Rusk, and Secretary of Defense McNamara, JCS representatives Lemnitzer and Burke – with the only CIA representative being Cuba Project Chief Bissell. None of the project military staff, with direct knowledge of conditions at the lodgment, participated - nor did CIA Director Dulles.[270]

Once again, we have no idea to what extent the president was briefed on tactical details, much less on the full state of the operation (including an update on the anticipated uprisings, defections, or plans for transition to guerrilla action). Certainly, he was not given information directly from the most knowledgeable sources, the CIA military leaders of the project. The only concrete result of the meeting was yet another authorization for Navy air cover and cover for a ground strike to be carried out by brigade aircraft, which would be flown by volunteer American National Guard pilots. Six Navy jets were to provide "positive, aggressive cover" during the hour long period scheduled for the B-26 strike as well as cover for the aircraft to be sent in another aerial resupply mission and supply landings by the LCUs.[271] Yet Lynch himself reports that he was ordered to hold offshore and simply waited, joined up with the Barbara J and the very late arriving freighter Caribe - only then beginning to unload its ammunition. There is also no record of any major air resupply mission arriving over the beach, only of the Air National Guard pilots flying the ground support air strike with no evidence of any Navy combat cover. Instead, the American pilots were met by Cuban jets, decimating the last of the brigade B-26's and resulting in the deaths of four of the National Guard airmen.

It had been a dramatic commitment, involving Navy jets and American volunteers in four brigade B-26's (one suffered engine trouble and returned to its base) - certainly something far beyond the earlier deniability restrictions placed on the operation. If all elements had been conducted as authorized, the lodgment would have had received a major ammunition resupply on the morning of D+2, advancing Cuban ground forces would have been badly hurt and the beachhead would have been protected for at least one more day, perhaps two. Yet it was clearly an act of desperation, with apparently no decisions made on any actions for longer term sustainment. The critical nature of the Navy support was reinforced in a communication from the strike base in Nicaragua directly to the carrier Essex. The Essex was advised that it was imperative that its combat air cover was given to the full beachhead, not just at the 12-mile limit. The message advised that strike and supply missions would involve Americans, and specified the radio frequency to be used by the Navy pilots for communications.

Secret Wars With Air Strikes And Tanks?

Separately a message went from the Joint Chiefs to Admiral Dennison, in overall charge of Bumpy Road, and to the commander of the Essex. It highlighted the importance of the air cover mission, noting not only the air strikes but supply missions from brigade aircraft (and C-130's; to be flown by the US Air Force). What followed was the total failure of the Navy to provide the critical combat air cover over the beachhead. It was that failure which revealed that the Navy did not know until D+2 that it was unable to communicate on the radio frequencies used by the brigade aircraft – something not reported to the strike base in Nicaragua nor project headquarters or the Joint Chiefs until a full three hours after it had received the mission parameters from the strike base in Nicaragua.

The failure also revealed that the CIA liaison officer on the Essex (Marine Colonel Frank J. Mallard) had apparently served largely as a bystander during the operations. When questioned about communications he offered very little information and when challenged as to his role in the activities Mallard's response was to claim that the Navy was "taking all its orders from Washington" – suggesting that rather than operating in conjunction with Cuba Project headquarters, the Navy task force had been acting at the direction of either Admirals Dennison or Burke.[272] As noted earlier, detailed activities of the task force were very difficult to reconstruct after the fact due to the fact that all of its operational records had been immediately destroyed, including the ships log and all communications to and from the Essex and destroyed before the command ship left its station off shore. The repeated failures of real time command, control, and communications during D+2 are well documented and they are most dramatically illustrated in one particular set of exchanges which occurred that morning. At 9 AM the strike base (JMTIDE) advised that its aircraft were being shot down over the beachhead – essentially demanding to know why the promised Navy air cover had failed – "where is your aggressive air support?" A series of messages from JMTIDE expressed its ongoing frustration over the loss of the aircraft and failure of support – "Today's air crews dispatched as last resort, confident of Navy cover. Will not send any more B-26's from base under present condition."[273]

Yet even following those communications, Cuba Project headquarters continued to message JMTIDE as if Navy air cover was in place, and would continue - "Complete Navy protection has been granted for the maximum number of B-26 strikes, upon receipt of this message until darkness tonight. Request you mount the maximum number of sorties for this period. Entire B-26 force to concentrate on support for the beachhead. Friendly Task Force Blue Beach throughout this afternoon." At that point in time the available B-26's had already been lost over the beachhead. The Navy aircraft had arrived far too late and finding no Brigade aircraft in view they had returned to the carrier Essex.

Equally confusing, the same early Joint Chiefs morning message to the Essex, which had ordered the combat air cover over the Brigade, had also advised that the beachhead was under ground attack and that "break out" plans (either as a force or in guerilla groups) were being discussed. If a breakout could not be developed the Navy had apparently been directed to begin plans for an evacuation effort, including protection for landing craft while still taking special measures for deniability. Based on that message traffic, it appears that senior personnel in

Washington were still discussing options, including a possible break out of the brigade, without an understanding of the tactical situation on the ground.

When Hawkins was later questioned about that issue, he responded that the military staff had fully understood that getting the troops out of the Zapata landing area had always been deemed to be virtually impossible (as he and Esterline had told Bissell privately), and the only option that had ever existed was evacuating the troops using the ships that had brought them. He had no comment at all when asked about any training or instruction in regard to "going guerilla."[274] Beyond that confusion, there is no record of any headquarters dialog directly with the brigade about either a break out or evacuation. Lynch, who was serving as radio relay for the brigade, mentions no communications at all of that nature up to the point in time at which he himself raised it as an option to Brigade commander, Pepe San Roman. It was only at noon of D+2 that Lynch received his first notice that evacuation was being discussed in Washington, with the Navy ordered to cover the effort with destroyers and combat air. He then personally raised evacuation with San Roman, who totally rejected the idea, while advising that Cuban formations were closing in on the beachhead from both sides. There is simply no indication that guerilla action or evacuation and re-landing had ever been previously discussed with the brigade leaders, including San Roman, or that any plans or preparation had been done for those contingencies.

Finally, at 2 PM on D+2 San Roman radioed Lynch that tanks were firing on his command post from both sides of the beach, he was preparing to destroy his radio, and had ordered his force to disperse into the woods and swamps around the bay. Two Navy destroyers did race into the bay on a reconnaissance mission, taking Cuban fire but not returning it. Shortly afterwards, with no radio contact from the Brigade, they retreated off shore in the face of increasing tank fire from the Cuban forces. As of the afternoon of D+2 (the third day on the beachhead), the Zapata Plan had failed.

From that point in time, for weeks, months, and decades, the dialog on the Cuban Project has largely be one of finger pointing and hyperbole. Accusations of blame (other than in the CIA Inspector General's report) would almost entirely focus on the 5 days of D-2 through D+2 - rather than the full Cuba Project which spanned some 13 months. That focus – and the degree of hyperbole brought to the finger pointing - stand out clearly in the title for Part IV of the study later prepared by the CIA's own historian – "Where Cuba was Lost." That work reserves its primary effort towards illustrating failures with the Navy's operations, as well as critiquing President Kennedy's ongoing decisions to maintain deniability through requesting air strikes be held to a minimum – as well as ultimately failing to order the American military into active combat operations against the Cuban Air Force and ground forces assaulting the beachhead.

In a broader view, one of the problems with all the subsequent debate and finger pointing is that criticism often failed to judge the failure at the Bay of Pigs in terms of the criteria established for the overall Cuba Project as a covert action. Instead, much of the criticism has been in terms of conventional military action. Yet the final Zapata Plan operation was developed with far more stringent constraints, and with assumptions that would never be found in conventional military planning. No military planning would assume 100% success in any air strike or any single supply effort as all would assume casualties in aircraft and transports. JCS chief Lemnitzer pointed that out during the Taylor Committee hearings. When he was asked what happens when something is not 100% successful, he replied that in war [combat] you never expect 100 percent success.[275] Operations against Cuba had actually begun on D-2 and it is an axiom of military planning that no battle plan survives first contact with the enemy. Contingency planning is integral to virtually all conventional operations.[276]

It's hard to imagine how any conventional military operation would have been planned in a manner that the cancellation (due to weather, enemy action, logistics issues) of a single attack could doom the entire effort. Given the loss of surprise created by the D-2 preemptive strikes, a plan assuming that absolutely all surviving Cuban aircraft (estimated at possibly half the original force) would be totally destroyed at multiple airfields in a D-Day strike simply gave no margin for either error or unforeseen events. Yet this was something that the projects senior leaders appear to have acceded to without any serious opposition, certainly not expressing concern to the point of discussing the potential need cancel the operation before landings began.

Despite later statements, the Taylor Committee hearings demonstrated that the option of cancellation had actually been available. At the time (10:30 PM) that the meeting between Bissell/Cabell with Dean Rusk concluded there was time to call off the landing (or to give President Kennedy that option). The brigade's troops and landing craft were still well off shore. The underwater team sent to mark the beaches did not deploy until 1 PM (Cuba and Washington are in the same time zone). There was some two and a half hours available to get the teams back on board, cease debarkation, and then to take the ships out of Cuban waters before daylight.[277] If the cancellation of the D-Day strike was seen by Bissell and Cabell to be as significant as they later represented, they could have made the point to the president, leveraging it with the cancellation option. If they had been in doubt, their military advisors appear to have been willing to reinforce the true degree of risk directly to the president.

Admittedly, calling out points of potential military failure in the Zapata Plan is no great challenge. That process began as months earlier with the February 3, 1961 Joint Chief's Study of the military elements of its predecessor, the Trinidad Plan (which provides the best available, detailed description of the CIA's own plans, which were not provided in writing for high level reviews and discussions). That feasibility study concluded that landing the brigade was indeed feasible, even without total surprise and in the face of limited initial opposition, which was done at the Bay of Pigs.[278] However, the JCS report began with the qualification that the actual mission, the overthrow of the Castro regime, would depend on support from inside Cuba. The CIA had given assurance that there was an active resistance, and an uprising was highly probable. Admiral Burke told the Taylor Committee that "great emphasis" had been placed on the uprising, with a great deal of effort put into organizing equipment for upwards of 30,000 Cubans who would be involved. Burke's own understanding of the plan was that the lodgment at the beachhead need only to be held for a limited time, "several days" before local volunteers and the broader uprising came into play.[279]

Secret Wars With Air Strikes And Tanks?

Beyond that consideration, the study assessed the initial air operations and paratroop assault at the beachhead as militarily feasible, but noted that centralized coordination and control was absolutely essential to overall success. Along with the need for centralized command and communications, logistics was identified as a major potential weakness – in terms of both personnel and plans for support. In the face of even moderate and determined resistance the planned logistics were judged to be inadequate. Supplemental material in the study specifically noted that logistics, including both shipping and supplies, was limited and allowed no margin for miscalculation or unforeseen contingencies.

The study also noted that plans should be made to involve guerrilla forces to support the effort from outside the landing area, and warned that without a popular revolution or the introduction of major follow-on forces the Cuban Army would retake the beachhead. It gave no estimate of how long the beachhead could be held. In the detailed material supporting the assessment, the study also noted that in addition to some 1,200 local militia and police forces there were 6,000 regular Cuban Army troops within 100 miles of the Zapata region beaches. The feasibility study estimated the beachhead would come under attack by a force of at least regiment size by D+1; the counter-assault would be supported by tanks and artillery at that point in time. It also noted that the CIA was assuming that the beachhead would be immediately sustained by some 1,500 local volunteers (doubling the force at the lodgment).

The "Air Annex" to the study noted that while the air strike plan was assessed as being "generally successful," the brigade combat force had only 18 trained pilots, almost a one to one relationship with its aircraft resulting in little margin for crew rotation or for aircraft losses. Other annexes noted the lack of amphibious training for the brigade, including potential problems in maritime element traffic control, the moving of materials onto and across the beaches, and the management and movement of supplies on the beachhead. Emphasis was given to the marginal nature of the logistics plan, noting that logistics would dramatically worsen as opposition built. Logistics and resupply were evaluated as insufficient to survive even moderate resistance for any extended period of time. A special point was also made that even a single Cuban attack aircraft operating over the beachhead could put the force's ships at risk, and given the logistics constraints that could easily jeopardize the entire operation.

A simple rereading of the assessments in the military feasibility study of the initial Trinidad proposal brings into focus the majority of the points of failure that did emerge in the actual Zapata operation. Yet beyond that, on April 3, the Cuba Project's own military leaders, the men most familiar with the details and assumptions of the plan, had specifically called out much deeper problems with the overall mission – stating that, as approved, the plan was literally doomed to fail.[280] They stated to the project chief that there was simply no reason to accept the proposition that a limited program of planned airstrikes would indeed take out all of Castro's combat aircraft, because no reasonable military plan assumes such total success. Any surviving fighters would very likely prevent resupply and would make B-26 operations over the beaches suicidal. In short, the landing would not cause Castro's overthrow and ultimately result in the loss of the landing force. While the terrain at the Bay of Pigs might slow Cuban assaults, it also would effectively trap the brigade and therefore, no "going guerilla" option remained or had been planned. Another vital problem with the area was it prevented any reinforcement of the beach by indigenous volunteers. Assuming total destruction of Cuban air power, the brigade could hold the lodgment for some days, but in time it would simply be overwhelmed by superior Cuban forces.

When Bissell chose to totally disregard his senior military staff and failed to take their issues into the strategic White House dialogs (with CIA Director Dulles supporting him), the two men were proceeding on their own, making judgements and arguing for military decisions well beyond the experience or expertise of either. Bissell himself had no military experience at all; he held a PHD in economics. Within the highest level of White House strategic reviews, the discussions did involve people with World War II military service, but that experience was not in conventional air or amphibious operations. Bissell was the project's senior officer, with military specialists advising him and the project's own military officers were the men most involved with the intelligence assessments and tactical details of the Zapata plan. They should have been used to provide the professional input for strategic decision making – yet Bissell appears to have intentionally avoided that, especially with the sidelining of Esterline during the weeks immediately preceding the landings.

As to the Joint Chiefs, the members personally involved in the White House discussions clearly took a limited role, viewing their involvement as limited to the military assessment of feasibility in regard to the amphibious landings. The details of the JCS staff studies (unlike the actual CIA plan itself, which was not in writing) were available to the Chiefs, and to the strategic decision

In Denial

makers. The extent to which those details were actually used or introduced into the highest level of dialogs remains an open question. Matters were made even more difficult because the new members of the Kennedy Administration (as well as President Kennedy himself) had no experience in communicating with the regular military officers participating in the meetings.

Years later, in an oral history interview, Admiral Burke explained how confusing strategy discussions could become in a political rather than a military context.[281] His career as a military officer had conditioned him to take statements as orders. As he put it, when the president said "well, gentlemen, this is the way it is," a decision had been made and an order given. Working under a former military president such as Dwight Eisenhower, such statements were clearly orders. Burke found that with President Kennedy such remarks were more of an academic nature, not final, literal commands, but more in the nature of "that's the way it looks now and let's go on and discuss it." Burke described really coming to appreciate the differences in decision making style between Eisenhower and Kennedy only after the Bay of Pigs, stating that initially there had been what he described as a "tremendous gap of understanding." That only became apparent to him some months later, following discussions of Laos in a National Security Meeting.

President Kennedy had expressed his appreciation of Burke for supporting a White House position and in response Burke told Kennedy that not only did he not support it, he didn't agree with it. Kennedy was surprised - they had both been in the meeting, and Burke had made no comments nor stated any issues or opposition. Burke responded that his opinion had not been asked, at which point Kennedy remarked, "Well, when you sit there and let it go by without saying anything, I think that you approve it." Burke took the admonition to heart and at a following National Security Council meeting spoke up, "Mr. President, I object to that; I don't agree with this." Everyone was shocked since the dialog was not on a military matter, and it was not something where Admiral Burke would be expected to have an opinion. Kennedy responded, "What is your opinion, Admiral?" I said, "I don't have any, but if the position of my ass determines my vote, and I don't know anything about this, I can't approve. Because I am here, and if my presence here signifies that I approve of this, then I want to know something about it. And I don't know anything about it." Kennedy took the point and began to pointedly ask for individual opinions during meetings, something he would later do consistently and effectively during the Cuban Missile Crisis.

Burke himself commented that those personal exchanges with the president had established a new working relationship. He didn't think Kennedy had intentionally been overlooking objections or opinions, "It wasn't that he did this deliberately; it was a difference in procedures." Burke's remarks are interesting not only in regard to personality factors, but in understanding the degree to which the military participants in the Trinidad and Zapata dialogs appear to have distanced themselves from what was fundamentally a CIA mission. Of course, the Joint Chief's did order staff studies of the military plans involved with the plans, but only to the extent to which operations were verbally described by CIA project staff. Admiral Dennison advised the Taylor Committee that it had been especially challenging, because there had also been difficulties in providing necessary support in the total absence of planning papers throughout the course of the activity.[282]

The absence of actual planning papers also makes it difficult to trace communications failures during the White House strategy sessions on the Cuba Project - in regard to either the Trinidad or Zapata Plans. We have no transcripts of those White House sessions or of individual dialogs between individuals such as President Kennedy and Richard Bissell, yet Secret Service logs reveal some thirteen off-the-record meetings with President Kennedy between Bissell and others during Kennedys first three months in office.[283] We don't even have the actual transcripts of the Taylor Commission Study which followed the failure at the Bay of Pigs. However, what we do have, "The Taylor Committee Investigation of the Bay of Pigs" (Volume 4 of the CIA Historian's work on the Cuba Project), offers us important insights into what key figures felt they knew and understood about the Zapata operation – correctly or incorrectly. Despite the obvious polemic in presentation, this material is invaluable and does include quotations from key individuals. It also reveals significant misunderstandings among the most senior parties involved, both in terms of operational facts, and in regard to the mission and rules of engagement specified by the Commander in Chief.

A first read of the Taylor Committee material is somewhat shocking, especially in terms of how much incorrect or conflicting information there was expressed by the most senior individuals who had been involved in strategic dialogs – ranging from intelligence about Cuban forces and the degree of resistance inside Cuba to important operational details. Senior administration officials such as Secretary McNamara had even continued with the belief that if the brigade failed to hold a lodgment at the Bay of Pigs it had been prepared to split up into groups and proceed to the Escambray.[284] Even more striking is Bissell's statement that it was not known that the Cuban T-33 jets were armed; a fact which was indeed well known to the project's air element staff, to his own military commanders, and was part of the national intelligence data on Cuban forces.[285] Some of the misunderstandings can be attributed to the normal compartmentalization and lack of written documentation for any covert operation. Others were clearly fostered by the unusual management structure of the project – in which high level direction from Deputy Director of Plans Bissell and his aide Tracy Barnes overlapped influence with the operational responsibilities held by WH/4 and effectively carried out by Esterline, who actually reported to WH/4 Director, J.C. King.

Exchanges during the Taylor Committee hearings made it rather obvious that J. C. King's actual role was largely unclear to everyone involved. King himself proved to be a font of misinformation and asked a number of obviously uniformed questions, as an example he questioned why all the operational Brigade aircraft were not launched for the D-2 Day strike - suggesting King had either not been privy to (or understood) the extended discussions related to preserving American deniability and President Kennedy's directives on that point. Beyond that, the separation of command and control related to air operations, conducted by individuals under Bissell's authority, and with only lateral communications to Hawkins (serving as the military chief of the final amphibious landings), not only had an impact on communications and response time, but further compartmentalized information about Cuban combat air capabilities. The degree of high-level misinformation and misunderstanding in regard to Cuban brigade air operations and air strike planning revealed in Taylor Committee study is overwhelming.

Even more disconcerting are the apparent misconceptions among the most senior CIA officers in regard to both the Cuba Project as a whole (as a politically sensitive covert action) and more specifically the Zapata Plan mission parameters - parameters specifically dictated by the Commander in Chief. To appreciate the full nature of those misunderstandings, or more accurately, "disconnects," it is important to restate the fundamentals of the project itself.

The Cuba Project was conceived and authorized as a strictly covert action by President Eisenhower as an activity in which the hand of the United States was not to show. It was to be a politically deniable operation, both domestically and internationally. In fact, it was so politically sensitive that the Eisenhower Administration refused to openly take a position supporting indigenous resistance to the Castro regime – while candidate John Kennedy was openly campaigning with exactly that as a significant element in his campaign for the presidency. All of the elements of the project – psychological, political and paramilitary – were to be fully covert and American involvement was to be totally deniable. The project was neither authorized by Eisenhower nor reauthorized by Kennedy as simply a clandestine military operation. Eisenhower had approved it as a covert regime change project, an effort to support and grow existing resistance inside Cuba to a point of overthrowing Castro, but with its military element having the appearance of only Cuban participation.

Secret Wars With Air Strikes And Tanks?

That had been the explicit direction and the nature of all the CIA's efforts between March and November, 1960. Eisenhower himself never directed a change in that mission, and in terms of creating the insurgency as initially conceived, the Cuba Project had literally failed by November, 1961 when it was overtaken by Castro's social and security actions inside Cuba, and by Soviet moves to support his regime militarily. The failure was sufficiently evident that by November President Eisenhower had become frustrated enough so that he was apparently prepared to support some sort of clandestine act of provocation which would allow overt American military action against Castro. Clearly the Cuba Project was initiated by Eisenhower as a deniable action, with considerations for both domestic politics and international politics. None of those concerns, or that direction, changed with President Kennedy's authorization of a mission to insert a force of anti-Castro Cuban volunteers into Cuba. That covert action was to be a stimulus for increased military opposition to Castro and a trigger for the rise of a broader insurgency.

As to deniability, Kennedy's own concern for American deniability was clear, even before his election the military leaders of the CIA project had discussed how political issues of deniability would place limitations on their plans, especially in regard to an air campaign. President Kennedy's demand for deniability was firm and consistent from the very first meetings between his new administration and the CIA. It was reasserted in his final directives, and in the rules of engagement for the Zapata Plan. The Cuban brigade was to be landed at night, all landing craft and brigade ships were to be at sea and outside Cuban territorial waters by daylight. Those directions were confirmed in the actual operations plan, which stated that the landing would be conducted entirely at night, and that for at least the first 24 hours all supply activity would be at night with troops deployed inland and "no observable beachhead." Brigade vessels were to return only during the nights of D Day and D+1 to discharge more supplies.[286] The Navy was authorized to provide screening for the brigade ships at sea and to protect the force outside the limit of territorial waters by engaging with and diverting Cuban aircraft or boats. Only in the event that US forces were fired upon were they allowed to return fire. No American citizens were to participate in the landings, and no Americans were to participate in brigade air combat strikes or combat air patrols. Neither were Americans to participate in air transport or re-supply of the brigade.

Those ground rules were actually nothing new and most of them had been in play from the very beginning of the project under Eisenhower. In the months and weeks prior to the actual landings concerns over deniability appear to have been understood and observed by the leaders of the project, to the extent that none of its specially trained paramilitary forces were inserted into Cuba for direct pathfinder operations to reconnoiter the landing area or even the general Zapata region. No specific contacts were established with resistance groups in the region or plans made for sabotage or diversions to undermine Cuban military operations against the beachhead. No efforts were organized to conduct sabotage operations against key Cuban airfields and aircraft, even those closest to the Bay of Pigs. In fact, it appears that there was no direct contact with even the closest resistance groups in the Escambray. Beyond that the Cuba Project leadership had determined not to inform or involve the resistance groups it was in contact with, including the largest united resistance organization, UNIDAD, in order to prepare a coordinated insurgency coordinated with the landings. The reasons given for that lack of action were a stated need for both operational security and deniability.

Yet once combat began, deniability was repeatedly and knowingly compromised. One by one most of the fundamental ground rules were waived - by whom is sometimes unclear, but several appear to have been with presidential concurrence. Americans were allowed to stay directly involved in the amphibious operations, assuming the role of landing and beachhead coordination. No effort was made to order Lynch and Robertson out of combat or to alter their unauthorized roles. An American civilian commanded one LCI and other civilians, commercial seamen, crewed both LCI's at the beachhead - all of them remained with the craft throughout the operation although none actually crewed the craft's machine guns as did Lynch and Robertson.

Americans were allowed to fly in operations in support of the lodgment – along with transport aircraft, in successful B-26 ground strikes against Cuban forces on D+1 and in a second, fatal series of planned ground strikes on D+2. United States Air Force transports were authorized to conduct air drops into the beachhead – only failing to do so due to lack of preparation and logistics issues. Brigade aircraft were authorized and did use napalm from American military stocks in air strikes. American pilots were authorized to fly Brigade B-26 aircraft in order to conduct D+1 B-26 ground attacks and did so successfully - but the Navy jets directed to fly combat air cover for those attacks failed to do so. American destroyers were sent directly off the beach to probe the landing area in advance of a US Navy evacuation mission. They took on Cuban tank fire while doing so, but did not return fire. Essentially the only sacrifice of deniability which was not authorized was the actual use of American jet combat aircraft to destroy the Cuban Air Force (as well as Cuban ground forces besieging the beachhead), which of course would have been an overt act of war.

All of which leaves us with some seemingly striking misunderstandings in remarks from experienced and senior CIA officers, almost all of whom would later complain that the failure at the Bay of Pigs was the result of President Kennedy's decision to not to openly commit the American military in preemptive and aggressive actions against Cuban forces. Such an action would have represented an act of war, without Congressional endorsement, and without a formal declaration of war. It would have been something far beyond anything associated with covert, deniable action projects, or with any mission previously assigned to the Central Intelligence Agency. All of which are "political" by their very nature – otherwise they would not be ordered to be covert and deniable.

Project Chief Bissell would later state that any prospect of deniability had been lost many weeks before the landing, yet he had not advised the president or his national security advisors of that fact. CIA Director Dulles moved that even further back in time, saying that he should have advised the president that it had moved beyond deniability months previously. Indeed, virtually none of the CIA officers involved maintained that the Trinidad and Zapata plans had anything beyond "technical" deniability, yet they had proceeded to propose, endorse, and carry them out under presidential authorization of a covert action assignment. It was a covert assignment that they themselves had converted into a conventional military operation, something well outside their charter either as an agency or in the presidential directives authorizing the mission (Kennedy's official national security directive had specified nothing more than inserting Castro volunteers into Cuba).

One of the more striking insights as to how far CIA officers had mentally drifted away from the presidential directives for covert action came from Jacob Esterline, the Cuba Project's operational head, and the senior officer involved in its military element. Esterline told the Taylor Committee that he and Marine Colonel Hawkins had both learned the lesson that "we [the CIA] cannot conduct an operation where political decisions are going to interfere with military judgement." Somehow Jake Esterline had become so subsumed by the project that he had lost touch with his own agencies' role in terms of being specifically legally chartered only for covert action – and with both President Eisenhower and Kennedy's direct orders not to let the hand of the United States show in the Cuba Project.[287] Esterline and the others had essentially been coopted by the desire for success, one of the major risks in any covert action.

Even Richard Bissell acknowledged that failure. When asked why, when it had obviously been constrained to the point where military success was uncertain, why didn't he say so, why didn't he just tell Dulles or tell Kennedy and recommend canceling it? His response was that he was psychologically and in every other way committed to the operation. Another senior officer in the project, Dick Drain, elaborated, "The operation began to have a life of its own and the intensity of the moment became a major factor in our working positively to achieve the goal, to the exclusion of objective examination of the likelihood of success."[288] Of course any objective concerns over deniability ultimately came to be viewed by those involved with the project as an obstacle, rather than an essential element of their assigned mission.

In contrast to what the senior CIA officers eventually did talk about, none of them ever clearly described what their plans for success had been, including preparations, details, or a timeline for the activities which were to follow the establishment of a lodgment at the Bay of Pigs. President Kennedy had been presented with something relatively simple in concept – the CIA would put a well-trained military force into Cuba and use it as leverage to organize broader Latin American support for resistance to Castro, in the best case creating diplomatic and military support for a provisional, anti-Castro government. That, and the probability of an island wide insurgency, was what the CIA had promised with the Zapata Plan. But were there actually any detailed plans beyond landing Brigade 2506 on the beaches? If so, they were never documented, discussed, or even referred to during the follow-on inquiries.

There was talk of ongoing covert re-supply, but no details of how that was going to occur. Certainly, there were a limited number of brigade transport air crews and aircraft in Nicaragua, but an ongoing series of flights out of the strike base would hardly have been deniable. During combat at the Bay of Pigs, decisions had been made to preserve the brigade ships, including the LCI's, by keeping them off shore during critical periods on Day+1 and Day+2, but how that might have been related to future supply plans remains an open question. Even the plans for ongoing air combat – a staple in any talk of the lodgment's long-term success - are unclear. All the brigade B-26's surely could not have been based at the small strip at the Bay of Pigs (under the imminent threat of concealed nighttime mortar or artillery bombardment from the surrounding forests and swamps) in order to conduct strikes across the island. Even with the total destruction of Castro's fighters, some B-26 aircraft and crews would have been lost to ground fire, as they already had been and there were no more trainees in the pipeline. Or were ongoing air strikes to continue out of Nicaragua, clearly visible to the world at large?

In short, even after all the official inquiries, we still have no clear picture of what was planned with a lodgment in place, including the actual plans for operating a provisional government and generating international support. Nor do we know anything of Cuban Revolutionary Council preparations for a provisional government or if there had been discussions with President Kennedy about when and how American combat support would be provided for such a government. Virtually no questions on such issues or about the longer-term mission were asked during the Taylor Committee inquiry, all the focus was on the failure at the Bay of Pigs. One other question also escaped any follow-on inquiry; its subject remains not only unclear, but mysterious. Were there "wild cards" in play to ensure Castro's removal, plans that even President Kennedy was unaware of at the time? Could such activities have essentially overturned the table in Cuba, making the amphibious landing not the "toss of the dice" it appears to have been, but something with far better odds? The potential "wild cards" of covert action are our next subject.

Notes

[256] Jack B. Pfeiffer, *Official History of the Bay of Pigs, Volume 1; Part 2, March 1960-April 1961*, Central Intelligence Agency, Washington D.C.,
September, 1979, 307

[257] Ibid, 337

[258] Ibid, 339

[259] Ibid, 342-344

[260] Grayston L. Lynch, *Decision for Disaster*, Brassey's, New York and London, 1998, 105

[261] Jack B. Pfeiffer, *Official History of the Bay of Pigs, Volume 4, March 1960-April 1961*, Central Intelligence Agency, Washington D.C., September, 1979, 29

[262] Jack B. Pfeiffer, *Official History of the Bay of Pigs, Volume 1; Part 2, March 1960-April 1961*, Central Intelligence Agency, Washington D.C., September, 1979, 344-345

[263] Ibid, 345-347

[264] Grayston L. Lynch, *Decision for Disaster*, Brassey's, New York and London, 1998, 123-124

[265] Ibid, 127

[266] Ibid, 123

[267] Jack B. Pfeiffer, *Official History of the Bay of Pigs, Volume 1; Part 2, March 1960-April 1961*, Central Intelligence Agency, Washington D.C., September, 1979, 351

268 Jack B. Pfeiffer, *Official History of the Bay of Pigs, Volume 1; Part 2, March 1960-April 1961*, Central Intelligence Agency, Washington D.C., September, 1979, 342-343

269 Grayston L. Lynch, *Decision for Disaster*, Brassey's, New York and London, 1998, 128

270 Jack B. Pfeiffer, *Official History of the Bay of Pigs, Volume 1; Part 2, March 1960-April 1961*, Central Intelligence Agency, Washington D.C., September, 1979, 366-367

271 Ibid, 367

272 Grayston L. Lynch, *Decision for Disaster*, Brassey's, New York and London, 1998, 370

273 Jack B. Pfeiffer, *Official History of the Bay of Pigs, Volume 1; Part 2, March 1960-April 1961*, Central Intelligence Agency, Washington D.C., September, 1979, 371-372

274 Jack B. Pfeiffer, *Official History of the Bay of Pigs, Volume 4, March 1960-April 1961*, Central Intelligence Agency, Washington D.C., September, 1979, 173-174

275 Ibid, 140

276 "No plan survives first contact with the enemy," remark attributed to Field Marshal Helmuth von Moltke (1880-1892), Chief of the Prussian General Staff.

277 Ibid, 55-56

278 Memorandum for the Secretary of Defense, "Military Evaluation of the CIA Paramilitary Plan, Cuba," February 3, 1961 https://www.maryferrell.org/showDoc.html?docId=1250#relPageId=3&tab=page

[279] Jack B. Pfeiffer, *Official History of the Bay of Pigs, Volume 4, March 1960-April 1961*, Central Intelligence Agency, Washington D.C., September, 1979, 119

[280] Don Bohning, *The Castro Obsession; U.S. Covert Operations Against Cuba 1959-1965*, Potomac Books Inc., Washington D.C., 2005, 32-33

[281] Joseph E. O'Connor, "Arleigh A. Burke, Oral History Interview, January 20, 1967 Location: Washington, D.C, John Fitzgerald Kennedy Memorial Library, National Archives and Records Service
https://www.jfklibrary.org/sites/default/files/archives/JFKOH/Burke%2C%20Arleigh%20A/JFKOH-ARB-01/JFKOH-ARB-01-TR.pdf

[282] Jack B. Pfeiffer, *Official History of the Bay of Pigs, Volume 4, March 1960-April 1961*, Central Intelligence Agency, Washington D.C., September, 1979, 58

[283] Don Bohning, *The Castro Obsession; U.S. Covert Operations Against Cuba 1959-1965*, Potomac Books Inc., Washington D.C., 2005, 63

[284] Jack B. Pfeiffer, *Official History of the Bay of Pigs, Volume 4, March 1960-April 1961*, Central Intelligence Agency, Washington D.C., September, 1979, 88

[285] Jack B. Pfeiffer, *Official History of the Bay of Pigs, Volume 1, Part 1, March 1960-April 1961*, Central Intelligence Agency, Washington D.C., September, 1979, 198

[286] Peter Kornbluh, *Bay of Pigs Declassified*, The New Press, New York, 1998, 130

[287] Jack B. Pfeiffer, *Official History of the Bay of Pigs, Volume 4, March 1960-April 1961*, Central Intelligence Agency, Washington D.C., September, 1979, 28-29

[288] Ibid, 161

In Denial

Chapter 7: Hidden Measures

One of the most obvious ways to remove the Castro regime from power was to remove Fidel Castro himself. Consideration for doing just that appears in a memorandum from CIA Western Hemisphere (WH/4) Chief J.C. King to CIA Director Dulles, written in December, 1959. In response to President Eisenhower's directive for new actions to deal with the Cuba problem, King recommended, among other options, the "elimination of Fidel Castro," as a move to "accelerate" the collapse of the revolutionary regime. Dulles approved the idea in concept, however in forwarding the proposal he substituted the phrase "remove from Cuba" rather than making a direct reference in writing to "elimination."[289] Eliminating Castro, and his senior leadership, certainly remained on King's mind. As mentioned earlier, he brought up the possibility in his very first meeting with the newly organized Cuba Task Force, in March, 1960. And the senior staff seconded to manage the Cuba Project within the Directorate of Plans had a history with assassinations activities. The Church Committee (United States Senate Select *Committee* to Study Governmental Operations with Respect to Intelligence Activities) would later review anecdotal reports that DDP Bissell and his senior aide Tracy Barnes had served as "cut outs" in regard to assassination activities within the agency, providing deniability to senior CIA officers in such activities.

In one instance, the approval of a 1950's plan to "incapacitate" an Iraqi officer accused of being a Communist sympathizer, the committees' report (Interim Report: Alleged Assassination Attempts on Foreign Leaders) concluded that Barnes had approved a poisoning attempt, acting on behalf of Bissell.[290] The device to be used in that attempt was a special monogrammed, handkerchief. In the Colonel's case, the handkerchief did not reach him prior to the CIA instigated coup, which resulted in his execution. The poisoning action itself had been endorsed by DDP Bissell and signed off on by Tracy Barnes and the committee found additional indications that Barnes was involved with other attempted assassinations.

Relatively early in the Cuba Project, Barnes was advised of CIA contacts who had made themselves available to plant a bomb on an aircraft in which Fidel Castro was scheduled to fly. Apparently on his own initiative Barnes ordered the action to proceed. However, when his superiors were advised they rejected the bombing plan and ordered him to cancel the attempt. In the interim the bombing had aborted, but only because the individual intended to carry it out had not received Barnes approval in time to carry out the bombing. [291] The Church Committee also found that Barnes had authorized the transfer of three rifles to the Dominican Republic in March, 1961. CIA surrogates later used the weapons in an assassination attempt against Dominican President Rafael Trujillo and one of the guns was found in the possession of the assassins after the shooting.

In Denial

In later years Richard Helms (CIA Director 1966-1973) expressed being upset when at one-point Barnes had been promoted to a level equal with him which he attributed to Barnes's willingness to conduct the sort of radical high risk actions which Alan Dulles and Richard Bissell had favored, but which Helms himself considered as "cowboy" behavior.[292] Given their backgrounds, it is certainly consistent that it was Richard Bissell who ultimately moved to add a serious assassination effort into the Cuba Project, initiating a "sensitive project" targeting Fidel Castro.[293] While there was talk of eliminating Castro and other senior leaders in the earliest days of the Cuba Project, it appears that movement in that direction actually did not begin until July, 1960, and then only in something of protracted fashion. On July 21, the Havana CIA station was advised that the possible elimination of the top three regime leaders (an idea J.C. King had introduced several months earlier) was being considered.[294] Normally it would be anathema to put that sort of thing on paper, and the message itself was quickly reversed (for the record) on the following day. While the message itself may have been rescinded, an assassination effort did indeed begin the following month.

Poison:

During August, 1960, Dr. Edward Gunn, CIA Office of Medical Services, transferred a box of cigar's (Castro's favorite brand) to the CIA's Technical Serviced Division to be treated with a lethal toxin. A full box of 50 cigars was treated with botulinum toxin, in sufficient strength to kill simply by handling the cigars; they did not have to be smoked.[295] The cigars were ready by October, but it appears that another option had emerged and was in play by September, leaving the somewhat challenging delivery of poisoned cigars as a lower priority. The use of poison in cigars, handkerchiefs, or with other types of delivery mechanisms was something the CIA had devoted considerable effort to developing as a tool for both assassinations and certain non-lethal activities.

The CIA's efforts along those lines were performed in conjunction with various military projects, largely centered on the Army's biological warfare program housed at the Edgewood Army Chemical Center and at Camp Detrick in Maryland. The CIA's Chemical Division was headed by Dr. Sydney Gottlieb of CIA Technical Services and it utilized the staff of the Fort Detrick's Special Operations Division (SOD) both for the production of the toxins and work on developing delivery systems. The CIA had begun its special materials program (MKNAOMI) in 1950, establishing an informal agreement with SOD to pursue designated projects; initial funding was on the order of $500,000 annually and reached a high of $675,000 by the mid-sixties. The program was "intended to stockpile severely incapacitating and lethal materials and to develop gadgetry for dissemination of these materials." A June 29, 1975 CIA memorandum confirmed the SOD/CIA relationship and noted that "no written records were kept; management was by verbal instruction and "human continuity." The memo notes that "some requests for support approved by the CIA had apparently involved assassination." [296]

In 1960, Richard Bissell first moved to bring assassination into the Cuba Project by contacting CIA Security Chief Sheffield Edwards in regard to "gangsters" who might have contacts with the former Havana casino crowd. Havana casino owners had been forcibly ejected from Cuba by Castro, losing businesses that had been both corrupt and amazingly profitable under Batista. It was no secret that they wanted revenge, wanted Castro out, and wanted the Havana casino business back. As it happened, Edwards referred Bissell to his operations Chief Jim O'Connell, who routinely worked with private contractors in a variety of largely illegal domestic activities not permitted by CIA personnel, including surveillance, wire taps, and prostitution stings targeting foreign diplomats in Washington D.C. and New York City. [297] One of his trusted assets in such assignments was Robert Maheu, formerly with the FBI, and at the time operating a private investigations firm.

Maheu had been an FBI special agent from 1940-1947, opening his own investigative agency in 1954, and being first recruited for special projects by the CIA in that same year. He was placed on a $500 a month retainer and granted a security clearance to perform assignments for the Operations (Plans) Directorate. Those activities ranged from "procurement of feminine companionship for foreign dignitaries" to wiretapping and bugging operations. In the latter activities he employed Alan Hughes who himself had formerly worked for the CIA's Technical Services Division at Camp Detrick under Sydney Gottlieb – the same division which would supply the poisons for several assassination attempts against Castro.[298]

As it turned out, both O'Connell and Maheu did know of a very well-connected individual named Johnny Roselli, a figure who seemed to be a good fit for the sort of contacts Bissell was seeking. Roselli was not a classic Mafioso although he had come up off the streets in New York and Chicago. He had developed a talent for making introductions and doing deals, first bringing East Coast mob money into "legitimate" the Los Angeles film industry, and then moving on to broker investment deals for major organized crime figures in Las Vegas casinos. He himself had worked as a trouble shooter for well-known mobster Jake Lansky in Lansky's Havana casino and knew all the key figures in the old Havana crowd and Roselli appeared to be an ideal individual to make the sort of connections Bissell sought.

The story of the poison plots which evolved out of the O'Connell, Bissell, and Roselli connection was certainly not known during the official follow-on inquiries on the Cuba Project. As with other CIA activities it only emerged in 1975–1976, during the investigations of the United States Senate Select Committee to Study Governmental Operations with Respect to Intelligence Activities (more commonly referred to as the Church Committee after its chair, Senator Frank Church). Bissell himself was called to testify before the committee, and generally gave vague and sometimes conflicting information as to the origin and evolution of the highly secret and compartmentalized effort against Castro. Edwards was also plagued by a relatively bad memory in his testimony, but O'Connell was specific – stating that Edwards and Bissell had come to him specifically looking to "eliminate" or "assassinate" Fidel Castro and that he had felt Maheu to be "tough enough" to handle that sort of project, first approaching him in late August.[299]

Edward's own testimony did summarize the overall nature of the assassination effort, specifically identifying Richard Bissell as the initiator. Edwards testimony also revealed that such activities were known as "sensitive operations" and that all dialog concerning them was strictly verbal: *"Approached by Mr. Richard Bissell, DDP, to explore the possibility of mounting a sensitive operation against Fidel Castro. It was thought that certain gambling interests which had formerly been active in Cuba might be willing to assist and might have intelligence assets in Cuba and communications between Miami, Florida and Cuba. Mr. Maheu was approached and asked to establish contact with a member of the gambling syndicate...Mr. Roselli showed interest...indicated that he had some contacts in Miami he might use...met with a courier going back and forth to Cuba...never became part of the project current at the time for the invasion of Cuba...no memoranda....no written documentation...orally approved by Senior Officials of the Agency."*[300]

O'Connell and Maheu first met with Roselli at the Hilton Plaza in New York City in September, 1960, and Roselli agreed to make introductions to people who knew the Cuban crowd. At a follow-on meeting in Miami, Roselli brought in two other men and introduced them simply as his Cuban contacts, one of whom he described as a courier. The CIA proposition was that Castro would be killed in a rifle attack, but that was rejected - apparently the individuals who would participate inside Cuba were not willing to risk that approach given Castro's well-known security precautions. Roselli's associates counter-proposed that poison would be much safer for all concerned. Later both Maheu and the CIA officers were shocked to learn that Roselli's associates were actually major Mafia figures from Florida and Chicago. But with the full nature of the project already discussed, they had little option other than to proceed and O'Connell requested six poison pills from CIA Technical Services.

Given the highly sensitive nature of such a project, especially one that was going to require significant funding (O'Connell testified that he had been authorized $150,000 in payments) one of the problems was how to actually obtain the money. It needed to come out of the Cuba Project funds, but that meant that someone in project operations would have to authorize the expenditure. In a 1997 interview with Don Bohning, Jake Esterline, operations chief of the Cuba project within WH/4 related that in the fall of 1960 he had received a mysterious request from his boss, J.C. King, for a large amount of money, money which was needed immediately. The amount was far beyond what he was routinely involved in authorizing for the Cuban operation. In response Esterline sent the request back to King stating that he would require some information/justification for that level of expenditure.

It appears that King actually had to obtain approval from Bissell to discuss the funding with Esterline. Apparently, he did so and the next day he "read in" Esterline on the general outlines of the assassination project, at which time Esterline agreed to approve the funding request. King also directed Esterline not to discuss the matter with the Cuba Project chief, Richard Bissell. Interestingly, Esterline ultimately came to believe that Bissell might have relied too much on the possibility of a Castro assassination in respect to some of some of his Cuba Project decisions: "If Bissell and others hadn't felt they had the 'magic button' I don't think we would have had all the hair splitting over air support." [301]

While the Congressional inquiries revealed a good deal in terms of the origins and nature of the Bissell/Roselli poison plot, they provide surprising little detail on how the effort was managed by Bissell, especially with the poison effort extending over some six months and with multiple "last minute" attempts. The initial outreach had been in September but the poison pills themselves were not ready until February, 1961. Then they were only delivered in March. The first individual recruited to actually poison Castro was Juan Orta, the General Director of the Office of Prime Minister Castro. Orta seemed an excellent candidate, with direct access to Castro, however he had fallen out of favor with Castro towards the end of 1960 and by the time he received the pills he simply returned them after some two weeks.[302]

With only some six weeks before the scheduled landings at the Bay of Pigs, the poison plot was suddenly very short on time. As a last resort Roselli's chief connection into Cuba, Santos Trafficante of Tampa Florida, called on a long-time association with Antonio "Tony" Varona, the head of one of the resistance movements inside Cuba and a member of the Cuban exile political leadership. With Varona already heavily involved in plans to oust Castro, he was more than willing to involve his own people inside Cuba and managed to get the poison capsules into Havana. A couple with access to one of Castro's favorite restaurants were in place and ready to conduct the poisoning, only awaiting Varona's final direction.[303] But, as noted, Richard Bissell apparently distanced himself from the operational aspects of the poisoning and appears to have had little appreciation for its timing and execution. That appears confirmed by the fact that he authorized the Cuban Revolutionary Council members, including Tony Varona, to be sequestered before and during the actual Zapata operation. Which in turn left Varona with no communications into Cuba, effectively aborting the very possibly successful attempt on Castro's life.

Due to the Congressional investigations, the plot to poison Castro, and Bissell's role in it, has become a relatively well-known part of the Cuba Project. What is much less known is that there were other "wild cards" in play in terms of eliminating Castro, both during 1960 and in the months immediately prior to the Bay of Pig's landings. Efforts, which appear to have been totally unknown to President Kennedy, and to some extent so compartmentalized that it remains uncertain exactly who, even inside the Cuba Project, was aware of them. CIA assassination activities are difficult to corroborate given that great care is taken not only to avoid documenting their discussion in written records – much vaguer terminology such as "elimination" or "removal" are used. Standard practice is that authorization or permission for assassination is never given in communications with surrogates who would carry out such missions, or with the CIA officers handling them.

The term "assassination" was simply never to be mentioned, never put on paper, and any communications would be strictly verbal. If someone who was in contact with the CIA mentioned assassination in a message, great care was taken not to comment or give any acknowledgement of the activity. The CIA expressed that point to Congress, admitting that CIA officers had been associated with individuals who were interested in or actually conducted assassination attempts, but the agency had never formally ordered them to conduct such actions – a response possibly true, but only in a purely technical sense. In that regard, we know that the CIA Guatemala Project (PBSUCCESS) was used as the model for the Cuba Project, and that senior CIA officers Esterline and Barnes were involved in both the Guatemala and Cuba projects. With considerable historical research available on the Guatemala project, it seems fair to say that its practices also reflected in measures which became part of the Cuba

Project activities and not just in an effort to poison Fidel Castro.

The CIA's own historical study of assassination as related to Guatemala (CIA and Guatemala Assassination Proposals 1952-1954) reveals that assassination was a frequent topic in the discussions of possible tactics to be used in that regime change project.[304] Even before the project had officially begun the CIA Directorate of Operations (Plans) officers had compiled a "hit list." The list contained the names of "top flight Communists whom the new government would desire to eliminate immediately in event of successful anti-Communist coup." Compiling and reviewing such lists (sometimes referred to as "black lists" given their high level of secrecy) remained an active part of the project. The focus on assassination was such that Castillo Armas, the coup leader, forwarded Headquarters a "disposal" list - the list called for the "execution through executive action" of some 58 "category 1" Guatemalans and the imprisonment or exile of another 74 designated as category 2.[305]

The training of an assassination team was actually discussed with Armas in February of 1954.[306] Preparation of selected personnel continued and project records of the Armas's organization show a "K" group. A June CIA headquarters briefing also mentioned that Armas's teams would assassinate known Communists once the invasion operations actually began. Of course, none of this discussion and planning related to CIA employees conducting such activities. The actual attacks were to be carried out by members of the rebel force. Generally speaking, the murders (the "disposal list") would be restricted to those "irrevocably implicated in Communist doctrine and policy" to "out and out proven Communist leaders," or "those few individuals in key government and military positions of tactical importance whose removal for psychological, organizational, or other reasons is mandatory for the success of military action."[307]

The CIA historical study actually acknowledges that "plans for assassination pervaded PBFORTUNE and PBSUCCESS, rather than being confined to an early stage of these programs. Even before official approval of PBFORTUNE, CIA officers compiled elimination lists and discussed the concept of assassination with Guatemalan opposition leaders. Until the day that Arbenz resigned in June 1954 the option of assassination was still being considered. Beyond planning, some actual preparations were made. Some assassins were selected, training began, and tentative "hit lists" were drawn up."

Evidence of similar lists can be found within the Cuba Project as well, one sample dated November, 1960 was located by a CIA historian in his research on the project. His exchanges with personnel associated with those lists are quite interesting. Needless to say none of them were willing to go on record confirming that the Cuba "Must Go" list was to be used in anything other than in a political context, a reference for organizing a new government following Castro's successful ouster.[308] Based on his interviews with senior personnel in WH/4, the historian ultimately concluded that assassination was definitely not an element in the Cuba Project's plans, and that none of WH/4's principals were even privy to the poison plots which occurred in conjunction with the project – a conclusion now proven to have been totally incorrect as related to both J.C. King and Jake Esterline, based on both later Congressional investigations and testimony and admissions from Esterline himself. Beyond that, it has become clear that certain CIA officers were also involved in a variety of assassination/elimination projects; projects which they absolutely refused to acknowledge, even in sworn testimony.

Snipers:

With documents and supplemental information now available to us, we can at least sketch in a picture of previously unknown plans, which were indeed developed for another type of assassination effort targeting Fidel Castro, something far different than the poison plot. The effort involved extremely well-prepared Cuban volunteers who were some of the first individuals who had joined the Cuba Project. They had gone through extensive paramilitary training, in Panama and Guatemala, who were redirected from the new infantry project of November, 1960 and sent on special infiltration and paramilitary missions into Cuba.

It appears that in the earliest planning for Cuba Project paramilitary activities, preparations were being made to insert individuals trained and equipped for sniper style attacks. A CIA memorandum of July 7, 1960 describes an organizational meeting in which the entire PM (paramilitary) staff were briefed on the new project. The briefing included the program's phases of operation and the initial plans for logistics, staging, and personnel. Beyond that the memorandum notes the specific training and equipment being provided for one of the earliest volunteers to be infiltrated into Cuba - Emilio Adolfo Rivero Caro, (cryptonym AMPANIC-7, pseudonym Rivero also known as "Brand" and "Pancho"). Rivero was given firing range training with a broad variety of weapons including silenced weapons and a "sporting rifle with telescopic lens attachment," a basic (and deniable) sniper class weapon. Related documents mention that Rivero himself described his mission as being to organize resistance groups for mounting sabotage operations and assassination of prominent Cuban Communist members in the Castro entourage.[309]

The first sign that paramilitary assassination was becoming a priority in the Cuba Project appears in a memorandum of February, 1961 (the month prior to the March effort Rivero described). Richard Drain, acting under Esterline as the head of operations for WH/4, proposed to Esterline and others the idea of using Cuban exile assets in an assassination effort against Castro. Specifically Drain proposed using Cubans affiliated with the DRE organization (AMHINT). Members of that group had shown their interest in assassination earlier, in January requesting delivery of rifles equipped with silencers and telescopic sights.[310]

It was only in February that the Cuba Project began sending a significant number of boat missions into Cuba, missions which could be used as a cover for a conventional sniper style attack. The majority of the missions departed from the CIA boat mission base at Key West Florida and were intended to deliver supplies, to infiltrate paramilitary personnel, and to exfiltrate Cubans. One of the larger boats used in those missions was the Tejana, although smaller boats including private yachts were being used in infiltration missions. The Tejana, a former US Navy submarine chaser, was well suited to supply missions as the ship was fast, relatively large, and modern. It was a deniable vessel, actually purchased by a Texan in order to establish a cover for the vessel and had originally operated out of the port of New Orleans before being retrofitted (at CIA expense) with radar, weapons, and gun covers.

The Tejana's crew consisted of Americans who had been with the vessel for some time, and of Cuban volunteers, many with Cuban navy experience.[311] During a limited number of missions (JEAN and MEGANO) the Tejana first went into Cuban waters beginning in early March, 1961 and concluded its operations on April 7. One mission failed due to lack of a contact at the designated rendezvous, and the last mission aborted due to a failure of the ship's engines. On its three successful missions Tejana covertly inserted 11 infiltration personnel, weapons, explosives, and some five tons of cargo.[312]

Documents show that one of the Cuban paramilitary personnel the Tejana carried into Cuba was Felix Rodriquez,[313] Rodriquez had been one of the earliest volunteers for the Cuba Project, taken into training first at the Panama Camp. He became one of the infiltration specialists, received special training, and participated in several missions into Cuba immediately prior to, but separate from, the amphibious landings. In the years following the landings at the Bay of Pigs, he joined other CIA projects, and was one of the few Cubans to become a long time CIA employee retained as a totally deniable field agent. In his own biography Rodriquez describes being paid as a CIA principal agent, but only under a verbal agreement with no contract and no paperwork.[314]

Following a short assignment to Venezuela, Felix Rodriquez, along with two other Cuban exiles, was moved into a project in Bolivia – a project specifically targeting Che Guevara. Operating under commercial cover,

Secret Wars With Air Strikes And Tanks?

Rodriquez became a key figure in the operation which ultimately led to Guevara's death. Afterwards Rodriquez continued activities across Latin America, conducting counter insurgency training under the cover of being an American military officer. Following that service, he was moved to Southeast Asia, where he supported Project Phoenix field operations out of Saigon and later was redirected back to Latin America, to a post in Argentina in 1972.

Rodriquez officially separated from the CIA in 1976 and received a virtually unique approval to publicly talk and write about his CIA employment. In his debriefing, prior to separation from the CIA, Rodriquez provided a statement that he had volunteered to kill Fidel Castro, stating that it was the only solution to the Cuban problem. He also stated that he had been supplied with a special sniper weapon for a mission into Cuba and that he and another CIA Cuban had also made multiple missions into Cuba. Rodriquez did not identify the CIA officer who had given them the assignments (and supplied the rifle) or state any details of the missions. The CIA memorandum covering the interview also states that a Miami Station officer who had known Rodriquez well during the period in question had confirmed his own knowledge of such an assassination mission.[315]

Corroboration of Rodriquez's statements is found in other CIA documents, as part of an internal inquiry into Castro assassination efforts conducted in the mid-1970s.[316] One of the memos mentions the names of two Cubans involved in the boat missions, "Felix" and "Segundo," the "Segundo" mentioned in the CIA document is possibly Segundo Borges Ransola. The two men are also mentioned in CIA documents as part of the same team on at least one

In Denial

February infiltration mission carried out by the Tejana, - serving on the SANDRA II team. In his own biography, Rodriquez later provided some detail on the assassination effort, describing a German bolt action sniper rifle with a telescopic sight. The rifle itself was pre-sighted according to the specifics of the mission, based on the exact location in which Castro was to be attacked. In media interviews, Rodriquez further described his participation in missions targeting Castro (and his own association with Segundo) – stating that both he and Segundo trained in Panama (in the training camp set up by Carl Jenkins).

Rodriquez noted that he and Segundo were only 19 years old when they entered training in the Panama camp and went through months of paramilitary training before they were sent on special missions into Cuba prior to the Bay of Pigs.[317] Borges was later involved in recruiting Rodriquez for a post Bay of Pigs covert action program against Cuba (AMWORLD) in 1963. Both men were involved in the AMWORLD project, with Borges leading a maritime infiltration team. [318] [319] Interestingly, Carl Jenkins also took a position as the chief CIA military liaison for the same AMWORLD project which involved both Felix and Segundo.

More recently, additional details have emerged on the plans to attack Castro with one or more snipers, disclosing that the attacks were planned to occur at the Veradero Beach resort, a favorite personal retreat of Castro. The CIA plans for attacking Castro at Veradero Beach appear to have been sophisticated, involving photographic reconnaissance and the preparation of detailed maps of the estate. The individuals involved in the Veradero Beach mapping work had been assigned to the Cuba Project and were later transferred to the National Photographic

Interpretation Center (NPIC) in Washington D.C. According to Edward Cates, the chief of the Image Exploitation Group at NPIC, "a number of our photo interpreters [8 individuals] supported Carl Jenkins of the DD/P (Deputy Directorate of Plans) concerning a plan to assassinate Castro at the DuPont Veradero Beach Estate, east of Havana. Castro was known to frequent the estate and the plan was to use a high-powered rifle in the attempt. The photo interpretation support was restricted to providing annotated photographs and line drawings of the estate." [320]

Other information used in the planning of the attack on Castro, including details of Castro's personal travel and activities, may have come from individuals previously close to Castro inside Cuba – specifically from Frank Sturgis (aka Fiorini) who is referenced in one assassination related document. Sturgis himself had played an active role in providing weapons for Castro's revolution, served with his forces, and later commanded a Cuban paratroop unit. He had become unhappy with Castro's turn towards communism, abandoning his support for him and returning to the United States. Prior to his departure from Cuba, Sturgis had personally and secretly made an approach to the CIA and offered to organize a lethal attack on Castro. At that time the Cuba Project had not begun and the CIA failed to respond to his approach. Sturgis's name appears in one January 20, 1961 document which includes a reference to "Pathfinder" – the document appears to relate to the Veradero attack plan. It is true that after his return to the United States, Sturgis became active in anti-Castro activities and records also show that he became an active source for the CIA and continued to report on intelligence from Cuba and within the Cuban exile community.

While further details on the actual Veradero Beach plan are lacking, it certainly appears that during March and early April, 1961 there was an active CIA effort to conduct sniper attacks against Fidel Castro. Reconnaissance was performed, maps made, one or more sniper rifles prepared and taken into Cuba, possibly on the Tejana, under cover of infiltration and supply missions - or perhaps separately. Felix Rodriguez himself described the missions being conducted on an unnamed yacht. However, when his details of the trips are correlated to Tejana mission reports, it becomes quite likely that the missions he described were carried out using the Tejana – specifically the Jean IV and Morgano III infiltrations conducted in April, 1961.

Rodriquez described two of the missions as aborting due to problems and the Tejana encountered exactly the same problems on those specific trips. During Jean IV the Tejana was unable to contact the local small craft scheduled to actually go on into Cuba and it failed to appear at their scheduled rendezvous point. On the Morgano III mission, problems with the Tejana's engine caused it to turn back from Cuba, taking it out of service past the landings at the Bay of Pigs. That appears to have been the end of the Veradero Beach attack plan. These plans for sniper attacks appear to have been quite serous but also very "last minute," coming into play only weeks before the amphibious landings, much as did the poison attempts.

Similar to the poison plot, ultimately the sniper attack simply failed to be carried out - not due to the failure of the poison or the sniper, but due to basic problems of logistics in delivering the attack. Beyond poison and sniper attacks, there were also other actions aside from assassination, which appear to have been concealed, and which might well have become "wild cards" in the operation, leading to the direct commitment of American forces. They remain speculative, documented to some extent but still not fully explained. We know they happened, exactly how, and under whose operational supervision remains a mystery.

Wild Cards?

Speculation as to possible efforts towards provoking Cuba into some action, which would have enabled an overt, conventional military response by American forces, begins with remarks made in December 1960 and January 1961, first by President Eisenhower's national security advisor to the Special Group and then, per Richard Bissell, by Eisenhower directly to Bissell himself. Where there is nothing in the official history of the Cuba Project, including the official inquiries, it has to be noted that neither of those sources proved reliable in revealing the poison plots or the sniper attack plan. It was only years later that information emerged about either of those efforts. Yet there are traces, events, and activities which either planned, or unplanned, could indeed have led to a conventional engagement, bringing major American military force into combat against the Cuban military.

The first indication (or mystery) has to do with the documented, but not explained, D-2 "diversion," mentioned in the official records – with absolutely no details provided. Certainly, it was important enough to have been scheduled (along with the preemptive air strikes) two days before the actual Bay of Pigs landings. Yet the little we do know about it is that it does not appear to support the extent of the remarks and criticism of its failure found in the official inquiries. The activity is described as a "diversion" and involved a relatively small force of several dozen men, led by Nino Diaz and sent to be infiltrated into Cuba with light weapons. The men involved had gone through only brief training at the Belle Chase facility, an abandoned Navy base outside New Orleans that had been turned into a training camp in late February, 1961. Grayston Lynch had been assigned there after being recruited for the project that month, managing the clearing and cleaning operation needed to establish the most basic camp type facility.

The Nino Diaz mission into Cuba sailed on the Santa Ana, an aging freighter, down the Mississippi and across the Caribbean to the southeast coast of Cuba, in Oriente Province. Ostensibly they were to land near Baracoa, only some fifty miles overland from the huge American Navy Base at Guantanamo Bay. Baracoa, near the Rio Mocambo, is on the coast of Cuba and during the Cuban revolution Nino Diaz, a Comandante in Castro's revolutionary army, had led a guerilla force in those same mountains. After turning against Castro, he joined various resistance groups and along with Manuel Artime helped organize the Movement to Recover the Revolution (MRR), with Diaz continuing to lead a guerilla group operating in the mountains near Guantanamo. He was reported to the CIA as being regarded as a "popular legend" in the Oriente.[321]

The general area of the landing site near Baracoa had no particular military targets, and it remains unclear how a clandestine infiltration of a small force - only destined for the mountains - would have drawn any special attention, serving as a serious diversion of Cuban military forces. Castro's militias and regular Army forces had dealt locally with several resistance groups of similar size over the past year, effectively crushing virtually all of them. On the face of it infiltrating Nino Diaz and his group back into the mountains where he had operated earlier would have done little more than put another small and lightly armed resistance group into an isolated part of far eastern Cuba – isolated other than the fact that the area was within some 50 miles of the Unites States Navy facility at Guantanamo Bay, across a terrain quite well known to Diaz.

Upon the arrival of the Santa Ana, Diaz claimed to have observed a heavy Cuban military presence in the designated landing area and determined not to attempt inserting any troops on D-2. Continuing to observe Cuban patrols the following day, Diaz refused orders to continue with his mission and was redirected towards the area of the amphibious landings, ultimately doing nothing at all to support the Brigade. There is no corroborating evidence that the Santa Anna was observed, challenged, or engaged in any fashion by Cuban forces during its time in the Baracoa area. Diaz himself later complained that neither he nor his group had received any specific briefing on his mission; they were not even given their destination until the Santa Ana was at sea.[322]

While the official inquiries offer no specific reasons for the failure, largely blaming Diaz personally, information now available suggests there had been plans to receive and support the Diaz diversionary effort, plans using a Cuban volunteer team deployed from the American base at Guantanamo. In coordination with Navy officers at Guantanamo, including Harold (Hal) Feeney, chief of base intelligence, a team of six to eight Cuban volunteers was to be trained, specifically in the use of high explosives, and dispatched to meet Nino Diaz's group - which was to be landed just east of the American base. The combined force would then create a major diversion in conjunction with the landings at the Bay of Pigs.

According to one of the leaders of the diversionary team, that effort actually got underway - out of Guantanamo - with the Cuban volunteers accompanied by two Navy officers from the base. The team then began to establish a covert training and explosives cache site near the base. On or about April 9/10 the group was handling explosives and detonators at the cache when a detonator was dropped, exploding some 250 other detonators.

All the personnel were badly wounded and it was only with the help of the Navy officers, including Feeney, that they were aided back to the base and medical treatment. It appears possible that the collapse of this very covert reception effort was not communicated effectively - or if it was, failed to result in the Nino Diaz mission being aborted.[323]

The official reports on the Bay of Pigs describe the Nino Diaz mission as a significant pre-landing diversionary effort and considerable criticism is directed against Diaz – all without any explanation of why his mission would have been considered to have been so significant to the overall operation. All of which fueled later speculation that Diaz's small force was not simply to go quietly into the mountains, but might have been intended to proceed towards Guantanamo, either staging some sort of provocation or at least drawing Cuban forces into military action in the area of the American base - focusing attention on it as a possible staging area for the anticipated arrival of the force which the United States was known to have been training. There was considerable Cuban suspicion of resistance activity associated with Guantanamo. The base had actually been used for infiltration and exfiltration of individual Cuba Project paramilitaries over a period of several months. Armed clashes in the vicinity of the base could have ended with some sort of local Cuban military response, and provided just the type of provocation that President Eisenhower had urged Richard Bissell to develop.

Which leaves us with an apparently critical mission that did fail, immediately before the Brigade landings. Was this attempt nothing more than a minor effort to insert a small guerilla force into the remote mountains of the Oriente province failing simply because it had been hurriedly put together at almost the last minute (as with the poison and sniper efforts)? If so it would be just one more failure due to poor planning and execution. Or perhaps the mission was intended as something far more significant, a true wild card, which failed because the force sent to execute it had neither been trained nor prepared for such an action?

From the mystery of the Nino Diaz diversion we proceed to yet one more mystery of the official Cuba Project record – that of the full story of US Navy involvement with the Bay of Pigs operation. As an example, we now know that the carrier Essex, which was screening the amphibious landing, had secretly loaded not only a squadron of ground attack aircraft, but extensive ordinance useful only in ground strikes – something entirely outside the scope of the Zapata Plan. No reference to that fact shows up in any of the follow-on inquiries. The only acknowledged role for the aircraft on the Essex were for reconnaissance in screening the ships of the brigade and in forcing off, or engaging, Cuban aircraft attempting to attack them while at sea. Nothing at all in the Task Force Alpha "Bumpy

In Denial

Road" mission plan called for ground attacks. Yet we know that the ordnance for such strikes was loaded (and noticed as being quite different than its normal weapons load out by the crew) due to a later interview with the Navy/CIA liaison for the operation, Captain Jacob "Jack" Scapa. Scapa also made it clear that the Navy force, Task Force Alpha, was operating under the direct orders of Admiral Burke. The real question appears to be whether Burke himself was prepared to exceed the mission directive of total deniability – by actively engaging the Cuban military? That possibility emerges in remarks both from Captain Scapa and from Admiral Burke himself.

In his interview, Scapa mentions that there was considerable conflict between Admiral Burke and President Kennedy during the actual landings, with Burke forcefully requesting the release of his entire task group to engage with Cuban forces in support of the beachhead.[324] Burke wanted to conduct ground air strikes as well as to send his destroyers into the bay to provide heavy fire support for the brigade.[325] Scapa states that Kennedy authorized Burke to prepare for Navy aircraft to perform ground attacks. Officially, based on documented message traffic, Scapa appears to be incorrect in that regard - Kennedy only ordered the Navy to provide jet cover for ground strikes by Brigade B-26's.[326] On the other hand, Lynch (in the command LCI communicating with the Navy) describes exchanges with the Essex in which he was setting up coordinates for Navy air strikes. The question as to exactly what Burke had personally authorized on D+2 remains open.

However, Scapa related something even more interesting (and historically mysterious). He states that Admiral Dennison, in Washington D.C., expanded on that strike directive – ordering not only the Essex to prepare for combat strikes, but that Dennison also authorized preparation for air strikes from the carrier USS Independence. Officially there was no second carrier assigned to Bumpy Road. But Scapa also related that at their personal initiative, Admirals Dennison and Burke had placed a major Navy force on "stand by" for action in Cuba. That force included the conventional super carrier USS Independence, the light missile cruiser Galveston (which had been operating out of Guantanamo only weeks previously), two destroyer squadrons, and a Marine Expeditionary Force.[327] Scapa states that the Bumpy Road, Task Force Alpha, was not informed of the standby force and it is unclear whether President Kennedy or anyone at the White House was advised of Dennison and Burke's action. Certainly nothing in the Taylor Committee report, the CIA IG's report, or the CIA Historians report mentions the action of such a major naval force. While Scapa says the units were placed on "stand by" we have no idea whether that meant some level of sea deployment or simply an increased state of readiness for the ships, stationed at Hampton Roads, near Norfolk, Virginia.

However, two specific remarks from Scapa suggest that the U.S.S. Independence was not only at sea but operating relatively close to the USS Essex, off the southern coast of Cuba. Scapa noted that when the Essex was "standing by" some 125 miles off shore from the Bay of Pigs (immediately prior to the landings), two A-1 propeller driven close air support Skyraiders were flown onboard Essex from the Independence, to supplement the Essex ground strike group.[328] It is true that the A-1 Skyraiders had an exceptional range, of some 1,300 miles. However, flying two aircraft from the Independence, if it were docked at

In Denial

Norfolk Virginia, would involve a direct flight over Cuba of some 1,200 miles, virtually the maximum range of the aircraft. Flying around the island would have exceeded the range of the aircraft. Flying propeller driven Navy aircraft directly over Cuba at that point in time seems unlikely, suggesting the Independence may well have been at sea within a few hundred miles of the Essex, possibly deployed closer to Guantanamo.

Scapa's second remark - that both the Essex and Independence were ordered to prepare their aircraft for strikes into Cuba would seem to confirm that both carriers were at sea, within striking range of Cuba, and the Bay of Pigs. Another point, which would support the deployment of a force separate from Task Force Alpha, comes from Grayston Lynch. Lynch wrote that when evacuation of the Brigade force at the beachhead was initially being discussed, he received a message from Washington that the Brigade would be evacuated using landing craft from the US Marine Amphibious Force, deployed just to the south of the Blagar's position, off the Bay of Pigs.[329] While it is known that the command carrier Essex did carry a contingent of Marines and had boarded a limited number of landing craft, there is no official record of any larger Marine group deployment.

Based on Scapa and Lynch's remarks, it certainly appears there may have been major elements of the American Navy at sea off the southern coast of Cuba, including a supercarrier (which would not have sailed without its own destroyer escort), and possibly even ships of a Marine Amphibious Force, with their own escort. Certainly nothing in the Zapata Plan called for such an overwhelming and visible American military commitment. Nothing that has appeared in the official history of the event mentions such a force nor how, or when, it would have been utilized.

Strangely enough, outside the government inquiries and reports, actual confirmation of the deployment of a major Navy force off southern Cuba, separated from Task Force Alpha, comes directly from Admiral Burke himself. In an oral history interview with the JFK Library, Burke stated that *"....during the operation, again because I had a lot of experience in war and I know things go wrong, I sent a force down there in case the operation went wrong and to pull the operation out of trouble if necessary. This was a US force, which I was forbidden to have anywhere near the operation."*330 Based on that remark, along with the observations by Scapa and Lynch, it seems reasonable to accept that Burke had indeed deployed a standby force as Scapa implied, away from Task Force Alpha, but in a position to support either the amphibious operation or any Cuban military activity against the Guantanamo base.331

It is true that President Eisenhower had approved the deployment of just such a US. Navy force off Guatemala – including a Marine Expeditionary group - and that its independent action had been a major element in the intimidation that led to successful regime change there. In terms of "hidden measures," the question arises as to who else within the Cuba Project was aware of Burke's orders. Certainly, Scapa knew and he was acting Navy/CIA liaison, working directly with Bissell. Did Bissell or someone else at his level picture the Navy force as a hidden element of intimidation or provocation? It appears that any such deployment was kept from the Special Group; it certainly appears President Kennedy was not advised of it. It would seem to have conflicted with directions personally given to Admiral Dennison by President Kennedy in a February 8,

In Denial

1961 meeting. In this meeting the president specified that he wanted an effort which involved no obvious support by United States ships or planes, even in supply missions.

If nothing else, as with the poison and sniper plots, there appears to have been an exceptional level of compartmentalization and "deniability" in play in regard to the US Navy element of the Cuba Project. Deniability of an extraordinary level, noted both in remarks by Scapa and in the official inquiries – deniability involving the total destruction of all Task Force Alpha communications. These official denials required the destruction of all the ships logs and orders relating to the Bay of Pigs operation (apparently ordered by Admiral Burke) – prior to the departure of the command vessel U.S.S. Essex from Cuban waters.[332]

Notes

[289] John Prados, Safe for Democracy: *The Secret Wars of the CIA,* Chicago: Ivan R. Dee, Inc., 2006, 209

[290] *Senate Select Committee to Study Governmental Operations with Respect to Intelligence Activities* (Church Committee), United States Senate, 1976, 181
https://www.aarclibrary.org/publib/contents/church/contents_church_reports_ir.htm

[291] Evan Thomas, *The Very Best Men*, Simon and Schuster, New York, 2006, 227

[292] This view of Barnes is conveyed in *Death in Washington* by Donald Freed, Lawrence Hill, 1980; Freed presents Barnes as being ultra-conservative, and fiercely anti-Communist

[293] *Foreign Relations of the United States, 1961-1963, Volume X, Department of State*, 337. Memo: May 14, 1962. Memo prepared for briefing the Attorney General of the United States.

[294] Interview with Richard Bissell, House Select Committee on Assassinations, 73-74 https://www.maryferrell.org/showDoc.html?docId=148865&#relPageId=76&tab=page

[295] *CIA Inspector General's Report, Cuba Project*, May 23, 1967, RIF 1993.06.30.17 also John Newman, Countdown to Darkness, 2017, 330

[296] The initial CIA/SOD agreement was later formalized in a 1952 Memorandum of Understanding between the CIA and the Army Chemical Corps Officer. H. P. Albarelli Jr, *A Terrible Mistake*, Trine Day, 2009, 64-66

[297] Bayard Stockton, *Flawed Patriot*, Potomac Books, 2006, 171

[298] H. P. Albarelli Jr., *A Terrible Mistake*, Trine Day, 2009, 659-653

[299] *Alleged Assassination Plots Involving Foreign Leaders*, United States Senate, Interim Report of the Committee to Study Governmental Operations, 1975, 75

[300] As with many CIA security cleared Lawyers, Doctors, professionals and business contacts, Maheu provided a totally deniable mechanism for contacts totally outside the Agency. *Foreign Relations of the United States, 1961-1963, Volume X*, Department of State, 337. Memo: May 14, 1962. Memo prepared for briefing the Attorney General of the United States.

[301] Don Bohning, *The Castro Obsession*, Potomac Books, 2006, 25-26

[302] *Alleged Assassination Plots Involving Foreign Leaders, United States Senate, Interim Report of the Committee to Study Governmental Operations, 1975*, 24-25 and 28, RIF 104.1005.10270 also John Newman, Countdown to Darkness, 338-339

[303] *Alleged Assassination Plots Involving Foreign Leaders, United States Senate, Interim Report of the Committee to Study Governmental Operations, 1975*, 82 also John Newman, Countdown to Darkness, 342-343

[304] Gerald K Haines, *CIA and Guatemala Assassination Proposals 1952-1954*, "Conclusions," CIA History Staff Analysis, June 1995, 9 https://www.cia.gov/library/readingroom/docs/DOC_0000135796.pdf

[305] Sources include memorandum *to [ ] "Guatemala Communist Personnel to be Disposed of During Military Operations of CALLIGERIS," (Castillo Armas), 18 September 1952, Box 134 (S)*

[306] Sources include *"Chief's CALLIGERIS Briefing Notes," J [ ] "Cost of Support for PBSUCCESS," 17 September 1954, Box 43 (S). He listed the 20 silencers resent. See also [ ] to Headquarters, 6 January 1954, Box 75 (S) and [ ] 2 to Headquarters, 21 January 1954, Box 1 (S). Also report #5. [ ] ." 18 September 1952, Box 73 (S) and [ ] Chief, memo for the record, "Pbt conference Held at [ ] " 13 February 1954, Box 74 (S). See also [ ] to Headquarters, 4 January 1954, Box 1 (S). The Headquarters Registry cop of the pouch manifest for 8 January 1954, Box 97 (S) list the manual "A Study of Assassinations." A handwritten note of the original manifest says the pouch was carried to [ ] by [ ]. The serial assassination study is in Box 145 (S)*

[307] Sources include: *Chief, Economic Warfare, [ ] memo to All Staff Officers, "Selection of individuals for Disposal by Junta Group." 31 March 1954, Box 145 (S)*. We know [ ] visited [ ] on this date from the [ ] visitors log book. He signed into [ ] on 31 March and [ ] *Log Book for 31 March 1954, Box 138 (S) also Memo, Box 145 (S)*

[308] Jack B. Pfeiffer, *Official History of the Bay of Pigs, Volume 3, Evolution of the CIA's Anti-Castro Policies, March 1960-April 1961*, Central Intelligence Agency, Washington D.C., September, 1979, 287-289

[309] AM-PANIC Cryptonym analysis, Mary Ferrell Foundation,
https://www.maryferrell.org/php/cryptdb.php?id=AMPANIC-7

Communications from Rivero to project headquarters describe a final effort in March of 1961 to sabotage the Havana power system and attack Castro during a public appearance [at the] Sports Palace. The CIA would later go to great lengths to characterize that any attempts at assassination were strictly at Rivero's own initiative, however now that we can see the details of his training and the weapons supplied him, such assertions become highly dubious.

[310] Ibid, 285-286
https://www.maryferrell.org/showDoc.html?docId=146518&#relPageId=297&tab=page

[311] Request for crypts for individuals who now crew and maintain the Tejana, CIA memorandum, February 22, 1961
https://www.maryferrell.org/showDoc.html?docId=35225&relPageId=1

[312] Boat Operations using Tejana, CIA Memorandum, March 6, 1961, National Archives, Washington D.C., RIF Number 104-10264-10126

313 Tejana will depart Key West Evening 27 Feb, CIA memorandum, February 27, 1961
https://www.maryferrell.org/showDoc.html?docId=35242&relPageId=1

314 Felix Rodriquez and John Weisman, *Shadow Warrior; CIA Hero of a Hundred Unknown Battles*, Simon and Schuster, New York, 1989

315 Memorandum for the Record, CIA Employee Claim on Aborted Castro Assassination Missions, Central Intelligence Agency, June 30, 1975
https://www.maryferrell.org/showDoc.html?docId=65964&#relPageId=2&tab=page

316 Felix Rodriquez, Castro Assassination, House Segregated CIA Collection, Central Intelligence Agency, Box 4 Committee
https://www.maryferrell.org/showDoc.html?docId=99953&#relPageId=4&tab=page

317 Felix Rodriquez interview, *Cuba Magazine*, 2005 as cited in Diario Gramma, Havana, Cuba, March 11, 2014
https://translate.google.com/translate?hl=en&sl=es&u=http://www.granma.cu/granmad/secciones/conclusiones/art005.html&prev=search

318 Cuban Exile Associates, FBI Memorandum, August 11, 1967, 56
https://www.maryferrell.org/showDoc.html?docId=88481&relPageId=56

319 The AMWORLD infiltration team trained at Camp Guillot on the Orlich ranch located in the Sarapiqui region of Costa Rica

[320] Memorandum for the Record, Dino Brugioni, Western Geographic Division, National Photographic Interpretation Center, Washington D.C, March 21, 1975
https://www.maryferrell.org/showDoc.html?docId=104139&relPageId=14

[321] True Revolutionary Situation Inside Cuba, CIA memorandum, August 18, 1960
https://www.maryferrell.org/showDoc.html?docId=186615&#relPageId=2

[322] Jesus Arboleya, *The Cuban Counter Revolution*, Ohio University Center for International Studies, Latin American Studies Number 33, Athens, Ohio, 1997, 84

[323] Ramon Machado, Brigade 2508, "Commander Harold Feeney, (Don Quixote), We've lost a Brother," article located and translation cited by David Boylan.
http://educationforum.ipbhost.com/topic/8572-harold-hal-feeney/page/2/

[324] Gordon Calhoun, "Task Force Alpha in the Bay of Pigs," *The Daybook*, Hampton Roads Naval Museum, Vol. 9, Issue 1, 2003, 15-16
https://www.history.navy.mil/museums/hrnm/files/daybook/pdfs/vol9issueone.pdf

[325] Ultimately Burke did order two destroyers into the beachhead, where they took on fire from Cuban tanks. But the Cuban forces had advanced far more rapidly than anticipated, the defense had collapsed under tank fire, and by the time the destroyers arrived the Brigade had destroyed its radio, scattered into the swamp and there was no force to support. The destroyers turned back out to sea with no exchange of fire.

[326] The author's discussions with an Essex crewmember suggest that Navy destroyers also sallied near the beachhead at nights to provide heavy fire support, later to return to sea for high speed daylight refueling for ongoing missions.

[327] Ibid, 13

[328] Ibid, 14

[329] Grayston Lynch, *Decision for Disaster*, Brassey's, New York, 1998, 131

[330] James E. O'Connor, Arleigh A. Burke, Oral History Interview, Administrative Information, Washington D.C., January 20, 1967, 23

[331] The author had verified the deployment of the Independence and its preparations for air strikes with Navy personnel directly involved, however even at this distance in time those individuals wish to remain anonymous.

[332] Jack B. Pfeiffer, *Official History of the Bay of Pigs, Volume 4, March 1960-April 1961*, Central Intelligence Agency, Washington D.C., September, 1979, 63

Secret Wars With Air Strikes And Tanks?

Chapter 8: Aspirations vs. Capabilities

The Cuba Project certainly illustrates the worst-case scenario for any covert military project. The project's official mission of deniable regime change involved strictly limited paramilitary activities, complemented by political action and propaganda campaigns. It anticipated creating a successful insurgency inside Cuba by November, 1962. That goal proved untenable, and major mission creep ended in a highly visible, conventional military action. Both CIA Director Dulles and Cuba Project Chief Bissell were ultimately forced to admit that political deniability had been sacrificed, well before the actual landings occurred at the Bay of Pigs.

Lessons learned from the failure of the Cuba Project were documented in the various inquiries and studies. But beyond issues of project oversight, of command and control, and the impact of personal egos, two warnings about covert action stand out most clearly. The first was concisely stated by Colonel Jack Hawkins years afterwards: "*[Policy makers] continue to harbor unrealistic, overblown ideas about what can be accomplished by covert, deniable means.*" The second comes from the initial, starkly objective, CIA Inspector General's report: *What was supposed to be a covert operation became a major overt military project "beyond the Agency responsibility as well as Agency capability."*

In Denial

It would seem clear that following the mission failure at the Bay of Pigs, policy makers and presidents should both have become aware that covert military action has definite limits, that mission creep is a fundamental danger, and that simply adopting the practices of deniability can become little more than an illusion. The question then is, following the events of April 1961, what changed in regard to American covert military action – did it stop, did it become more limited, or more realistic? Did President Kennedy and his successors take a more prudent course in authorizing and overseeing covert military projects? In this and the following chapter we will attempt to answer those questions by examining four American covert military actions - all projects which began under President Eisenhower and continued under Eisenhower's successors. Each of them consumed substantial resources, all involved surrogate fighters who lost their lives (in either small or very large numbers), and all extended over periods far longer than the Cuba Project.

15 Years of Covert Action against China in Tibet:

The Communist Chinese government began a military expansion into Tibet in 1950. By October of that year China sent some 10,000 People's Liberation Army forces across the Yangtze River, fully prepared to occupy as much territory as needed to force Tibetan compliance with Chinese political rule. By October, with the Korean conflict diverting the rest of the world, the small Tibetan forces in the eastern region of that country had been overwhelmed and eastern Tibet was effectively surrendered to Chinese rule.[333] With Korea holding center stage in international affairs, during the next three years China proceeded to build an extensive network of roads and airfields inside Tibetan territory, establishing the infrastructure for the

Secret Wars With Air Strikes And Tanks?

actions required to fully integrate Tibet under Chinese political control. That move began in 1955, and included not only the control of religion in Tibetan schools, but the introduction of a rigid Chinese-style collective agricultural system. Armed uprisings over Chinese dominance followed, and Tibetan tribal forces briefly blocked further road building and inflicted serious Chinese casualties. In response China sent heavy bombers against Tibetan villages, killing thousands.[334]

The brutality, and success, of the Chinese military move into Tibet prompted President Eisenhower to launch a comprehensive covert action program, with the objective of encouraging and enabling Tibetan military resistance.[335] There is no indication that the question of the huge imbalance in forces was ever seriously discussed, nor that the project goal was ever clearly stated. The best that can be said is that any effort to harass or otherwise impede China in extending its area of political control was seen as desirable. As would become routine, the CIA was tasked with all elements of the Tibet project – propaganda, political action, and the paramilitary element.[336] The program would have limited periods of early success, however due to a suspension of project air supply from May to November, 1960 (Eisenhower cancelled all covert flights across communist bloc countries during that period; a move prompted by the U-2 crisis with Russia), a significant number of the CIA's trained Tibetan paramilitary surrogates inside Tibet were left to their own resources and exposed to serious losses in encounters with the Chinese army.

When President Kennedy entered office in 1961, the CIA effort inside Tibet was clearly floundering, and remained in that state during his first year in office. During that first year Kennedy was dealing with other challenges, not just in Cuba but in Laos, Vietnam, and the Congo. It quickly became clear that he had no intention of immediately cancelling the various Eisenhower covert action projects already in play – or even removing them all from CIA control, despite the disaster at the Bay of Pigs. Regardless of how he might have felt about the CIA and its effectiveness, it should have been no surprise that he was unlikely to abandon the containment actions begun by Eisenhower.

As early as 1952, in his first campaign for the Senate, he had spoken of the Communist threat as "... power[full], unrelenting and implacable," maintaining that a balance of military power had to be maintained and that containment would be needed in both the political and economic spheres as well.[337] Following his election, President Kennedy reinforced that position in his well-known 1961 inaugural address: "*Let every nation know, whether it wishes us well or ill, that we shall pay any price, bear any burden, meet any hardship, support any friend, oppose any foe, in order to assure the survival and the success of liberty.*" He continued on with his remarks to personally commit himself, "*In the long history of the world only a few generations have been granted the role of defending freedom from its hour of maximum danger. I do not shrink from this responsibility – I welcome it.*"[338]

Given the far more pressing problems of Cuba and Laos, the president and his new special group did not actually move to address the ongoing CIA Tibet Project until early in 1962. At that time a survey of the project estimated that over the previous seven years that the CIA had managed to establish contact with some 2,000 combatants inside Tibet – arming some 800 of them in covert and highly risky airdrops. However, China had deployed tens of thousands of troops into Tibet during that same period, crushing any and all resistance by Tibetan tribal factions. The original thought of creating a viable Tibetan insurgency had clearly failed and was increasingly unlikely in the future. At that point, rather than allowing the project to continue into some form of mission creep, President Kennedy accepted a recommendation from his Special Group that the project continue, but with a new, and much more pragmatic goal.

From 1962 on the Tibetan volunteers would be redirected to create a series of road and border watch teams, reporting on Chinese military movements and any potential buildup suggesting further advances along the Tibetan borders.[339] That move was deemed especially important in view of Kennedy's hope to improve relations with India and the fact that the Chinese Army's success in Tibet had led to a new level of Chinese assertiveness in the Indian border areas. China was strengthening its military presence across the border regions, clandestinely constructing secret roads into areas which could be used to stage attacks into disputed territories, or into India itself.[340] Following American support for India during major Chinese incursions into its territories in late 1962, India itself became supportive of maintaining a Tibetan guerilla force, useful for road watch and possible harassment of Chinese supply lines.

   India then became actively, and covertly, involved in the CIA Tibet project, even organizing a special tactical force of Tibetan guerrillas, under Indian cover designation as the 12th Gurkha Rifles. In a secret ceremony Indian Prime Minister Jawaharlal Nehru assured the Tibetan force of his countries backing and "vowed that they would return to an independent country."[341] Armed resistance to China inside

Tibet had virtually ceased by 1964, but with Indian support the CIA's project simply continued on and on, with no new definition of goals set under President Johnson. As one of the nation's longest covert actions it simply went into sustainment mode, only to cease in 1971, in line with President Nixon's goal of improving American relations with China.

Throughout that time, from 1954 to 1971, the Tibet military project remained within the province of the CIA. While President Kennedy had certainly been unhappy with the CIA, he had accepted covert military action as an option, something that the CIA was allowed to manage as long as it involved limited military action, with up to a few hundred fighters. That was in line with the assessments following the Cuba Project, and President Kennedy was consistent in terms of placing limits on the CIA's military activity. He also rejected a proposal from the State Department to actually strip covert action from the CIA.[342]

Ten Years of Covert Action against Russia and Cuba in the Congo and Angola:

American covert action in Africa began in the Congo under President Eisenhower, continued under Kennedy and Johnson, and eventually extended into Angola during the Ford Administration. The initial CIA covert action activities in the Congo began in 1960, but were never officially authorized or formalized as a specific project. Under Eisenhower efforts in the Congo ran the gamut from political action to effect regime change through a variety of assassination plots. Under Kennedy and Johnson CIA efforts were turned to covert and highly deniable conventional military action, with CIA surrogates acting under commercial covers.[343]

Secret Wars With Air Strikes And Tanks?

President Eisenhower was particularly concerned that European colonies in Africa were vulnerable to socialist or communist control as they became independent nations. The Belgian Congo, with huge mineral resources in its Katanga Province, was seen as ripe for nationalist agitation and potential Soviet influence. Eisenhower's concerns were amplified by CIA Director Alan Dulles, who repeatedly and consistently agitated against Patrice Lumumba, a popular figure seeking to become the independent nation's first prime minister. Dulles's litany of warnings about Lumumba, beginning early in 1960, were remarkably similar to the same dialog he had used to urge Eisenhower to approve the CIA proposal for the Castro regime change project of March of that same year. In National Security Council meetings Dulles described Lumumba as a charismatic leader, but corrupt and with communist support. Deputy CIA Director Cabell joined Dulles in several of the meetings, and as he had in remarks about Castro, reinforced Eisenhower's communist fears – positioning Lumumba as a strong man, an opportunist with a "leftist tinge" who was taking money from communists.[344]

In the Congo election results, local parties largely related to tribal affiliations carried the day in each of the provinces, with the highly pivotal provinces of Katanga and Oriental being controlled by the parties of Moïse Tshombe and Patrice Lumumba, respectively. On a national basis Lumumba won a quarter of the total seats, and managed to organize a coalition that put his chosen president in control of what was fundamentally a Lumumba regime in the new Democratic Republic of the Congo. Yet within a month of its June, 1960 independence, a major segment of the Congolese Army mutinied and the civil government dissolved within several areas of the country. Belgium responded by sending in troops to protect large numbers of its citizens living in the Congo – a move viewed by the government of the Congo as foreign intervention, and a less than subtle effort to reassert some level of colonial influence. Matters were immediately made worse in July, when the mineral rich mining province of Katanga (heavily influenced by Belgian financial interests) declared its independence as a separate State of Katanga, under a regime led by Moise Tshombe.

In August, a second eastern mining province, diamond-rich Kasai-Occidental, also declared itself to be an independent nation, South Kasai. Belgium had invested heavily in the mining infrastructure of both regions, especially in Katanga, and Tshombe retained the support of Belgian business interests, a large Belgian military detachment, and a well-trained force referred to as the Katanga Gendarmerie. Tshombe, supported by Belgian mining interest money, further enhanced his military control by bringing in mercenaries from Belgium, Rhodesia, and South Africa - one of the best-known of the units being Major Mike Hoare's "4 Commando" unit from South Africa. The end result was that within months of its independence the Congo's central government had lost control over a good deal of its territory in its southeastern region.

The Lumumba government immediately appealed to the United Nations for help in the removal of the Belgian "security" force and to the United States and other countries for military aid and assistance to help restore control over the Katanga and South Kasai territories. With no reply to the Congo from the United States or other Western nations, the end result was a UN Security Council resolution demanding Belgium withdraw its forces, the dispatch of a UN peacekeeping force, and direct Soviet support to Lumumba in the form of Russian transport aircraft, maintenance personnel, and advisors. The political situation in the Congo had become complex and increasingly fluid due to Belgian intervention and the succession of the Katanga Province. However, Dulles remained almost totally focused on Patrice Lumumba, whom he described as inept, but highly susceptible to Soviet influence. Dulles's campaign against Lumumba reinforced President Eisenhower's concerns over African nationalism, as did Lumumba's rejection of ongoing Belgian influence in the Congo.

The ambivalence of American foreign policy towards African independence was not going to moderate until the election of John Kennedy. In 1960 Kennedy himself had gone on record with a totally different view of the emerging African nationalism, with a June, 1960 speech on the floor of the Senate: "We much greatly increase our efforts to encourage the newly emerging nations of the vast continent of Africa – to persuade them that they do not need to turn to Moscow for the guidance and friendship they so desperately need…we can no longer afford polices which refuse to accept the inevitable triumph of nationalism in Africa – the inevitable end of colonialism…"[345]

However, as of summer, 1960 it was President Eisenhower's tendency to lean towards the European powers that was driving American policy in Africa (as it had in Southeast Asia). Even with no official covert action program in place, Dulles's own views were already being reflected in the political action practices of the Congo CIA Station Chief Lawrence Devlin. CIA station chiefs routinely directed CIA political action efforts towards opposing or

In Denial

undermining the political success of any leftist leaning or communist supported political figure. Devlin had begun doing just that as soon as Lumumba had appeared as a major figure of political influence in the Congo.

As of the summer of 1960 the Eisenhower Administration's official policy towards the Congo was that of overtly walking a fine line, publicly supporting United Nations reconciliation activities, and efforts to unify the Congo while covertly working to minimize Soviet influence and access to Lumumba. Lumumba was viewed as the key to Soviet bloc influence in the Congo, just as Castro was viewed as the key of Soviet influence in Cuba. That view had solidified in July, with CIA Director Dulles, the American Ambassador to the Congo (William Burden), and the CIA station chief all lobbying for American action against Lumumba – as revealed in a seminal cable from Burden: "Lumumba has now maneuvered himself into a position of opposition to the West, resistance to the United Nations and increasing dependence on the Soviet Union...Only prudent therefore, to plan on the basis that Lumumba government threatens our vital interests in Congo and Africa generally. A principal objective of our political and diplomatic action must therefore be to destroy Lumumba government as now constituted...." [346]

Dulles personally continued to position the Congo as a key "domino" nation, much as Cuba, and Lumumba as a key figure of Soviet influence on the same order as Fidel Castro. In fact, Dulles specifically described Lumumba as a person who was a "Castro" or worse. By August the State Department weighed in with their assessment – describing Lumumba as "messianic," not rational, and in fact "irrational and almost psychotic."[347] With that ongoing CIA and State Department focus on Lumumba, by August the

National Security Council formally reached the conclusion that the United States should be prepared to take direct measures, acting "*at any time to take appropriate military action to prevent or defeat Soviet military intervention in the Congo.*"348 Eisenhower himself joined that position, apparently swayed by the Soviet agreement to provide airplanes, weapons, and military advisors to assist Lumumba's central government in moving against the secession of Kasai and Katanga, the Congo's richest provinces.

Yet President Eisenhower did not turn to the option of conventional intervention, nor even to a formalized CIA project. Instead, during a National Security Council meeting of August 18, Eisenhower turned to CIA Director Dulles and made a remark to the effect that "Lumumba should be eliminated." Several individuals in the meeting felt that Eisenhower had expressed a directive for Lumumba be killed.349 While the literal nature of that remark can, and will be argued by historians, it is clear that DCI Dulles interpreted the remark as authorizing an assassination. That assassination effort is now well documented, including the fact that Richard Bissell became tasked with the effort, and personally directed Sidney Gottlieb of the CIA's technical services division to prepare a special poison (polio was selected; a disease still indigenous to Africa) for use against Lumumba. Gottlieb himself was later sent to personally deliver the material to the CIA's station chief in the Congo.350

During August, 1960, Richard Bissell (evidently tasked into the assassination project by Dulles) also began personal contacts with CIA Africa Division Chief Bronson Tweedy, directing him to begin working with the CIA Congo station to explore assassination possibilities and identify assets which might be used against Lumumba. Tweedy himself later testified that poison was high on the list of possibilities.351 Of course in that same period of time Bissell was also driving the effort to assassinate Fidel Castro, working through the CIA's Office of Security to identify surrogates for that effort. American crime figures involved with former casino operations in Havana provided a link into Havana, but carrying out a murder effort in the Congo was something even more challenging.

On the ground in the Congo the political action efforts, including the organization of coup attempts, and the new assassination effort all remained almost entirely in CIA Station Chief Devlin's own hands, something Devlin very much understood. The failure and success of either was to be on him, and not on the CIA – "they would be at least partially off the hook."352 For Cuba there was a massive, sanctioned Cuba Project involving hundreds of people and large numbers of Cuban volunteers; in the Congo it appears to have been something much more limited, largely a personal quest for Dulles and Bissell, but operationally a task for Devlin, who needed his own separation from the assassination aspect, and his own surrogates.

It appears that by October, 1960 Bissell and Congo Station Chief Devlin had decided they required a CIA headquarters staff officer to assist in running the assassination operation against Lumumba in the Congo.353 To manage that, Bissell turned to the CIA's Staff D. It was Staff group D which conducted "dirty tricks" overseas – things like burglaries, safe cracking, wire taps, and other activities normally required to obtain items including adversary's documents, code books, communications equipment, and other materials of value to both the CIA's intelligence collection activities and to the National

Security Agency (NSA). The group was designated as "Staff D," whether or not the "D" stood for "dirty tricks" is arguable, but descriptive. Staff D undertook tasks which involved some of the roughest aspects of CIA activity, including collecting material for foreign blackmail, and intercepting foreign couriers on occasion – using whatever force was required.

As described in Dr. John Newman's research on the Lumumba assassination, the problem was that nobody in Staff D wanted to be directly involved with murder.[354] The first individual contacted by Bissell, Staff D Chief of Operations, Arnold Silver, weighed in with a resounding "no" to the assignment. Not to be deterred, Bissell then went to Silver's own Staff D deputy, Justin O'Donnell with the mission. O'Donnell responded that he also wanted no part of an assassination, but despite that he was encouraged to contact Sydney Gottlieb at CIA Technical Services for the poison to be used against Lumumba. As a counter, O'Donnell did agree to take on an assignment in the Congo, essentially to serve as a staff cut-out to find foreign surrogates to assist in the effort. However, his own focus was to assist Station Chief Devlin in an operation to place Lumumba in the hands of his political enemies (which would still likely end with Lumumba's death, just not directly and with the approved level of CIA deniability). To assist him in that plan, O'Donnell arranged for a European Staff D CIA asset, under the control of the Luxemburg station, to be recruited and sent to the Congo. Other Staff D European assets were also sent in for support, however in the end none of them appear to have been directly involved with the events that ultimately led to Lumumba's death.

In Denial

The same can be said for the rather sensational poison plot. Sydney Gottlieb was personally dispatched to Leopoldville in late September with the poison (in various forms, one in a tube of toothpaste) and with confirmation of the orders for Devlin to use the material in killing Lumumba. But by then Devlin himself was already engaged with a variety of local individuals in multiple plots, including pursuing placing an assassin in Lumumba's residence, arranging for a small group armed attack on him, or arranging for him to be kidnapped and turned over to his political opponents. Gottlieb's poison was simply another option, and never actually came into play. The reality in the Congo was that there were multiple CIA political action efforts in play to garner influence in Leopoldville, while at the same time Station Chief Devlin was pursuing several different plots to eliminate Lumumba, either politically or permanently. [355] Unlike the Cuba Project, the CIA Congo focus seems not only to have been on regime change – which did happen, Lumumba was ousted - but equally with an obsessive effort directed personally against Patrice Lumumba.

Given Develin's broad and ongoing political action efforts (and funds) he was able to reach out to any and all anti-Lumumba factions, using money as the weapon of choice. If anything, covert action (other than the assassination efforts) in the Congo proved to be much more on the order of earlier years in Iran, with across the board offers to anyone anti-Lumumba, to remove him from office one way or the other. Just as in Iran, there was a premature political coup and Lumumba was dismissed (temporarily) from office, only to reassert his authority and return to power within days. As of September 7, the CIA's initial political action effort has been defeated and Dulles complained of inadequate planning, expressing himself on the point that it was extremely hard to run a coup in the Congo.[356]

Yet as in Iran (and not in Cuba) the CIA efforts did manage to turn up a major Congolese military figure who had both the desire for political power and the support of local commanders in the area of the nation's capital, Leopoldville – Colonel Joseph Mobutu, Chief of Staff of the Army. Station Chief Devlin was impressed with Mobutu's military assets and with his offer to oust the elected regime, throw out the Soviets, and ally himself (and the Congo) with the United States. Devlin extended American endorsement and followed that up with cash for Mobutu. A second coup then went into play, placing Mobutu and the military in power for the next nine months, before control was handed back to parliament.[357]

The events of late 1960 in the Congo are a chaotic mix of CIA political action with different factions, of a successful military coup funded by the CIA and, overlaid over it all, multiple ongoing tracks towards assassination of Patrice Lumumba – all fully revealed years later in CIA communications documents and in the personal testimony of station chief Devlin. What comes through quite clearly in it all is that the CIA success in regime change in the Congo worked because it found a military leader, with enough support within the ranks of the army to back his move; a leader who could take control of the nation's capital and who was willing to take American money and support in order to place himself and his commanders in political power. During the Cold War it would become a familiar CIA regime change scenario, successful in Iran, Guatemala, the Congo, and ultimately in Vietnam. In those instances where such a figure did not exist, as in Indonesia, Cuba,

Laos, Angola and Nicaragua, no amount of covert or overt military effort proved sufficient.

The Mobutu coup was a political victory (although American involvement was hardly deniable) for the Eisenhower Administration as Mobutu was seen as western-leaning. He had quickly confirmed that orientation with an order for all Soviet technical personnel and advisers to leave the Congo. Still, while holding supreme power in Leopoldville, both he and the CIA were well aware that Lumumba retained a large degree of popular support in the Congo's eastern territories. Governance in the Congo remained "fluid" to say the least; Mobutu would not actually become president of the Congo until 1965.[358] Dulles continued to advance his view of Lumumba as a threat; he presented him as too popular, too nationalistic, too independent, and too "slippery."

Even with Mobutu in power, Lumumba remained a CIA target. As noted earlier, the Staff D officer assigned to support Congo activities was Justin O'Donnell. O'Donnell did not actually arrive in the Congo until November, 1960, following the ascendency to power of Mobutu in October. O'Donnell still opposed any direct assassination of Lumumba, but he was convinced that Lumumba would be neutralized (most likely executed) if he could be maneuvered into the custody of his Congolese opponents. As matters developed, CIA station personnel, led by Station Chief Devlin, actively worked with Mobutu and his aides on plans to capture Lumumba, who had managed to break out of protective custody. Devlin provided details of which routes were most likely and recommended which roads to block.[359]

Secret Wars With Air Strikes And Tanks?

Plans were in play to send the deniable asset from Luxemburg to assist in the capture attempts, but before that could happen local forces seized Mobutu in Kasai province. In the end Lumumba's death came about much as O'Donnell had anticipated; he was taken from prison, tortured, and brutally murdered. To what extent those directly involved were encouraged by CIA efforts remains a matter of debate, certainly Lumumba had a wide variety of political enemies and brutality was in play across the Congo in December, 1960 when he was killed. There is, however, no doubt that he was an American target and that months of CIA effort were spent in various efforts to eliminate him, in any fashion possible.

During 1961 the overall political problem in the Congo became that of dealing with Moise Tshombe, the Katanga secession, and the central government's loss of control over something on the order of half the nation's territories. Aiding the government in Leopoldville to stay in power and reconstituting the Congo as an example of western support for an emerging African democracy was the challenge faced by the incoming Kennedy Administration. Kennedy chose to meet that challenge through overt support for the Leopoldville central government as well as the United Nations forces involved in attempts to end the successions. Both Kennedy and United Nations were forced to deal with the fact that Moise Tshombe was showing no sign of actually honoring his pledge to reunite Katanga into a Congo unified government.

Tshombe was sustained by Belgian financial and military support, which enabled him to employ experienced mercenary groups and he even managed to organize a small air force, which successfully carried out attacks on Congolese Army units. Tshombe was not alone in his resistance to the Leopoldville government. One of the other newly declared independent regions was led by Antoine Gizenga, the region under his government covered the entire northeast of the country and Gizenga was being actively supported by the Soviets, Fidel Castro's Cuba, and a number of left-wing nations across Africa. Congolese Army and UN Forces were initially successful in South Kasai but suffered embarrassing defeats in Katanga. In the fall, UN peacekeepers were captured and military efforts against Tshombe largely stalled. Earlier in 1961, preoccupied with events in Cuba and Laos, the Kennedy Administration had not been initially prepared to make any major new commitment in the Congo - only to find that the American ambassador had actually taken just such action, on his own initiative and without informing the president, State Department, Secretary of Defense, and Joint Chiefs.

In March, 1961 Ambassador Clare Timberlake personally directed the US Navy to send a small regional contingency force including two destroyers and two Marine landing ships into Congolese waters. President Kennedy learned of the vessels Navy's arrival off the Congo only from media coverage. He was clearly not pleased with the Timberlake's initiative, especially as it had the same appearance of overt Western intervention which had consistently provoked nationalist responses throughout the Congo. Among other remarks on the situation he expressed a strong desire to both Secretary of State Dean Rusk and Defense Secretary Robert McNamara that he would like the opportunity to review such deployments in the future.[360] Kennedy found himself in the same position as his predecessor, facing a chaotic situation in the Congo which continued into 1962, with both the national government and the United Nations frustrated by Tshombe and the Katanga succession. The

Secret Wars With Air Strikes And Tanks?

Katanga Air Force had proven itself to be a special threat and Kennedy even considered direct American action to eliminate it. Certainly, without any air element of its own, the central Congo government was limited in supporting military operations over its vast territories and UN air units or even overt American air intervention against Katanga could only have been strictly temporary measures.

It was at that point, in mid-1962, that a new and highly covert American military operation was initiated in the Congo. Its goal was to provide the central government with both ground attack and transport aircraft. The CIA was tasked with the effort and its solution was to organize and send a group of Cuban exile pilots, mechanics, and support staff. Volunteers were once again recruited to fight communism and the effort was carried out strictly under commercial cover. Even decades later details of the project's initiation and even its level of authorization remain sketchy. We know what happened in the Congo, exactly how it was handled operationally within the CIA remains unclear.[361]

What we do know is that summer, Roberto Medell, a Cuban veteran of the Bay of Pigs, was approached and recruited to organize a group for military air action in the Congo. The cover for the unit would be strictly commercial; the Cubans would work for the Caribbean Marine Aero Corporation (Caramar), a Florida corporation with an address at Miami International Airport. Personnel would be issued visas by the Congolese Consulate in New York and the recruiting was done in a rented office in a building just outside the Miami airport, and all contacts were made by word of mouth among the anti-Castro community in Miami. The unit which came into being would continue operations over some five years, ultimately expanded to include a marine element to fight in eastern Congo, on and around Lake Tanganyika.[362]

The CIA cover business itself was under contract to the Congolese government and the CIA worked with the US Ambassador to the Congo and the State Department in facilitating and handling its logistics. The first Cubans to join the company were hired as trainers for a new Congolese air force, flying AT-6 "Texan" trainers. Serving six-month tours, the first six pilots arrived in late 1962 and referred to themselves as the Cuban Volunteer group but Congolese Army personnel named them, in Swahili, *Makasi*, meaning– "strong and powerful." A cable from Ambassador Timberlake discusses the need to keep the contract arrangement in place through at least 1965. The cable was transmitted to the State Department, the CIA, and the White House, and mentions the need to keep the relationship confidential.[363] In 1962 the Cubans flew unarmed missions, not for training purposes, but on intimidation flights over rebel positions.[364]

However, by the fall of 1962 the UN military mission had prepared itself for another major advance against Katanga. This advance was to be supported by a combination of jet fighters and fighter bombers from the Swedish Air Force and the Ethiopian Air Force, as well as Canberra bombers from the Indian Air Force. Kennedy had committed the United States Air force for transportation and logistics support and in December, 1962, new clashes between UN and Katanga forces, along with the shoot down of a UN helicopter, triggered a major UN response. The UN air elements proceeded to eliminate the Katanga Air force, including the destruction of all its airfields and runways.

Secret Wars With Air Strikes And Tanks?

By January 1963 Katanga was subdued and the UN forces began their withdrawals from the Congo. Up to that point the American involvement in the Congo had been quite overt and successful - the establishment of an anticommunist leadership in control of the central government, and the overall loss of Soviet influence in the Congo had been a significant strategic victory for the Western bloc and both the Eisenhower and Kennedy Administrations. In the spring of 1963, President Kennedy met with Congolese leader Joseph Mobutu at the White House, congratulating him on standing up to communist expansion. Kennedy's praise for Mobutu was effusive: *"General, if it hadn't been for you, the whole thing would have collapsed and the Communists would have taken over."*[365] Unfortunately, the following months proved that much of the Congo was still very far from under control of the central government – violence became widespread, as did extreme brutality towards both opposing factions and foreigners.

There was general outrage over Lumumba's murder. It was jointly blamed on the central government and on foreign influence. Emotions were especially high in the Eastern territories, where Lumumba had held broad popular support. The UN intervention was seen as an invasion; nationalism and anticolonial hatreds surged. Westerners of any nation became targets for the new rebel movements and within a year the Leopoldville government had lost control over large sections of territory to a variety of rebel factions as regional and tribal political figures raised their own armies, assuming roles as regional and local warlords. The most violent and fanatic fighters belonged to a group calling themselves *Simbas*, "lions" in the Congo's dominant Swahili language.

In Denial

The Simbas, managed to gain broad popular support and their use of witch doctors, native magic, and certain drugs also turned them into fierce fighters, with little fear and no self-control. Their treatment of captives was so brutal that it panicked units of the Congolese Army, turning them in to a very real threat to the Leopoldville government. The Congolese Army (ANC), proved largely ineffectual in battle against the Simbas and with the UN gone, it had no air transport or ground support of its own. In response the CIA approved arming several Makasi aircraft with machine guns and air-to-ground rockets. Makasi planes began to make ongoing attacks against the rebels, both on independent missions and in support of the ANC.366

The Cuban volunteer air unit was significantly expanded during 1963, and by October it included twelve T-28 fighters and seven B-26 bombers, plus a small number of transport aircraft. At that point there were some twenty Cuban exile pilots flying, as well as a number of Cuban exile maintenance crews. Given how sensitive the situation in the Congo was in regard to foreign interference, the Cuban group continued to operate strictly under commercial cover, as a contractor to the central government. To that end, during 1963 a new cover firm had been created for further recruiting. The company, Anstalt Wigmo, was registered in Lichtenstein; WIGMO was an acronym for Western International Ground Maintenance Organization.367 The cover proved especially effective as the government was also contracting other groups, including South African mercenaries, in its desperate fight against the Simbas. The United States agreed to the mercenary force, and provided funding, "providing they were neither Belgian nor American."368

316

Secret Wars With Air Strikes And Tanks?

The next American move came in 1964, under President Johnson, the United States opened the Military Mission, Congo (COMISH), under Colonel Frank Williams in the summer of that year. The new and overt military support involved the supply of six T-28 fighters, six helicopters, and ten C-54 twin-engine transports directly to Congolese Army; it also provided a cover for American's going into the Congo in support of the Makasi effort.[369] The US Air Force aircraft were accompanied by American air crews, maintenance and security personnel and a complement of paratroops.[370] To some extent the new commitment to an American military presence had become a matter of little choice, because the situation in the Congo had become truly desperate as the Simba advances continued. By August, the Simbas had gained control over major cities, including Stanleyville in Orientale Province during August 1964.

The Simba capture of Stanleyville, with a population of over 30,000 including a large European community, had given the rebels some 1,600 foreigners to use as hostages. The emboldened Simbas were openly calling for and accepting military aid from both the Soviets and the Chinese – worse yet, several of their factions and leaders openly positioned themselves as communists, going as far as declaring a "People's Republic of the Congo." The situation became increasingly dangerous as Makasi air strikes began to hurt the Simbas, not only causing them to blame the United States (American military officers assigned to COMISH had been observed in the field with Congolese Army forces) but inflamed their hatred of all of all Americans and Europeans. Torture became common, and all captives were treated as enemies, either killed or made hostages. Simba forces were ordered to arrest and

In Denial

"judge without mercy" all Americans. This order amounted to a virtual death sentence.[371]

In October, 1964, Makasi air strikes, field operations by Hoare's 4 Command group and American military logistics support had begun to encourage Congolese Army troops and the central government had begun to regain territory. The effectiveness of the Cuban air group became apparent in a radio intercept of October 1; the Simba commander in Stanleyville had been ordered to kill one European or American for every Congolese killed in an air strike.[372] With thousands of civilians in imminent danger, President Johnson ordered direct military action and the US and Belgium hurriedly assembled a complex airborne rescue operation designated "Dragon." Dragon forces were on the ground in the Congo in November, 1964, accompanied by a small and highly deniable CIA force of Cuban volunteers under Rip Robertson, sent specifically to rescue American diplomatic personnel. Five of the Cubans were killed during the mission, which rescued a number of hostages including missionaries. Belgian paratroops jumping into Stanleyville from American military aircraft managed to save large numbers of hostages, although the Simbas had already killed 47 people and another 30 were brutally murdered during the assault. The Makasi air unit conducted targeted strikes in support of the Dragon mission and were a key element in its success.[373]

The Dragon missions and continuing Makasi air attacks provided a major impetus for the Congolese Army, as did the continued advances by Hoare's 4 Commando units.[374] It was estimated that as many as 10,000 rebels were killed during central government advances during the last half of 1964. By early 1965 a new series of government campaigns reclaimed over half the ground lost to the Simbas during

1964. Equally importantly, by May 1965, Hoare's commando units and the Congolese Army advanced to the point of being able to cut a vital rebel supply route coming into the Congo from Sudan.

Not only was the Sudan road critical in terms of truck supply to the Simbas, but it also brought a direct confrontation with a Cuban Army detachment, formed in Algeria and sent by Castro to support the Congo rebels.[375] It was the final series of Congo central government offensives, into the eastern regions of the Congo and across Lake Tanganyika, which brought the CIA's Cuban volunteers into direct combat with old enemies - Cubans sent by Fidel Castro to support and act as advisors to the rebels. Castro had sent one of his best-known commanders, Che Guevara, to lead the effort. Castro himself viewed the anti-colonial, nationalist movements across Africa as fertile ground for spreading a revolutionary message.

In order to engage with rebels in the eastern lake region, Hoare's commandos were provided with new equipment and additional forces. The CIA arranged for tugs, barges, and SWIFT boats (the same type the CIA was using in covert missions against North Vietnam). It also recruited and sent in yet another group of Cuban volunteers, a naval force to operate on the "Great Lakes" of the Congo. The Cubans were recruited from a highly secret, autonomous force that the CIA had begun to organize during the Kennedy Administration, in the second half of 1963. That force was discontinued under President Johnson, however Cubans eager to continue their fight were recruited by the CIA. They were told that they would play a vital role in stopping the communist overthrow of yet another country, and be returned to the struggle against Castro in Cuba following their African service (something which did not happen).376

With the new resources, a central government initiative in the eastern Congo, Operation Banzai, was launched across Lake Tanganyika towards rebel supply sites in Tanzania.377 By September the new Cuban maritime unit was on the lake with CIA-armed "Swift" boats and the Makasi unit's aircraft began patrolling the lake (the main supply route for the rebels) during the day.378 The CIA's volunteers went into action against some 180 Cuban Army combatants operating in the area of Lake Tanganyika. The Cuban Army personnel also faced a number of problems, including missing weapons parts, the wrong caliber ammunition for the Soviet weapons provided to the rebels, and totally inexperienced recruits. They did manage to organize ambushes of Congolese Army troops and one major attack on an ANC camp, but beyond that they were unable to put together any organized assaults.

In their most serious attack, they were defeated, with five of the Cuban Army troops killed and the others unable to recover their bodies. A diary recovered from one of the dead Cubans (kept against all orders) revealed that Che Guevara was personally leading the Cuban unit.379 In June, 1965, Makasi aircraft located and strafed the Cuban camp. At the same time, the Congolese government managed to bring an end to the Katanga succession, removing the Katanga communist leaders. With that the rebellion largely ended and all foreign troops were called to leave the Congo.380 Castro ordered Che Guevara and his force out of the Congo in November and the CIA Cuban volunteers (over 100 volunteers) departed during 1966 and 1967; the Makasi air group being last out of the country. Castro's force had been larger, over 200, but arrived late to the action, only in 1965 when the rebels were largely defeated and retreating.

Mobutu was officially elected to the presidency of the Congo in 1965 and ultimately banned all opposition parties, taking full control of the Congo (renamed as Zaire in 1971) until 1974. He maintained cordial relations with the Johnson and Nixon Administrations, becoming involved with the United States and the CIA again in a civil war in the neighboring nation of Angola. In that conflict, the United States (via the CIA) and Zaire would face off against both China and Cuba for influence. Although the CIA's involvement in covert military action in the Congo has to be considered one of its few military successes, its second effort, in Angola, would be a far different story.

Taking Sides in Angola:

President Eisenhower's concerns in regard to the wave of nationalism in Africa extended far beyond the Congo. Eisenhower himself described the advent of the African independence movements as a "destructive hurricane." His Assistant Secretary of State had gone further, warning that, "...premature independence and irresponsible nationalism may present grave dangers to dependent peoples."[381] It would only be a new administration and a new president, which would move the United States into a firmer position against colonialism in Africa.

As early as 1956 Senator John F. Kennedy had declared that position: "...*we shall no longer abstain in the UN from voting on colonial issues, we shall no longer trade our vote on other such issues for other supposed gains. We shall no longer seek to prevent subjugated peoples from being heard.*"[382] In 1961 Kennedy's views would put the United States in direct conflict with the Portugal's 72-year-old leader Antonio Salazar. Salazar himself totally opposed any move towards independence and was strongly on record that "no quarter" would be given to agitators in Portugal's extremely profitable African colony of Angola. Yet despite his own personal sympathies, Kennedy was forced to face the basic fact that Portugal was not only a member of NATO, but that the US air bases in the Portuguese Azores islands were considered to be absolutely vital to the Strategic Air Command and its capability to operate across both Europe and the Middle East. Salazar, very much aware of the strategic importance of the bases, made it clear that any US support for independence in Angola would jeopardize American's welcome in the Azores.

President Kennedy's only leverage in the matter came from the US military assistance mission to Portugal and the possible restriction of American weapons and military supplies being provided to the Portuguese government. Those materials, supplied to Portugal as a NATO member, were being used against Angolan rebels. Their use had been observed and reported on by a number of foreign observers and NBC News had threatened to air a special on the subject, including the Portuguese use of American supplied napalm in Angola.[383] One American, John Marcum had watched Portuguese planes bomb and strafe Angolan villages. He copied information from spent 750-point napalm bomb cases; the cases carried stickers reading "Property of U.S Air Force."[384]

But Kennedy's hopes for using weapons sales as leverage were undercut by the terms of a secret agreement with Portugal, which Eisenhower had reaffirmed shortly before leaving office. The agreement stipulated that there would be no "prior consent" usage approval related to the weapons sales. Even invoking such a restriction would provide grounds for Portugal to cancel its treaties with the US, including the Azores's SAC base lease. After a series of ongoing diplomatic exchanges, President Kennedy was forced to face the fact that Portugal was in position to stonewall the Angolan issue based on the strategic value of the US presence in the Azores. The Joint Chiefs insisted that the bases were indispensable, pointing out that they represented a vital element of the American early-warning system, and that the Azores were a key element in American anti-submarine warfare (the Chiefs were correct; the bases did play a key role in the Cuban missile crisis of 1962). By fall 1962, the Kennedy Administration was forced to accept the status quo in Angola. In response to a list of complaints from Lisbon, Washington responded, *"Our efforts ....are not designed to force Portugal to leave Africa but to encourage measures which we are convinced are necessary to enable her to stay and complete work which she has begun."*[385] Sensing the American dilemma, Portugal further hardened its position by not only refusing to support the US during the Cuban missile crisis, but by allowing the Azores lease to expire with no renewal. They would only allow its use to continue on a "day to day" basis.

That status quo would remain in place until 1973/74, under the Nixon/Ford Administration, and most importantly with the personal involvement of Henry Kissinger (in the dual roles of National Security Advisor and Secretary of State). As with CIA Director Dulles in earlier years, Kissinger was very much concerned about African independence movements. He viewed the Portuguese as fighting against Soviet and Chinese sponsored rebels in Angola. At his own initiative Kissinger began exploring covert options for weapons sales for Portuguese use in Angola, only to have his efforts overtaken by events in Portugal itself. In 1974 the long time colonial oriented regime in Lisbon fell in a coup. The new government proved more than willing to work out an exit strategy for Portuguese colonialism in Angola.386

Covert but Conventional Warfare in Angola:

In April 1974, Secretary of State Kissinger directed a comprehensive review of "Military Assistance and Arms Policy in Black Africa" by the National Security Council Interdepartmental Group for Africa. The report was to be submitted in May for presidential review.387 What was missing from the official study was any specific mention of Angola, and in particular that covert military assistance was already being provided to selected Angolan factions or that Zaire (previously the Congo), encouraged by the United States, was already providing training and logistics support to rebel forces targeting the newly independent Angolan regime.388 During the summer of 1974, the CIA began a new round of payments to this insurgency, doing so without approval of the 40 Committee (the then current name for the covert action oversight group) and while a public American policy of neutrality in regards to Angola was in effect. 389

Following the coup in Portugal, during 1975 Angola was granted independence, with a power sharing agreement among its various political factions - an agreement that survived no more than weeks. As in the Congo following its independence, Angola quickly moved into what amounted to full scale combat among the various insurgent movements. And in that new chaos, it was Henry Kissinger who personally moved the United States, and the CIA, into a major covert action, a major military effort involving full scale military combat with Zairean and Angolan surrogates. The earlier Cuban experience appears to have had no impact on Kissinger, as he consistently pushed for greater and more extensive CIA military involvement in

Angola. Under his urging, mission creep in the project became a constant.

Kissinger's position (which can objectively only be described as an obsession; similar to Dulles's obsession with Lumumba in the Congo) appears to have been based in both a general need to preserve American "great nation" status by maintaining the super power confrontation with the Soviets across Africa and an equal need to demonstrate "will and determination" following the fall of South Vietnam. Kissinger was outspoken on the need to maintain America's image: *"In addition to our substantive interest in the outcome [in Angola] playing an active role would demonstrate that events in Southeast Asia have not lessoned our determination to protect our interests..........at a time of great uncertainty over our will and determination."*[390] Without any presidential directive, without any formal program, and without a stated goal, Kissinger's own influence over the covert action 40 Committee resulted in $265,000 in payments to the leader of the FNLA rebel movement simply to assist him in being competitive in securing a position in the future power sharing arrangement.

A CIA communication noted that Secretary Kissinger favored a $14 million dollar commitment to covert military action in Angola, but that the Assistant Secretary of State for African Affairs (Nathanial Davis) opposed any such program. Overwhelmed by Kissinger's influence, and seeing no hope for a diplomatic initiative Davis remained firm and submitted his resignation.[391] Davis was not the only person to challenge Kissinger's *"Cold War" view of the situation in Angola. In his study of the Angolan war, Jonathan Kwitny writes that "...one really has to question the sanity of someone who looks at an ancient tribal dispute over control of distant coffee fields and sees in it a*

In Denial

threat to the security of the United States."[392] Kissinger's goal, and the American funding, was intended to undermine, and if possible oust, the regime that had come to power in the new Angolan government. That faction, the declaredly Marxist leaning MPLA (Popular Movement) was indeed receiving offers of Soviet support and a modest amount of military supplies. Its primary opponent, was Roberto's FNLA (National Front) – operating in the north of the country and out of bases in Zaire. A third, smaller anti-regime group (UNITA), headed by Jonas Savimbi, was located in the south of Angola. All three factions maintained a presence in Luanda, the Angolan capital, although the city itself was stronghold of the MPLA.

With the new, covert American funding, both Mobutu and Roberto appeared to have been encouraged enough to actually move against the MPLA. Up to that point Mobutu had given Roberto's group sanctuary and military training. Then, in a significant escalation, Zairian aircraft arrived in the Angolan capital of Luanda, carrying uniformed FNLA troops. On January 26, the FNLA troops in Luanda attacked the government radio station and kidnapped its assistant director, an MPLA member. Beginning on February 3 and through March, the FNLA attacked MPLA headquarters and several other MPLA installations in the capital. Portuguese efforts to broker a cease fire failed, and in April the FNLA began assaults on the MPLA in other Angolan cities.[393] The FNLA attacks and the descent into full scale civil war stimulated a significant increase in Soviet supply to the MPLA both by air and ship. It also moved the MPLA to formally request military support from Cuba.

The first Cuban advisors arrived in May, 1975 and immediately joined in counterattacks that pushed back the FNLA in the north, and UNITA in the south. The first cycle

Secret Wars With Air Strikes And Tanks?

of escalation had thus been completed (solidifying MPLA control) well before the CIA's own covert military operation, designated as IAFORTUNE, had been formally proposed or approved.[394] The presence of Cuban advisors and Soviet military aid had reinforced Kissinger's views and at his urging, President Ford requested that the CIA provide a proposal for covert action inside Angola. CIA Director Colby promised an operations plan by early July, 1975, but had not delivered one as of the oversight committee meeting on July 13. Kissinger then personally gave Colby 48 hours to produce an operation. On July 17 President Ford approved "Project Feature" and by June 27, 1975 the first planeload of American arms was on its way towards Zaire, where it would be transported by Zairian aircraft to the US backed rebels inside Angola.[395]

President Ford did advise appropriate Congressional committees of the IAFEATIRE program; however, the advisory gave no details, set no goals, and did not even specify that the project was intended for Angola. It merely referred to the authorization of a new national security action in Africa. [396] Of course, as in the majority of its earlier covert military assignments, the CIA was facing the fact by the summer of 1975 that it had once again been tasked with ousting a firmly established regime, already receiving Cuban and Russian military support, and doing so in classic deniable fashion. Their directives stated that no CIA officers or American military personnel would go into Angola and that the operation was to be totally managed out of Zaire. In fact, 40 Committee directives specifically forbid putting CIA personnel into Angola. The American military aid program was to be conducted in isolation, through Zaire, and with no coordination with other powers involving themselves in Angola.

In Denial

While official details of the project are slim, we are fortunate to have a unique firsthand view into CIA operations on the ground during IAFEATURE, straight from the CIA Angola Task Force leader, John Stockwell.[397] He provides full lists of the weapons shipped in during the two year conflict; a partial inventory includes 622 crew served mortars, rockets and machine guns; 4,210 antitank rockets, and 20,860 rifles (primarily of obsolete WW II vintage). Some 10,000 FNLA and UNITA fighters would be involved in the Angolan rebellion. The CIA was back to managing a covert, but conventional military action several times larger than the Cuba Project of earlier years. The CIA's military effort inside Angola was actually far larger in every respect and there were no constraints on the use of American military assets for support and supply.

By the end of 1975, 83 CIA officers were dispatched to stations in Zaire, Angola, and South Africa to work air and ground transport as well as logistics and propaganda activities. Initially three supply flights by Air Force C-141 Starlifters carried small arms and supplies from a CIA storage facility near San Antonio, Texas directly to Kinshasa, Zaire. A large inventory of 12 M-113 tracked amphibious vehicles, 60 trucks, 20 trailers, 5,000 M-16 rifles, 40,000 rifles of other types, 1,000,000 rounds of ammunition and additional rockets, mortars and recoilless rifles were transported by the US Navy transport Challenger sailing out of Charleston, South Carolina. By the end of August, President Ford had authorized over $24 million for the Angola operations. Under Mobutu's orders, the Zairian Army hauled or flew materials into FNLA bases in Angola, enough arms for two full infantry battalions as well as additional armored cars. US C-130 transport aircraft sales to Zaire were expedited to ensure sufficient aircraft for the supply operations. As usual, while officially denied, American support to rebel factions inside Angola was quite visible to everyone in the region.

Given the size of the effort, the order to keep all Americans out of Angola was once again simply ignored by CIA personnel in the field. Stockwell himself was the first officer to go into Angola, but by the fall of 1975 CIA communications personnel, paramilitary trainers, and case officers were working inside the country. As we have seen, the paramilitary professionals assigned to the mission did what they needed to do, and reported only what they had to. Advisors placed inside Angola were designated as "intelligence gatherers"; officers as high as retired Army colonels were placed on contract and sent into Angola.

An American infantry training team was dispatched to Kinshasa in Zaire, and then rerouted to an FNLA camp inside Angola. Personnel wore utility uniforms and on occasion even referred to themselves as mercenaries.[398] When CIA Director Colby later wrote in his own book, *Honorable Men*, that "no CIA officers were permitted to engage in combat or train there [in Angola]," officially - based in the reports being filed at headquarters - that was true. But, as we have learned, CIA project staff was perfectly capable of practicing deniability up their own chain of command. Stockwell describes the fact that even at the CIA headquarters level, the chief of the African Division allowed no verbatim transcripts to be taken of group meetings. He refers to such practices as "several levels of untruth functioning simultaneously," a strikingly accurate description, and certainly something not unique to the Angolan operation.[399]

In September, 1975, things appeared to be coming together for the diverse CIA factions, which opposed the MPLA. Zaire used American supplied C-130 transports to lift its 4th and 7th Commando Battalions into Angola and advanced towards the Angolan capital. The offensive was joined by troops from the FNLA as well as Portuguese mercenaries. At first it appeared that the advance might indeed force its way into Luanda. Then Cuban advisors joined the MPLA forces in the field and resistance stiffened around the capital.

The MPLA forces then came under a surprise attack when a South African assault group crossed its borders with 50 armored cars and some 1,000 troops. The South Africans, with artillery and logistics vehicle trains, moved to join with UNITA forces in the south. Some 2,000 additional South African troops provided logistics support from their side of the border, flying transports and operating fuel trucks. Two separate South African columns literally rolled through opposing MPLA units and began a successful advance to the north. By November the MPLA was estimated to have only maintained control over the capital and three of fifteen Angolan provinces.

The United States maintained that it was totally uninvolved with the seemingly coordinated South African advance - to acknowledge any joint association would have been politically disastrous across Africa. In reality, CIA officers had been quite active in South Africa and that nation was even covertly supporting certain of the highly secret logistics and supply efforts for the American backed rebel factions in Angola. South Africa officially denied its military involvement, but that was simply a matter of form since no other force existed which could have advanced into Angola from the south in such strength. The exposure and intense international condemnation of the South African assault led to immense pressure on that nation. The immediate response was for its forces to cover themselves by joining with and operating to support the

Secret Wars With Air Strikes And Tanks?

UNITA rebel forces. As 1975 ended, it appeared that the Ford Administration's covert action in Angola, an effort which once again put the CIA in charge of a major conventional military force, might prove to be a major CIA success. Within months, in early 1976, any such thoughts were quickly being quashed, through the actions of a long time CIA adversary which been building its own force inside Angola.

Fidel Castro had been officially silent about sending Cuban aid to the MPLA. There was a general African opposition to any foreign forces intervening in what were viewed as Angolan internal affairs. But once the presence of South African forces in Angola became more broadly known, there proved to be little opposition to Cuban aid to the central government - felt to be literally under siege by foreign interests. The Cuban ships Vietnam Heroico, La Plata, and Coral Island had sailed to Angola, carrying weapons, combat supplies, and additional military advisors. The Cubans themselves were very sensitive to accusations of being invaders, especially with the build-up occurring shortly before the date set for the official declaration of Angolan independence. The Cubans took great pains to quickly move their arriving forces to select, remote MPLA camps.[400]

As it had in the past, the CIA was very thoroughly, and in huge quantities, supplying its surrogates the weapons used by regular infantry forces. In contrast, the MPLA had already received Soviet medium-range rocket artillery systems which would prove invaluable under the tactical guidance of its new Cuban combat advisors. The range of those weapons outdistanced the mortars provided by the CIA to its forces by several miles; they even outranged the light field artillery brought to the fighting by the South African units covertly deployed with the FNLA forces.

In Denial

In November, on the day Angolan independence became official, a CIA supported force of 1,500 FNLA, Zairian commandos, and Portuguese mercenaries advanced across the Angolan plains towards Luanda. They were supported by four artillery pieces, manned by South African artillerymen. As the units advanced, they were first bracketed and then utterly smashed by round after round of 122 mm. rocket fire from the Russian rocket launchers. Over 2,000 rockets, roughly 100 salvos of 20 rockets apiece, battered the FNLA fighters, utterly routing the advance. The South African artillery was largely held out of the action, and when it was able to fire, was totally outranged. [401] That engagement was the first in which Cuban advisors had actively joined and fought with the MPLA. Over the weeks that followed, a slow, highly methodical advance by Cuban/MPLA forces drove the FNLA units back to the Zaire border.

The long-range fire proved devastating in stopping what had been organized as the key FNLA advance against the MPLA. But beyond that, the combat on the Angolan plains illustrated one of the major consequences of pursuing deniability in covert military action. Limited by the constraints of deniability, weapons for surrogate troops generally have to be sourced outside the US military inventories – the presence of main line US Army tanks at the Bay of Pigs is truly unfathomable in terms of standard CIA practices, as is the fact that none of the follow-on inquiries commented on that issue. Obtaining deniable weapons means covertly purchasing them from international arms dealers, obtaining them from allies, or negotiating complex surplus weapons deals. While that works for standard infantry weapons, even including machine guns and mortars, it becomes another matter entirely for heavy weapons, antiaircraft weapons, and armored vehicles. Angola Project chief John Stockwell noted that the United States had no immediate choices for weapons to match the Russian field rocket systems, even in standard Army weaponry.

The defeat of the FNLA advance relieved any immediate pressure on the Angolan capital and during the fall of 1975, the Cubans deployed an "air bridge" (Operation Carlotta) to take fully equipped Cuban Army combat brigades into Angola. The 2,800 troops already there were joined by another 10,000.[402] Having no concerns about deniability, the Cuban Army formations were fully equipped with Russian and Eastern bloc tanks, armored cars, helicopters, and trucks. The MPLA forces also continued to receive massively increased Soviet supplies, including more of the deadly medium range rocket batteries. The FNLA advance (clearly coming from Zaire and US backed) as well as the South African thrust into Angola had created an air of international sympathy for Angola and allowed for unrestrained and truly massive support from both the Soviets and the Cubans. Russia sent in seven full shiploads of military equipment, estimated at $225 million. In comparison the CIA was spending only $25 million on its surrogates. While 100 Soviet supply flights had gone directly to the MPLA, the CIA had sent 9 flights into Zaire to supply its forces.

During 1976, the Cuban/MPLA forces continued to overwhelm the rebel factions, with superior weaponry, firepower, and tactics. A well-organized Cuban attack stopped a South African column dead at the Battle of Ebo. The South Africans halted their advance and a full Cuban heavy artillery regiment arrived in three more Cuban freighters followed by four additional Cuban ships with full units of motorized infantry.[403] The South Africans were left with the choice of either a major move into full scale warfare or managing a quick, relatively quiet exit from

Angola. With no major American commitment in view, the South Africans disengaged, withdrew back behind their own border, and were out of the picture in Angola.

During 1976, the American Defense Intelligence Agency reported some 44 Soviet flights into Angola plus 9 Soviet ships making deliveries transshipped to Angola through the Republic of the Congo.[404] Once again the CIA found itself having started a conventional, deniable, and basically limited military effort only to provoke an unconstrained and much stronger military response from its adversaries. It had essentially handed the MPLA and the Angolan central government the moral high ground among the African nations by what appeared to be (and actually was) a coordinated military effort with the generally detested apartheid government of South Africa. The Organization of African States was incensed by the South African incursion and voted by 42 to 4 to recognize the MPLA in Luanda as the official government of Angola.

The CIA Angola Project struggled with other options, ranging from sending more advanced weapons to actually putting numbers of American military advisors into the field. Bringing in additional mercenary fighters was also a consideration and perhaps most amazingly, given the overall goal of opposing Cuban, Russian, and even Chinese influence, virtually all the CIA station chiefs involved pushed for stronger cooperation with the South Africans. The Kinshasa station was especially active in that regard, and sent officers to Pretoria for discussions. Once again, the urge to succeed with an operation at all cost – despite almost universal condemnation by the majority of the African nations which it wanted to influence – had set into motion a CIA covert action.

Secret Wars With Air Strikes And Tanks?

That commitment was exacerbated by Henry Kissinger's constant pressure to oppose the Soviets at all costs. Kissinger was quite open to stronger involvement with South Africa as well as in fielding deniable units via mercenary operations (ignoring the fact that mercenaries from the former colonial powers were considered as one more symbol of colonial power still being in play in Africa).[405] In China, during conversations with Vice–Premier Deng Xiaoping, Kissinger discussed the Angolan situation, stating that "we are prepared to push South Africa as soon as an alternative military force can be created."[406]

Henry Kissinger was not someone to let go of a failing project, in the face of either the realities of combat or Congressional objections. Almost solely in response to his pressure, the Angola Project team continued support for Angolan insurgent groups for much of 1976. The Agency was given access to additional funds and five more Air Force Starlifters were sent off with cargos to Kinshasa, Zaire, some 22 transshipment flights carried the supplies on into Angola. Even as the FNLA totally ceased to be an effective fighting force, Secretary Kissinger sent a cable to the American State Department representative in Kinshasa to be passed on to UNITA. The message was that America would continue to support them as long as they demonstrated they could effectively resist the MPLA. In the following chapter, we will see that message to be eerily familiar to a similar communication from Kissinger to CIA surrogate forces in Laos – urging that fighting and resistance continue "at all costs."[407]

Kissinger was as loath to accept military reality as Richard Bissell had been during the Cuba Project. During one last period of virtual desperation the CIA Angola Project team had proposed sending the American military into Angola. Edward Mulcahy, acting assistant secretary for African Affairs, took their proposal to Kissinger for approval. At the next team meeting he described Kissinger's reaction; Kissinger had not really approved or disapproved, he had read the paper and then just grunted. Not a clear pro grunt or a con grunt, just a grunt and the team pondered the grunt. They decided it would be best to defer on sending in Americans, Mulcahy would comment later, "It was a strange way to run a war."[408]

Limits to Covert Military Action:

The assignments given to the CIA in Tibet and in Africa provide us with confirmation that there are indeed serious limits to what can be expected from covert military action. Both reinforce the point that policy makers routinely harbor unrealistic ideas about what it can accomplish – how any could have thought that a Tibetan insurgency could somehow slow, much less block the full weight of the Red Chinese Army remains unclear. The Indian Army was barely able to slow even a relatively minor border incursion by China in 1962. While President Kennedy allowed the project to continue, he demanded it be focused into something realistic, turning it into essentially a road and border watch intelligence collection activity and nothing more.

The same can be said by his authorization for the Makasi covert air combat program in support of the central government of the Congo. It addressed a very specific need, involved a very limited force, and at least to some extent was deniable, shielded by an American military mission to the legitimate government of the Congo. As for the Angola Project of Ford, and primarily Kissinger, it went through major mission creep even within two years, much as had the Cuba Project. The forces deployed were never a match for those being sent in by the adversary governments and it moved the CIA into the position of trying to remotely manage full blown conventional combat. The same language found in the CIA IG's report on the Cuba Project could very well be applied to Angola – "it was beyond Agency responsibility as well as Agency capability." Certainly, the lessons learned at the Bay of Pigs had been well and truly forgotten (or willfully discarded) by the mid-1970's. In the following chapter we will examine two operations that suggest that loss of memory actually occurred several years earlier.

Notes

[333] Kenneth Conboy and James Morrison, *The CIA's Secret War in Tibet* (Lawrence, KS: University of Kansas Press, 2002), 7–8

[334]Ibid. 26

[335]*Foreign Relations of the United States, 1964–1968, Volume XXX*, China, Document 342
http://history.state.gov/historicaldocuments/frus1964-68v30/comp2

[336]Jeffrey T. Richelson, *The U.S. Intelligence Community* (Boulder, CO: Westview Press, 1999), 17

[337] JFK on the Containment of Communism, 1952, Address to the Massachusetts Chapter of the American Federation of Labor, August, 1952, The Gilder Lehrman Institute of American History.
https://www.gilderlehrman.org/content/jfk-containment-communism-1952

[338] Inaugural Address of John F Kennedy, January 20, 1961, The Avalon Project at Yale Law School
https://web.archive.org/web/20070514235348/http://www.yale.edu/lawweb/avalon/presiden/inaug/kennedy.htm

[339]*Foreign Relations of the United States, 1964–1968, Volume XXX*, *China*, Document 337
http://history.state.gov/historicaldocuments/frus1964-68v30/comp2

[340] *Foreign Relations of the United States, 1958–1960, China,* Volume XIX, Document 388
http://history.state.gov/historicaldocuments/frus1958-60v19/ch5

[341] Ibid. 187

[342] Schlesinger, *A Thousand Days; John F Kennedy in the White House*, Mayflower Dell, New York, 1965, 428

[343] The details of the various CIA actions in the Congo during the Eisenhower Administration - none of which occurred in a coordinated, project like fashion - are complex and convoluted; the related documents themselves are disconnected and involve numerous pseudonyms and aliases. The situation in the Congo went through several political stages, and the CIA response reflected the political chaos. For the most current study of exactly what individuals and activities were in play under Eisenhower and Dulles at a particular time, the reader is referred to the work of Dr. John Newman in his book *Countdown to Darkness*, chapters 10, 16, and 17. CIA activity in the Congo under President Kennedy was a totally different matter and is best described in separate sources. John Newman, *Countdown to Darkness*, CreateSpace Independent Publishing, 2017

[344] *Foreign Relations of the United States, 1958-1960, Volume XIV Africa*, Document 106 also John Newman, *Countdown to Darkness*, 154-156

[345] John F. Kennedy, Senate speech, June 14, 1960, reprinted in John F. Kennedy; *The Strategy of Peace*, Harper and Brothers, New York, 1960

[346] *Foreign Relations of the United States, 1958-1960, Volume XIV Africa*, Document 136, Telegram from the Embassy in the Congo to Department of State. Also **see** John Newman, Countdown to Darkness, 161. As Dr. Newman points out,

In Denial

Ambassador Burden's views of the Congo crisis and Katanga succession were likely influenced by the fact that while he was acting as the American ambassador, he was also on the Board of American Metals Climax, a corporation with major and critical interests in the Katanga mines.

[347] Madeleine G. Kalb, *The Congo Cables*, Macmillan Publishing, 1982, xii

[347] Ibid, pp. 14-16, 27-22-39

[348] Richard D. Mahoney, *JFK: Ordeal in Africa* (New York: Oxford University Press, 1983), 40

[349] Madeleine G. Kalb, *The Congo Cables: The Cold War in Africa—From Eisenhower to Kennedy* (New York: Macmillan Publishing, 1982), 54–55

[350] *Alleged Assassinations Plots involving Foreign Leaders, Interim Report on by the Select Committee to Study Government Operations*, 21-23

[351] Bronson Tweedy Deposition to the Church Committee, October 9, 1965 RIF 157-10014-10089 and RIF 157-10014-10067; also, John Newman, *Countdown to Darkness*, 235-239

[352] Larry Devlin, *Chief of Station Congo*, Perseus Books Group, New York, 84

[353] CIA Leopoldville Cable to Director, October 15, 1960, RIF 157-10014-10089 also John Newman, *Countdown to Darkness*, 287-288

[354] William Harvey Church Committee deposition 1, 9, RIF 157-1002-10105 and Summary of Expected Testimony of Justin

Secret Wars With Air Strikes And Tanks?

O'Donnell, RIF 147-10014-10106 also John Newman, *Countdown to Darkness*, 287-289

[355] CIA Leopoldville Cable to Director, *Alleged Assassinations Plots involving Foreign Leaders, Interim Report on by the Select Committee to Study Government Operations*, 15

[356] *Foreign Relations of the United States, 1958-1960, Volume XIV Africa*, Document 199

[357] Larry Devlin, *Chief of Station Congo*, Perseus Books Group, New York, 81-82

[358] "Kasavubu Regime Ousted by Army Coup in Congo," Reuters as reported in the New York Times, November 25, 1965 https://archive.nytimes.com/www.nytimes.com/library/world/africa/651125kasavubu.html

[359] Larry Devlin, *Chief of Station Congo*, Perseus Books Group, New York, 115

[360] Kalb, *The Congo Cables*, 240–241; Thomas P. Odom, *Dragon Operations: Hostage Rescues in the Congo, 1964–1965* (Fort Leavenworth, KS: Combat Studies Institute, U.S. Army Command and General Staff College, 1988), 12. Timberlake's successor, Ambassador Godley, an action-oriented former Marine nicknamed by certain of his staff as "CINCCONGO" (Commander in Chief, Congo), was equally assertive. In 1964, during the hostage crisis in Stanleyville, Godley developed his own rescue plan, requesting naval assets to support it. After approval from the State Department, he organized "Operation Flagpole," under command of the chief of the American military mission, using embassy marine security personnel and with support from Makasi aircraft. The mission was practiced, but aborted at the last moment due to reports of rebel forces near the consulate.

361 Stephen R. Weissman, "Why is U.S. withholding old documents on covert ops in Congo, Iran?" *The Christian Science Monitor*, March 25, 2011. The lack of clarity is largely due to the fact that significant State Department Foreign Relations material on Africa for the period 1960–1968, which is required by law to be published, is still being withheld—even though the State Department Historical Advisory Committee called for its release in 2003. The same 1991 records access law that initially provided us with so much detailed insight into events in Guatemala appears to have been successfully compromised by CIA objections over the Africa material. An exceptionally protracted Agency review and re-review process had also blocked release of the material.
http://www.csmonitor.com/Commentary/Opinion/2011/0325/Why-is-US-withholding-old-documents-on-covert-ops-in-Congo-Iran

362 Frank R. Villafaña, *Cold War in the Congo: The Confrontation of Cuban Military Forces, 1960–1967* (New Brunswick, NJ: Transaction Publishers, 2009), 37–38

363 George Lardner Jr., "Cuban Surrogates in Africa: An Old Issue," *The Washington Post*, June 6, 1978, A14

364 Villafaña, *Cold War in the Congo*, 68

365 Kalb, *The Congo Cables* 372–373

366 Lardner, Jr., "Cuban Surrogates in Africa," 70

367 Villafaña, *Cold War in the Congo*, 81

368 Mike Hoare, *Congo Mercenary*, (Boulder, CO: Paladin Press, 2008), 27

³⁶⁹ Ibid., 6

³⁷⁰ "U.S. Sends Four Big Planes to Aid Tshombe," *The New York Times*, August 13, 1964 https://www.nytimes.com/1964/08/13/archives/us-sends-four-big-planes-to-congo-to-aid-tshombe.html

³⁷¹ Odom, *Dragon Operations*, 22

³⁷² Ibid., 33

373 Ibid., 1

³⁷⁴ Ibid., 91, 103, 131

³⁷⁵Ibid., p. 108

376 Villafaña, *Cold War in the Congo*, 40–411

³⁷⁷ Hoare, *Congo Mercenary* 253

³⁷⁸ Ibid., 144–145

³⁷⁹ Considerable detail of combat operations (including several fierce battles) between Hoare's Commandos, the Cuban exile volunteers, and the Castro detachment may be found detailed in *Cold War in the Congo*

³⁸⁰ Ibid.,162

381 Richard Mahoney *JFK: Ordeal in Africa*, Oxford University Press, Mahoney, 1983. 35

³⁸² Ibid, 187

383 Ibid, 196

[384] William Blum, Angola 1975 to 1980s, The Great Powers Poker Game, Common Courage Press, 2008
http://www.thirdworldtraveler.com/Blum/Angola_KH.html

[385] Ibid, 218

[386] Piero Gleijeses, *Conflicting Missions: Havana, Washington and Africa, 1959-1976*, The University of North Carolina Press, 2002, 230-232

[387] *Foreign Relations of the United States, 1969–1976, Volume E–6, Documents on Africa, 1973–1976*, Document 1, April 25, 1974

[388] *Foreign Relations of the United States, 1969–1976, Volume E–6, Documents on Africa, 1973–1976*, Document 21, Response to National Security Study Memorandum 201, Washington, October 8, 1974
http://history.state.gov/historicaldocuments/frus1969-76ve06/d21

[389] John Stockwell, *In Search of Enemies, a CIA Story*, New York, W.W. Norton & Company, 1978, 67

[390] John Prados, *William Colby and the CIA*, Lawrence, KS, University Press of Kansas, 2009, 317. NSC Staff memorandum, Henry Kissinger to Gerald Ford, June, 27, 1975

[391] John Stockwell, *In Search of Enemies, a CIA Story*, New York, W.W. Norton & Company, 1978, 53

[392] Walter Isaacson, *Kissinger*, New York, Simon and Schuster, 1992, 675

[393] Piero Gleijeses, *Conflicting Missions: Havana, Washington and Africa, 1959-1976*, The University of North Carolina Press, 2002, 250-252

[394] Walter Isaacson, *Kissinger*, New York, Simon and Schuster, 1992, 676

[395] John Prados, *Keepers of the Keys*, Lawrence. KS, University Press of Kansas, 2009, 318

[396] Ibid, 55

[397] John Stockwell, *In Search of Enemies, a CIA Story*, New York, W.W. Norton & Company, 1978

[398] Ibid, 177-179

[399] Ibid, 179

[400] Piero Gleijeses, *Conflicting Missions: Havana, Washington and Africa, 1959-1976*, The University of North Carolina Press, 2002, 261

[401] Ibid, 268-269

[402] Interagency Intelligence Memorandum, Soviet and Cuban Military Aid to Angola during January, 1976.

[403] Piero Gleijeses, *Conflicting Missions: Havana, Washington and Africa, 1959-1976*, The University of North Carolina Press, 2002, 319-321

[404] *Foreign Relations of the United States, 1969–1976, Volume E–6, Documents on Africa, 1973–1976,* Document 3; Intelligence Appraisal DIAIAPPR 4-76 Prepared by the Defense Intelligence Agency, Washington, January 9, 197
http://history.state.gov/historicaldocuments/frus1969-76ve06/d33

[405] The Nixon Administration in general, had little confidence in the nationalist independence movements and leaned towards supporting the stability of existing African governments. In 1969, NSSM 39 had concluded that insurgent movements were ineffectual and neither "realistic nor supportable" alternatives when compared to the continuation of colonial rule. That report was based in an interdepartmental review and Kissinger himself had expressed doubt in "the depth and permanence of black resolve" and the chances of any black nationalist movement succeeding. The 1969 finding seems to have been an extension of the assessment in the National Intelligence Estimate Number 70-1-67, The Liberation Movements of Southern Africa. That estimate concluded that "the liberation movements stand little chance of significant progress toward deposing any of the White Regimes of Southern Africa through 1970 and probably for some significant time thereafter." The estimate was however quite accurate in projecting that only a civil revolt within Portugal, ejecting the existing leadership, could lead to Angolan independence.

[406] . Records of the Department of State, Policy Planning Staff, Director's Files (Winston Lord), 1969-1977, *"White House Memorandum of Conversation with Chinese Officials, "The Soviet Union; Europe; the Middle East; South Asia; Angola."* George Washington University National Security Archive. National Archives Record Group 59, Box 373
https://nsarchive2.gwu.edu//NSAEBB/NSAEBB67/gleijeses4.pdf

Secret Wars With Air Strikes And Tanks?

[407] John Stockwell, *In Search of Enemies, a CIA Story*, New York, W.W. Norton & Company, 1978, 233-235

[408] Walter Isaacson, *Kissinger*, New York, Simon and Schuster, 1992, 678-679.

Chapter 9: Inertia

Tasking the CIA with covert military missions beyond its experience and capabilities, especially when the mission itself is unrealistic, has proved to be a prelude to both failure and exposure. But underlying such mistakes is the possibility of an even more fundamental failure, one called out by the CIA's own Inspector General in his Cuba Project study. Lyman Kirkpatrick concluded that the Cuba Project chief and the senior officers in the agency had failed in a key responsibility: *"[They] failed to advise the president that success had become dubious....at some point in the degenerative cycle they should have gone to the president and said here are the facts, the operation should be halted."*[409]

In exploring the Cuba Project in great detail, that failure becomes more than evident, confirmed in extreme fashion by the effort of its senior operational and military efforts to actually resign prior to the dispatch of the Cuban Expeditionary Force to the landings at the Bay of Pigs. That assessment was actually confirmed, after the fact, by the personal admissions of both Cuba Project Chief Richard Bissell and CIA Director Allen Dulles. Yet perhaps that element of failure is not an issue in all covert action, but rather an aberration, a matter of personal egos, of career aspirations? Perhaps it had to do with a project proposal that was being presented to a new president – by officers hesitant to actually admit that the agency itself had failed in the first phase of the project, and had not openly acknowledged that to President Eisenhower or his Special Group? Such an admission would not have been helpful in gaining the acceptance of President Kennedy for the new amphibious landings plan.

We have seen that missions can be reassessed and at least refocused rather than be forced into mission creep and escalation. President Kennedy demonstrated that with the Tibet Project and in placing strict limits on covert military action in the Congo. In contrast, the Angola Project demonstrated that high level policy makers can force covert military action forward in the face of seemingly unsurmountable odds - forced to the point of not only exposing the mission, but of seriously compromising diplomatic efforts throughout an entire geographic region. An exploration of the following projects reveals that "inertia" in covert action, even covert military action, is indeed a fundamental problem and a very real risk, involving the temptation to proceed in the face of reality both by those who order it, and those who become operationally and mentally committed to mission success. The urge to success can override caution, objectivity, and reality. When it does, regard for the consequences and concerns for the surrogates actually involved in the missions appears to fade far into the background to become submerged in another type of denial.

14 Years of Surrogate Warfare in Laos

The United States first became involved in Laos under President Eisenhower, as part of the overall American effort to contain communist bloc expansion globally and across Asia. The initial American involvement was limited, focused on political action, foreign aid, and limited military assistance, all intended to support the central government and prevent a takeover by a communist faction known as the Pathet Lao. But much as in the Congo, within a short time it became clear that providing diplomatic support and foreign aid was not enough. Even the presence of an overt military aid mission (consisting primarily of advisors) was not sufficient to sustain a neutral central government against rebellion and threats from communist factions, especially with the Soviet Bloc eager to support such movements around the globe.

Laos was emerging from a long history of French colonial control and, as with the Congo, was heavily factionalized, highly distrustful of any foreign intervention, and heavily influenced by existing armed resistance forces who had been in combat for years against the French colonial governments. The official American military mission in Laos involved sending advisors to the Royal Lao Armed Forces (FAR), assisting with planning and tactics to be used in operations against communist and other antigovernment factions around the country, including operations against mutinous army units. Beyond that overt support, as early as 1959, President Eisenhower began covertly sending United States Special Forces into Laos.

Over a hundred men were sent in the initial deployment, under cover as members of a special program ostensibly created to evaluate the effectiveness of both civilian and military aid going to that country. That project was designated as the Programs Evaluation Office (PEO). The Special Forces personnel, wearing civilian clothing and with identity covers, went into Laos in Operations Hotfoot and White Star.[410] They were organized into mobile teams, assigned to work with battalions of the Royal Lao Army as trainers, but authorized to engage in combat as the situation might demand. The first White Star commander was Lieutenant Colonel Arthur "Bull" Simons. In order to preserve deniability, both covert military and CIA operations in Laos were placed under the joint control of the Ambassador and the CIA station chief. While that seemed reasonable enough in the early years, that covert approach would ultimately result in major combat operations being directed by individuals with no particular military experience.

As early as 1960, the major covert action focus in Laos began to shift from maintaining an ostensibly neutral government, first to intelligence collection, then guerilla action, and finally to major surrogate military operations. All activities aimed at the constantly growing North Vietnamese support of the Pathet Lao, and the establishment of a major infiltration and supply route coming down through eastern Laos and into South Viet Nam. The initial creation of an American surrogate military effort in Laos involved both Bull Simons, who recruited Laotian tribesmen on the Bolaven Plateau in northeast Laos, and efforts by Bill Lair, a highly experienced CIA field officer who brought in volunteers from Thailand. Lair was moved into Laos from Thailand (where he had been working in counter insurgency activities with the Thai government) and brought some ninety-nine Border Patrol Police (PARU) advisors with him. They not only began conducting their own missions, but were also assigned as advisors and trainers for Hmong tribal irregulars in northeastern Laos. The CIA's goal for both initiatives was to establish the deniable military capability to harass and divert both Pathet Lao and North Vietnamese Army units

In Denial

who were themselves developing a buffer zone around the rapidly growing supply line into South Vietnam.[411]

At first that supply line was little more than a series of foot trails running down the Laotian side of the Vietnamese border, used by North Vietnam to infiltrate supplies and a limited number of both political and military cadre. Later those foot trails evolved into a multi-road transportation corridor down the length of the Laotian border, carrying North Vietnamese troop formations, truck convoys, and even tanks to the south. To retain American deniability, with an official foreign policy position of strict neutrality in Laos, the CIA conducted its covert military missions against the "trail" using Laotian indigenous tribal groups, generally referred to as "irregulars."

By the early 1960's the situation on the ground in Laos had become almost as fractionalized and chaotic as that of the Congo. The Pathet Lao, receiving large quantities of weapons and military supplies via Soviet air transport, had become a serious threat to central government control of much of the north and east of the country. North Vietnamese security forces were establishing themselves into buffer zones around the trail into South Vietnam, forcing out central government forces and tribal groups. There were irregular tribal military forces, often acting autonomously, yet formally classified as being under general central government and Royal Lao Army command. In addition, there were US military assistance advisors, Thai military advisors, and CIA paramilitary officers all working with the Royal Lao Army.

The first, and seemingly the most serious, national security decisions that President Kennedy faced involved Laos, Vietnam, and Cuba. President Eisenhower had focused him on Laos as he left the White House – both Cuba and Vietnam came to Kennedy as something of a shock. Intuitively Kennedy's view was that Laos was emerging from colonialism, and as with the African colonial nations, he publicly stated that Laos should be allowed to move into a position of neutrality – free from political domination by either East or West.[412] Unlike Eisenhower, Kennedy accepted the concept of neutrality and would effectively use that acceptance to immediately improve relations with self-declared neutral nations such as India.

Still, a neutral Laos with the communist Pathet Lao in control of large amounts of territory and providing access to North Vietnamese for unrestricted use of a cross border feeder route into South Vietnam was simply not acceptable. For any neutrality plan to work (and to keep the United States from becoming involved in Laotian combat – overtly or covertly), the central government had to maintain some degree of territorial control, especially in its eastern regions. As of February, 1961, that remained a possibility. A Special National Security Estimate predicted that central government forces would be able to recover ground from the Pathet Lao in an upcoming offensive.[413] In reality that critical offensive never came together, instead the Pathet Lao launched their own assault, overwhelming and shattering a substantial amount of the Laotian government force.

President Kennedy's desire for a neutrality-oriented solution in Laos remained jeopardized by ongoing Pathet Lao attacks, and the inability of the Royal Laotian Army to defend government territories. The immediate questions were whether the communist faction could even be brought into negotiations leading to a neutral regime or whether the capital itself might fall to them. Given the ongoing Pathet Lao military successes, it seemed likely that they would only pause if met with meaningful force. The only obvious force available would be the commitment of United States forces in a conventional American military intervention. To that end, on March 9 a special task force on Laos submitted a seventeen-step military escalation plan to the new president.

Designated as Operation Mill Pond, the plan began with more military advisors and advanced to deploying small Army units, all the way to large American military formations.[414] President Kennedy accepted the concept, but only approved initial preparations for such an effort. Yet even preparations had to face the fact that the terrain and logistics of Laos necessitated both extensive air transport supply and combat air support. Acknowledging that fact, approval was given to deploy American helicopters with Marine, Army, and Navy to support the White Star group already in place in Laos. In addition, three hundred Marine maintenance personnel were sent to Udorn, Thailand to provide maintenance and servicing for the helicopters.[415]

During the next few weeks, briefings and discussion on the amphibious operation targeting the Castro regime became overshadowed by proposals and dialog as to the possibility of immediate American military intervention in Laos. Those meetings were conducted in an air of urgency (and some desperation) as ongoing Pathet Lao attacks continued to consume the Laotian central government forces. The State Department wanted to deploy troops to key locations in a holding action, the Seventh Fleet was ordered to concentrate in the South China Sea, and the Joint Chiefs raised the specter of North Vietnamese or even Chinese intervention. Details of those strategy sessions

during March and April, 1961, the positions advocated and the ongoing changes through the final decision by President Kennedy not to commit conventional forces are explored in detail by Dr. John Newman in his seminal work on the Vietnam conflict, *JFK in Vietnam*. For additional detail, readers are referred to Newman's writing, particularly his chapter "Straight to the Brink over Laos."
416

While the strategy dialogs continued, President Kennedy began to act, going public to demonstrate American commitment to Laotian neutrality. On March 24 (only weeks before the landings in Cuba) he announced the deployment of three US Navy aircraft carriers - carrying 1,400 Marines – into the South China Sea. Designated as Task Force 77 the carriers moved to a point some 200 miles off Danang, South Vietnam, taking up station for air operations into Laos. Two Marine fighter squadrons were deployed from Japan to forward bases in the Philippines and additional Marine forces set sail for Okinawa. More Marines were sent to Thailand, with an additional 2,600 stationed on Okinawa activated for immediate deployment. For the next few weeks (through and following the disaster in Cuba) negotiations continued in Laos, as did ongoing losses of territory by the central government. However, on April 24, the Laotian negotiations did result in setting a date for a ceasefire, but as that date approached the Pathet Lao continued to take territory. The outstanding question was whether they would overrun the entire country before the agreed cessation of hostilities, or whether the United States would openly commit military forces to prevent that? In the end neither event occurred.

April 27, 1961 saw the beginning of a series of dramatic meetings concerning American intervention in Laos.

In Denial

Admiral Burke (a familiar figure, involved in our previous examination of the independent deployment of a major American Navy task force off Cuba during the Bay of Pigs landings), attended as the representative for the head of the Joint Chiefs of Staff. Burke personally pushed for a massive Southeast Treaty Organization intervention, putting a military force across both Laos and South Vietnam. Such a huge intervention ran the risk of forcing a Chinese military response. Burke responded to that possibility by reviewing contingency plans for the seizure of China's Hainan Island (defended by three Chinese battalions), deploying 240,000 American troops into both South and North Vietnam as a blocking force, and the use of nuclear weapons if those troops faced being overrun by massive Chinese forces.[417]

Burke received no real support for his proposal from the other military participants at that meeting. Marine General Shoup provided a sanity check, pointing out that given the lack of air fields in Laos, as well as limitations on American air logistics, no more than 1,000 troops a day could be put on the ground in Laos - such small contingents would be quite vulnerable.[418] The Joint Chiefs did become more animated about military intervention towards the end of April, the problem being that each of the Chiefs appeared to have a different view of exactly how much force to commit, and even exactly where to deploy it. Their individual proposals included open deployment of units not only to Laos, but to Thailand and Vietnam. Since any such major intervention ran the risk of Chinese military action, the Chiefs stressed the possibility of having to use tactical nuclear weapons.

As of the end of April, Kennedy remained open to preparations for major ground deployments if the communist forces did not honor the pending ceasefire. The Commander in Chief Pacific was ordered to develop contingency plans which would move brigade sized forces (5,000 troops) to both Udorn, Thailand and Danang, Vietnam.[419] While the Joint Chiefs and many of his own advisors had become convinced of the need for intervention, the experience at the Bay of Pigs appears to have had made it clear to the new president that he needed to be far more probing in questioning plans for military action. Generalities and assurances were simply not sufficient.

Comments from a May 1, National Security Council meeting indicate that the president began asking the chiefs for details of their plans, in particular raising issues of logistics and support for the large forces being discussed (a major issue in the recent failure at the Bay of Pigs). It appears the Chiefs had little more detail to present, and still held their own differences of opinion. The answers to Kennedy's questions on logistics and supply were particularly concerning, because there were only two airfields in Laos. They were only usable in day light and in good weather and both were particularly vulnerable to attack. In addition, the president was told that deploying 10,000 troops would virtually empty the nation's strategic manpower reserve.[420]

By the end of that meeting, President Kennedy was not ready to commit to immediate military action in Laos, or more broadly in Southeast Asia. Although he stated that he was simply deferring any final decision, no further buildups or deployments were authorized and ultimately Kennedy compromised by turning to a combination of both overt political action, and deniable military action in Laos. Once again, when the tests for conventional intervention (probability of success and consequences) could not be met, but national security (and political concerns) dictated a response, the compromise was covert action.

Surrogate Forces in Laos

In pursuit of neutrality in Laos, American military action was going to be deniable and by definition, covert. President Kennedy allowed the existing programs to continue under CIA auspices, initially limited to intelligence collation, trail watch, and guerilla style harassment operations. Based on initial successes, he did authorize expanding the surrogate forces and providing them with heavier infantry weapons. Following his death, under Presidents Johnson and Nixon, both restrictions and constraints on the surrogate forces would disappear. As with the early CIA failure in Cuba, new proposals would equip and deploy the Laotian surrogate forces as conventional infantry formations, aided by air support extending to "covert and deniable" saturation bombing by American B-52 Strategic Air Command bombers. Once again there was first mission creep, then inertia in the face of failure, and finally…consequences.

To expand convert military action in Laos, the CIA turned to surrogate fighters whom it had already begun to work with during the Eisenhower Administration – in particular the Hmong. The Hmong hill tribes of northeastern Laos (referred to by Laotians as the Meo people) lived in the region of the Plain of Jars, to the west of North Vietnam. Of Chinese origin, the Hmong were independent and both fiercely anticommunist, and anti-Vietnamese. During the ongoing Laotian coups and counter-coups of the early 1960s, the Hmong had proved to be more combative and more effective than the central government forces, fighting for their homeland against all comers, the Pathet Lao in particular. That made them particularly attractive as potential surrogates and in a show of support from the Eisenhower Administration, the CIA had supplied them with two thousand rifles in late 1960.[421]

Due to their independent nature, the Hmong enjoyed no particular favor within the Laotian central government. Yet with their homeland threatened by the Pathet Lao, and increasingly by North Vietnamese Army security forces expanding a security perimeter to protect their supply route south to Vietnam, the Hmong came to depend on constantly increasing financial and military support from the United States, covertly via the CIA. CIA officers assisted in recruiting Hmong fighters with the enthusiastic endorsement from the preeminent tribal chief, Vang Pao. A large number of the individual Hmong tribal groups were under Vang Pao's umbrella of influence. In direct contrast to how it had managed its Cuban surrogates, small Hmong units were trained, equipped, and deployed with minimal direction by CIA paramilitary officers; it was accepted they knew their own home territories best and could carry out their own missions. Only a minimum number of CIA field officers were deployed and the Hmong initially proved quite successful in independent action, collecting vital information on the Pathet Lao movements and successfully preventing any of their attempts to consolidate new territory.

Those first efforts proved so successful that in February 1962, President Kennedy approved a plan to significantly enlarge the Hmong combat forces. His authorization approved training and support for up to 11,000 Hmong "irregulars." In addition, the Hmong were to be equipped with 75 mm recoilless rifles. Kennedy also gave the

In Denial

authorization to recruit additional tribal irregulars in both the far north of Laos and in its southern panhandle. In the south, the Kha tribes were armed, and their operations would be supported by US Special Forces; coordination was to come from a substantial new CIA regional base located at Pakse, Laos. The effort to restrict supplies coming through Laos into South Vietnam was largely going to be up to the CIA's surrogate forces, rather than those of the Royal Lao military. It had proved so ineffective that virtually the entire Laotian–Vietnamese border became "denied" to the government and the lack of any central government control allowed the North Vietnamese ongoing access to South Vietnam via the Ho Chi Minh trail. A minimum of 4,000 North Vietnamese infiltrators moved down the trail in 1961, 5,300 in 1962, and 4,700 in 1963.

In response, the CIA requested that the Hmong, who were increasingly facing actual North Vietnamese Army units, be further equipped for conventional combat. Guerilla operations were simply not going to be enough to deal with an increasingly well-equipped adversary, and as in the Cuba Project, the CIA once again lobbied for a move to conventionally equipped and armed surrogates. With no other options available, President Kennedy approved the initial CIA requests, issuing National Security Action Memorandum 240. That directive authorized the CIA to provide the Hmong with artillery howitzers, heavy mortars, some aircraft, and additional funding. In addition, Kennedy also gave conditional approval to NSAM 256. That directive called for covert US military aerial reconnaissance in Laos, as well as action to pressure the Royal Lao Air Force for aggressive air and ground attacks.

This effort was intended to buy time for the establishment of conventional, but deniable American military air support operating out of bases in Thailand.[422] That support would come to involve a huge number of covert/deniable missions flown by the US Air Force and by the CIA's proprietary commercial cover company, Air America. Air America's contract work led them into a broad variety of Laotian missions ranging from routine supply flights, to missions for combat support, as well as search and rescue activities for downed Air America and US military pilots. Covert air support in Laos grew to involve some twenty helicopters, and a limited number of propeller-driven attack aircraft. CIA field officers were also allowed to call on air strikes from the USAF 7th and 13th Air Force at Udorn, Thailand.[423] In addition, a variety of shorter-range air transports for supply and personnel transport were operated by Air America.[424]

In Laos, the Kennedy Administration had become caught in the same diplomatic bind as Eisenhower had been with Cuba. Both presidents had officially taken a position of neutrality, eschewing public support for regime change. Yet in each instance, major covert military projects resulted and in both instances the CIA was designated to manage the combat. It appears that, in the case of Los, the most fundamental lessons of the Cuba Project and the Bay of Pigs were fading, due the demands of the moment. By the end of summer, 1963, the Hmong units were being reorganized from guerrilla teams, into infantry formations directed into conventional military missions. The CIA immediately moved to support those missions with greatly expanded covert air support, including heavy-lift military helicopters to move in weapons authorized by NSAM 249.[425] In one assault a thousand Hmong engaged Pathet Lao forces near the Plain of Jars for over five days. The

In Denial

budget for Hmong support exploded, growing to over $300 million a year.

Yet any covert commitment the United States was prepared to mount was literally being overwhelmed by the massive effort North Vietnam, heavily supplied by the Soviet Union, was conducting using its regular army units. By 1964, what had been a trail was now a corridor containing a series of actual roads; carrying some twenty to thirty tons of supplies each day, and over 9,000 NVA regular army troops had moved down the corridor and into South Vietnam.[426] The North Vietnamese had no concerns over deniability, but President Johnson remained unprepared to overtly commit to conventional warfare in Laos, or to go to Congress to justify it. As for Congress, the Gulf of Tonkin resolution of August, 1964 placed all the onus for expanding combat operations in the region directly on the president, specifically authorizing him to take those military measures required to repel armed attacks against US forces, and repel further aggression. The resolution also referred to the security of Southeast Asia Treaty Organization (SEATO) members, however neither Vietnam nor Laos were formal members of the organization and Laos was a self-declared neutral in the Vietnamese conflict.

With President Johnson retaining the Kennedy era position of neutrality in Laos, the United States became increasingly mired in covert, but expanding conventional military action. In doing so it increasingly found that its surrogate indigenous fighters were facing not only Pathet Lao Guerillas but heavily armed and battle-hardened North Vietnamese Army units. The results would be tragic, proving once again that in conventional warfare the larger, better equipped force almost always prevails. That had been true for the CIA's military operations in Indonesia, in Cuba, in the Congo, and would prove to be true again Laos, and later in Angola and Nicaragua.

The early successes of 1962-1964 did obscure that reality for a time; at first there had been some indication that covert military efforts could produce results in Laos. In 1964 Thai pilots in "Operation Mill Pond" flew covert air missions in southern Laos, using fighter bombers identical to those flown by the Lao Air Force.[427] President Johnson also approved "Operation Barrel Roll," the first covert US military air strikes against the trail inside Laos in 1964. The CIA began "Operation Hardnose," deploying twenty radio-equipped road watch teams to collect intelligence on the Ho Chi Minh trail. The teams themselves were composed of native "irregulars," trained by the Thai PARU teams that Lair had brought into Laos.

The Thais also fielded first four, and later ten, of their own six-man road watch/trail watch intelligence teams, under White Star. What the road watch revealed was that the North Vietnamese were proceeding with an unprecedented building and supply effort and by 1965 the trail had developed into a complex network of roads capable of supporting extensive heavy truck traffic. The amount of supplies moved equaled the total of the previous five years, and some seven North Vietnamese Army (NVA) infantry regiments and twenty battalions came down from the north. Literally hundreds of trucks were moving each direction each week. The only recourse appeared to be increased (but clandestine) action by regular American military units against the corridor.

In March 1965, concurrent with the first major round of American air strikes against North Vietnam ("Operation

Rolling Thunder"), Johnson approved escalated attacks on the trail, with Barrel Roll strikes continuing in the north and a wave of air strikes designated "Operation Steel Tiger" going against the trail in the southern panhandle of Laos. The American Military Assistance Command, Vietnam (MACV) was granted control over strikes in the southern panhandle across the border from Vietnam. Given the official US position on Laotian neutrality, all such operations from South Vietnam were highly secret. From 1965 on, CIA covert military action in Laos would become a matter of increasing surrogate attacks against the Pathet Lao and North Vietnamese and deniable American air strikes against the "trail." Deniability practices as well as the various covers developed for the American efforts burdened military operations while the air effort would grow to be so vast it was literally impossible to conceal.

Military supplies destined for the Hmong were concealed within routine military assistance shipments to Thailand or the Royal Laotian military, and Air America performed challenging and dangerous distribution missions under contract to USAID. It was all very efficient; daily supply flights destined for the Hmong were sent into Laos from Udorn air base in Thailand. Daily Air America missions distributed them from Vang Pao's main base at Long Tieng, dropping rice, foodstuffs, and supplies to Hmong villages. Air America missions also carried combat personnel, advisors, and military supplies out from Long Tieng into field bases (Lima sites) and even into live combat operations. All the Laotian activity occurred with presidential, NSC, and Congressional oversight.[428]

The CIA briefed key legislators who sat on its appropriations subcommittees as well as the senior Congressional leadership. For example, Senator Stuart

Secret Wars With Air Strikes And Tanks?

Symington was routinely briefed on the warfare in Laos by senior CIA officers, including Laos Chief of Station Ted Shackley (reassigned from Cuban operations at the domestic CIA station in Miami). Shackley personally introduced Symington to Vang Pao during a trip Vang Pao made to the United States. Later, during an inspection trip to Southeast Asia, Symington was given a personal tour of Vang Pao's Laotian headquarters at Long Tieng. Yet neither Johnson nor Nixon ever authorized an official CIA project for Laos and Congress never approved a budget for the Laotian secret war. Funds were approved by "small CIA subcommittees of the armed forces committees."[429]

The initial successes of the Hmong, against the Pathet Lao and North Vietnamese security patrols had been encouraging. The Hmong were fighting for their homeland, they didn't flee from combat and into 1965 CIA they stand out as an example of what a highly motivated indigenous force can accomplish. The same success characterized CIA work with the Lao and other tribal irregulars in the south during that same period. However, by 1966, major changes in force structures and combat began to change the dynamic of surrogate warfare in Laos. The North Vietnamese supply routes though eastern Laos began to be defended by full sized North Vietnamese Army groups with units equipped with everything from artillery and tanks to antiaircraft guns. What had begun as a loosely patrolled buffer region, largely controlled by the Pathet Lao, became a tightly organized security zone operated by the regular North Vietnamese Army – a zone expanded by advances into Hmong homeland, across both the Plain of Jars and on the Bolaven Plateau.

North Vietnam responded in force to Johnson's 1966 escalation of American ground combat in Vietnam, as a consequence the surrogate warfare in Laos became increasingly challenging, even in terms of logistics. That year Air America, under contract to the CIA, moved some six thousand tons of supplies a month in support of indigenous forces.[430] A further indication of a changing battle ground and the new military pressures on the Hmong was the deployment of US AC-130 gunships in their support, by the end of that year, US aircraft were being shot down on covert missions within Laos. During 1966/1967 the balance of forces in Laos dramatically shifted. In 1964 the Royal Lao Armed Force numbered 50,000 men plus some 23,000 CIA irregulars (73,000) and they faced 20,000 Pathet Lao and around 11,000 North Vietnamese regulars (31,000). With two to one superiority, even given the poor fighting record of the Royal Laotian Army, the CIA's irregular surrogates were in a viable fight.

Yet by 1968 the Lao government and CIA forces faced an adversary numbering over 100,000 fighters, including some 30,000 regular North Vietnamese infantry. Worse yet, as the North Vietnamese sent in larger and larger units, the Hmong manpower began to bleed away. Even with the maximum American support and aggressive recruiting practices, Vang Pao only managed to field a force of 40,000 potential combatants. Of that number, about 25,000 had to be retained for local defense activities; leaving some 15,000 assigned to special mobile units developed to face ongoing assaults. From 1967 on Vang Pao faced an increasing shortage of manpower, even as he increasingly turned to teenagers during the following three years.[431] As new, regular North Vietnamese Army units continued to enter Laos, the Hmong's only source for combat replacements were younger and younger fighters.

Secret Wars With Air Strikes And Tanks?

The same change in mission and force structures for CIA irregulars was also occurring in the southern Laotian panhandle, although with smaller sized tribal units. When Ted Shackley arrived in 1966 as the new Chief of Station in Laos, he canceled most of the development programs in the south, focusing resources on sending irregulars against the Ho Chi Minh trail. In 1967, CIA irregulars in the south were tasked with a helicopter-inserted attack against a position on the much expanded and improved "trail." That small force of a hundred men attacked with no air support only to suffer an immediate counterattack, being overrun and losing fifteen men. That defeat was small but illustrative of what was happening further north, to the Hmong. The North Vietnamese Army and its Pathet Lao continued the counter attack with a series of purging assaults to suppress any and all guerilla activity.[432] During 1967 the North Vietnamese Army had expanded its security perimeter in the south, overrunning virtually all of the irregular tribal centers the CIA had established in that region.[433]

By 1968 the covert action program that President Kennedy had initiated in Laos – one of intelligence collection, road watch, guerilla assaults and harassment operations – was a thing of the past. Its initial successes were long gone. Beyond that, the calculus of forces had entirely changed, shifting heavily in favor of the Pathet Lao and North Vietnamese. From a purely pragmatic view, North Vietnam didn't need to control the central government or occupy the Laotian capital of Vientiane; they merely needed to secure sufficient territory to fully protect their supply corridor into South Vietnam. That would have been the time to revisit the fundamental mission in Laos, to question from a purely military standpoint whether the mission was failing and whether the concepts of covert action and deniability still made any sense. However, by 1968, military operations in Laos, including the use of American covert ground and air elements, were still being run by the CIA. They were organized and directed by former Miami Station chief, Theodore Shackley, a CIA officer with no military or combat experience at all.

Shackley carried on covert military action in Laos in what can only be considered a single-minded fashion, focused entirely on success. In doing so he displayed an extreme aggressiveness, and a tendency for ordering extremely risky actions, with limited forces. He also demonstrated little apparent regard for either the imbalance in forces or for surrogate combat losses. One particular operation illustrates Shackley's overall approach, which he openly expressed as taking the war to the North Vietnamese. To do so he conceived of the idea of placing irregular forces directly on the North Vietnamese border in north-central Laos. With American Embassy agreement, Lao army forces and irregulars were sent to expand the Nam Bac garrison in northern Laos.

The experienced staff members in the embassy disagreed, as did the "old man" of Laotian covert operations, Bill Lair. Lair told Shackley that the logistics were impossible, and that sending troops to Nam Bac would only provoke an overwhelming counter attack. Given their aggressiveness in the buffer zones, a base only forty-five miles from the North Vietnamese border would be intolerable. Regardless of staff protests, several thousand Laotian Army FAR and a limited number of CIA irregulars were deployed to Nam Bac. The garrison was supplied with howitzers, and promised support in the form of both

Secret Wars With Air Strikes And Tanks?

Laotian and covert American Air Force ground attacks. The US Air Force began large-scale supply drops out of Udorn Thailand, and individual Air America supply missions were also flown.

As predicted, the North Vietnamese Army launched a massive attack on Nam Bac and, less than a month after it had been reinforced, the entire outpost had been totally overrun by the North Vietnamese. No more than a third of over 3,000 Lao troops sent there were ever heard from again. Many of them were recruits, so new to the Lao military that they had no combat experience at all. In contrast, the North Vietnamese Army forces consisted of battle-hardened regulars.[434]

The military reality in Laos had become obvious. Given the force imbalance, the lack of any manpower pool among the Hmong, and the ongoing failures of the Lao Army, Shackley's tough talk about taking the fight to the North Vietnamese suggests that he was either fundamentally incompetent in regard to military operations or in something resembling a state of denial. From that point on the Hmong themselves came under increasing assault in their own homeland. When they were deployed in conventional attacks the irregulars required extensive America air support; American B-52 carpet-bombing strikes would become common in Laos.

Vang Pao's own base at Long Tieng was repeatedly besieged by forces equipped with tanks and artillery; massive air attacks and B-52 bombing was required to stem the assaults. From 1968 on, the "commercial" pilots and flight crews of Air America would increasingly be called on to operate under fire, both in transport and supply missions. More and more frequently they were also requested to fly rescue missions, either for downed American pilots or American special operations personnel trapped by hostile forces. In some instances, entire Hmong villages had to be evacuated by air, as the North Vietnamese began to occupy the Meo homeland.

Objectively, by 1969/1970 there was simply no way for the CIA's irregular forces to perform any substantive military mission; instead of harassing or disrupting North Vietnamese operations they were simply fighting for their lives. The amount of logistics and combat air support required simply to sustain them had grown dramatically. While all the standard practices of "deniability" continued to be followed, consuming time and resources, the thought that American involvement in Laos could be concealed was no better than an illusion, particularly so given that both American military and Air America personnel were increasingly being lost in the Laotian combat.[435]

In short, just as in Cuba, the CIA had been given a military mission that had failed, but instead of acknowledging that, mission creep and inertia had taken over – and so apparently had personal egos. The same "degenerative" cycle that Kirkpatrick described in his Inspector Generals' report of 1964 had set in again within a handful of years.

Once again, in addition to failure, there would be public exposure. The existence of irregular armies was no secret within certain Congressional circles, and neither was the extremity of their combat situation. As the Hmong were driven totally off the Plain of Jars, and as the core of their territory, including Long Tieng, came under attack, the whole indigenous army strategy began looking more questionable to people in Washington. A 1968 CIA

Headquarters memorandum had provided a blunt and accurate assessment of the proxy armies: ."..*the guerrilla operation in the north [of Laos] has survived only on the sufferance of the North Vietnamese. It will continue only as long as the enemy calculates that the harm done to him is not worth the effort to stop it.*"[436]

In 1969 the North Vietnamese made that calculation and sent a full Army regiment plus two additional battalions against the Hmong. In response, the CIA encouraged the Hmong to counterattack and, in the end, brought literally all its Laotian irregulars into the battles - even its surrogate forces from southern Laos were flown into the fight by Air America. More than ten battalions of CIA irregulars were supported by over 200 air strikes a day. That massive effort enjoyed some early success, only to be shattered in the end. The only thing it accomplished was to significantly raise both Congressional and media interest into just what was going on in Laos.

Senator John Cooper began hearings on US involvement in Laos and an amendment was introduced aimed at restricting the use of the American military in Southeast Asia. Equally important, the *New York Times* published a series of articles about American military involvement in Laos. A low-key media response from the Nixon Administration maintained that any such involvement had been extremely limited, so limited that there had been no American military casualties - only 25 "contractors" and one dependent had been lost. The press quickly fact checked that statement, discovering numbers of unexplained American deaths. Embarrassingly, Nixon was forced to backtrack on the earlier statement and admit that 200 Americans had died and 193 were missing in Laos.

In Denial

The scope of American involvement in Laos was further revealed when press touring the USAID office on the other side of the hill from Long Tieng simply walked over the hill. They quickly noted the extensive military operations at the base. The press counted about a dozen transports on the ground, along with ten light planes, a dozen or more unmarked T-28 fighter bombers, and several helicopters. Air traffic was so dense that an air traffic control program was obviously in place, with aircraft holding slots in a landing and takeoff pattern.[437] The revelations about Long Tieng, news of ongoing the B-52 strikes, and the American casualties in Laos fully exposed what had been chartered to be a program of fully deniable covert military action.

While the Nixon Administration was embarrassed, the consequence of the CIA's actions to the Hmong were truly horrendous. In 1970 another 12,000 North Vietnamese Army troops had been sent against them and they were in constant retreat across their homeland. By that March Hmong families were being evacuated from points all across the Meo homeland and Long Tieng was barely being held. At that point the Hmong had fewer than 5,000 fighters available and they were facing a force of some 67,000 North Vietnamese Army regulars. During the course of the year they would take huge casualties, with 1,000 killed and an additional 1,500 wounded—a 50 percent casualty rate. With many of the Hmong having already fled from their villages, they were almost totally dependent on American supply and support.

Yet in Washington, the Hmong appear to have been viewed only as a tool, with Nixon and Henry Kissinger (as national security advisor) ordering repeated Hmong harassment attacks against the North Vietnamese supply corridor; the same fruitless orders were being sent to the other Laotian irregular forces as well. The irregulars were used as a bargaining tool in Kissinger's peace negotiations. A study of the situation in the final years of the Vietnam conflict objectively (but far too politely) describes their treatment "...the plight of the Hmong could perhaps not be ignored...but it would not be the operative factor in Washington's policy decisions."[438] The essentially sacrificial treatment of the CIA's surrogate forces in Laos is fully revealed in a final series of orders from Nixon and Kissinger, orders which directed that a new campaign against North Vietnam be carried out by sending in irregulars as special guerrilla units, to conduct sabotage within North Vietnam. The motive for the missions was strictly political, in support of negotiations with Hanoi. A CIA briefing on those "Commando Raider" operations was surprisingly honest about the operation's goal – describing it as simple harassment of the North Vietnamese, "...to prick the political and military sensitivities within their own borders."[439]

Beyond being largely suicidal for those involved, the Commando Raider assaults illustrated the bravery of the fighters sent into one of the most denied territories on the planet at that time. The raiders did successfully blow up one pipeline and attacked a North Vietnamese divisional army headquarters, as well as other targets. However, the ground infiltrations were extremely lengthy, and in the end only twelve of some twenty-two missions carried out actual attacks. Overall the Commando Raider missions cost $3 million and resulted in twenty-nine casualties for the Laotian irregulars. Official evaluations describe the effort as producing "meager" results with little reason to expect anything more. The penetration project was canceled in May, 1971. As some observers had feared, the remaining

In Denial

Hmong military capability had ended up being little more than a sacrificial element in the final American political negotiations with the North Vietnamese.

Inside Laos, the North Vietnamese responded as had always been expected, totally overrunning the Hmong homeland.[440] When the North Vietnamese Army moved to cross the north–south demilitarized zone and invaded the south, there were few resources left for Laos. Still Kissinger kept pushing (as he would later in Angola) for the Hmong to counter attack. They did so, but there had been no time for any real planning of the assault and virtually all United States air power in the region was consumed in opposing the North Vietnamese invasion of South Vietnam. There was no chance that any last-ditch Hmong effort could be sustained.[441]

From the American perspective, it all came to an end in February, 1973, with a formal cease-fire agreement for Laos. As a part of that agreement, the Hmong forces were to be fully merged with the regular Laotian military. The practical result was that in May, Vang Pao left Long Tieng, and the Hmong came under the oversight of a central government that had little real use for them, even with the CIA funding their integration into the Laotian army. Beyond that, a number of Laotian political factions had a great many scores to settle, and the Hmong had very few friends in the capital of Vientiane. Yet the Hmong did have 250,000 refugees outside their homeland, 12,000 war widows, 16,000 orphans, and 2,000 disabled veterans.

In 1975, following the final massive North Vietnamese move into South Vietnam, Vang Pao was asked to resign. He in turn went to the United States, pleading for help in evacuating those of his people who were the most at risk.

The State Department agreed, but committed to bring out only a few hundred persons.442 Communist forces surrounded Long Tieng, American aircraft evacuated no more than 500 people, and Long Tieng fell. In the end some 2,400 Hmong had been airlifted to Thailand; eventually something like 8,000 made it by themselves across the border as refugees. Ted Shackley, head of the CIA's Far Eastern Division at the time, rejected further pleas to help resettle Hmong refugees, and simply left it as an internal problem for Thailand.443 Some 30,000 Hmong people ended up in Thai refugee camps, and eventually another 55,000 Laotians were resettled in the United States.444 There had indeed been consequences.

"Going North" - Black Operations against North Vietnam

Covert military operations against North Vietnam evolved out of the Eisenhower Administration efforts to oppose communist control in Vietnam following the signing of the Geneva accords of 1954. The accords were a diplomatic agreement (including a ceasefire) intended to resolve the conflicts arising from France's loss of political control over the nations which had been part of its former empire in Indochina. While the United States participated in the negotiations, the Eisenhower Administration refused to sign the final accord, largely due to the fact that it called for a temporary partition of Vietnam until elections could be held and there was American concern that the popularity of the major political figure in Vietnam, Ho Chi Minh, would result in a communist regime in control of the unified nation. His lifelong nationalist struggles against first the French, and then the Japanese occupation, had given him an immense political reach within the Vietnamese public.

In Denial

The Geneva agreement called for a general election to be held by July, 1956, resulting in a unified Vietnamese nation. However, given the earlier, post-World War II, successes of the highly organized communist parties in Eastern Europe, Eisenhower feared that any unified government in Vietnam would quickly come under communist control. In anticipation of the agreement's signing, in June 1954 CIA teams were dispatched from the already established CIA station in Vientiane, Laos. The southern team, primarily a political action effort, was led by a military officer detailed to the CIA, Colonel Edward Lansdale. Lansdale's cover was as a member of the American Saigon Military Mission, which had been established during the earlier American efforts to support the French in their efforts to retain control in Indochina.

A separate covert action team was sent into the North, to the Hanoi and Haiphong regions. That team was led by a veteran CIA paramilitary officer, Lucien Conein. Conein had served with the American Office of Strategic Services (OSS) during the war, operating with the French Resistance movement and afterwards serving in Indochina. The initial mission for Conein's team was not unlike earlier CIA and American military missions that were being carried out in Europe, establishing the framework for opposing new Communist regimes. In the three hundred days left before the national referendum, he was to develop "stay behind" teams to remain should Ho Chi Minh come into power.

In that event, the groups would be directed in covert military actions, conducting sabotage, harassment, and guerilla assaults to destabilize a neutral, or communist leaning government. The concept for such teams had become embedded in CIA practices, based on its earlier efforts in Europe. Officially the CIA had never admitted exactly how badly that effort had failed, with team after team "rolled up" during insertions into denied territories, captured, tortured and/or pressured to broadcast misleading radio reports which only led more teams into captivity. Conein's mission, activated after the partition of Vietnam into North and South, was quite aggressive. Not only was he directed to create political unrest in the North (the base of the Viet Minh nationalist movement under Ho Chi Minh), he was to conduct sabotage operations to destabilize its economy. In preparation for that, he recruited anti-communist volunteers who were sent to a highly secret Navy facility on Saipan, the same facility that had been used to train paramilitary teams for Korea and China, and which were used to train the initial recruits from Tibet.

More than two hundred recruits were trained and infiltrated back into the stream of Viet Minh sympathizers who began moving into the northern zone. Other personnel were covertly infiltrated by both air (Air America) and sea (covert United States Navy missions). A small Navy task group was detailed to support the missions into the north and carried in over eight tons of supplies for the anticipated northern guerrilla actions. The supplies included explosives, pistols, rifles, radios, and ammunition.445 Conein's network was to focus on attacks against transportation, specifically on the northern railroads. Oil for the trains was laced with acid and explosives were concealed in coal to be used in the engines. Some damage was done, but almost all the teams ended up under arrest, then prominently displayed in anti-American show trials.446

In Denial

In the south, Lansdale became heavily involved with political action (primarily political bribes) and anti-communist propaganda. The focus of the CIA mission in the south was to create sufficient fear of what would happen under communist rule to block the pending elections and ensure that at least "South Vietnam" (no such name existed in the Geneva accord) became isolated and independent, thereby blocking the formation of a unified Vietnam (either communist or simply neutral). That first period of political warfare in the south included "dirty trick" propaganda such as planting rumors that Chinese troops had begun moving into the North, aggressively violating Vietnamese villages there. Lansdale also managed to produce rumors that local soothsayers were predicting doom under communism.

While such measures appear trivial in retrospect, Lansdale's political action success was far greater. He personally managed to gain the favor of a Catholic anticommunist leader, Ngo Dinh Diem, and provided major, covert funding for Diem's campaign for leadership in the south. The CIA also funded bribes of more than $3 million to the leaders of rival groups, in turn for their declarations of support for a Diem regime. With American political maneuvering in his support, Diem became secure enough to declare that the south was rejecting the Geneva-mandated referendum, declaring South Vietnam to be an independent state. The initial CIA covert guerilla campaign in the north faded away relatively quickly, leaving efforts focused on political action in the south. During the following years factionalism and a limited communist insurgency (with the Viet Cong) dominated matters in Vietnam just as the same factionalism and a separate communist insurgency (with the Pathet Lao) prevailed in

Secret Wars With Air Strikes And Tanks?

Laos. With inherent weaknesses within the ruling political regimes of both nations, their central governments remained unable to totally deal with the communist rebel groups.

Upon assuming his new office, America's President John F. Kennedy faced resurgent communist pressure in both nations. Kennedy immediately ordered an in-depth review of the Vietnam situation and Edward Lansdale was invited back from Saigon to attend a National Security Council meeting. With his extended experience in Southeast Asia and in Vietnam in particular, Lansdale impressed Kennedy and brought suggestions for bold moves to the discussion. One of those moves proved of special interest to the new president, the idea of covert action against the north as leverage to end their support for the Viet Cong insurgency in the south. Given that the covert action in the north was to be military, but highly deniable and limited in scope, the project was initially assigned to the CIA. On May 11, 1961, Kennedy issued a National Security Action Memorandum (NSAM 52); the directive covered both covert actions to support the Diem regime in the south and assigned the CIA the task of organizing deniable, destabilizing military actions against North Vietnam.

The earlier effort in the north, with Conein's recruits, had been followed by a small number of infiltration missions during 1956–1957, in hopes of contacting anticommunist networks rumored to be in existence. All those efforts proved fruitless, because without exception such networks turned out to be nonexistent.[447] Certainly North Vietnam was going to be an extreme challenge for infiltration activities and one of the fundamentals for success in such operations was, and remains, connecting with an organized resistance movement. That had been true in Europe where both British SAS and the American special operations groups had enjoyed great success in such activities. The same had been true in Indochina where indigenous, nationalist groups had been extremely active against the Japanese occupation. The bad news was that fighters from those same groups, highly organized, well trained, and experienced now constituted the adversary (the Viet Minh) in North Vietnam (as they did in Laos and South Vietnam - the Pathet Lao and Viet Cong)

Beyond that, the native Vietnamese remaining in North Vietnam, or moving there from the South, were by and large supportive of the communist leadership, still highly anticolonial, highly nationalist, and proud of ejecting the French. They also proved to be very observant and routinely reported unknown persons or any sort of abnormal activity; a sighting of a parachute, a suspicious boat, or the appearance of strangers not known to the locals was quickly known to local authorities and security forces. Even the noise of a low flying aircraft, or relatives of local families who suddenly appeared, all routinely triggered security reports. By its very nature, the new communist government in the north was extremely control oriented; it exercised very tight regulation over individual movements throughout the country, especially near the coast and borders. To make matters even more challenging, there was little or no noncommunist commercial traffic across the borders or into port; the use of business covers for infiltration was generally not an option. In the end almost all the individuals and teams sent into the north by the CIA faced having to operate independently, isolated from contacts with the locals that would result in their exposure.

In 1961, based on the initial experiences of Conein's teams, and the lack of success in the few missions attempted against the north more recently, the CIA's Far East Division held no illusions about black operations in North Vietnam. An earlier 1959 memorandum on the subject described such operations as a "complete waste of time." In even stronger language it assessed the probabilities of success as nonexistent, with little hope for recruits or volunteers - "we might as well shoot them."[448] Yet, as we have previously seen, field experience and recommendations often seem to have had little impact on high-level policy decision making, or on commitments by senior CIA officers.

CIA Covert Action against North Vietnam

Saigon CIA Chief of Station William Colby directed the initial covert missions against the north during 1960–1963. The operation was designated as "Project Tiger" and the first agent was sent north across the Demilitarized Zone between the north and south during late 1960. He was never heard from again.[449] To provide deniability, and to compartmentalize covert actions against the North from its activities in the South, a section of the American military support mission (the Combined Studies Group) was used to house the CIA's activities in its northern operations.[450] In further pursuit of secrecy and compartmentalization, the actual agents and agent teams would be inserted into the north by yet another CIA proprietary airline, Vietnamese Air Transport (VIAT), registered in Delaware, and manned with Nationalist Chinese flight crews. With no indigenous resistance inside North Vietnam, the Project Tiger teams were given a very basic mission of simple sabotage and harassment. Colby would characterize Tiger as only a "modest effort," with the longer-term goal of establishing guerrilla operations.[451] To most of the personnel involved it proved to be fatal, rather than "modest."

Beginning in 1961 and continuing through 1963, four to six-man teams of volunteers were inserted in air drops as guerilla fighters. They carried no false identification, had no resistance elements to receive them, and most were dropped into relatively isolated areas. They operated totally independently with no local support and other teams were inserted by slow boats designed and built to resemble local fishing junks, but specially configured for infiltration and sabotage teams. In total thirty teams and several "singleton" individual agents were sent in on sabotage and harassment missions. At the end of the three years it was believed that four teams and one individual might still be operational, or at least not dead or jailed. The rest had been killed, captured, or worse yet, forced ("doubled") to send back radio transmissions requesting follow-on agent and supply drops.

The North Vietnamese success in coercing false transmissions from CIA team radio operators (identical to the CIA experience in Eastern Europe) resulted in a loss of an entire series of teams, gutting the entire operation. The first radio equipped-agent had been captured after two months, the first air-dropped team (Castor) captured and turned after four days, the next (Echo) caught and its radio operator doubled immediately. Team Dido lasted one week in the field and others suffered the same fate. In addition, one supply plane was shot down, junks were captured, and in the end the only notable sabotage success was a frogman attack on two gunboats in June, 1962. [452] The personnel losses for Colby and the supposedly "modest" Tiger Project were brutal: 26 men lost in 1961, 68 in 1963, and no less than 123 in 1963.[453] [454]

At that point Colby did objectively report on the failure of the Tiger Project, even noting that it was having the same lack of success as the earlier missions against Eastern Europe and the Soviet Union. In June, 1963 he advised the CIA's Director of Operations that "no intelligence of value has been or likely will be obtained from such operations."[455] Remarkably, and in another tragic illustration of inertia in covert actions, Colby himself neither suspended nor canceled any of the ongoing black entry or maritime operations sabotage missions – continuing to send in as many teams as could be trained. When Colby met with Defense Secretary Robert McNamara later in 1963, there is no indication that he reported his suspicions that the majority of the Tiger teams had been compromised or that there were serious concerns of security issues within the South Vietnamese side of the program. That concern was later confirmed, but only well after the end of fighting in Vietnam. Only then was it revealed that infiltration team mission information had been routinely passed to North Vietnamese agents by informants within the South Vietnamese military forces.

Given the CIA's performance in the Cuba Project, President Kennedy had seriously begun to consider transferring larger scale covert military operations from the CIA to the Department of Defense and the military. During 1961, the president issued several National Security Action Memorandums (NSAMs 55, 56, and 57), which directed certain changes in covert action operations. In particular, NSAM 55 removed the previously existing exclusive authority given to the CIA in regard to planning and executing deniable military actions. The overall change in role and authority was designated as "Switchback." As part of this change in direction, Kennedy also directed General Lansdale to participate in a study that would generate recommendations for the Joint Chiefs of Staff at the Pentagon, assigning it a new level of responsibility for covert operations. By October 1961, the planned shift of covert paramilitary activities from the CIA to the Army began as Switchback was implemented in Vietnam. The transition would take some time to accomplish.

Switchback represented a significant shift in global responsibility, and required a new command structure under control of the Joint Chiefs of Staff. In February 1962, the Joint Chiefs began implementing the new office of Special Assistant for Counterinsurgency and Special Activities (SACSA). That office and its staff were established inside the Office of Special Operations of the Joint Chiefs of Staff, and its first head was Major General Victor Krulak of the Marine Corps. SACSA would play a role around the world during the 1960s and 1970s. The transfer of covert action against North Vietnam from the CIA to the Army is of interest for several reasons, not the least of which is whether it answered the question of whether a professional military organization can do deniable covert military action more effectively than a professional intelligence organization. In regard to the switch in Vietnam, William Colby personally advised President Kennedy there was no reason to think that military-led denied entry operations in North Vietnam would prove any more productive than the CIA's efforts, either earlier in Eastern Europe or against North Vietnam.

President Kennedy, apparently heavily influenced by Defense Secretary Robert McNamara, was not convinced by Colby's opinion, and authorized the switch in Vietnam.

To McNamara, the former CEO of General Motors, success in covert action was a matter of scale and resource commitment, as with projects in industry. McNamara felt the CIA had been running a minimalist effort (Colby had indeed described it as "modest") with limited resources. Surely the military had the assets, skills, and overall clout to make covert action in denied territories work. In broad terms McNamara's attitude appears to have been that the CIA dabbled in paramilitary operations, but the military were the true professionals.

Military Covert Action against North Viet Nam

The end result of the exchanges was the development of Operational Plan 34A (OPLAN 34A), which outlined a significant escalation of American covert warfare across Southeast Asia. As written, OPLAN 34A plan was comprehensive and aggressive. More would be better; the military would carry the day by applying more resources, more organization, and tighter control. Whether or not President Kennedy would have accepted the plan remains a standing question, before he could review it, Kennedy was tragically killed in Dallas, Texas. Four days later, approval was granted by a new president, Lyndon Johnson. Yet following its approval, a series of policy reviews eliminated elements of the plan related to its more aggressive goals, such as creating resistance movements inside North Vietnam. Concerns were raised that if the US was too obviously active in North Vietnam, the north would escalate its activities in the south. There was once again a fear of triggering some level of Chinese intervention.[456]

Beyond policy limitations, operational realities soon began to make themselves felt, causing a slip well beyond the proposed mission start date of February, 1964. It became clear that the high-level decision makers, including both Secretary McNamara and the Joint Chiefs themselves, had not considered the fact that the Army was going to have to build its own covert operations team in Saigon, and more importantly locate staff to run it. Deniable action simply was not a conventional Army career specialty and the Army did deal with the tactics of guerilla warfare, but in terms of countering it – not conducting it.[457]

Maritime missions against North Vietnam

Actually, the Army was not the only segment of the military to switch into covert action programs against North Vietnam. The CIA had been conducting a series of missions using indigenous junks and small, high powered SWIFT boats to infiltrate agents. The SWIFT boats were fast, and they were armed with both .50 caliber machine guns and .81 mm mortars. However, they had a seriously limited range and could only penetrate a short way along the North Vietnam coast. Yet by 1964 larger and much longer-range fast patrol boats had been added to the operation by the Navy and those boats were operated by a Naval Advisory Detachment, which also trained and prepared crews and Vietnamese commandos for missions against targets in coastal North Vietnam.[458]

The first of the new maritime missions began in February, 1964, and over the next four months deniable attacks were carried out on targets including North Vietnamese patrol boat bases, key bridges, fuel storage facilities, and even North Vietnamese fishing vessels. The initial raids were almost total failures, with a half of the two dozen personnel involved either captured or killed in action. By June the missions began to make some impact, bridges and pumping stations were destroyed, and North Vietnamese naval bases were shelled.[459] Those June successes prompted an aggressive response from the North Vietnamese forces and patrol boats were sent against the raiders.

On the night of July 30, a quick reaction group of four North Vietnamese patrol boats chased South Vietnamese raiders for some 45 nautical miles. On their return north the North Vietnamese boats passed within four miles of the US Destroyer Maddox, which was conducting electronic intelligence in the Gulf of Tonkin.[460] The United States Navy had independently been tasked with conducting electronics and signals intelligence, although research has determined that the American military mission commander in Saigon had specifically requested the Navy patrols collect information on targeted North Vietnamese costal installations.[461] As the pace of the covert maritime raids accelerated, American Navy destroyer patrols were moved inshore, from 20 miles out to only 4 miles off the North Vietnamese Coast.[462] At that point signals intelligence revealed that the North Vietnamese were committed to repelling further raider attacks, and believed that the Navy destroyers had been moved to support the small boat raids. North Vietnamese boats were being mustered near the destroyer's patrol route and intelligence analysts warned that the Maddox was likely to be engaged if it continued its close in shore patrols.

On August 2, as the Maddox proceeded with its mission, Marine signals intelligence units in the South intercepted radio traffic and orders indicating that the North Vietnamese thought the Maddox was supporting new raids and they were preparing to engage the destroyer. A warning message was sent to all commands and a tactical

In Denial

warning was sent to destroyer Maddox. What followed was in no sense a surprise attack; signals intelligence provided a complete picture of the incident.[463] Three North Vietnamese patrol boats attacked the Maddox, causing no significant damage, but themselves taking casualties and heavy damage from Maddox gunfire and attacks by Navy jets called to provide air support for the destroyer.

In a show of resolution, the American destroyer patrols continued and accelerated the pace of the deniable maritime attacks on the North Vietnamese. On the evening of August 3, three South Vietnamese boats attacked a North Vietnamese military garrison and a radar site. Some 770 rounds of high explosive were fired during the attacks and in total four separate maritime attacks on North Vietnamese military targets were made over five days.[464] During that time, the American destroyer patrol commander had moved his ships further offshore to provide maneuvering room in case of attack. He was also concerned about reports from both the American destroyers involved in the patrols because each was experiencing technical problems with their radars; the Maddox's air search radar and the Turner Joy's fire control radars were both inoperative. While no specific signals were intercepted in regard to pending attacks, it began to be assumed that the North Vietnam would again target the destroyers.

Operating at night and anticipating a night attack, the destroyers began to report a variety of air and surface contacts. The destroyers opened fire on a number of tenuous radar and visual sightings. The carrier Ticonderoga dispatched a Navy jet to the scene, the pilot easily located both destroyers – quite visible by their wakes – but found no sign of any other vessels in the area. Navy

Commander James Stockdale, in the air over the destroyers was adamant: "*I had the best seat in the house to watch that event and our destroyers were just shooting at phantom targets—there were no PT boats there . . . there was nothing there but black water and American firepower.*"[465]

    In the dark and with a mix of chaotic and intermittent radar, sonar, and visual observations, both American destroyers continued to fire on perceived targets, and reported themselves under attack. The incident occurred over some two hours, and within three hours the Maddox commander transmitted an after-action report advising that the Maddox had never positively identified an enemy vessel. However, despite repeated advice from the field commanders, President Johnson responded by ordering a series of air attacks on North Vietnam and Congress passed legislation which led to a major expansion of the American military commitment in Vietnam. At that point, further covert, deniable missions against North Vietnam were conducted against the background of full-scale American air and ground warfare, including massive aerial strikes inside North Vietnam. Yet rather than revisiting the reality of further guerilla action in the North, senior policy makers simply left the Army to continue with its original mission, as if nothing had changed.

    In turn, the Army officers newly assigned to the mission had come into covert action with no particularly relevant experience, and something of a lukewarm attitude towards it: "*It was all a guess and by golly, step by step type of operation,*" observed Colonel Clyde Russell, the first of some five chiefs of Military Assistance Command, Vietnam Studies and Observations Group (MACVSOG). [466] He elaborated that he and the other officers assigned simply had no background or training in "denied area" operations. They felt that it should have been obvious it would take time for them to learn how to operate in that sort of environment.467 Russell was supported by only thirteen CIA personnel during 1964, primarily psychological warfare officers – the experienced CIA paramilitary and covert operations people were rapidly being assigned to new CIA projects in the south.468 As the war expanded during the next two years, the Army did add certain improvements to covert air insertion and supply, more efficiently inserting teams into the North. However, the results on the ground proved little different than the CIA's preceding three years of failed efforts.

The Army continued with the CIA's recruits, then formed and sent in new teams to follow them. Nothing changed in either in terms of practices or operations, and again, time after time, the South Vietnamese teams were killed, captured, or doubled by the North Vietnamese. By 1966 the Army was forced to accept that sabotage and guerilla operations inside North Vietnam were simply not feasible. At that point the ground mission was limited to putting in teams for road watch, monitoring the feeder routes to the Ho Chi Minh corridor. Yet that proved a huge challenge, continuing the program was simply producing more casualties. Ultimately research determined that not a single one of the long-term agents infiltrated into the north had successfully made it back out of North Vietnam alive!469

Secret Wars With Air Strikes And Tanks?

Notes

[409] Peter Kornbluh, *Bay of Pigs Declassified; The Secret Report On The Cuba Invasion*, The New Press, New York, 1998, 6-7

[410] Robert M. Gillespie, *Black Ops, Vietnam: The Operational History of MACVSOG* (Annapolis, MD, Naval Institute Press, 2011), 39

[411] John Prados, *William Colby and the CIA: The Secret Wars of a Controversial Spymaster* (Lawrence, KS: University Press of Kansas, 2009), 171–172

[412] John F Kennedy, *Public Papers of the Presidents of the United States, 1961-1963, Volume 1, 8*

[413] John Newman, *JFK and Vietnam*, Western Books Inc., New York, New York, 1992, 10-11

[414] Charles A. Stevenson, *The End of Nowhere; American Policy Towards Laos Since 1954*, Beacon Press, Boston, 1973, 142

[415] Harry Felt, message to CP, quoted in Edward Marold and Oscar Fitzgerald, *The United Stations Navy and the Vietnam Conflict*, Washington DC US Government Printing Office, 1986, 60

[416] John Newman, *JFK and Vietnam*, Chapter One, "Straight to the Brink over Laos," 9-23

[417] Charles A. Stevenson, *The End of Nowhere; American Policy Towards Laos Since 1954*, 301-302 also Walt Rostow interview of Richard Neustadt, April 11, 1964, as cited in Arthur Schlesinger, *A Thousand Days; John F Kennedy in the White House*, 315

418 Edward Marold and Oscar Fitzgerald, *The United Stations Navy and the Vietnam Conflict*, 69; apart from inserting American troops the logistics problem of supplying them – almost entirely by air – was far beyond the immediately available resources in the region, and would remain so for up to at least the first two weeks.

419 John Newman, *JFK and Vietnam*, 51 and 62 end note #18

420 Ibid, 53

421 Thomas L. Ahern, Jr., *Undercover Armies: CIA and Surrogate Warfare in Laos 1961–1973* (The Center for the Study of Intelligence, CIA History Staff, 2006), 23.

422 Ibid., 184

423 Richard Secord and Jay Wurts, *Honored and Betrayed: Irangate, Covert Affairs, and the Secret War in Laos* (New York: Wiley & Sons, Inc., 1992), 59

424 For further details on American military activities in Laos, readers are referred to the definitive work on special military operations in Vietnam and Laos, *Black Ops, Vietnam* by Robert Gillespie; and *Honor Denied: The Truth about Air America and the CIA,* by Allen Cates (Bloomington, IN: iUniverse, 2011).

425 Ibid., 117

426 Ibid., 45

427 Ibid., 100

428 Ibid, 56–57

[429] John Prados, *Presidents' Secret Wars: CIA and Pentagon Covert Operations from World War II Through the Persian Gulf War* (Chicago: Ivan R. Dee, Inc., 1996), 273–274

[430] Ibid., 281

[431] Ibid., 282

[432] Thomas Ahern, *Undercover Armies*, 252

[433] Ibid., 144–145

[434] David Corn, *Blond Ghost: Ted Shackley and the CIA's Crusades* (New York: Simon & Schuster, Inc., 1994), 153–155

[435] Allen Cates, *Honor Denied*, 94–107. Due to the practice of deniability, the losses of the Air America personnel were never acknowledged; a listing of their actual losses has only recently become fully available and is documented in Cates's writings on Air America.

[436] Ibid., 300

[437] John Prados, *Presidents' Secret Wars*, 290–291

[438] Thomas Ahern, *Undercover Armies* 431

[439] Ibid., 349–351

[440] Ibid., 428. A CIA headquarters memorandum of 1972 notes that many in the State Department had been saying for some six years that "the North Vietnamese military moves in North Laos been strictly reactive."

[441] Ibid., 461–462

442 Thomas Ahern, *Undercover Armies*, 511–515

443 Ibid., 516–517

444 John Prados, *Presidents' Secret Wars*, 296

445 John Prados, *William Colby and the CIA: The Secret Wars of a Controversial Spymaster* (Lawrence, KS: University Press of Kansas, 2009), 64

446 Stanley Karnow, *Vietnam: A History*, 221–222

447 Ibid.7

448 Thomas L. Ahern, Jr., *The Way We Do Things: Black Entry Operations into North Vietnam, 1961-64,* Center for Intelligence Studies, May, 2005, 57

449 John Prados, *William Colby and the CIA*, 74–75

450 Richard Shultz, *The Secret War Against Hanoi* 4–6

451 Ibid., 28–29

452 Thomas Ahern, *The Way We Do Things,* 13–27

453 John Prados, *William Colby and the CIA*, 80

454 Ibid., 44–5

455 Thomas Ahern, *The Way We Do Things*, 41

456 Shultz, *The Secret War Against Hanoi*, 37–40

457 Robert M. Gillespie, *Black OPS Vietnam: The Operational History of MACVSOG,* Naval Institute Press, 2011

458 Robert M. Gillespie, *Black OPS Vietnam: The Operational History of MACVSOG*, 20-21

459 Pat Patterson, Lieutenant Commander, United States Navy, "The Truth About Tonkin," *Naval History Magazine*, Volume 22, number 1, February 2008
http://www.usni.org/magazines/navalhistory/2008-02/truth-about-tonkin

460 Robert Gillespie, *Black Ops Vietnam: The Operational History of MACVSOG*, (Annapolis, Maryland, Naval Institute Press, 2011), 23

461 Robert Hanyok, "Skunks, Bogies, Silent Hounds and Flying Fish: The Gulf of Tonkin Mystery 2-4 August 1964," *Cryptologic Quarterly*, National Security Administration, 5
http://www2.gwu.edu/~nsarchiv/NSAEBB/NSAEBB132/relea00012.pdf

462 Robert Gillespie, *Black Ops Vietnam: The Operational History of MACVSOG*, 24-25

463 Ibid, 14

464 Pat Patterson, Lieutenant Commander, United States Navy, "The Truth About Tonkin"

465 Jim and Sybil Stockdale, *In Love and War*, (Annapolis Maryland, Naval Institute Press, 1990), 5-8

466 Richard Shultz, *The Secret War Against Hanoi*, 42–42

467 Ibid. 37–38. Shultz also points out that army doctrine and training were oriented strictly towards the use of guerrilla operations in support of conventional warfare and that even the Special Forces personnel assigned to MACVSOG were trained

for counterinsurgency as part of maintaining "friendly" regimes, not clandestine warfare to undermine hostile regimes in denied territories.

[468] Ibid, Chapter 2, 40-65

[469] Ibid., 58

Chapter 10: In Search of Deniability

National leaders turn to covert military action for two simple reasons, as an alternative to openly engaging a perceived adversary with conventional forces (and running the risk of escalation to large scale warfare) and in pursuit of deniability – both in consideration of domestic politics and international relations. One constant in all such actions is that they are designed and executed with the intent of concealing national sponsorship in order to enable official government deniability. In exploring decades of American covert military actions, we examined the standard measures taken in pursuit of deniability. Those measures included concealment of funding, proscriptions against the participation of both CIA and US military personnel and the use of weapons and equipment that could not be traced back to either the CIA or the American military. Perhaps the most challenging practice of all was recruiting and "managing" surrogate combatants in military actions in which Americans were not supposed to be directly involved.

Over the decades huge amounts of money, logistics effort, and administrative recourses were devoted to establishing and maintaining the proscribed deniability for covert projects – an especially demanding task in regard to covert military action. Elaborate commercial and financial covers were created through proprietary companies and financial structures established and operated by the CIA. Special units of the Air Force and even of the Joint Chiefs of Staff were created to support deniable CIA activities, military personnel were detailed from regular service and put under cover within the CIA, and the CIA itself turned to contract personnel and foreign recruits for paramilitary training and in some instances actual combat missions.

Yet in spite of all that effort and of constant orders by presidents, from Eisenhower on, to "keep the hand of the United States from showing" we have seen strange, inconsistent behavior on the part of the CIA itself, starting from its earliest years by leaking confidential information on its Iranian coup success seemingly only in the interest of promoting the Agency's own reputation. We saw statements from its own senior officers declaring that the Cuba Project was actually "technically deniable" - or even more strikingly, that "we [the CIA] cannot conduct an operation where political decisions are going to interfere with military judgement." In terms of deniability practices themselves, we have also seen considerable inconsistency, verging on the ridiculous in certain instances.

In the case of the US Navy support for the amphibious landings at the Bay of Pigs, sailors on American destroyers were ordered to wear civilian clothes, the ship's hull numbers were painted over, and the national ensign was taken down, burned, and then the "tattered remains" hoisted – ostensibly disguising the destroyer as a "Central American ship." US Navy jets operating from the carrier Essex were repainted a solid gray, with all markings obscured - whose jet attack bombers they were supposed to be is unclear.[470] The ships in the operation were even ordered to burn all communications traffic logs on a daily basis. Yet at the same time all that was occurring, regular

Secret Wars With Air Strikes And Tanks?

US Army tanks – only in active service with the American Army – were being landed on the beaches.

United States deniability in the amphibious landings in Cuba was simply an illusion, as much so as denying American sponsorship of the Guatemalan coup with a US Navy task force sitting off shore and conducting a naval blockade of all shipping. Other examples of American exposure include the CIA's delivery of weapons and arms to rebels in Indonesia with US markings on the crates and routing numbers showing them having been processed at the huge American airbase in the Philippines, the B-52 bombing raids over Laos and Cambodia[471], the provision of US Navy developed mines to CIA surrogate forces in Nicaragua[472], and the shipment of American shoulder launched Stinger antiaircraft missiles to CIA sponsored fighters in Afghanistan.[473] Historically, the temptation to deniable action has led to some extremely complex practices in its pursuit, and in more contemporary times, to some quite simple alternatives. In this final chapter we will explore both complex and simple deniability measures in detail, evaluating both the resources devoted to such efforts, and the end results and consequences for each approach.

Autonomous Action against Cuba – Project AMWORLD

The original Cuba Project had been a disaster for the United States, Fidel Castro's grip on Cuba had been strengthened, the Soviet Union had assumed a far stronger role in Cuban (and Latin American affairs), and in 1962 the Cuban Missile Crisis had resulted in an official assurance that that the United States would not conduct conventional military action against Cuba.[474] Yet a declared communist

In Denial

regime, still with Russian military support, was in place some ninety miles off the coast of the United States. It continued to represent both a major national security concern, and a major political exposure for the Kennedy presidency. It was the sort of quandary that leads national leaders to the option of covert action, and during 1963 that was exactly what happened, with the Kennedy Administration committing itself to yet one more deniable effort to oust Fidel Castro from power in Cuba. Given the circumstances, the new effort was to be extraordinarily deniable, with extreme efforts taken to conceal any American involvement. Fortunately, the documents now available allow us another unique view into covert operations in one of the most sophisticated efforts ever undertaken to achieve total deniability.

As of 1963, any new covert military action against Cuba was going to have to be exceptionally deniable in all its aspects, including funding, equipment, logistics, and personnel. Certainly, it would have to be totally isolated from any indication that it was being supported by American personnel, from American bases (or even from the continental United States) or with American funding; money for its activities would have to appear as coming from other nations, either in Latin America or Europe. Those were the criteria that were to drive the new CIA covert operation, developed during 1963 and conducted over some three years. Kennedy left the military project (AMWORLD) assignment with the CIA; its activities were to be relatively limited – sabotage and harassment assaults. [475] A separate CIA political action project (AMTRUNK)[476] was created, with the goal of actually bringing about a military coup against the Castro regime. The AMWORLD military project was to be largely a matter of using high profile attacks to demonstrate that Cuban opposition to Castro was still very much alive.

The thrust of what was referred to as the "autonomous group" approach was the creation of a relatively small, but extremely well-equipped, Cuban exile military group, whose missions would primarily be of a naval nature. The Kennedy Administration was willing to trade the types of direct control normally found in CIA covert action for increased deniability and aggressiveness. A very small and highly compartmentalized CIA unit supported the autonomous group effort with logistics, intelligence, and training, but it would not be in charge of actual military operations. Recruiting, mission planning, personnel assignments, and the assaults themselves would all be under total control of the small Cuban paramilitary force. CIA logistics support was going to involve providing money, contacts, and introductions to vetted CIA companies and weapons vendors.

The AMWORLD group would operate from Caribbean bases, supplied and provided with the ships and aircraft to conduct military operations against Cuba. In the context of autonomous action, the CIA officers assigned to work with the group functioned as advisors and administrative support. The CIA AMWORLD support staff was extremely small, Henry Hecksher (a veteran of the Guatemala, Laos, and Cuba projects) played the lead role, with oversight from an office in Washington D.C. He also provided political and media advice for the group's leaders, headed by Manuel Artime, another familiar figure from the original Cuba Project. Carl Jenkins (paramilitary trainer for the Cuba Project) assisted in arranging training, coordinating contacts, and support for the Artime led effort.

In Denial

The autonomous group strategy evolved over five months beginning in the spring of 1963, following the release of the Brigade 2506 prisoners who had been taken captive at the Bay of Pigs. Attorney General Robert Kennedy had been very much involved in negotiating the return of the prisoners, and that solidified his personal relationships with a number of exile leaders including Manuel Artime. Artime personally met with both Robert Kennedy and President Kennedy and maintained those contacts during the early months of 1963. Artime also made trips to Central America in March and May, soliciting aid for a new anti-Castro effort. The March trip took him to avowedly anticommunist regimes in Nicaragua, Costa Rica, Honduras, and Venezuela asking for financial aid as well as access to bases that could be used for efforts against Castro.

In addition to his outreach for international support, Artime criticized the CIA for earlier "over-controlling" the Cuban exiles, essentially micromanaging all their activities against Castro.[477] In his conversations with the Kennedy's and with various CIA officers he promoted the concept of a more "cooperative" relationship, one in which the CIA would furnish advice and funds as well as assist in logistics and making arms available. The caveat was that any such new effort would have to be totally from outside the United States.[478] His views proved to be a good match to the thinking about a new, very covert project, and in May the concept for the new project was authorized. In an early success Artime reached agreements for operating facilities in Nicaragua and Costa Rica, both countries with regimes having close ties to the US. By the end of July, he was deeply involved in the initial stages of personnel selection, and the creation of draft purchasing lists for supplies, weapons, and equipment, including a variety of naval vessels.

The CIA had reserved the right to give Artime and his officers' advice, and if necessary raise issues, but there was one caveat: "the stipulations…were designed to obtain one single purpose; namely, to make sure that 'no one can say you and your group are being run by Americans.'"[479] In terms of logistics, the plan was to equip his group with weapons and military equipment by way of clandestine transfer to Artime through the Nicaraguan government. Purchases would be financed with money from the US government, not the CIA itself. The relationship was to be quite simple, "We'll give you [Artime] the money and they get the arms."[480]

A Swiss bank account was established for Artime, to provide funds for operating expenses as well as for reimbursements to third parties for the purchase of supplies and equipment. Over the span of the project some $7 million was directed towards Artime's accounts.[481] Working accounts were opened in both the name of Artime and a personal friend, Sixto Mesa, who had been secretary of finance for Artime's own counterrevolutionary group *Movimiento de Recuperación Revolucionaria (* Movement to Recover the Revolution/MRR); the accounts were to be maintained at an amount of $25,000 each.

Two and perhaps three Swiss accounts were required because Artime needed a small base of operations inside the United States. A Miami office was used for covert personnel contacts ("letter drops"), and the purchase of materials only available domestically. In the interest of deniability and compartmentalization, separate accounts and funds were used for domestic US vs. off shore operations and money from the Swiss accounts was transferred using a financial "cutout," at the First National Bank of Miami. The Bank was well known to the CIA, described as an institution "with which HQS [headquarters] Monetary Branch maintains special relations."[482]

The CIA staff assigned to AMWORLD included Hecksher and his secretary, Jenkins, and no more than half a dozen administrative and logistics personnel.[483] It was isolated from other Cuban related activities which were conducted out of the CIA station in Miami. That may have been just as well, because senior officers at the Miami station were less than excited about the whole autonomous group idea. Miami station chief Shackley made no effort to hide his appraisal, "The whole operation was set up as a result of Artime's discussion with the Kennedy's; I was asked my opinion of it and I said it was a lousy idea…the whole thing was an exercise in futility."[484] Artime was covertly given access to American military bases and personnel for recruiting, but at the same time he was publicly denying any connection to the American government. That did produce a good bit of confusion within certain US military units, and they became more than a little interested in finding out exactly what was going on with their trainees.

One report from the 112th Military Intelligence Group gives a good insight to the story line being used with the AMWORLD project. Its report states that Artime was obviously recruiting for a revolutionary camp in Nicaragua. He was quoted as telling recruits that the US government was not going to do anything for Cuba, and that he had obtained aid and instructors from Europe. Recruiters working with Artime reinforced that message in separate contacts with the recruits, telling them that they could no longer rely on America and were turning to other countries for weapons, funding, and bases.

Artime's cover story included his purported feelings that the U. S. had decided to coexist with Cuba but the good news for the exiles was that a Latin American country was buying planes from England for Artime and had promised its support for his military operations. The Somoza government was very involved and the group would have bases in Nicaragua. Artime and other leading Cuban exiles had recently had meetings with Somoza and had gained his personal support. Overall Artime's cover story was a credible one for the public.

On the other hand, certain US Army and Air Force commands were rightly confused in receiving high level orders allowing him to recruit trainees for a project ostensibly at odds with official American policy. Establishing the autonomous action cover story, without any reference to American support, was also a personal challenge for Artime. Numerous AMWORLD memoranda from Hecksher and Jenkins deal with the cover story and give advice to Artime on how to maintain it, especially with the press. In order to do so he was expected to be highly visible, soliciting independent support for his campaign and appealing to anticommunist groups and corporate interests, all while complaining about a lack of any official American administration support.

It was clear from the beginning that Artime's military actions were going to be largely naval in nature. He was going to need serious maritime assets and his activities would require at least one relatively large "mother ship," and there would also be a need for a variety of smaller transport/landing craft as well as for attack boats of the "swift" type - light naval craft fitted for exceptional speed. Setting up that sort of naval force while leaving absolutely no paper trail to the CIA or the United States was a challenge, it ended up taking the better part of a full year. The first vessel acquired for Artime's force was the Colombia-registered *Olga Patricia,* a light cargo ship. It had originally been built for the Army, later acquired by the Navy and in the summer of 1963 was sitting in Biscayne Bay Harbor off Miami.[485] Artime turned the purchasing and supply activity over to his newly designated Secretary of Finance, Manuel Gutierrez. The CIA assisted by advising Gutierrez that the purchase of the *Olga Patricia* could be facilitated by contacting the "Ads & Cargo Corp." Apparently Ads & Cargo of Miami was yet another CIA proprietary, possibly for leases and charters of temporary-use assets.[486] The purchase of the ship, and other maritime resources, was to be conducted through a newly established Artime commercial front, a Panamanian company named Maritima BAM.

Another transport vessel was identified, apparently for charter rather than purchase.[487] The *Joanne* was berthed in Baltimore and it was ideal for hauling and/or barge-towing activity for large military cargo. A Cuban exile crew had to be recruited as the ship would be an "operational" vessel, used to carry not only military supplies but combat personnel.[488] When the *Joanne* sailed out of Baltimore it covertly exfiltrated (in a concealed cargo hold) one of Artime's new combat teams, designated the "black nine." It also carried several electrical generators, two radio sets, and fourteen silenced pistols with some 1,400 rounds of ammunition. The ship's destination was Artime's new base at Tortuguero, Costa Rica.[489]

Secret Wars With Air Strikes And Tanks?

Artime needed large quantities of military equipment, but he was to be operating from very isolated bases that lacked port facilities and that meant barges and landing craft were also going to be required. Finding a barge was relatively easy: JMWAVE had a list of known suppliers in Florida. Using CIA cutouts, Artime's people were referred to a "vetted" marine supplier in Tampa who would lease an appropriate barge. The landing craft were a bit more challenging; they had to be purchased through a military cutout and that was accomplished by using Artime's Costa Rican contacts to purchase two LCMs for the sum of $120,000. The transaction was made through the Cooper-MacDonald National Marine Bank in Baltimore, and the vessels were to be delivered to the Nicaraguan National Guard.[490]

Then there were the smaller transport craft and attack boats. For those the CIA also turned to the US military, and four vessels were supplied. Of the four, one came from the Navy and the other three from the Air Force; two in service craft were transferred from a location in Miami and a third (declared surplus) from Port Canaveral in Florida.[491] While Artime's new maritime force was being put into place, arrangements also proceeded to obtain the quantity of weapons and ammunitions that would be needed.

AMWORLD documents show that to obtain deniable weapons for Artime, the CIA turned to one of its standard overseas sources of the period, Interarms/Interarmco (International Armament Corporation).[492] By November of 1963, a comprehensive list of desired military weapons had been prepared, ranging from rifles to four-barrel cannons. There were some problems in that Interarmco did not have all the items on the list, in particular certain Czech and Russian weapons that had been included. Artime's own personnel appear to have actually gone to Europe to work through those issues.

By mid-December some $80,000 had already been sent to Interarmco and accepted in payment for the first shipment.493 The balance of the purchase, some $240,000 worth, was to be due upon delivery. A total sum of $326,262.82 was to go into Interarmco's bank, the Banque Genevoise de Commerce in Geneva, Switzerland.494 Delving into all these commercial details is a bit tedious, however it illustrates the amount of work, the amount of money, and the extent of the "cut-outs" required to set up what was in truth a rather modest maritime guerilla unit – one operating outside the United States, ostensibly with foreign sponsors, but in reality with nothing but agreements for remote, undeveloped bases. The quest for an absolutely autonomous and deniable operation proved to be extremely expensive, and time consuming.

As to the personnel for the guerrilla force, recruiting proved to be relatively easy, however the need to create covers and arrange transportation so that the individuals could be covertly sent to Nicaragua and Costa Rica also proved exceptionally time consuming. Many of Artime's recruits were individuals well known to him, and to us, from the initial Cuba Project. They included Felix Rodriquez and Segundo Borges Ransola, individuals who appear to have been involved in the February/March 1961 infiltration missions that included plots for sniper attacks on Fidel Castro. Both had been among the earliest anti-Castro volunteers to go into the Panama and Guatemala training camps with Carl Jenkins. In the summer of 1963, Segundo Borges joined Manual Artime for a recruiting trip to Fort Benning, Georgia; he later became the leader of one of Artime's AMWORLD commando teams.495

Secret Wars With Air Strikes And Tanks?

Another of the earliest 1963 AMWORLD recruits was Carlos "Batea" Hernandez (Cuban Brigade trainee 2523). Hernandez was a black belt in Judo and a sharpshooter and it was his expertise in Judo and his friendship with Artime that led to Artime to request Hernandez as his personal bodyguard while Artime was traveling in Latin America early in 1960. Carlos Hernandez also trained in Panama and Guatemala and was moved first to the Belle Chasse camp and then into the 1961 maritime infiltration missions.[496] Rodriquez, Borges, and Hernandez illustrate the quality of Artime's recruits; the AMWORLD personnel were experienced and extremely well trained in all facets of guerilla operations.

The AMWORLD project had been approved with the caveat that it was to be completely autonomous in terms of funding, equipment, bases, personnel and operations. To a great extent that was achieved, although it took more than a year to reach the point of it being able to launch actual missions against Cuba. Yet with all the work on disconnecting it from the CIA, its personnel remained quite closely connected to the Cuban community in Miami. During 1964 and 1965 the AMWORLD Cubans maintained a relatively large office and staff in Miami, and key personnel were allowed to rotate from the offshore camps back and forth to Miami - gossip and rumors about a secret American operation against Castro once again became rife.

Word had begun to spread about some sort of new effort against Cuba from almost from the beginning. In July, 1963 the *Miami News* carried an article by Hal Hendrix titled "Backstage with Bobby." Hendrix wrote about Robert Kennedy's activities in reaching out to Cuban exiles in regard to new military actions against Cuba. Two days later Hendrix interviewed Artime, focusing on possible connections between RFK, who he had been publicly associated with him, and Artime's new, self-proclaimed effort to create a new military effort based outside the United States.

Artime stayed on script with the approved AMWORLD story line, talking about gaining new support from wealthy Latin American citizens, anti-communist political parties, and Central American governments. He adamantly denied any support from RFK or the US, yet regardless of the denials, the newspaper stories had established the context for some sort of relationship between Artime and the Kennedy Administration and other reporters continued to aggressively pursue that story. The early exposure was discouraging and it was discussed as an issue at Special Group meetings and viewed as an extremely serious matter. Yet other than continuing denial, little could be done after the fact and the media would be watching for US government connections to Artime.

Given his earlier experiences in the CIA Cuba projects, senior AMWORLD Project officer Henry Hecksher was quite aware of such media issues and was very much concerned about operational security. So much so that in arranging for two field officers to support the logistics of delivering boats and aircraft, he added another element to their assignment. Along with their support role, the officers were also directed to evaluate the degree of operational security being practiced by the Cuban personnel. The first individual assigned in the dual role was US Air Force Lt. Colonel Manny Chavez, detached from the CIA's Miami station (JMWAVE) to support the AMWORLD effort in October 29, 1963.

Secret Wars With Air Strikes And Tanks?

Chavez had served as a US Air Attaché in ten Latin American countries including El Salvador, Honduras, Nicaragua, Costa Rica, Peru, Bolivia, Venezuela, the Dominican Republic, and Haiti. He had been the American military attaché to the Guatemalan government at the time of the CIA's Guatemala Project. Later he was attached to the American Embassy in Venezuela, serving there during 1957-1959 with CIA officer David Morales, another veteran of the Guatemala project.[497] The two men were then assigned to the initial Cuba Project and shared desks for a time at the CIA's Miami station, both serving in Miami from 1960 – 1964. By late 1963, Morales was involved in providing training support for the AMWORLD project, for both Artime and his senior officer, Rolando Quintero.

Chavez's roles in the early months of AMWORLD were threefold. He assisted with the logistics of moving major pieces of equipment and shipments of weapons for the project, he appears to have done some contact work to set up the logistics for the project's air support, and he was quietly but directly charged with monitoring and reporting on the operational security of the project. Chavez worked on air logistics in the early days of the project, assisting with both aircraft purchases, and the establishment of covers for the foreign operation of the aircraft. In November 1963, Chavez (using the pseudonym of Mr. Sambora aka "the Mexican") traveled to Mexico City, meeting with Mexican Air Force officers and also consulting with the point man for AMWORLD media/propaganda outreach in Central America, David Phillips, who had been the former head of propaganda for the Cuba Project.[498]

Chavez was also involved in coordinating the logistics of the transfer of the weapons purchased from Interarmco and shipped from Europe. His logistics work gave him considerable insight into the use of the covers being provided by the CIA as well as the internal communications among the Cubans involved in the project. Considerable caution was taken in introducing Chavez into the project, ostensibly in a support role, but in reality, as an observer ("penetration agent") within the group, tasked with reporting on it.[499] His reports include observations on the security, effectiveness, and leadership involved in AMWORLD operations, and those reports became increasingly unfavorable as the first months of the project passed.

Colonel Napoleon Valeriano was also assigned to propaganda and psychological warfare activities in support of the AMWORLD project. He had a long history with the CIA including paramilitary activities and covert actions supporting psychological warfare. Valeriano had served in the Philippines, and under Carl Jenkins in the Cuba project, at both the Panama camp and the Guatemala training base. Apparently, Chavez's negative AMWORLD assessments were shared by Valeriano, as well as by David Morales in Miami, who independently reported back to CIA headquarters on personal issues with Artime (pseudonym Dr. Gonzalez) which threatened to compromise security of the project. In a familiar vein, the early complaints from all three officers were simply filed, in the interest of getting on with the assaults. Within eight months inertia was already setting in at AMWORLD – getting the teams operational had become the priority.

In spring 1964, with considerable logistics help from the CIA, the initial Artime maritime operation was in place at Monkey Point in Nicaragua. A paramilitary camp had also been set up at Puerto Cabezas in Costa Rica, where

Secret Wars With Air Strikes And Tanks?

Artime's people were sharing the use of a private airstrip with the brother of the owner. The brother was running his own air operation, which involved whiskey smuggling, at the time that seemed of little concern, but would ultimately produce some major headaches for Artime. In addition, a refueling base had been established in the Dominican Republic and overall some 300 men were involved in AMWORLD operations. Those operations included the use of a pair of 250 foot "mother ships," two Swift attack boats, one C-47 transport aircraft, and two Cessna light aircraft. By mid-1964, AMWORLD was just beginning to carry out attacks against Cuba. However, Chavez's reports on Artime and the project as a whole were becoming increasingly troubling - in all aspects, from leadership to security.500 Yet while Chavez's assessments of operations, security and leadership were accepted at headquarters, pursing the mission continued to be given the priority. CIA headquarters actually characterized the security of the project as "deplorable"; a key criticism given that the project had been established on the fundamental premise of extreme security and deniability.

Yet rather than elevating the security issue, project leadership chose to focus on autonomy over deniability. In an attempt to preserve Chavez's full role as a "penetrating agent," he was directed to do no more than confront Artime and demand a fuller role in what was viewed as Artime's project - with access files, bases, and all operational information. Chavez was even obliquely criticized for compromising his position by being too demanding and confrontational with Artime over issues such as security. The upshot of what had become a fundamental problem for an exceptionally covert project was that Artime was simply counseled, and Chavez was given the approval to transfer out of the AMWORLD project entirely, at his discretion.[501] It appears that he chose that option within only a few months.

During the latter half of 1964 and through 1965, Artime's maritime commandos staged some fourteen missions, with only four of them being at least partially successful.[502] Actually their very first mission, in May 1964, (an attack on the Pilón sugar mill in Oriente Province) turned out to be their only major operational success. That mission destroyed several warehouses and up to seventy tons of sugar, worth $1 million in desperately needed revenue for Cuba. The success was enough to secure ongoing CIA funding for the project for a total of $225,000 each month.

However, in September 1964, one of Artime's attack boats engaged what they thought was the pride of the Cuban shipping fleet. In reality, they attacked the Spanish commercial freighter *Sierra Maestra* off the Cuban coast and during the battle its Captain, first mate, and engineer were killed. Several other crewmembers were injured, and the ship itself heavily damaged in the assault. The attack created an international incident, Spain was outraged and Artime was ordered to stand down for a time. By November, there were further news stories in Miami papers about scandals in Artime's Central American camps, including reports that Costa Rica was investigating Cuban exile participation in smuggling inside its borders. That was followed by a December 1964 article stating that Costa Rica was expelling the exiles. The story was not accurate, but it became part of an ongoing negative media coverage of Artime and his operations.

Despite the extreme measures used to establish all the covert aspects of the AMWORLD project, the media and the international community continued to directly, and correctly, assume American support, and by early 1965, the State Department was increasingly unhappy about the association. President Johnson himself had never been really focused on Cuba, and was not prepared to weigh in on continuing covert action against the Castro regime. Laos and Vietnam had begun to consume the Johnson Administration, and to siphon off a good deal of CIA resources. By February 1965 the project began to be quietly wound down and ultimately Artime's funding was simply eliminated. The cessation of American support for the project was communicated both to Artime and the governments that had been supporting him.

AMWORLD, the last major covert action CIA project against Cuba and Fidel Castro, had been a uniquely complex experiment in establishing autonomous and deniable surrogates. In the end it proved neither deniable nor militarily successful. As we have seen, in the following years, from Laos to Angola, the CIA would return to its more classic role in organizing and directly managing covert military actions. In contemporary times, post-Cold War and post 9/11, the CIA has been moved into a support role, combined with the military in special operations around the globe. In many of those operations the Joint Special Operations Command and even some Military Assistance Missions utilized CIA support in operations organized under national security authorities, but conducted as intense, but low-profile actions – not deniable, but highly classified and covert.

In contrast, by the second decade of the 21st Century, other nations have begun to pursue deniable military activities, generally in a far simpler fashion and with a great deal less expense and bureaucracy than we have seen in Cold War era CIA projects. Exploring a few of those efforts provides a contrast to the American Cold War approach, and also reveals the truly ongoing temptation of deniable action. It also allows us to examine one of our earliest questions, which is whether any such actions can truly be conducted in a manner to escape exposure – and consequences.

A Return to Covert Military Action in the 21st Century

Beginning in 2012, Russian Federation President's Dmitry Medvedev and Vladimir Putin began to clearly express the contemporary Russia geopolitical position that their nation is entitled to claim a sphere of economic, political, and even cultural influence – influence which stretches beyond the actual physical territory of the Russian Federation.[503] President Medvedev specifically claimed "privileged interests," stating that the Russian sphere of influence extended beyond its "border regions."[504] His successor, President Putin in his third term became equally adamant about that position and *TIME Magazine* had noted Putin's expansive view of Russian influence as early as 2007. In naming Putin as their Man of the Year in 2007 *Time* observed: "Putin has put his country back on the map. And he intends to redraw it himself."[505]

Of course, claiming such a sphere of national political/economic influence is not unique to Medvedev and Putin or to Russia. President Monroe of the United States had proclaimed an American sphere of continental influence in 1823.[506] The Monroe Doctrine stated that any further efforts by European nations to take control of any independent state in either North or South America would be regarded as a sign of "unfriendly" intentions towards the United States and treated accordingly. Monroe's declaration was in response to the fact that several Central and South American nations had only recently achieved independence from European colonial powers.

In the 20th Century, Japan asserted an economic sphere of influence in Asia, both prior to and during World War II.[507] In the 21st Century, China has moved to assert its own sphere of natural resource control over a vast region of the South China Sea. Iran has also asserted a sphere of political and influence across the Persian Gulf region, claiming special rights over the Strait of Hormuz, a critical access route to Gulf state oil production.[508] These claims are of special interest to our subject because each of these 21st Century sphere of influence actors is turning to covert action, and covert military activities, in pursuit of establishing and maintaining their political and economic rights. This return to covert military action began in the context of Russia's repeated concerns that both economic and political pressure from Western nations, including both America and NATO (the North Atlantic Treaty Alliance), posed an existential threat to Russia's borders.

Russia's leaders viewed western economic and democracy initiatives as simply covert political action, threatening the long-established Russian sphere of influence across what had formerly been the Soviet Union (and before that, the Russian Empire). Russian concerns cited the inclusion of new nations into NATO (including nations who had been part of the former Soviet Union). Joint military and security exercises with non-NATO treaty nations on Russia's borders were another irritant. Russia also objected to the European Union's 2009 announcement of a new "Eastern Partnership" initiative, focused on the former Soviet republics of Armenia, Azerbaijan, Belarus, Georgia, Moldavia, and Ukraine.

President Putin was particularly concerned over a variety of democracy initiatives in nations around the Russian Federation's borders, activities conducted both by the European Union and by various Non-Governmental Organizations, including groups officially funded by the United States. The European nations, and the United States, rejected those concerns, citing traditional western support for democratic initiatives and open economies but from the Russian perspective its protests simply were not registering with Europe or the United States. It maintained that Russian influence was clearly being targeted and the Russian media illustrated Western targeting with headline stories in both the *Moscow Times* and *Izvestia*. In one example the Russian press reported that $500,000 in funding was being offered out of the American embassy in Lithuania, made available to regional media organizations with the objective of promoting journalism to combat Russian "propaganda." One of the grants available as part of the offer included money for a research project – the title of the study being "Investigative Journalism Training to Counter Russian Messaging in the Baltics."[509]

In 2014, Russia turned from diplomatic protests, to deniable military action against one of its historically closest allies, the Ukraine. The Russian operation occurred during a period of political chaos in Ukrainian internal affairs, resulting from a contested election. On March 4, 2014 Russian's UN ambassador presented a letter signed by the incumbent (Russian backed) president of the Ukraine, requesting Russian peace keeping forces to restore order in his nation. Not coincidentally, the Russian Parliament had already voted to approve a request by

Secret Wars With Air Strikes And Tanks?

President Putin to deploy Russian troops to the Ukraine if requested. However, Putin did not actually send conventional Russian forces into the Ukraine, an action that would have quickly escalated into open warfare.

Instead, during March 2014, uniformed troops wearing no national insigne, but well organized and well-armed, began seizing government buildings in the Ukrainian region of Crimea. The troops showed every sign of being regular military units, and were quickly dubbed "the little green men" by the international press. Initially both the Russia government and President Putin strongly denied any involvement in those Crimean activities. Putin publicly stated that Russia was certainly not involved in the Crimea and had no intentions of annexing the region but within a matter of weeks new political groups had been formed, pro-Russian activists were engaged in extensive media campaigns, with major broadcast Russian media support, and there were dramatic calls for Crimean separation from the Ukraine. The separatist activities also involved the port of Sebastopol, which housed a major Russian Navy base and a large local contingent of Russian Navy forces (including Russian Marines). With the arrival of the little green men in Crimea, those Russian units had quickly established conventional military control over the area by isolating and disarming major elements of the Ukrainian Navy and Air Force.

Almost immediately a Crimean referendum was organized, with overwhelming votes being cast for succession. By March 18 President Putin signed a document granting The Russian Federation membership to both the Crimea, and the port of Sebastopol. The economic and political integration of Crimea became a major priority for Russia, pursued with great fervor and widely supported inside Russia. It was an accomplishment praised in the Russian press, citing the quicker than anticipated "adaptation" of the population.[510] Within some two years Russia deployed significant numbers of missile systems into Crimea, including anti-aircraft, anti-ship, and wide area systems capable of broad air suppression over the Black Sea and the Ukraine. Such deployments increasingly fueled air and naval confrontations with both Ukraine and other nations in what has previously (and legally) been the neutral waters of the Black Sea.[511]

Russian involvement in the Crimean operations had been so obvious (and the success so overwhelming) that President Putin himself later chose to take credit for the initially deniable action. He admitted to personally sending in Russian forces, expressing his satisfaction with the decision on Russian television and citing approval from the Russian Parliament to intervene to "protect Russian interests."[512] The actual military deployment of the Russian personnel was conducted under full deniability, with a mix of Russian paratroops (Pskov 76th Guards Division with all identifying insignia and unit badges removed) flown into Sevastopol in ten aircraft, and the follow on insertion of a smaller number of civilian "volunteers." The paratroops quickly deployed and seized the Supreme Council building (the headquarters of the Crimean regional government), and the main Crimean airfield. Russian air forces also established airspace control over Crimea to support the landing of the troops.

A series of deniable "civilian" surrogates were flown in within two days, some 170 Russian military veterans from Afghanistan and Chechnya as well members of various political "clubs" known to be strongly supportive of President Putin. Russian FSB and GRU officers were also covertly inserted, and orchestrated the veterans in various public appearances, representing them as local, completely indigenous Crimean partisans. Russia's deniable, covert action in Crimea was totally successful within a matter of days; no particular constraints were placed upon it other than the removal of insigne from the Russian military and a well-run propaganda effort involving "volunteers" from the Putin political clubs. The Russian operation in Crimea was intense, surgical, and of very short duration. Compared to Cold War era CIA operations, it was extremely efficient and economical, conducted clandestinely but with no resource constraints, fully using Russia bases as well as air and maritime military assets.

The next stage of Russian covert action – against Ukraine - turned out to be something far different, something far more reminiscent of a Cold War era CIA project. It was protracted and "evolutionary" in nature, suffering ongoing mission creep into full scale conventional military action. In some aspects it resembled the 1960s American involvement in Laos. The context for the follow on actions in Ukraine was strictly geopolitical, described in President Putin's own remarks in referring to Ukraine as "Novorossiya"" – a term from the era of the tsars.[513] Putin's use of the term Novorossiya expressed his own personal belief that large sections of eastern Ukraine were not simply Russian speaking, but deeply linked to traditional Russian culture, making them inherently receptive to a direct political linkage with Moscow. That view went back centuries, to when Novorossiya had been simply a territory of the Russian Empire, annexed in 1774.

Culturally, most of southern Ukraine had been settled by a broad mix of peoples, only more heavily populated with native Russians during the Soviet era when the region had been designated part of the Ukrainian People's Republic. There was a history of separatism in the region. However, it was not until 1990 that a new Novorossiya movement had campaigned for either autonomy or for status as a "special state" within Ukraine. That effort did not gain wide popular support at the time. In contrast to Putin's assumptions, while the Ukrainian east had its own issues with central government in Kiev, it would eventually prove to be even less excited about political control from Moscow.[514] Subsequent events would demonstrate that only in the Donbass region, specifically in the Donetsk and Luhansk administrative areas, was there any extensive support for union with Russia.

At first there was no violence and no actual declarations of independence in the Ukrainian east. However, there were discussions about separatism, and political groups were formed to promote an independent Novorossiya (which would include the Crimea). Activists from eastern Ukraine went back and forth to Crimea, attracting the attention of the volunteer paramilitary groups, which had been brought in as key public support for the Russian seizure of the Crimea. Those "volunteers" were led by led by Colonel Igor Strelkov. Strelkov proceeded to move a small paramilitary force from the Crimea into Slavyansk, a small city in the Donetsk area of eastern Ukraine. Strelkov later described selecting a location where his small, but aggressive, group might make a major military impact.[515] Strelkov (who called himself "shooter") did indeed have a highly visible impact – very bloody and brutal, but in the end not sustainable simply by his own force. His financing was coming from local, pro-Russia, Ukrainian oligarchs; with their encouragement he began to acquire a number of local volunteers and the violence began to increase.

Strelkov's fighters initiated the first real violence in the east by seizing a police station, then taking control of the local municipal government.

The next phase of the effort to break away at least sections of the east from the central Ukrainian government involved pro-Russian groups in both the Donetsk and Luhansk regions of Ukraine. Each declared itself as a fully independent People's Republic. To some extent Strelkov, as the largely self-appointed defense minister for Donetsk, became the popular face of the independence movement in the east, publicly calling for Russia to intervene. Initially no overt Russian response was required and no formal Russian recognition of the insurgent Ukrainian republics. It was at that point that Russian covert military action began to escalate.

Russian surrogate forces began to be inserted into the Ukraine, composed largely of private company paramilitary units, serving in companies owned and operated by President Putin's own political supporters. The Russian fighters were also brought into the Donetsk region of eastern Ukraine with funding from pro-Russian Ukrainian oligarchs.[516] While private military companies were formerly illegal in Russia, in 2012 then Prime Minister Putin had endorsed the concept, and private Russian companies began to be organized outside Russia. One of the best known private military contractors, Wagner Group, provided civilian "troops" to the separatist oligarchs in Donbass region of eastern Ukraine.[517]

Beyond that, large conventional Russian military forces were deployed on the Russian side of the Ukrainian border. In some respects, the move was reminiscent of the Cold War US Navy intimidation efforts off Guatemala and Cuba.

In contrast, the Russian intimidation was far larger, and eventually far bolder. At their peak, estimates put between 30,000 and 40,000 Russian troops on Ukraine's border in the spring of 2014. However, the central government in Kiev proved not to be intimidated and refused to accept the loss of its territories in the east.

By early July, under increasing Ukrainian Army pressure, Strelkov was forced to shift his forces to the city of Donetsk, initially undefended by the Ukrainian Army. The resulting combat in a heavily urban area largely devastated Donetsk. It appears that by that time Moscow had begun to appreciate that a much broader Novorossiya was not emerging as an independent political entity. In late June, 2014 Putin asked the Russian parliament to cancel its earlier resolution on the use of Russian forces in Ukraine, and the Federation Council did so, making it officially illegal to use the Russian military in eastern Ukraine.[518] At the same time, both the Ukrainian Army and an increasing number of nationalist volunteers in the east began to enjoy gains against the separatists.

The initial Russian response to the central government pressure involved Russian weapons shipments, covert deployment of Russian military trainers, and a limited number of volunteers. Although officially denied in the strongest terms at the time, Putin himself later admitted that Russian fighters and advisers, if not official Russian Army units, had indeed been present in eastern Ukraine: "We never said there were not people there who carried out certain tasks including in the military sphere."[519] In addition to supplying weapons (including artillery) to the eastern separatists, there is also evidence that on occasion the Russian military itself engaged regular Ukrainian Army forces from within Russian territory.

Secret Wars With Air Strikes And Tanks?

One the most devastating such attacks occurred in July 2014, when a three-minute artillery bombardment targeted four Ukrainian Federal Army brigades which had been assembled for an advance. The Russian artillery barrage destroyed dozens of vehicles and killed several dozen Ukrainian troops. Damage assessment determined that the attack had used advanced dual-purpose munitions including air dropped mines and top-down anti-tank sub-munitions along with fuel air explosives.[520] The attack had employed some of the most advanced artillery available to the regular Russian Army.

Beyond that, Russian shoulder launched anti-aircraft missiles were provided to the separatists, along with even more advanced anti-aircraft systems. Verified counts of Ukrainian Federal aircraft losses included 9 combat aircraft, 3 cargo planes, and 10 helicopters.[521] One of the cargo planes was determined to have been brought down by a Buk missile system; the same type of weapon which an official Dutch study determined to have brought down a commercial Boeing 777 airliner transiting at high altitude above the combat in the Ukraine.[522] A Dutch Safety Board report concluded that the weapon which destroyed the airliner was a very specific Buk surface to air missile rocket, noting that it had obtained photos showing a Buk system being driven into the Ukraine, around the suspected launch area and then departing over the Russian border. In turn Russia adamantly denied the Safety Board conclusions.

Despite the Russian weapons and direct artillery support, the Ukrainian Federal Army and a growing number of eastern Ukrainian volunteer groups began to surround the separatists, threatening support from across the Russian border. Separatist calls for Russian military support increased, stressing that the Donetsk insurgency might well be overwhelmed within two weeks.[523] It began to appear that many of the locals in the Donbass, much less all of "Novorossiya" were far more nationalist and less pro-Moscow than Putin had originally believed. It was at that point in time in which something very familiar occurred – major mission creep. At the end of July, 2014, the Russian Army began a heavy shelling of Ukrainian forces from across their joint border.

What followed next was the arrival in Ukraine of large organized military formations of Russian "vacationers." Russia adamantly denied it at the time, but later President Putin was forced to acknowledge the appearance of large numbers of "volunteers," ostensibly all on leave and acting strictly on their own accord. The Russian "vacationers" were tasked with stopping the Ukrainian central government advance by diverting the Ukrainian Federal Army with a move against the second largest city in the region, where no serious fighting had yet occurred. The separatist spokesman, Strelkov, was quite specific about the Russian deployment: "It was mostly the vacationers who attacked Mariupol...they could have taken it without a fight but they were ordered not to...the order was simply to halt the [Ukrainian] offensive...they were told not to occupy the city under any circumstances."[524]

The combat that followed the initial Russian military intervention became extremely bloody for the Ukrainians, but with substantial Russian losses as well. As Russian deaths began to mount, military death benefits payments were kept secret and burials obscured with warnings to family members. In addition, Putin quietly issued a low key, but highly consequential, order directing that military deaths occurring during peacetime "special operations" be classified. That order provided the authority for a formal declaration of secrecy in regard to any military death, especially those which occurred on even those which occurred outside announced military activities – or on vacation.[525]

By the end of August, it was clear that the initially covert, relatively small scale Russian military activity in the eastern Ukraine had escalated into full scale warfare involving a large, if still technically deniable, Russian military force. The Russian formations sent into Ukraine involved full combat brigades, self-propelled artillery, and tank units. The Russian forces also employed extensive use of surveillance drones and electronic warfare equipment. As a consequence, the Ukraine's Ministry of Foreign Affairs officially announced on August 27, 2014 that an invasion was in progress.

Ironically, the scope of the Russian advance was exposed by the extent and severity of Ukrainian Army losses. Following one round of combat, media coverage revealed two destroyed Russian main line T-72 battle tanks, advanced tanks of a type not previously exported or made available outside Russia itself.[526] The tanks had been part of a major armored engagement with Ukrainian Federal Army forces and the Ukrainians had been routed, leaving dozens of their own tanks and armored vehicles behind. Similar engagements during August and into September demonstrated that even regular Ukrainian Army groups could not stand up to a mix of new Russian weapons and tactics. When the regular Army shattered, the inexperienced Ukrainian volunteer units became totally exposed to the push by armored forces. During August they were routed and trapped, suffering hundreds of casualties during the Russian advance.[527]

In Denial

By September the denied, but conventional, Russian offensive had succeeded, leaving solid blocs of pro-Russian separatists within the two self-declared independent republics in south-east Ukraine. Those separatist enclaves wanted nothing to do with Kiev. They considered themselves under attack by the central government and viewed the Russian's as defending them. Outside of the separatists' enclaves, the bloody Russian incursion had provoked equally virulent anti-Russian emotions, leading to an increase in nationalist volunteer military groups in the region. Still, it had become clear that any new central government military initiative against the reinforced separatists was going to be fruitless.

The result was a cease fire accord (the Minsk protocol) defining lines of control and buffer zones that allowed Kiev to cease its offensive in the east, and led to the withdrawal of some larger and more visible units of the Russian military. In spite of the Minsk agreement, the military reality was that having certain strategic locations in the separatist areas still under federal government control, such as the Donetsk Airport, was viewed as a tactical weakness by both the separatists and Moscow. While it was little more than an irritant – the Ukrainian central government in no way was equipped or supplied to pursue any military initiative against the separatist enclaves – what happened next illustrates one of the fundamental risks of covert action.

At that point the Russian operations against the Ukraine, driven by Vladimir Putin, appear to have developed into the something of a personal obsession, as with several of the earlier American covert operations we have explored – Dulles and Bissell in Cuba, Shackley and Kissinger in Laos, and Kissinger in Angola. Putin's first covert military action against Ukraine, in the Crimea, had been tightly focused, limited in terms of the force deployed, and successful, in some respects, not unlike the CIA's use of the Cuban volunteers in the Congo. Putin's follow on effort in what he viewed as "Novorossiya" had begun covertly enough, then moved through major mission creep first with Russian artillery engagements and then the deployment of a major conventional force into Ukraine. At that point deniability was lost, but Russian prestige had taken something of a blow even with a simple cease fire agreement. What happened next was of little strategic value to Russia, something more of a display of will – on the same order as B-52 carpet bombing in Laos. Inertia had clearly taken hold, deniability was no longer a concern, brute force and intimidation came into play.

With no obvious strategic or tactical motivation, other than proving to Kiev that Russia was prepared to use massive force in the face of any central government action in the east, a second major Russian Army offensive was launched. It proved to be both tactically sophisticated and brutal, once again overwhelming both volunteer and regular Ukrainian Army forces.[528] Ostensibly the new fighting was triggered by Kiev's decision to maintain its military presence at the Donetsk airport and in response, Russian forces deployed tactical units to surround the airport and slowly squeeze its parameter. Separatist forces supported by Russian tanks and armored vehicles entered the airport, supported by artillery and rocket barrages. The Ukrainian infantry was once again battered and the airport was not just occupied by the separatists but rather totally destroyed. The assault also destroyed much of the central government's military equipment which had remained in the east.

In Denial

More significantly, in separate assaults, combined Russian and separatist forces reduced the remaining cities in the region which were still defended by central government forces, resulting in an estimated 6,000 civilians killed in the fighting before yet another cease fire came into place. The best available estimates suggest that from August 2014 to the time of that second cease fire in January 2015, a combined force of separatists and regular Russian Army units had shattered the remaining government forces in the east, some eight thousand regular Ukrainian Army and volunteer military units. It was conventional warfare in all respects, with each phase denied by the Russian government, only to be later acknowledged after each success of the Russian forces.

In the following year the sniping, firefights, probes, and limited shelling across the border continued along the boundaries of the separatist regions. There were recurring Russian troop build ups directly across the joint Ukraine/Russian border, fears of new interventions, and a general sense of instability. No major military initiative was taken by Kiev nor has there been any new large-scale deployment of regular Army forces from Russia. In December, 2018, Russia once again moved to demonstrate its ability to intimidate the Ukraine, through denial of Ukrainian access to the Black Sea from the Sea of Azov. Upon completing a huge new bridge across the straits of Kerch, Russian forces stopped more than 150 vessels over a period of six days, ostensibly over security threats to the bridge.

Following that, Russian Navy units deployed from its huge Crimean base intercepted, fired upon, and took possession of three Ukrainian Navy ships (a tug boat and too armed patrol vessels) transiting the Kerch Strait from the Black Sea. The ships were on their way to the Ukrainian port of Mariupol, on the Sea of Azov. Mariupol is the Ukraine's third largest port.[529] It took almost a year for Russia, in September, 2019, to agree to a prisoner exchange which included the Ukrainian sailors taken prisoners in the Kerch incident. As part of the agreement between Russia and Ukraine, the naval personnel from the Kerch incident were freed, along with a number of other prisoners taken into captivity during the prior years of combat in Eastern Ukraine.[530]

As for the separatist Ukrainian enclaves, as of 2019 it still appears that Moscow retains hope for at least a limited version of what Putin had visualized in the spring of 2014. The ultimate goal is that Kiev will tire of the drain on its resources, the tension that undermines its own internal politics, and accede to some sort of independence for the breakaway enclaves as well as officially accepting the acquisition of Crimea and Sevastopol by the Russian Federation. That would represent an acknowledgement of Russian claims in regard to the concept of a sphere of influence and its hegemony over the southeastern Ukraine. As it is, the continuing faceoff leaves an estimated 800,000 civilians living near the contested demarcation lines with another 100,000 in the buffer zones in between.[531] Beyond that, an estimated three million or more people have simply moved out, going west to Ukraine or east into Russia.

Certainly, those numbers illustrate what happens when a covert military operation takes on a life of its own. In terms of sheer quantity, they are reminiscent of the Hmong experience in Laos. There were other consequences as well. In September, 2017 the Ukraine entered into an initial association agreement with the EU, a relationship involving the converging of regulations, workers' rights, movement of people, access to the European Investment Bank, and a free trade zone.532 September, 2017 also saw an expanded multi-nation training and interoperability exercise (Rapid Trident) between the Ukraine, the United States, and some 14 other nations including Bulgaria, Canada, the United Kingdom, and Georgia. The exercise involved both battalion and platoon level training, as well as an integrated air and ground logistics operation.533

With Ukraine's signing of the EU agreement, Ukraine's President Poroshenko cited the "high price" which Ukraine had paid to be able to make such a move towards the EU. Since then, the United States has advanced its own military partnering with the Ukraine, most recently moving beyond the supply of various types of military equipment to the sale of highly lethal tactical weapons such as Javelin anti-tank missiles.534 At present it remains to be seen whether the attitude of a new Ukrainian president, the recent prisoner exchange, and signs of a possible new Russian peace initiative might lead to an agreement with Russia, an agreement which might well limit any further engagement between the Ukraine and the European Union.535

Private Armies:

In American Cold War era covert operations, it was not uncommon to find military personnel "detailed" to the CIA for professional duties as trainers or even field advisors. Some moved on to become full time CIA employees. American civilians and even foreign nationals also served as contract pilots, both for logistics and on occasions in combat, such as in Guatemala, Indonesia, Laos, and the Congo. What we did not find in our explorations of those operations were groups of American military or civilians actively deployed in ground combat. That would have been a violation of standard CIA practices of deniability.

However, in the 21st Century, in the Ukraine, we find both Russian military units and employees of private military companies (such as the Wagner Group) serving as "troops" for the separatist oligarchs in the Donbass region of eastern Ukraine. By 2018 those same types of private army personnel were being sent into Syria, fighting along with Syrian regular army units.536 It is true that the United States employed private military companies to perform security duties in both Iraq and Afghanistan, however, security details are one thing - deployment of conventionally armed paramilitary units as surrogate combat forces is quite another. Even though the Trump Administration reportedly considered such an option in Afghanistan, as of the time of this writing the United States has never turned to private military contractors as a military force – and certainly not as a deniable force, independent of American policy or control.537

In contrast, as of 2018 Russia, appears to have taken exactly that tack, allowing the Syrian government to contact commercial Russian paramilitary company employees to supplement its own forces, as well as the conventional military units (primarily air force) that Russia had openly deployed in Syria.538 The Wagner Group, first identified as the source for Russian military contractors serving in the eastern Ukraine, fielded a combat unit to serve along with Syrian government groups during a major offensive against ISIS territory in eastern Syria. If it continues, this new Russian tactic may come to represent a transformation in the practices of covert military operations. Commercial military contractors not only provide official deniability for the Russian government, they also avoid a particular type of problem which arose in the Ukraine. As Russian "volunteers" began to be used in Ukrainian combat, bodies began to return to Russia. Funeral services and burials led to questions as to cause of death, especially as no regular Russian Army personnel were officially in combat.

Those questions began to make it into the media, embarrassing Putin and eventually forcing him to acknowledge some level of military involvement in Ukraine. The Russian government responded by enacting new laws which classify information about deaths resulting from "national security" service. This prevented official inquiries, but did nothing to deal with questions among families and friends. Most recently, the deaths of Russian military contractor personnel in Syria illustrates that there is a degree of deniability that comes with this new tactic, even though combat in Syria proved to be bloody for the Russian military contractors.

On two separate occasions at least 500 Syrian government fighters, along with Wagner combat units, advanced across a declared deconfliction line. The line had been established to mark off territory in which American military forces were operating against ISIS. The Syrian/contractor formation was accompanied by tanks and employed heavy weapons in its assault, which resulted in fire going into the American zone. Following a lack of response to requests to cease fire, American heavy artillery fire and armed drones where brought into what evolved into very intense fighting.

During these engagements a considerable number of attackers were killed and wounded. Russian casualties were significant, exceeding a hundred personnel, possibly far greater.[539] Once again, Russian families began to deal with deaths of veteran military personnel in what they had perceived as some type of government service.[540] Yet even with media reports of 100-200 contractor casualties in Syria, the Russian government was able to remain officially disconnected (with a new type of "technical" deniability) from the deaths, simply referring all inquiries back to the companies involved.

It appears that the use of private military contractors (PMCs) may provide Russia with yet another useful, and deniable option – that of securing access to natural resources and the associated mining and production facilities associated with them. Russian corporate contractors have begun to provide military style security in both Libya and the Central African Republic. The presence of well-organized and heavily armed, professional paramilitary forces provides considerable leverage in chaotic territories with weak or non-existent central government forces. That security leverage is apparently being used by the Russian companies to negotiate separate business arrangements related to the resources (and related production facilities) being protected. As of 2019, Russian military contractors were identified operating in the Sudan, the Central African Republic, and in Venezuela.

Wagner's presence in the Central African Republic is particularly interesting. It appears to be one of the most obvious examples of Russian private military contractor activity, deniable in terms of official Russian sponsorship, but highly successful in securing Russian commercial investment in gold and diamond mining concessions. Russian contractors guard facilities, provide training for government forces, and even serve as a security force to protect that nation's leader, Faustin-Archange Touadéra.

In Denial

It's a unique sort of visibility, deniable for the Russian government, but actively promoted by the Russian business firms which are directly involved. There are posters in the capital proclaiming "Russia: hand in hand with your army." Yet to be technically accurate, the signs should read "Russians, hand in hand with your army."

The Russians mentioned are all ostensibly private citizens, associated with a business conglomerate called Lobaye Investments. That company does everything from funding a Central African Republic radio station to training the government's army recruits. It has also deployed Russian military contractors, some 250 with more on the way, in a variety of "security" operations. Yevgeny Prigozhin, a longtime confidant of Vladimir Putin, is the organizing force behind the Wegner paramilitary contracting group, the source of the paramilitary personnel in the Central African Republic.[541]

Seemingly both economical and efficient, this new practice provides an interesting alternative to the much more complicated, and expensive, military assistance program approach taken by the United States during the Cold War – programs still very much in existence across certain regions of Africa. In fact, the concept of using commercial contractors as surrogates has, at least to some caught most of the world off guard, including the United Nations. In 2017, the UN approved a Russian training mission in the Central African Republic. Such missions have been routinely conducted by national military forces, under the rules, regulations and responsibility of the sponsoring nation. Instead, in the Central African Republic, Russian private military contractors appeared, along with associated commercial companies with no official Russian government oversight or ties.

Secret Wars With Air Strikes And Tanks?

At the time of this writing in 2019, Russian private military companies are involved with at least 15 African nations, and Russian military aid is being offered to the same nations, in exchange for mining rights and energy partnerships.[542] In touting its growing military/commercial relationships, Russia has announced that 35 African leaders will be attending the first ever Russia/Africa Summit, co-chaired by Russian President Vladimir Putin and Egyptian President Abdel-Fattah el-Sisi. The event will be held in Russia's Black Sea resort city of Sochi, in October. This new type of surrogate approach is unique in offering the element of deniability, being extremely efficient in terms of requiring little to no Russian government support or funding and beyond that being economically attractive.

Russia's companies doing business in Africa have increased trade with that continent almost three-fold over the past few years, up to $17.4 billion dollars in 2017. All in all, the combination of deniable private military contractors, Russian private enterprise, and access to natural resources seems far superior to comparable, and much larger scale, American surrogate action operations of the Cold War era. There are of course negatives in this Russian variant of deniable, surrogate action. Many of the regimes being supported with private Russian paramilitary security are dictatorial, repressive, and arguably corrupt. There are also reports of brutality against civilians and even the murder of Russian journalists investigating the extent of the highly secretive Russian business involved, most recently of foreign reporters mysteriously murdered in the Central African Republic. It appears that this form of deniable action has its own particular consequences.

In Denial

It does need to be noted that, in the 21st Century, the United States still publicly undertakes military operations across the African continent, as part of its long-standing practice of military assistance programs. Although they are conducted in a low-profile fashion, they are not deniable and occur largely in northern and eastern Africa, focused on combating jihadist insurgencies. Circa 2018 there were American missions in progress in some 20 African nations, mostly on a small scale with limited numbers of personnel. Still, American military personnel have been deployed across the entire African continent and continue to perform assistance, which can include actual combat.[543]

In most military assistance missions, the Americans advise, assist, and train African militaries and do not perform security or combat roles. In certain flashpoint regions, including Nigeria and Somalia, where there is active jihadist fighting in progress, the military assistance personnel are supplemented with personnel from the Joint Special Operations Command. On occasion they also work with local militaries and other national forces, examples include the French military in Nigeria and Italian and pan African national units in Somalia. Those forces do come into combat and do suffer casualties. In 2017 four American and five Nigerian troops were killed during an ambush while the group was on a mission in Niger. More recently, in September, 2019, American and Italian military personnel came under attack in Somalia; one American service member was injured during a jihadi attack on an airfield outside the capital of Mogadishu; the Baledogle facility, which has been important as a source of reconnaissance drone flights over Somalian insurgent territories.[544]

Secret Wars With Air Strikes And Tanks?

Variations on a Theme – Overt but Deniable

The Russian use of private military contractors as surrogates is only one example of how deniability practices are being adapted to the projection of power in the 21st Century. Generally speaking, all of the new efforts are aimed at intimidation, associated with the goal of establishing spheres of influence without provoking military retaliation. While the tactics themselves can be quite aggressive, involving actual assaults and attacks on the designated adversaries, they are ostensibly carried out either by "patriotic" civilians, or by surrogates willing to accept blame – providing a high risk but seemingly effective type of deniability.

China's solution for deniability in intimidation efforts across the South China Sea rests in the fact that it has a large, dual role maritime militia, composed of small merchant boats and a very large number of fishing trawlers. The sea going militia is composed of ships that have normal commercial functions, but are under military control of the People's Armed Forces Departments. As with any militia, they can be activated for specific tasks or in support of a broader coastal defense military mission. What makes them especially deniable is the fact that certain of the craft are crewed by demobilized troops who may serve either in uniform or in civilian clothes, with their vessel either serving in an official Chinese military role, a routine commercial role, or tasked for covert, deniable duties (reporting to either the Navy or to other agencies) such as harassment of foreign vessels in waters considered as within the Chinese sphere of influence.

Flexibility in the militia reporting structure also provides a certain type of cover since the maritime craft cannot only be given orders by their militia unit, but also be tasked for maritime law enforcement (MLE), for coast guard duties, or to regular PLA Navy activities.545 When charged with regular military duties, maritime militia boats can simply serve as small transports, perform costal patrols, or serve as search and rescue units. However, recent investigative reporting suggests that some craft and crews are trained for more sophisticated missions, including intelligence collection and harassment/interdiction activities. A number of recent intimidation incidents suggest the involvement of militia craft.546

In recent years Chinese vessels, ostensibly working as fishing ships, have taken the time to shadow and engage in "non-fishing" maneuvers such as repeatedly crossing the bows of US Navy ships operating in the South China Sea near man made islands China is building and arming as territorial defense installations. Other nations are also claiming portions of the South China Sea, and experiencing much more aggressive treatment from Chinese "fishing vessels." During a Philippines government effort to assert its legal presence in the South China Sea, it stationed a naval ship at a disputed atoll (the Second Thomas Shoal). During that time Chinese boats, ostensibly manned by patriotic and angry Chinese civilians, repeatedly harassed Philippine's supply vessels. More aggressively, the same type of patriotic and angry Chinese fishermen continued repeatedly harassing Vietnamese boats operating around an oil drilling rig. During a three-month period of 2014, these Chinese craft often rammed Vietnamese boats, actually sinking one of them.

Reportedly special ships and crews are used for such aggressive missions, one source states that the militia personnel are provided with a "disability pension" of over

Secret Wars With Air Strikes And Tanks?

$8,000 a year if they are injured on a military or other special mission; the same benefit given to other government employees. Equally important, the source described observing specially built "fishing boats" with "T Bar" structural reinforcements – unnecessary for commercial fishing but quite helpful in "ramming" and other such harassment type activities. Militia craft have actually been photographed loading crates labeled as light weapons, with larger craft (clearly not standard fishing vessels) equipped with water cannons, collusion absorbing rails, and even more strongly reinforced hulls.[547] One of the advantages of this type of deniability is that actions which could lead to armed conflict, such as the ramming of the Vietnamese fishing vessels, can be blamed on private citizens.

China has also elevated official deniability to a new level. In December 2016 an American Navy survey ship's crew, the U.S.N.S. Bowditch, was forced to simply observe as a regular, marked, Chinese Naval vessel (DALANG III-Class ship/(ASR-510) quite literally stole an American remotely piloted submersible that the ship was using in oceanic research.[548] The incident occurred in the South China Sea, but only some 50 nautical miles northwest of Subic Bay in the Philippines, an area never previously contested by China. The Bowditch had deployed an unmanned underwater vehicle (unclassified and nonmilitary) with the capability of testing ocean salinity, temperature, sound transmission, and other such characteristics. Such survey work is done around the globe, and openly published for scientific purposes. The data is also used in building US Navy oceanographic data bases used in submarine operations, which is why the Navy funds it.

In Denial

The Bowditch observed the Chinese Navy ship, and made radio contact with it, identifying itself and its mission. However, when the underwater vehicle returned to the surface, the Chinese ship moved in and lifted the submersible aboard, departing the area and ignoring all further radio communications. A formal protest was registered with the Chinese government and ultimately the vehicle was returned. The official Chinese government response was that a Chinese Naval vessel had routinely discovered a piece of "unidentified equipment" in the ocean, recovered it and examined it in terms of being a potential hazard to navigation, having no idea that it was a piece of American equipment. The official response rebuked the United States for dramatizing the entire incident.[549]

This particular incident illustrates overt yet deniable action in its most classic form. Then again, deniable action can be even more aggressive, and more overt. For such an example it is only necessary to move from the South China Sea to the Persian Gulf, and the nations bordering the Strait of Hormuz. In that region, we find covert and deniable military action being carried on at its most extreme - in actual warfare.

Operating on the Edge – Iran in the Gulf

In retrospect it's hard to conceive how the United States ever truly felt that it could maintain deniability with main line American tanks on shore at the Bay of Pigs. The same could be said with B-52 Stratofortresses carpet bombing in Laos. Yet it is true that American military action was conducted across Southeast Asia for years – officially denied all the while, with protests but no overt military response from its major geopolitical adversaries.

The decision to go covert is always accompanied by a calculus as to the possible consequences, although not a calculus of collateral damage or surrogate losses - that hardly ever comes into the decision making. The calculation is in terms of consequences to the actor. Russian President Putin wanted the Crimea. He calculated that the west would not go to war over its seizure in a covert action, and was proved correct, enough so that he later admitted personally ordering the operation. There were national consequences to Russia in terms of sanctions, a price Putin was ready to pay. But a covert military action did not escalate to conventional warfare – his basic calculation proved correct.

Beginning in 2019, Iran moved into a series of extremely aggressive covert military actions in the Persian Gulf. Already under American financial and trade sanctions, the calculation appears to have been that Iran could enforce its self-declared sphere of influence, demonstrate that it could close the Strait of Hormuz to international oil shipments, and significantly intimidate its primary regional adversary, without an escalation to open combat. The full scope of the Iranian calculation only became visible once all its elements had come into play.

A series of May/June limpet mine attacks were conducted against foreign shipping in the Gulf of Oman, with the most blatant occurring on June 13. Commercial vessels were attacked and one ship (Front Altair) was seized and taken into port in Iran. As part of that operation one of the small boats involved in the attack appears to have tried to shoot down an American surveillance drone, using a shoulder fired anti-aircraft missile. These attacks were conducted brazenly, with small paramilitary boats clearly traceable to Iranian forces. Virtually no effort was made to disguise the attack, other than recovering failed limpet mines in broad daylight. [550]

On June 20, 2109, an American military surveillance drone was shot down by an Iranian missile battery while operating over the Strait of Hormuz. Iran took full responsibility for the action, maintaining that it might also have justifiably shot down a manned American military surveillance aircraft, but determined to act prudently in asserting its rights.[551] The night of September 14/15 a massive series of air strikes was carried out against the Khurais oil field and the Abqaiq oil processing facility in Saudi Arabia. Best estimates are that 4 cruise missiles and some 18 suicide drones were used in the devastating attacks, which for a time shut down half of Saudi's oil exports.[552] Some of the weapons crashed short of their targets and were recovered while other fragments were recovered at the strike locations. The recovered parts and materials strongly suggest Iranian weapons. But Iran has provided a variety of similar weapons to its proxy forces fighting against Saudis in Yemen and those forces, the Houthi's, claimed responsibility for the Saudi oil facility attacks, pointing out that they had been conducting similar strikes against Saudi forces for years, even attacks using ballistic missiles.

No military action was taken in response to the attacks, neither by Saudi Arabia or any other actor in the region. The only specific response came from the United States, with further sanctions on Iran and promises to send air defense weapons and troops to protect the Saudi oil facilities. Saudi Arabia had already deployed an extensive air defense system against the previous Houthi attacks, and it remains unclear as to what defense against cruise missiles and suicide drones will work across a broad geographic parameter. If the Iranian goal was to point out the vulnerability of the Saudi oil infrastructure – or that of Saudi's regional allies – that certainly was accomplished in the attacks.

Several factors may have gone into the apparent Iranian decision to undertake such bold and barely covert military actions. First, they had tested the potential for military retaliation in a prolonged series of increasingly overt ship attacks, ultimately shooting down an unmanned American surveillance drone, with no military consequences. Second, they were maintaining military surrogates in their efforts against Saudi Arabia, and those surrogates (referred to as "proxies" in contemporary terminology) had been conducting a long series of relatively high-profile attacks, including sending intermediate range missiles against Saudi forces on a regular basis. Finally, and not to be disregarded, the history of weapons shipments into the region had begun with covert sales of North Korean missile technology as well as Cold War era Soviet weapons.

By 2019 there were a wide variety of foreign, locally modified, and locally manufactured weapons in use in the area, thereby making it hard to specifically identify the origin of any given device. A drone or a cruise missile might well show evidence of components from several sources, establishing some level of deniability even as to weapons. It has to be noted that the Iranians proceeded in a step by step process, only turning to a massive drone and cruise missile attack on Saudi oil facilities after seeing a lack of military response to their previous actions. New sanctions, yes, but sanctions were already in play. What they did not see in response to covert military action was an overt conventional military response. Despite the apparent irrationality of each individual step, there appears to have been a calculus in play which suggests a far more coherent and planned intimidation operation.

In Search of Deniability

In exploring almost 70 years of covert, deniable military action we have reviewed Cold War era American operations which were limited, short term, and successful (Guatemala and the Congo), highly sophisticated and protracted, but failed (Indonesia, Cuba Project, AMWORLD, North Vietnam, and Angola), and operations initiated to be totally covert but which underwent mission creep to the point of full scale, conventional military action (Cuba, Laos, and North Vietnam). In contemporary times we see the return of covert military action, both successful and failed, with Russia imminently successful in the Crimea, and largely failing in Ukraine. Other examples include restrained, but successful, variants including the use of technically deniable private military contractors by the Russian government, of covert but seemingly effective intimidation operations by China, and bold, high risk and seemingly successfully deniable military action by Iran.

Our detailed examination of the Cuba Project revealed how complex and conflicted covert action can be - conflicted to the point of not recognizing failure, as well as a refusal to acknowledge total loss of deniability, a fundamental charter for the mission. It also revealed a risk we would see in later operations with the emergence of a level of blindness among those tasked with the operation, to such a degree that they become unable to accurately assess the chances of success. That left them unable to accurately describe the risk of failure, isolating them from what was clearly visible to officers in the field.

President Eisenhower had ordered the Cuba Project to oust the Castro regime without showing the hand of the United States. Despite the best efforts of many officials, no matter how well designed an operation seems, denial cannot assure secrecy. The actors always become visible to their adversaries, to the media, within domestic politics, and to the international community. The reality we have found is that neither in that operation, nor in virtually any other covert military action, is full deniability feasible.

While full deniability may be an illusion, claims of deniability are often sufficient to defer any immediate military response. In that regard deniability does work, at least for the short term. Its consequences are often fatal to surrogates, proxies, civilians, and in terms of collateral damage, but not often for the sponsor, at least not immediately. Which is why it remains a perennial temptation. Covert action always remains "on the table," repeatedly requested, accepted and endorsed by national leaders. It is a gamble, but one which works frequently enough to be addictive. Still, as with any addiction, it has consequences – short-term or long-term – there are always consequences.

Notes

[470] Gordon Calhoun, "Task Force Alpha in the Bay of Pigs," *The Daybook*, Hampton Roads Naval Museum, Vol. 9, Issue 1, 2003, 8-9

[471] *Maximillian Wechsler,* "America's 'Secret War' and the bombing of Southeast Asia," *The Big Chill, April 19, 2017 also William P Head, Bombing From Above the Clouds, The Fairchild Papers, United States Air University, Air University Press, July, 2002*
http://www.thebigchilli.com/feature-stories/americas-secret-war-and-the-bombing-of-southeast-asia

https://media.defense.gov/2017/May/05/2001742911/-1/-1/0/FP_0007_HEAD_WAR_FROM_ABOVE_CLOUDS.PDF

[472] Doyle McManus and Robert C. Toth, "Setback for Contras : CIA Mining of Harbors 'a Fiasco'," *Los Angeles Times*, March 5, 1985
https://www.latimes.com/archives/la-xpm-1985-03-05-mn-12633-story.html

[473] Ted Mann, Twenty-Five Years of Stingers And Jihad in Afghanistan, *The Atlantic*, October 1, 2011
https://www.theatlantic.com/international/archive/2011/10/uncomfortable-anniversary-stinger-missiles-jihadi-hands/337231/

[474] "The Cuban Missile Crisis, 1962," Department of State United States of America, Office of the Historian
https://history.state.gov/milestones/1961-1968/cuban-missile-crisis

Secret Wars With Air Strikes And Tanks?

[475] Also known as Second Naval Guerilla. Plan for offensive military operations against Cuba from offshore, led by Manuel Artime (AMBIDDY-1). Based at Monkey Point in Nicaragua. https://www.maryferrell.org/php/cryptdb.php?id=AMWORLD

[476] AMTRUNK OPERATION: Reel 48, Folder LL - AMTRUNK OPERATION (WHAT CASTRO MIGHT HAVE KNOWN) (BACKGROUND FILE ON 7), Mary Ferrell Foundation, CIA Cryptonyms Database, The objective of AMTRUNK "was to overthrow the Cuban government by means of a conspiracy among high-level military and civilian leaders of the government culminating in a coup d'état which would oust both Castro and the Communists from power...in retrospect, the activity appears to have been insecure and doomed to failure from its inception primarily for lack of compartmentalization, and loose talk on the part of its principals."
https://www.maryferrell.org/php/cryptdb.php?id=AMTRUNK

[477] National Archives and Records Administration, RIF 104-10241-10174, Meeting with Ambiddy/1, on May 3, 1963. https://www.marryferrell.org/mffweb/archive/viewer/showDoc.do?mode=searchResult&absPageId=407095

[478] Ibid

[479] RIF 104-10241-10139, Meeting between Chief, SAS and Ambiddy-1 on 1 July, 1963
https://www.maryferrell.org/showDoc.html?docId=43338#relPageId=1

[480] Ibid

[481] Ibid

449

[482] RIF 104-10241-10131, Notes for your meeting with Ambiddy-1 during week from July 1, 1963

[483] RIF 104-10241-10170, Cable: Ambiddy/1, Arr ZRMETAL NAT FLT, 224, May 9, 1963

[480] Ibid

[485] RIF 104-10241-10136, Maritime Assets
http://www.maryferrell.org/mffweb/archive/viewer/showDoc.do?mode=searchResult&absPageId=494731

[486] Ibid

[487] RIF 104-10241-10122, Telephone Conversation between Ambiddy-1 and R. Hernandez, December 12, 1963. The *Joanne* appears to have been rented from a company named BAUM by Maritime BAM on a monthly basis. The first month's rental was for November, 1963, and the ship sailed from Baltimore in December.

[488] RIF 104-104-10077-10204, MV *Joanne* left Baltimore Port 1 Dec AM

[489] Ibid

[490] RIF 104-10240-10440, Director Cable Re Delivery Subject Cooper-McDonald
https://www.maryferrell.org/showDoc.html?docId=21316#relPageId=1

[491] RIF 202-10001-10028, CIA Cuban Operations and Planning
https://www.maryferrell.org/showDoc.html?docId=10246#relPageId=1

[492] RIF 104-10275-10051, Contact Report #15; Pass Instructions Re Procurement of Material. It is interesting to note that in at least one document, Interarmco is referred to as a CIA proprietary company although clearly by 1963 it was a quite successful international business. https://www.maryferrell.org/showDoc.html?docId=66912#relPageId=1

[493] RIF 104-10241-10109, Memo: Telephone Conversation between Ambiddy-1 and R. Hernandez, 18 Dec. 1963

[494] RIF 104-10241-10118, Memo Conversation between Ambiddy-1 and Raul Hernandez, Dec. 1, 1963.

[495] The AMWORLD infiltration team trained at Camp Guillot on the Orlich Ranch located in the Sarapiqui region of Costa Rica. This camp could be reached from the landing at Tortuguero by traveling the Rio Sarapiqui to Cornelio Orlich's finca (farm). This team consisted of nine men plus Borges. The team members were: Julio Yanez Pelegrin, Aramis Pinon Estrada, Armando Caballero Parodi (Brigade 2716), Miguel Penton (Brigade 2579) was with Felix Rodriguez in Cuba before and during Bay of Pigs., Victor Herrera (Brigade 3215), Porfirio Bonet "El Nino" was later associated with Frank Castro, Mamerto Luzarraga (Brigade 3516) and Humberto "Che." Humberto was most likely Humberto Solís Jurado (Brigade 2510). https://www.maryferrell.org/showDoc.html?docId=178367&#relPageId=5

Additional MRR members were training at the Starke ranch in Costa Rica before political circumstances forces both Borges team and the MRR Cubans to relocate to Nicaragua. The Starke ranch was owned by Ludwig Starke Jimenez a Costa Rican ultra-right-wing political figure.

[496] There remains a possibility that certain of the trainees may have also trained at Camp Stanley in Texas.

[497] Evelyn S. Gonzalez, "94-Year-Old Alumnus on Live, Love and Being a Spy," *Florida International University News*, May 24, 2014
https://newsarchives.fiu.edu/2013/05/94-year-old-alumnus-on-life-love-and-being-a-spy

[498] CIA Memorandum to Mexico City re Zambora cover travel, AMWORLD Project
https://www.maryferrell.org/showDoc.html?docId=30904&#relPageId=2&tab=page

[499] "Letter to Ambiddy-1 [Artime], CIA Memorandum, Director to Mexico City December 3, 1963
http://documents.theblackvault.com/documents/jfk/NARA-Oct2017/docid-32397696.pdf

[500] AMWORLD Review of Deficiencies, CIA Memorandum to Chief Western Hemisphere, June 14, 1964
https://www.maryferrell.org/showDoc.html?docId=147600&#relPageId=44

[501] AMWORLD, Possible Basis for Entente between Ambiddy-1 [Artime] and Zambora [Chavez], CIA Memorandum to Deputy Chief Western Hemisphere, June, 22, 1964
https://www.maryferrell.org/showDoc.html?docId=147600&#relPageId=33

[502] Rodriguez, *Shadow Warrior*, 119

[503] Fiona Hill, testimony before the United States House Representatives Armed Service Committee, "The Russian Security Challenge," Washington D.C., February 10, 2016, Brookings Institute

https://www.brookings.edu/testimonies/understanding-and-deterring-russia-u-s-policies-and-strategies/

[504] Paul Stronski, Richard Sokolsky, *The Return of Global Russia: An Analytical Framework*, December 14, 2017, Carnegie Endowment for International Peace
https://carnegieendowment.org/2017/12/14/return-of-global-russia-analytical-framework-pub-75003

[505] Richard Stengel, "Choosing Order Before Freedom," *Time Magazine*, December 19, 2007
http://content.time.com/time/specials/2007/personoftheyear/article/0,28804,1690753_1690757,00.html

[506] Monroe Doctrine, 1823, Our Documents, National Archives and Records Administration
https://www.ourdocuments.gov/doc.php?flash=true&doc=23

[507] Nathaniel W. Giles, *"The Greater East Asia Co-Prosperity Sphere: The Failure of Japan's "Monroe Doctrine" for Asia,"* Honors Thesis, East Tennessee State University, May 2015
https://dc.etsu.edu/cgi/viewcontent.cgi?article=1265&context=honors

[508] Suyin Haynes, "The Strait of Hormuz Is at the Center of Iran Tensions Again. Here's How the Narrow Waterway Gained Wide Importance," *Time World New*, July 23, 2019
https://time.com/5632388/strait-of-hormuz-iran-tanker/

[509] Drew Sullivan, "Journalism or Propaganda; Let's Help Russian Media the Right Way," *Global Investigative Journalism Network*, August 19, 2015
https://gijn.org/2015/08/19/journalism-or-propaganda-lets-help-russian-media-the-right-way/

510 "Crimea's Integration in Russia is Quicker than Expected – Official," *TASS*, November 19, 2016
https://www.rbth.com/news/2016/11/19/crimeas-integration-in-russia-is-quicker-than-expected-official_649175

511 Ryan Browne, "US show of force sends Russia a message in Black Sea," February 20, 2018, *CNN Politics*
https://www.cnn.com/2018/02/19/politics/us-russia-black-sea-show-of-force/index.html

512 "Putin Acknowledges Russian Military Servicemen Were in Crimea," *RT / Russia Today News*, April 17, 2014
https://www.rt.com/news/crimea-defense-russian-soldiers-108/

513 Paul Sonne, "Novorossiya' Falls From Putin's Vocabulary as Ukraine Crisis Drags Revival of Czarist-era term for 'New Russia' fades ahead of European decision on sanctions," *The Wall Street Journal*, May 29, 2015
https://www.wsj.com/articles/novorossiya-falls-from-putins-vocabulary-as-ukraine-crisis-drags-1432936655

514 The Russia idea that Ukraine could be separated due to by creating a "construct" state was not dissimilar from the American effort to split Vietnam in a purely political North/South construct. No such "state" as South Vietnam existed before the United States literally declared it into being. As with the British and French experience in the Middle East, the creation of construct states via lines drawn on maps has proved to be a very disruptive and inherently unstable practice.

515 A. Prokhanov, "Who Are You Shooter?; An interview with the former Minister of Defense of the Donetsk People's Republic, *Zavtra*, November 20, 2014

516 Eli Watkins, "Key Russian oligarch in touch with Russia, Assad before mercenaries attacked US troops," February 22, 2018
https://www.cnn.com/2018/02/22/politics/russia-syria-us-troops/index.html

517 Op Cit

518 "Federation Council cancels resolution on using Russian Troops in Ukraine," *TASS*, June 25, 2014
http://tass.com/russia/737674

519 Shaun Walker, "Putin Admits Russian Military Presence in Ukraine for First Time, *The Guardian*, December 17, 2015
https://www.theguardian.com/world/2015/dec/17/vladimir-putin-admits-russian-military-presence-ukraine

520 Shawn Robert Woodford, "The Russian Army Strike that Spooked the U.S. Army, *Land Warfare*, The DuPuy Institute
http://www.dupuyinstitute.org/blog/2017/03/29/the-russian-artillery-strike-that-spooked-the-u-s-army/

521 Jacek Siminski, "Analysis of Ukrainian Air Force Losses in Eastern Ukraine Clashes," *The Aviationist*, December 2, 2014
https://theaviationist.com/2014/12/02/analysis-of-ukrainian-air-force-losses-in-eastern-ukraine-clashes/

522 "MH17 Ukraine Disaster; Dutch Safety Board blames missile, *BBC News*, Blames, October 13, 2015
http://www.bbc.com/news/world-europe-34511973

523 Taras Kuzio, *Putin's War Against Ukraine, University of Toronto*, Toronto, Canada 2017,
252-253 also Mikhail Zygar, *All The Kremlin's Men*, Perseus Books, 288

[524] A. Prokhanov, "Who Are You Shooter?, cited from Mikhail Zygar, *All The Kremlin's Men*,
Perseus Books, 285-286

[525] Karoun Demirjian, "Putin Denies Russian Troops are in Ukraine; Declares Certain Deaths Secret," *The Washington Post*, May 28, 2015
https://www.washingtonpost.com/world/putin-denies-russian-troops-are-in-ukraine-decrees-certain-deaths-secret/2015/05/28/9bb15092-0543-11e5-93f4-f24d4af7f97d_story.html?utm_term=.c88c22223610

[526] Maria Tsvetkova, Aleksandar Vasovic, "Charred Tanks point to Russian Involvement," *Reuters World News*, October 23, 2014
https://www.reuters.com/article/us-ukraine-crisis-tanks-exclusive/exclusive-charred-tanks-in-ukraine-point-to-russian-involvement-idUSKCN0IC1GE20141023

[527] Lucian Kim, The Battle of Ilovaisk: Details of a Massacre Inside Rebel-Held Eastern Ukraine, *Newsweek*, November 14, 2014
http://www.newsweek.com/2014/11/14/battle-ilovaisk-details-massacre-inside-rebel-held-eastern-ukraine-282003.html

[528] Amos C. Fox, "The Russian–Ukrainian War: Understanding the Dust Clouds on the Battlefield," Modern War Institute, *West Point Military Academy*, January 17, 2017
https://mwi.usma.edu/russian-ukrainian-war-understanding-dust-clouds-battlefield/

[529] "The Kerch Strait Incident," *Institute for Strategic Studies*, December, 2018
https://www.iiss.org/publications/strategic-comments/2018/the-kerch-strait-incident

Secret Wars With Air Strikes And Tanks?

530 "Ukraine and Russia exchange prisoners in landmark deal," *BBC World News*, September 7, 2019
https://www.bbc.com/news/world-europe-49610107

531 Adrian Bonenberger, "The War No One Notices in Ukraine," *The New York Times*, June 20, 2017
https://www.nytimes.com/2017/06/20/opinion/ukraine-russia.html

532 "EU-Ukraine Association Agreement officially enters into force," *Euromaidan Press*, September 1, 2017
http://euromaidanpress.com/2017/09/01/eu-ukraine-association-agreement-officially-enters-into-force/#arvlbdata

533 Sgt. Kyle Larson, Rapid Trident demonstrates multinational proficiency in Ukraine, United States Army Europe, September 30, 2019

http://www.eur.army.mil/RapidTrident/

534 Kyle Rempfer, "More lethal aid to Ukraine? US trainers, Javelins have already made Russians a little more nervous," March 6, 2019
https://www.militarytimes.com/news/your-military/2019/03/06/more-lethal-aid-to-ukraine-us-trainers-javelins-have-already-made-russians-a-little-more-nervous/

535 UK-EU Relations, *Global Security*, September 1, 2017
https://www.globalsecurity.org/military/world/ukraine/forrel-eu.htm

536 Eli Watkins, "Key Russian oligarch in touch with Russia, Assad before mercenaries attacked US troops," February 22,

2018
https://www.cnn.com/2018/02/22/politics/russia-syria-us-troops/index.html

[537] Mujib Mashal, "As Afghanistan Frays, Blackwater Founder Erik Prince Is Everywhere," *New York Times*, October 4, 2018

[538] Andrew Linder, "Russian Private Military Companies in Syria and Beyond," Center for Strategic and International Studies, Issue 16, October 7, 2016
https://www.csis.org/npfp/russian-private-military-companies-syria-and-beyond

[539] Joseph Trevithick, "Russian Mercenaries Take the Lead In Attacks On US And Allied Forces In Syria," *The War Zone*, February 15, 2018
https://www.thedrive.com/the-war-zone/18533/russian-mercenaries-take-a-lead-in-attacks-on-us-and-allied-forces-in-syria

[540] Andrew Roth, "There's no one to help': Russian mercenary industry's toll on families," World News, *The Guardian*, August 26, 2019
https://www.theguardian.com/world/2019/aug/26/russia-drive-into-africa-shines-light-on-mercenary-industry

[541] Tim Lister, Sabastian Shulka, and Clarissa Ward, "Putin's Private Army," *CNN Interactive*, August, 2019
https://edition.cnn.com/interactive/2019/08/africa/putins-private-army-car-intl/

Secret Wars With Air Strikes And Tanks?

542 Nick Turse, "U.S. Generals Worry about Rising Russian and Chinese Influence in Africa," Documents Show, *The Intercept*, August 13, 2019
https://theintercept.com/2019/08/13/russia-china-military-africa/

543 Greg Myre, "The Military Doesn't Advertise It, But U.S. Troops Are All Over Africa," *Parallels*, National Public Radio, April 28, 2018
https://www.npr.org/sections/parallels/2018/04/28/605662771/the-military-doesnt-advertise-it-but-u-s-troops-are-all-over-africa

544 Omar Nor, Michael Callahan and Ivana Kottasová, "Double attack hits US military base and Italian convoy in Somalia," *CNN World News*, October 1, 2019
https://www.cnn.com/2019/09/30/africa/baledogle-base-italian-convoy-mogadishu-attacks-intl/index.html

545 Andrew Erickson and Connor Kennedy, "Beware of China's "Little Blue Men" in the South China Sea," *The National Interest*, September 15, 2015
https://nationalinterest.org/blog/the-buzz/beware-chinas-little-blue-men-the-south-china-sea-13846

546 Christopher P. Cavas, "China's Little Blue Men Take the Navy's Place in Disputes," *Defense News*, November 15, 2015
https://www.defensenews.com/naval/2015/11/03/chinas-little-blue-men-take-navys-place-in-disputes/

547 Andrew Erickson, "China's 'Little Blue Men' Prepare for Hybrid Warfare," War is Boring, December 17, 2016
https://medium.com/war-is-boring/chinas-little-blue-men-prepare-for-hybrid-warfare-22bd2ec08e8d

548 Statement by Pentagon Press Secretary Peter Cook on Incident in South China Sea, United States Department of Defense, Washington D.C., December 16, 2016
https://www.defense.gov/Newsroom/Releases/Release/Article/1032611/statement-by-pentagon-press-secretary-peter-cook-on-incident-in-south-china-sea/

549 Ben Blanchard and Steve Holland, "China to return seized U.S. drone, says Washington 'hyping up' incident," *Reuters World News*, December 16, 2016
https://www.reuters.com/article/us-usa-china-drone-idUSKBN14526J

550 Joseph Trevithick, "Navy Explosives Expert Shows Off Evidence Of Iranian Involvement In Tanker Attacks," *The War Zone*, June 19, 2019
https://www.thedrive.com/the-war-zone/28602/navy-explosives-expert-shows-off-evidence-of-iran-involvement-in-tanker-attacks

551 Joshua Berlinger, Mohammed Tawfeeq, Barbara Starr, Shirzad Bozorgmehr and Frederik Pleitgen, "Iran shoots down US drone aircraft, raising tensions further in Strait of Hormuz," *CNN World News*, June 20, 2019
https://www.cnn.com/2019/06/20/middleeast/iran-drone-claim-hnk-intl/index.html

Secret Wars With Air Strikes And Tanks?

[552] Joseph Trevithick, "Here's All The New Info You Need To Know In The Aftermath Of The Saudi Oil Facilities Attacks," *The War Zone*, September 18, 2019 https://www.thedrive.com/the-war-zone/29918/heres-all-the-new-info-you-need-to-know-in-the-aftermath-of-the-saudi-oil-facilities-attacks

About the Author

Larry Hancock is considered to be one of the essential contemporary writers in the areas of intelligence and national security. He is the author a number of works including *Nexus: The CIA and Political Assassination*, and coauthor of *The Awful Grace of God*, a study of religious terrorism, white supremacy, and the murder of Martin Luther King Jr. A graduate of the University of New Mexico, he earned his BA with honors, majoring in history, cultural anthropology and education. Following service in the United States Air Force and a professional career in computer/communications and technology marketing he returned to his long-term interest in historical research. Known as a "document geek," he researched and published several collections of CIA, FBI, and military documents prior to beginning his writing efforts. *In Denial* is his tenth book dealing with Cold War era history and issues of military history and national security.

Other Books Published By Campania Partners

Judyth Vary Baker: In Her Own Words by Walt Brown, PhD, Campania Partners, 2019.

Human Time Bomb: The Violence Within Our Nature by Carmine Savastano, Campania Partners, 2020.

The War State: The Cold War Origins of the Military-Industrial Complex And The Power Elite by Michael Swanson, Campania Partners, 2013.

Index

A

AEDEPOT, 27

Afghanistan, 399, 420, 433, 448

Ahern, Thomas, 393–94

Ambiddy-1, 131, 449–52

AMTRUNK OPERATION, 449

AMWORLD project, 276, 404, 409, 411–12, 414

Angola Project, 335–36, 349

Artime, Manuel, 83, 90, 113, 124, 131, 209, 280, 401–2, 449

B

Barnes, Tracey, 167–68, 170–71, 202, 261, 269, 288

Bay of Pigs operation, 60–65, 98, 130–33, 283, 288

Bissell, Richard, 51–52, 84–86, 89–90, 94–95, 99–100, 123–24, 136–37, 155–56, 161–63, 170–72, 195–99, 201–2, 204, 243, 246, 261–63, 265, 267–68, 287, 305–7

Brigade 2506, 211, 213, 223, 234, 254, 284

Burke, Arleigh, 145, 162, 175, 233, 235, 240, 244–45, 284–85, 287, 293–94, 356

C

Calhoun, Gordon, 65, 175–76, 218, 220, 293, 448

Castro, Fidel, 48–49, 69, 76–79, 87, 124–27, 149–50, 183, 249, 260–66, 268–69, 272–73, 275–78, 304, 319–20, 401–2, 408–9, 449

Castro assassination efforts, 58, 275

CAT (Civil Air Transport), 34, 61, 105–6, 119, 129

Central African Republic, 435–37

Central Intelligence Agency, 27–29, 32, 60–65, 97–98, 100–101, 129, 131, 133–34, 174–80, 219–21, 256–59, 291–92, 294

China, 1, 105, 296–97, 299–300, 321, 335–36, 338–39, 377, 441, 446, 459–60

CIA Covert Operations in Indonesia, 130

CIA's Secret War in Tibet, 129, 338

Civil Air Transport. See CAT

Colby, William, 344, 384, 391, 394

Cold War, 1–2, 5, 12, 16, 26–28, 32, 97, 99, 342–43, 416, 421, 436–37

Cold War Strategy, 26, 31

Conboy, Kenneth, 4, 129–30, 338

CRC (Cuban Revolutionary Council), 47, 84, 90–92, 183–84, 216, 230, 268

Cuban Brigade, 52, 209, 249, 409

Cuban combat aircraft, 197–98, 204–5, 210, 213

Cuban military, 36, 69, 89, 114, 119, 197, 279, 284

Cuban Missile Crisis, 245, 323, 399

Cuban pilots, defecting, 195, 200

Cuba Project, 2–4, 40–42, 44–47, 50, 52–56, 58–59, 67–68, 95–96, 110, 122–27, 135–36, 142–43, 189–90, 248–49, 260–63, 267–69, 271–74, 287–89, 295–96, 335–37

Cuba Project Team, 49, 89, 127, 139, 144, 193, 250

D

Devlin, Larry, 304, 306, 308–10, 340–41

Dulles, Allen, 121–22, 125, 127, 197, 200, 233, 243, 252, 260, 295, 304–5

E

Eisenhower, Dwight, 14, 17–18, 33–37, 45, 47, 49, 77, 108, 110–12, 124–27, 136–38, 300–301, 303, 305, 349–50

Eisenhower Administration, 13–14, 69, 127, 138–39, 248, 304, 310, 339, 358–59, 375

Eisenhower covert action projects, 298

Eisenhower Special Group, 49, 136, 139

Erickson, Andrew, 459–60

Erskine, Graves, 82, 99

Essex, 188–89, 224, 234–36, 283–86, 288

Esterline, Jacob, 63–64, 131, 134, 136, 138, 160–61, 167–69, 171–72, 191, 199, 202, 253, 267, 272–73

F

FBI, 183, 218, 264, 462

Fitzgerald, Oscar, 391–92

Ford, Gerald, 17, 327–28, 344

Fort Detrick's Special Operations Division, 263

G

Gillespie, Robert, 4, 392, 395

Guantanamo Bay, 280–81

Guatemala Assassination Proposals, 98, 270, 290

Guatemala operation, 38, 109

Guatemala project, 13, 39–40, 73, 103, 269, 411

Gulf of Tonkin, 387, 395

H

Haines, Gerald, 97–98, 290

Hawkins, Jack, 49–52, 63–65, 115, 117, 125–26, 128, 160–61, 163, 167–71, 191, 194, 196, 198–99, 202–3

J

Jenkins, Carl, 113, 117, 276, 401, 408, 412

JMMATE Project, 27

JMTIDE, 141, 196, 225, 236

Johnson, Lyndon, 14, 300, 317–19, 358, 362–63, 385, 389, 415

Joint Chiefs of Staff, 7, 14, 37, 53, 142, 145, 161–62, 176, 199, 356, 384

K

Kalb, Madeleine G., 340

Katanga Air Force, 313–14

Kennedy, John, 44–46, 48, 50–53, 58–59, 144, 150–53, 156–58, 160, 162–63, 170–71, 193–95, 200–201, 203–4, 244, 246–47, 254–55, 296–300, 352–55, 357–60, 383–85

Kennedy Administration, 2, 4, 52, 244, 312, 315, 319, 323, 361, 400–401, 410

Kennedy presidency, 400

Kennedy's deniability issues, 51

Kirkpatrick, Lyman, 54, 348, 370

Kissinger, Harry, 323–25, 327, 335–36, 344–47, 373–74, 428

Kornbluh, Peter, 20, 63–65, 100, 179, 258, 391

L

Lansdale, Edward, 376, 378–79

Laos, 3–4, 18–19, 43–45, 298, 310, 312, 349–58, 360–74, 376, 391–92, 399, 401, 415, 428–29, 431–32

Laos and South Vietnam, 35, 356, 380

Laos in Operations Hotfoot and White Star, 350

Laotian secret war, 365

Leopoldville government, 312, 315–16

Lumumba, Patrice, 301, 303, 308–9

Lynch, Grayston, 218, 220–21, 256–57

M

MACVSOG (Military Assistance Command, Vietnam Studies and Observations Group), 389, 391, 394–95

Marold, Edward, 391–92

Martin Luther King Jr, 462

Mason, John T., 175–76

McGeorge Bundy, 173

McManus, Doyle, 448

McNamara, Robert, 385

Mexico City, 411, 452

Mobutu, Sese Seko, 309–10, 315, 321, 326

Morrison, James, 129–30, 338

MPLA, 326, 329–35

N

National Committee for a Free Europe (NCFE), 10, 27

National Security Council, 12, 37, 103, 111–12, 121–22, 126–27, 133, 157, 305

NATO, 322, 417

Navy destroyers, 150, 187, 214, 237, 294, 387

Newman, John, 4, 174–76, 178, 289–90, 339–41, 355, 391–92

Nigeria, 438

Nino Diaz mission, 280, 282

Nixon, Richard, 128, 174, 358, 365, 371–73

North Vietnam, 352, 356, 358, 363, 365, 367, 373, 375, 379–81, 384–86, 388–90, 394, 446

North Vietnamese Army (NVA), 359, 362–63, 367, 369, 372, 374

O

Operation Carlotta, 333

Operation Flagpole, 341

Operation Haik, 39, 109

Operation HANCE, 109

Operation Hardnose, 363

Operation Hard Rock Baker, 23

Operation PBSUCCESS, 28, 62

Operation Steel Tiger, 364

Operation Switchback, 384

OSS (Office of Strategic Services), 376

P

Panama, 27, 113, 190, 272, 276, 409

Pathet Lao, 350–53, 355, 359, 365–67, 378

PEO (Programs Evaluation Office), 350

Pfeiffer, Jack, 60–65, 98, 131

Pfeiffer, Jack B., 129, 174, 176–77, 179–80, 219–21, 256–59, 291, 294

Portugal, 321–24, 346

Prados, John, 20, 30, 60, 62, 99, 101, 131–33, 288, 344–45, 393–94

Puerto Rico, 142, 147–48, 187, 200, 223

Putin, Vladimir, 416, 418–21, 423, 426

R

Radio Swan, 74–76, 83, 98

Robertson, Rip, 42, 141, 143, 149, 167, 193, 208, 210–11, 215, 222, 251

Rodriquez, Felix, 274, 292

Roman, San, 186, 193, 208–9, 237

Roselli, Johnny, 264–66

Roselli's associates, 266

Royal Lao Army, 43, 351–52

Rusk, Dean, 139, 201, 205, 239, 312

Russia, 6, 8, 11, 297, 300, 416–23, 425–27, 429–37, 443, 446, 454–55, 457

Russian forces, 420, 424, 427, 429–30

Russian government, 430, 433–36, 446

Russian military, 421, 424–25, 428, 455

Russian military contractors, 433–35

S

SACSA (Special Assistant for Counterinsurgency and Special Activities), 384

Saudi Arabia, 444–45

SEATO (Southeast Asia Treaty Organization), 362

Shackley, Theodore, 365, 368–69, 428

Simbas, 315–19

South China Sea, 2, 354–55, 417, 439–42, 459–60

South Vietnam, 35, 43–44, 352–53, 355–56, 360, 362, 364, 367, 374, 378, 380

Soviet Union, 6–7, 9, 27, 304, 346, 362, 383, 399, 417

Stockwell, John, 30, 328, 332, 344, 347

Sturgis, Frank, 277

Symington, Stuart, 18, 365

T

T-28 fighters, 316–17

T-33 jets, 200, 227

T-72 battle tanks, 427

TASS, 454–55

Taylor Committee, 239–40, 245, 247, 253, 285

Thailand, 107, 129, 351, 354–57, 361, 364, 375

Tibet, 2, 4, 35, 59, 106–7, 112, 129, 296–300, 336, 338, 377

Training Bases, 100, 116, 122

Trinidad Plan, 40, 46–47, 49, 51, 58, 145, 147, 154, 183, 188, 240

Truman, Harry, 8–9, 12–13

Truman Administration, 5, 11–12, 17

Tshombe, Moise, 302, 311–12

U

Ukraine, 2, 106, 418–34, 446, 454–57

United States Air Force, 230, 251, 314, 462

United States Naval Institute, 175–76

United States Navy, 23, 108, 143, 387, 395

V

Vang Pao, 359, 364–66, 369, 374

Venezuela, 274, 402, 411, 435

VIAT (Vietnamese Air Transport), 381

W

Washington Post, 342, 456

Z

Zapata Plan, 158–59, 164, 182, 185, 238, 240, 243, 246, 249, 252, 254, 283, 286

Zygar, Mikhail, 455–56

Made in the USA
Monee, IL
18 August 2021